The Road to Mobocracy

THE ROAD TO
MOBOCRACY

Popular Disorder in New York City, 1763–1834

P A U L   A.   G I L J E

Published for the
*Institute of Early American History
and Culture
by the University of North Carolina Press
Chapel Hill and London*

The Institute of
Early American History
and Culture
is sponsored jointly by
The College of William and Mary
and the
Colonial Williamsburg Foundation.

© 1987 The University of North Carolina Press

Manufactured in the United States of America

Library of Congress Cataloging-in-Publication Data

Gilje, Paul A., 1951–
The road to mobocracy.

Originally presented as the author's thesis
(Ph.D.—Brown University, 1980) under title:
Mobocracy.
Bibliography: p.
Includes index.
1. Mobs—New York (N.Y.)—History—18th century.
2. Mobs—New York (N.Y.)—History—19th century.
3. Riots—New York (N.Y.)—History—18th century.
4. Riots—New York (N.Y.)—History—19th century.
I. Institute of Early American History and Culture
(Williamsburg, Va.) II. Title.
HV6483.N7G54 1987   302.3'3   86–30852
ISBN 0–8078–1743–0

To my mother

and father

Preface

The focus of this work is both rioting and perceptions of rioting. Primarily, this is a social history of rioting from the era of the American Revolution to the Age of Jackson. It addresses basic questions of modern studies on popular disorder in both Europe and America: What happened in the riots? Who were the rioters? What were the methods of riot control? How do the riots fit into the overall socioeconomic context? In pursuing answers to those questions, it takes into account changes in the intellectual temper through which riots were viewed.

That eighteenth-century milieu stressed the idea of corporate communalism. Although there may never have been even a near-perfect single-interest community, the world of the eighteenth century was far closer to that ideal than was the world of the nineteenth. Despite occasional riots representing cleavages in society, the legitimacy of rioting in the eighteenth century depended upon this corporate ideal. As long as consensus was the goal, a community might join together and riot to purge itself of deviants or to protect itself from outside intrusions. Those who did not participate in such disturbances often condoned them. Moreover, the eighteenth-century mob respected both persons and property; seldom did it lash out in murderous assault. Instead, rioters minimized conflict by focusing their ire upon an object—like an effigy—which symbolized their grievances.

By the beginning of the Jacksonian period the ideal of the easily defined community interest, under assault for more than a century, finally broke down. A new form of democratic politics emerged, aiming to moderate the many competing interests and channel them into some ill-defined greater good. Some groups were shortchanged by this new political system; with the supposed homogeneity of the community stripped away, intense and bitter rivalries, hatred, and prejudices were revealed. Moreover, these animosities were aggravated by clearly defined special interests arising from the new socioeconomic conditions. Religious, ethnic, racial, and class differences came into prominence and created divisions that periodically erupted into bloody collective action. A riot in the Jacksonian period, then, tended to have diverse goals, employ violence, and attack persons as well as property. By the 1830s popular disturbances betrayed a deeply fractured social order. To many Americans, rioting had become an illegitimate activity to be resisted by whatever force necessary. All moments of public license were to be curtailed, and civic leaders moved cautiously toward a new conception of riot control.

The transformation of popular disorder outlined above was neither sharp nor linear. Rioters throughout the period joined in popular disorder for their own reasons. Yet despite the nuances of each incident and the varied motivations of each participant, the pattern that emerges reflects the major social and intellectual changes of this period.

I have opted to limit this examination of popular disorder to New York City. Questions surely can be raised about the typicality of this experience. But I decided early on that it was far better to trace in detail the story of rioting in one central place than to scatter my efforts all over the map. For nearly every riot in New York, there was a similar riot in Philadelphia, Boston, or even the small towns in the interior. The conclusions from a study of New York popular disorder may not hold for every riot in every community in Revolutionary and post-Revolutionary America, but they offer a model that other studies might test and measure if not incorporate.

The staffs of several institutions and libraries were very helpful to my research. These include the University of Oklahoma libraries, the Brown University libraries, the American Antiquarian Society, Butler Library of Columbia University, Bobst Library of New York University, the New-York Historical Society, the New York Public Library, the Library of the Museum of the City of New York, the New Jersey Historical Society, the Historical Documents Collection at Queens College, City University of New York, the Library of Congress, and the Municipal Archives and Record Center of New York City. Certain individuals stand out for their aid in pointing the way toward important sources. I want to thank especially Idilio Gracia Peña of the Municipal Archives and Record Center, Leo Hershkowitz of Queens College, and Thomas Dunnings of the New-York Historical Society.

I have benefited immensely from being a member of the Department of History at the University of Oklahoma since 1980. My colleagues have been encouraging and have offered me every assistance possible. The office staff has typed and retyped countless versions of the manuscript. I want to thank particularly Barbara Million and Martha Penisten. The University Research Council of the University of Oklahoma has provided two travel grants for research and one other grant to prepare the maps and obtain illustrations.

Portions of this book were offered first as papers on two separate occasions at symposia at the New-York Historical Society. Those essays are being published by the New-York Historical Society through the University Press of Virginia. The first essay, "Republican Rioting: Traditions of Anglo-American Mob Behavior in Revolutionary New York City," is to appear in *New Approaches to the History of Colonial and Revolutionary New York* and includes some material from Chapters 1 and 2 of this volume. The second essay, "Culture of Conflict: The Impact of Commercialization on New York Workingmen, 1787–1829," will appear in *New York and the Rise of American Capitalism* and includes some material from Part III of this volume. Those sections of this book which repeat what is in those essays are included here with the permission of the New-York Historical Society.

My research on popular disorder began well over a decade ago in a seminar paper for Gordon Wood. It grew into a dissertation under his invaluable guidance and, with several more years' effort, has emerged as the present work. The number of people who have added to my ideas, corrected my mistakes, and helped me along this tortuous path is almost endless. The following (in alphabetical order) were of special help: Drew Cayton, Gary Cohen, Shank Gilkeson, Rob Griswold, Bruce Laurie, David Levy, Judy Lewis, Pauline Maier, Bill Pencak, Carl Prince, Bob Shalhope, Don Spaeth, John Thomas, Sean Wilentz, Conrad Wright, Jr., and Alfred Young. I am also very grateful to the staff at the Institute of Early American History and Culture, but I would like to thank in particular Philip Morgan and Gil Kelly for their willingness to use their blue pencils. I am equally indebted to Mary Goodman for creating the maps. As much as those mentioned and unmentioned have aided me, the errors and mistakes of interpretation and fact remain mine.

Finally, I want to thank those who are closest to me. My parents have always encouraged me to strive to do what I wanted to do, and to do it the best I can. I hope I can teach Erik and Karin, my children who came along when this project was well on its way to completion, the same lessons. Each member of my family has supported and aided me whenever I was in need, but I must acknowledge the special debt I owe to my best friend, and wife, Ann.

Contents

xi

Illustrations and Tables

FIGURES

TABLES

Abbreviations and Short Titles

MCC	*Minutes of the Common Council of the City of New York* (New York, 1917)
NYC	New York City
NYCA	New York City Municipal Archives and Records Center
NYCGS	New York City Court of General Sessions
NYCOT	New York City Court of Oyer and Terminer
NYCMMPO	New York City Magistrate's Minutes, Police Office
NYCSCPC Bonds	New York City Supreme Court, Police Court, Bonds
NYCSCPCC	New York City Supreme Court, Police Court, Cases
NYHS	New-York Historical Society
NYPL	New York Public Library

Unless otherwise indicated, newspapers cited are from New York City and are cited by short titles; fuller titles are supplied in the Bibliography.

PART I

Traditions

ONE

Pre-Revolutionary Traditions of Anglo-American Mobs

A mobocracy . . . is always usurped by the worst men in the most corrupt times; in a period of violence by the most violent. It is a Briareus with a thousand hands, each bearing a dagger; a Cerberus gaping with ten thousand throats, all parched and thirsting for fresh blood. It is a genuine tyranny, but of all the least durable, yet the most destructive while it lasts. The power of a despot, like the ardour of a summer's sun, dries up the grass, but the roots remain fresh in the soil; a mob-government, like a West-India hurricane, instantly strews the fruitful earth with promiscuous ruins, and turns the sky yellow with pestilence. Men inhale a vapour like the Sirocco, and die in the open air for want of respiration. It is a winged curse that envelops the obscure as well as the distinguished, and is wafted into the lurking places of the fugitives. It is not doing justice to licentiousness, to compare it to a wind which ravages the surface of the earth; it is an earthquake that loosens its foundations, burying in an hour the accumulated wealth and wisdom of ages. Those, who, after the calamity, would reconstruct the edifice of the publick liberty, will be scar[c]ely able to find the model of the artificers, or even the ruins.

Fisher Ames, 1799

When Fisher Ames decried mobocracy in 1799, he was reacting to the political storms swirling about him: to the madness of the Parisian sansculottes who were just then turning from the violence of the guillotine to the despotism of Napoleon, to the frightening specter of racial warfare in the West Indies, and to the bitter, volatile political battles threatening the young American republic. Arch-Federalist and conservative that Ames was, such upheaval in the name of the people and in the guise of mob action seemed all too threatening. Thus he believed that, of all the classical forms of government, the corruption of democracy—mobocracy—was the most destructive. A monarchy could degenerate into despotism or an aristocracy into oligarchy, yet the damage inflicted upon liberty and property might not be permanent: the despot or oligarch seized property but rarely destroyed it. Mob government, however, might be compared best to natural disasters like a "West-India hurricane," sweeping all before it, or an earthquake burying knowledge and property under the rubble of a dying civilization. Mobocracy led inevitably to the worst of all possible worlds: the abandonment of the social contract and a regression to barbarism. Mob government was no government.[1]

Although the fear of mobocracy so vividly portrayed by Fisher Ames grew out of the eighteenth-century Whig science of politics, most Anglo-Americans earlier in the century viewed popular disturbances with less apprehension. Patricians—the merchants, lawyers, and gentry—feared any disorder, but they also believed that riots helped protect them from tyranny. They tolerated moments of license as part of the way society operated. Plebeians—apprentices, laborers, mechanics, and others on the lowest stratum of society—enjoyed the moments of revelry, challenged social authority without directly threatening the social system, and expressed an ideology of their own that emphasized communal welfare and individual fair play. Both sources of support for rioting converged to give the eighteenth-century rioter a sense of legitimacy in his own mind and in the minds of many others. This idea Fisher Ames was incapable of understanding.

For many Anglo-Americans in the mid-eighteenth century, then, popular disorder assumed a quasi legitimacy. Based on an image of society that recognized a single all-encompassing communal interest, this attitude reflected a belief that the people in the street often (but not always) acted in

1. *Works of Fisher Ames* (Boston, 1809), 96–97 (first appeared as Laocoon No. 2 in *Russell's Gazette* [Boston], Apr. 29, 1799). For similar statements, see 2–5, 18, 98–99, 104, 108.

defense of common, shared values. From this perspective, mobs had certain acknowledged social and political functions. Rioting in the eighteenth century, however, was a complex phenomenon. The ideal of a corporate, single-interest world did not go unchallenged. Self-interest persistently gained wider acceptance, and divisions emerged along economic, ethnic, racial, and religious lines.[2] These developments affected patterns of mid-eighteenth-century rioting and prevented the mob from achieving full legitimacy.

To understand this popular disorder, we must first examine more closely the intellectual origins of the mixed attitude toward rioting and then relate them to the popular image of corporatism—an image not necessarily reflective of reality. But these perceptions of society only begin to reveal the true character of the problem. We must then look at the tumultuous crowd itself, dissecting its behavior to understand fully its functions in the eighteenth century and discovering, insofar as possible, who participated therein.

The Commonwealth Writers

The mixed attitude toward rioting in the mid-eighteenth century and Fisher Ames's vitriolic attack on mobocracy shared the same intellectual source—the collective work of English coffeehouse radicals known as True Whigs, or commonwealthmen. These writers created an elaborate critique of English society and politics, identifying corruption and luxury as threats to liberty. Their essays and books were reprinted in America and became very popular among the colonial elite. The ideas and even the language of the commonwealthmen appeared repeatedly in political controversies in the 1730s, 1740s, and 1750s and again during the resistance movement of the 1760s and 1770s, and they form the major intellectual influence on America in the eighteenth century.[3]

2. The best discussions of these developments are Gary B. Nash, *The Urban Crucible: Social Change, Political Consciousness, and the Origins of the American Revolution* (Cambridge, Mass., 1979); and James Henretta, *The Evolution of American Society, 1700–1815: An Interdisciplinary Analysis* (Lexington, Mass., 1973).

3. The literature on the impact of the commonwealthmen is now vast. For a general review, see Robert E. Shalhope, "Toward a Republican Synthesis: The Emergence of an Understanding of Republicanism in American Historiography," *William and Mary Quarterly*, 3d Ser., XXIX (1972), 49–80. See also Caroline

Thus, although Fisher Ames's indictment of mobocracy reflected specific historic circumstances at the close of the century, it also stemmed from the recognition by these earlier political thinkers that rioting was potentially dangerous.[4] Mobs were unpredictable and often uncontrollable. Thomas Gordon, one of the commonwealth writers, cautioned in the 1720s that "one may at any Time gain an Interest in a Mob with a Barrel of Beer" or "by Means of a few odd Sounds, that mean nothing, or something very wild or wicked." He argued that, although "some Quacks in Politicks" ventured "publick Disturbances," believing that they could guide them for their own purposes, the likely outcome was the rise of a demagogic dictator like Caesar or Cromwell.[5]

Writing before the Age of Revolution, thinkers like Gordon still had faith that the people could discern right from wrong. Gordon advised: "It is certain, that the whole People, who are the Publick, are the best Judges whether Things go ill or well with the Publick." "Every Cobler can judge as well as a Statesman, whether he can sit peaceably in his Stall; whether he is paid for his Work; whether the Market, where he buys his Victuals, be well provided; and whether a Dragoon, or a Parish-Officer, comes to him for his Taxes."[6]

These commonwealth writers adhered to the same tripartite classical theory of politics used by Ames, but focused not on the fear that democracy might lead to mobocracy. Instead, they concerned themselves with a threat rooted in the experience of the seventeenth century; their greatest apprehension was that the monarchy would gain too much power and lead to tyranny. In fact, Thomas Gordon went so far as to argue that, even if a

---

Robbins, *The Eighteenth-Century Commonwealthman: Studies in the Transmission, Development, and Circumstance of English Liberal Thought from the Restoration of Charles II until the War with the Thirteen Colonies* (Cambridge, Mass., 1959); Bernard Bailyn, *The Origins of American Politics* (New York, 1968), 54, 117, 137, 141, 143–144; Bailyn, *The Ideological Origins of American Politics* (Cambridge, Mass., 1967), 42–93; H. Trevor Colbourn, *The Lamp of Experience: Whig History and the Intellectual Origins of the American Revolution* (Chapel Hill, N.C., 1965); Gordon S. Wood, *The Creation of the American Republic, 1776–1787* (Chapel Hill, N.C., 1969), 3–45.

4. Ames's language in his antimobocracy quote is very similar to Thomas Gordon's language decrying monarchical despotism. See [John Trenchard and Thomas Gordon], *Cato's Letters; or, Essays on Liberty, Civil and Religious, and Other Important Subjects,* 3d ed. (London, 1733), I, 190.

5. *Ibid.,* IV, 247–254; I, 184–194.

6. *Ibid.,* I, 87.

tumult led to a mobocracy, the resulting anarchy was preferable to tyranny, since "all tumults are in their nature, and must be, short in duration"
and "must soon subside, or settle into some order." Gordon held that "Tyranny," by contrast, "may last for ages, and go on destroying till at last it has
nothing left to destroy."[7]

Under certain circumstances—to oppose tyranny, for instance—many
Anglo-Americans held that they had a right, almost a duty, to riot. The
source of that sense of duty lay in a distinction between natural law and
civil law that was fundamental to the Enlightenment of the mid-eighteenth
century. "The Essence of Right and Wrong," Thomas Gordon wrote,
"does not depend upon Words and Clauses inserted in a Code or a Statute-
Book . . . but upon Reason and the Nature of Things, antecedent to all
Laws."[8] Natural laws, then, depended upon nature and reason, and civil
laws were the statutes and edicts of the government. In a good and free
republic, civil law largely coincided with natural law, but even in the best
of governments there was some space between the two. That gap was to
be bridged by the people themselves, either through participation in the
political process or, when that was not possible, through the enforcement
of their collective will as expressed by crowd action. In short, politics in-
doors, the normal channel of government, was to be checked by politics
out-of-doors, the people in the mob.

Moreover, the commonwealth writers saw a contest between power and
liberty, which affected their attitude toward popular disorder. Because of
the need to safeguard liberty from the power of government and ensure
that mobs could, when the occasion warranted, assert the natural law over
the civil, a wide variety of popular collective activity was accepted. A permanent police establishment or persistent use of the military to curb potential disorder would have threatened liberty and might have strengthened the executive to the point of despotism. In this view holiday frolics,
Pope Day processions, and other tumultuous crowd behavior as well as
more spontaneous riots protesting unjust practices were all lumped together and labeled as mob activity. Such mobs were to be tolerated as long
as they did not go too far, as long as the amount of property destroyed
remained small, and as long as not too many people were hurt seriously.
Those are nebulous limits indeed, but they most accurately describe the
boundaries between toleration and suppression, because those boundaries

7. Thomas Gordon, trans., *The Works of Tacitus,* II (London, 1731), 61. See
also Pauline Maier, *From Resistance to Revolution: Colonial Radicals and the Development of American Opposition to Britain, 1765–1776* (New York, 1972), 42.
   8. [Trenchard and Gordon], *Cato's Letters,* II, 65–67.

depended on the changing *perception* of danger as much as on the changing *amount* of violence and damage. Given the eighteenth-century fear of tyranny, the accompanying disorder was a small price to pay to guarantee liberty and the protection of property.[9]

The Corporate Ideal and Its Problems

The high-minded ideals of the commonwealthmen cannot alone explain the mixed attitude toward rioting among Anglo-Americans in the mid-eighteenth century. Perhaps of greater importance was the popular image of society as a single corporate entity—an image which was under strain as more and more persons sought their private interest and thereby divided society.

The corporate image of society had its roots in the idea of the organic community, containing certain agreed-upon gradations but sharing a single identifiable interest. In the words of Thomas Gordon, "Nothing is so much the Interest of private Men as to see the Publick flourish." Not only will everyone be happier, but "every Man's private Advantage is so much wrapt up in the publick Felicity."[10] Tied in some ways to the ideas of men like Gordon, the ideal reached beyond the readership of the commonwealthmen and included a set of expectations shared by those on top as well as those on the bottom of society. In New York City, for example, corporatism was built into the duties of local government. The city corporation (the term was used purposefully) set the price of bread, regulated the butcher stalls, granted licenses to cartmen, and guaranteed the supply of firewood. In times of exceptional hardship, the city corporation stepped in to alleviate somewhat the suffering of the poor. The distribution of food and fuel in such instances was not the action of a distant, impersonal government. Rather, the magistrates and those of the city's elite who often privately joined such efforts perceived their acts of charity in a highly personal way. They knew many of the poorer members of the community and

9. Maier, *Resistance,* 3–48; William Ander Smith, "Anglo-Colonial Society and the Mob, 1740–1775" (Ph.D. diss., Claremont Graduate School, 1965); John Phillip Reid, "In a Defensive Rage: The Uses of the Mob, the Justification in Law, and the Coming of the American Revolution," *New York University Law Review,* XLIX (1974), 1043–1091; Gordon S. Wood, "A Note on Mobs in the American Revolution," *WMQ,* 3d Ser. XXIII (1966), 635–642; Wood, *Creation of the American Republic,* 18–28, 319–321.

10. [Trenchard and Gordon], *Cato's Letters,* III, 192–199.

believed they had both the responsibility and obligation to protect them.[11]

Although this corporatism stood as an unattainable ideal, it was fundamental to the general tolerance for rioting. The sense of solidarity implied in corporatism supplied the theoretical framework that allowed the mob to believe that it acted for the benefit of the community. The commonwealth distinction between natural law and civil law could be translated on the local level as the distinction between the community's single interest and the intrusions of private, divisive, or outside interests. The problem arose, however, in identifying that true interest of the community.

The eighteenth century was marked by a contest between the ideal of corporatism and an increasing sense of individualism. The classic study of the English bread riot offers an insight into the clash between the ideal and the real. Popular motivation in these disturbances was rooted in a "moral economy" based less on profit than on the greater good of the community. A baker did not charge whatever price the traffic would bear. Instead, he charged the "just price"—the price set by tradition and ancient law as being fair and equitable for both himself and his customer. When fluctuations in the market system enticed the baker or grain merchant to charge more than the just price and when the local officials were unwilling or unable to stop him, very often the townspeople rioted, seized the disputed bread, and either sold it for the baker at or a little below the just price or simply walked off with it.[12]

The moral economy and community interest in these English bread riots reveal a continued faith in the corporate image of society. But they also demonstrate how much that single interest had become a fiction. The baker raised the price of bread or exported grain to more profitable markets because he put his personal aggrandizement above the needs of the community.

11. Edward Countryman, *A People in Revolution: The American Revolution and Political Society in New York, 1760–1790* (Baltimore, 1981), 56–60; Hendrik Hartog, *Public Property and Private Power: The Corporation of the City of New York in American Law, 1730–1870* (Chapel Hill, N.C., 1983), 13–58. For a discussion of this concept in Philadelphia, see Eric Foner, *Tom Paine and Revolutionary America* (New York, 1976), 19–69.

12. E. P. Thompson, "The Moral Economy of the English Crowd in the Eighteenth Century," *Past and Present,* No. 50 (Feb. 1971), 76–136. For further examination of this subject, see George Rudé, *The Crowd in History: A Study of Popular Disturbances in France and England, 1730–1848* (New York, 1964); Rudé, *Paris and London in the Eighteenth Century: Studies in Popular Protest* (New York, 1971); John Bohstedt, *Riots and Community Politics in England and Wales, 1790–1810* (Cambridge, Mass., 1983); Alan Booth, "Food Riots in the North-

New York City did not experience bread riots like those in England, or like those in Boston where crowds on several occasions rioted to prevent the export of grain in times of dearth.[13] But New York City did experience the warring of marketplace and moral economy. During the fall of 1748, when merchants exported grain out of the city at the expense of the local supply and thereby raised its price, every cartload of flour taken to the wharves brought "at Least twenty Cursses from the Common People with many hard Wishes for sending it away."[14] Such grumbling, however, did not produce a riot, largely because city officials, in the spirit of corporatism, sympathized with the "Common People" and, on this and similar occasions, petitioned the provincial government to halt further shipments of grain.[15]

By the middle of the eighteenth century, in both England and America, a new, aggressive individualism emerged to compete with the ideal of communal solidarity. Without the intrusion of the market economy, there would have been no riots in defense of the moral economy. Yet the older ideal remained alive, attested to by the action of English and Bostonian bread rioters, the curses of New York's common folk, and the petitions of New York's city leaders. Thus, even as social and economic change propelled them to a new materialistic and capitalistic order, Anglo-Americans tenaciously held on to their traditional values and extolled the virtues of forgoing private gain for the public good.[16]

The challenge to the corporate image of society did not end with indi-

West of England, 1790–1801," *Past and Present,* No. 77 (Nov. 1977), 84–107; Elizabeth Fox Genovese, "The Many Faces of Moral Economy: A Contribution to a Debate," *Past and Present,* No. 58 (Feb. 1973), 161–168; Walter J. Shelton, *English Hunger and Industrial Disorders: A Study of Social Conflict during the First Decade of George III's Reign* (Toronto, 1973); Roger Wells, "The Revolt of the South-west, 1800–1801: A Study in English Popular Protest," *Social History,* II (1977), 713–714; Dale Edward Williams, "Morals, Markets, and the English Crowd in 1766," *Past and Present,* No. 104 (Aug. 1984), 56–73.

13. Nash, *Urban Crucible,* 76–80, 133–135.

14. Philip L. White, ed., *The Beekman Mercantile Papers, 1746–1799,* I (New York, 1956), 61–62.

15. *Evening Post,* Jan. 9, 1749; Countryman, *A People in Revolution,* 57.

16. Thompson, "Moral Economy," *Past and Present,* No. 50 (Feb. 1971), 76–136; Joyce Appleby, *Capitalism and a New Social Order: The Republican Vision of the 1790s* (New York, 1984), 9–50; Appleby, "The Social Origins of American Revolutionary Ideology," *Journal of American History,* LXIV (1977–1978), 935–959; Henretta, *Evolution of American Society,* 95–107; Wood, *Creation of the American Republic,* 53–70, 75–83, 93–124, 606–607.

vidualism. An emergent market economy increased social divisions, casting rich against poor, white against black, and one ethnic group against another. In this swirling world of conflicting loyalties, it became ever more difficult to identify the true single interest of the community. But the corporate ideal persisted and served groups in conflict as each claimed to protect the real interest of the community.

One major division emerging in the mid-eighteenth century was between patrician and plebeian. Both groups remained linked through paternalism and deference, and both groups remained committed to the corporate ideal. Their differences lay outside the explicit class conflict of the nineteenth century and consisted, instead, of contrasting perceptions of the community interest. The eighteenth-century world was hierarchical; the upper levels of society, in good paternalistic fashion, held that they were the stewards of the community. As part of this charge, the elite believed that they, in their greater wisdom, knew what was best for the community. This assumption meant that, as far as the patricians were concerned, the one interest in society was their interest. More than deference supported this view. Bolstering their position was the elite's control of government and law.

The plebeian, on the other hand, although willing to defer to his betters most of the time, thought that he and his neighbors were the final arbiters of communal welfare. Common folk believed that the community's interests took precedence over any individual's interest. The basis for this simple faith in fair play was the sense of solidarity bred in a small, face-to-face world. As a tradition the notion of community interest reached back, in plebeian minds, for centuries, to the days before the Norman yoke. Although not directly challenging the standard notions of deference, in its extreme form it represented a rough kind of egalitarianism which asserted that every member of the community was entitled to a decent living.[17]

Patrician and plebeian did not always agree on how to determine the community interest, but at times their views of what was good for the community coincided. New York City, for instance, experienced several impressment disturbances, ranging from public demonstrations and the burning of a navy longboat, such as occurred in July 1764, to more vio-

17. E. P. Thompson, "Patrician Society, Plebeian Culture," *Journal of Social History,* VII (1973–1974), 382–405; George Rudé, *Ideology and Popular Protest* (New York, 1980), 27–38; Christopher Hill, "The Norman Yoke," in Hill, *Puritanism and Revolution: Studies in Interpretation of the English Revolution of the Seventeenth Century* (New York, 1958), 50–122.

lent immediate resistance to the press-gang, as in 1758 and 1760, when men were killed.[18] The seamen and laborers susceptible to the press-gang participated in these disturbances because their lives and freedom were at stake and because the gang wrenched men from the community. The patrician, of course, was immune to the ravages of the press-gang but opposed the practice because of its effect on commerce and its drain on the local labor supply. Whenever there was a threat of impressment, local coasters refused to come to the city, and provisions of wood and fuel became scarce.[19] Moreover, as Cadwallader Colden explained to British officials after the incident in 1760, "the Merchants of this Port had suffered by the Seamens removeing to the neighbouring colonies where they were free from any press."[20] When there was this coincidence of interest, even though patrician and plebeian came to it for very different reasons, the patrician might excuse, if not condone, the riot; and the social conflict evident in a moment of popular disorder was minimized.

There were times, however, when the differences between plebeian and patrician visions of the public good sharply diverged, pitting the interest of the poor against the interest of the rich.[21] A controversy over the exchange rate of copper pennies in the winter of 1753–1754 brought this division into the open. The problem began when a self-selected group of leading merchants in New York decided to devalue pennies in relation to the shilling. The ratio set by the assembly to attract specie to the colony had created an exchange imbalance with the mother country that adversely affected trade and, so the merchants claimed, the interests of the province.

Not everyone agreed. To many in New York, the merchants' arbitrary

18. *Gazette: Post-Boy,* July 12, 1764; I. N. Phelps Stokes, *The Iconography of Manhattan Island, 1498–1909* . . . , IV (New York, 1922), 698; *Mercury,* Aug. 11, 1760; Nash, *Urban Crucible,* 266. See also Jesse Lemisch, "Jack Tar in the Streets: Merchant Seamen in the Politics of Revolutionary America," *WMQ,* 3d Ser., XXV (1968), 381–395; John Lax and William Pencak, "The Knowles Riot and the Crisis of the 1740's in Massachusetts," *Perspectives in American History,* X (1976), 163–214.

19. See *Mercury,* Mar. 27, 1758, Sept. 14, 1761.

20. *The Colden Letter Books* (New-York Historical Society, *Collections,* IX–X [New York, 1877–1878]), Pt. I, 14–17.

21. For a discussion of this clash in 18th-century England, see Thompson, "Patrician Society, Plebeian Culture," *Jour. Soc. Hist.,* VII (1973–1974), 382–405; and Thompson, "Eighteenth-Century English Society: Class Struggle without Class?" *Soc. Hist.,* III (1978), 133–165.

action was for personal gain at the expense of the common welfare. One critic argued that the devaluation hurt the poor, because they bought with pennies and were paid in pennies. The merchants' action thus raised the price of bread, fixed in pennies by the city government, and decreased the wages of "all Labouring men." Distraught over this violation of the moral economy, riotous crowds gathered in the street on the morning of January 11, 1754; "armed with Clubs and Staves," with a drummer at their head, they demonstrated their opposition to the proposed devaluation.

The plebs may have viewed the issue one way; the city's elite certainly viewed it another. One newspaper, speaking for the merchants and others who supported the measure, asserted that the new valuation was correct and "calculated for the real Benefit of every Individual in this Province." The grand jury, which made a report on the riot within a week, reiterated this position and claimed that the disorder came from the mistaken zeal of a "deluded People, most of them Strangers, who know as little the true Interest of the Colony, as they themselves were known in it." It was only from "Ignorance" that the rioters could think that they were "defending the Cause of the Poor." Obviously, both plebeians and patricians believed that they knew the true interest of the community, and the patricians, at least, were unwilling to recognize the legitimacy of the plebeian position. Wedded to the notion of a single-interest society, the grand jury ignored the argument of the rioters and declared that "general Harmony . . . prevails in both publick and private Life." The rioters could be so easily dismissed because the grand jury believed that the antidevaluation demonstrators were a "weak People" and "extremely low" and because it questioned whether they really belonged to the community at all—for the rioters "seemed to be Inhabitants of the World," outsiders who were "assembled here by mere chance."[22]

Controversies directly pitting plebeian against patrician, like the 1754 coinage riot, were rare in New York. When they did occur, the poor invariably lost. In 1754 the mayor and aldermen went along with the merchants' new exchange rate, and at least half of the grand jury, nominally acting for the entire community, either were merchants who signed the devaluation agreement or were related to those merchants.[23] When the plebeian contested the power of the patrician, the outcome was rarely in doubt.

22. *Gazette: Post-Boy,* Jan. 14, 21, 1754; *Mercury,* Dec. 24, 31, 1753, Jan. 7, 21, 1754; Nash, *Urban Crucible,* 229.
23. Six men on the grand jury signed the merchant devaluation agreement of December 1753, and six others shared the last names of some of the merchants who signed the agreement. Although the identifications here are not absolute, the

Other divisions in society occasionally surfaced in disturbances during New York's colonial period. In 1712 and again in 1741, racial hatred flared in the city. In the first case, blacks seized the initiative, attempted to burn the city, and killed several whites. In the second instance, no real rebellion took place. Instead, whites acted upon the slightest suggestion of a conspiracy and, supported by the weak circumstantial evidence of suspicious fires and questionable confessions, engaged in an orgy of legal executions. The only extralegal crowd action in 1741 occurred when two convicted blacks broke down on the scaffold and identified others supposedly involved in the plot. Normally this confession would have spared their lives, at least temporarily. But when the sheriff began to return the captives to jail, the crowd became tumultuous and insisted upon an immediate hanging.[24]

Intracommunity conflict in the guise of ethnic and religious animosity was evident in mob activity against Jews. Although a part of New York society for over a century, Jews were a barely tolerated minority; and, during the 1740s, there were at least two anti-Semitic disturbances.[25] One New Testament–quoting correspondent reported in the *Weekly Journal* in May 1743 that "a Rabble" of "Rude unthinking Wretches" harassed a Jewish burial. The leader of this mob, who "by dress" appeared "to be a Gentleman," held out a crucifix and "Mutter'd in Latine . . . his Pater-Noster" as the coffin was let down into its grave. The mock ritual here, interestingly, mimicked hated papist ceremony while interrupting the Jewish last rites.[26] The second report of anti-Semitic crowd action was in a letter written by Governor Clinton to discredit Oliver De Lancey. On Feb-

---

convergence of names is fairly conclusive, particularly since it does not take into account individuals who may have been related through marriage or who were cousins with different names. For the merchants' agreement, see *Mercury*, Dec. 24, 1753; for the grand jury list, see Jan. 21, 1754. See also *Gazette: Post-Boy*, Jan. 14, 1754.

24. Daniel Horsemanden, *The New York Conspiracy*, ed. Thomas J. Davis (Boston, 1971 [orig. publ. New York, 1744]), esp. 109–117. See also T. Wood Clarke, "The Negro Plot of 1741," *New York History*, XXV (1944), 167–181; Thomas J. Davis, "The New York Slave Conspiracy of 1741 as Black Protest," *Journal of Negro History*, LVI (1971), 17–30; and Ferenc M. Szasz, "The New York Slave Revolt of 1741: A Re-examination," *NY Hist.*, XLVIII (1967), 215–230.

25. On the general position of Jews in colonial New York, see Jacob R. Marcus, *The Colonial American Jew, 1492–1776* (Detroit, Mich., 1970), I, 305–312, 397–411, II, 863–873, 890–892.

26. *Weekly Journal*, May 16, 1743.

ruary 2, 1749, De Lancey and a number of his followers borrowed a plebeian practice and blackened their faces, then assaulted the home of a newly arrived Jewish family. The immigrant husband and wife had lived in grand style in Holland but had arrived in New York in straitened circumstances. The rioters smashed all the windows of their house, "afterwards broke open his door," entered the building, "and pulled and tore away every thing to pieces." If this indignity was not enough for this once-affluent Jewish family, De Lancey and his friends "then swore they would lie with the woman," because, as De Lancey declared, the wife "was like Mrs Clinton, and as he could not have her, he would have her likeness."[27]

Despite—perhaps because of—the divisions within society evident in the attacks against Jews, the festering racial hatred, the struggle between plebeian and patrician in the coinage controversy, and even the differences in approach to the issue of impressment, plebeians clung to the corporate image of society. Battered, distorted, and strained, the ideal of the single-interest community remained somehow intact. Jews could be harassed because they were outsiders: the anti-Semitic rioters were merely expressing their opposition to an alien group in their midst. The sheriff could comply with the wishes of the tumultuous crowd in 1741 and hang the confessing blacks because the so-called slave conspiracy threatened the entire white community. Plebeian and patrician each stood his ground in January 1754 because each believed he protected the true interest of the community. Similar faith in corporatism lay behind patrician and plebeian opposition to impressment. Social reality may have reflected increased divisions, but the image of corporatism remained in the minds of many Anglo-Americans and helps to explain why they, at times, eagerly ran into the streets to riot.

Rules and Rituals of Mob Behavior

To understand why popular disorder was quasi-legitimate for mid-eighteenth-century Anglo-Americans, we must look beyond the writings of the commonwealthmen and the somewhat tarnished ideal of corpo-

27. It should be noted that the report of the attack on the Jewish family came from Governor Clinton, and that Clinton and the De Lanceys were political enemies. See E. B. O'Callaghan, ed., *Documents relative to the Colonial History of the State of New York; Procured in Holland, England, and France,* VI (Albany, N.Y., 1855), 471.

ratism to the behavior of the mob itself. What did rioters do in the streets? Why did they act the way they did? Answers to these questions are difficult and varied: each rioter joined in the tumult for his own reasons. Each moment of disorder, as evident from the examples cited, was different. Yet some generalizations can be ventured. Crowds were integral to everyday life: some crowds formed at the behest of colonial leaders, some formed at the behest of plebeian organizers, and others formed extemporaneously. All had the potential for tumult. When the people assembled in the street in a riot, unspoken rules guided their collective behavior. In many cases, these rules provided a set form of popular ceremony and became a type of ritual. The rules were not always followed, but both plebeian and patrician knew what they should and should not do in a riot. One result of this awareness was to minimize physical violence by the mob and by the authorities. The emphasis both on ritual and on the avoidance of violence derived from the sense of communal solidarity behind the activities of most mobs. This concern with ritual and the attendant lack of violence also reflected the need to express social divisions while suppressing overt conflict. Rioting, then, acted to ease social tensions and to express special plebeian concerns.

Despite the lower-class orientation of mid-eighteenth-century crowds, the colonial elite encouraged some public activities that brought the people clamoring into the streets. The intention of these occasions was to tie the worlds of patrician and plebeian closer together in moments of popular celebration. Several times a year the colonial leadership organized public theater to reinforce the traditional bonds of deference and patronage. On the King's Birthday, the anniversary of his coronation, the arrival of a new governor, and the celebration of a great military victory, patricians marched in processions, escorted by the army and local militia. They ordered the cannons of Fort George to fire a salute, they called for bonfires and for all the windows in the city to be illuminated with candles, and they often treated the crowd to food and drink while secreting themselves in a private banquet.[28] For example, in 1745 to commemorate the colonial victory at Louisbourg, the New York elite held a dinner for themselves. But the officials, besides ordering the usual illuminations, had a bonfire built on the edge of the city (to prevent it from spreading to buildings) and distributed twenty gallons of good wine to the crowd.[29] The displays of pa-

28. For examples of such public celebrations, see Stokes, *Iconography*, IV, 533, 535, 537, 539, 541, 543, 554, 585.
29. *Weekly Post-Boy*, July 15, 1745.

triotism and communal good will on holidays showed the elite to be benef-
icent. And even though they dined separately, they also demonstrated a
shared national identity and pride.

The elite used dramatic public ritual in other circumstances as well.
The magistrates, sitting high on the judicial bench, frequently ordered
convicted criminals to be punished publicly. Thus officials in November
1752 had one thief "whipped at the Cart's Tail, from the City-Hall, thro
Wall Street, Hanover Square, and Broad-Street, up to the Hall again."
The path brought the carted criminal through the central parts of the city.
The judges wanted crowds to form, to shout, to jeer. They wanted the
public to see the ignominy of the criminal, and they wanted the public to
join in the punishment.[30] This public punishment revealed, to all who
would behold, the penalties for transgression of the law. It, too, fostered
interclass identity by singling out the offender as a miscreant who no
longer fitted into the community. As in moments of popular celebration,
the elite eagerly embraced the public forum and saw the standing and
shouting of the crowd in the street as natural.

To be most effective, this public theater had to be orderly, exhibiting
"Decency and Decorum." But any time a crowd formed, as everyone in the
eighteenth century knew, tumult was always possible. During the celebration of the fall of Louisbourg, "young Gentlemen-Rakes" showed "their
unchristian Way of rejoicing" by going about the city smashing windows
and shutters. The annual celebration of the King's Birthday also had a degree of disorder. Frolickers echoed the roar and boom from the cannons at
Fort George by firing their own guns, firecrackers, and squibs. Not only
did the din intrude upon the city's peace and quiet, but the actions themselves were dangerous, with harm to property and injury to persons possible. In 1750 a house near Whitehall Slip caught fire, reportedly from
some squibs thrown by boys. Aware of these dangers, officials frowned
upon such activities. But the efforts to stifle such excesses, if the repeated
reports of rowdy incidents are any indication, met little success.[31] Perhaps
more extensive patrols, limiting the official celebration, or not distributing
liquor could have prevented the disorder. But such measures would have
curtailed the effectiveness of the dramaturgical moment, and the elite was
not ready to do that.

30. *Ibid.,* Nov. 27, 1752.
31. *Evening Post,* Nov. 7, 1748; *Weekly Post-Boy,* July 15, 1745; Stokes, *Iconography,* IV, 554, 617, 623, 703, 709.

If misrule surfaced in official celebrations, it was even more evident during explicitly plebeian holidays like Pope Day, New Year's Eve, and Pinkster Day.[32] On these occasions the world was turned upside down. On November 5 (Pope Day) and New Year's Eve the lower orders took over the streets in carnival activity. Pinkster Day, a colonywide celebration during Pentecost, belonged to the black slaves. They were allowed to drink, collect in public, dance, and make merry. At times, they even briefly exchanged roles with their masters. The rowdiness of official celebrations became routine on these days.[33] Unwritten rules—rituals—guided crowd behavior during this seasonal disorder. The established ceremony during moments of misrule, whether on plebeian or official holidays, affected the behavior of the people in the street whenever a crowd formed. Examination of this ritual opens up the deeper meaning of crowd action and reveals some of the interplay between patrician and plebeian in mid-eighteenth-century New York City.[34]

Evidence on popular practices of crowd ritual is often hard to find. Passed on by word of mouth or simply through personal experience, there is often little documentation for the historian to explore. How much of the ritual of English popular culture was transferred across the Atlantic, when it was transferred, and how it might mix with strains of popular culture

32. For citations on Pope Day, see n. 53, this chapter. For rowdiness on New Year's, see *Mercury*, Jan. 7, 1765; New York, *The Colonial Laws of New York, from the Year 1664 to the Revolution, . . .* V (Albany, N.Y., 1894), 532–533; Alice Morse Earle, *Colonial Days in Old New York*, 2d ed. (Port Washington, N.Y., 1965), 185–202.

33. Earle, *Colonial Days*, 185–202; E.A.A., "Sassafras and Swinglingtow; or, Pinkster Was a Holiday," *American Notes and Queries: A Journal for the Curious*, VI (1946), 35–40; A. J. Williams-Myers, "Pinkster Carnival: Africanisms in the Hudson River Valley," *Afro-Americans in New York Life and History*, IX (1985), 7–17. The Pinkster Day celebration parallels the burlesque voting on election days of blacks in New England. See Joseph P. Reidy, "'Negro Election Day' and Black Community Life in New England, 1750–1860," *Marxist Perspectives*, I (1978), 102–117.

34. For a general anthropological discussion of ritual and symbolic action, see Max Gluckman, ed., *Essays on the Ritual of Social Relations* (Manchester, 1962); Gluckman, *Order and Rebellion in Tribal Africa: Collected Essays, with an Autobiographical Introduction* (London, 1963); Victor W. Turner, *The Ritual Process: Structure and Anti-Structure* (Chicago, 1969); Turner, *Dramas, Fields, and Metaphors: Symbolic Action in Human Society* (Ithaca, N.Y., 1974); Turner, "Symbols in Ndembu Ritual," in Max Gluckman, ed., *Closed Systems and Open Minds: The*

from other ethnic groups remain difficult questions to answer with any real precision. Although much of the exact knowledge of specific ritual may have been lost, it is clear that New Yorkers, like most colonial Americans, were conscious of many English popular traditions. If New Yorkers did not always practice the ritual of a certain tradition, the custom was often filed away in the collective mentalité to be resuscitated when the need arose, in its old form or in a new form more responsive to popular needs.[35]

Traces of four overlapping types of Anglo-American ritual can be detected in the popular disorder of New York and its environs before 1765. The first of these is the ritual of communal regulation known as the *charivari*. Called *shivaree, skimmington,* or *rough music,* it was a ritual that singled out a wide variety of misbehavior. In the eighteenth and nineteenth centuries in England, it ordinarily included treating the victim to a midnight concert of pots, pans, and improvised drums as well as shouts and screams. The musicians serenaded all kinds of miscreants, from the wife beater to the shrewish wife, and from the sexual deviant to the worker that broke an agreement with his fellow laborers. The range of activity also extended beyond simple noisemaking to include mock (as well as real) attacks on the object of ridicule.[36] Evidence of rough music in New York City in the mid-eighteenth century has not been found, but there is a reference to a "skimmington ride" in Poughkeepsie in 1751, and in nearby

---

Limits of Naïvety in Social Anthropology (Edinburgh, 1964), 20–51; and Clifford Geertz, *The Interpretation of Cultures: Selected Essays* (New York, 1973).

35. For a discussion of the transference of popular culture across the Atlantic, see Alfred Young, "English Plebeian Culture and Eighteenth-Century American Radicalism," in Margaret C. Jacob and James R. Jacob, eds., *The Origins of Anglo-American Radicalism* (London, 1984), 185–212.

36. This brief summary is based on Violet Alford, "Rough Music or Charivari," *Folklore,* LXX (1959), 505–518; Natalie Zemon Davis, "The Reasons of Misrule," in Davis, *Society and Culture in Early Modern France: Eight Essays* (Stanford, Calif., 1975), 97–123; Davis, "Charivari, Honor, and Community in Seventeenth-Century Lyon and Geneva," in John J. MacAloon, ed., *Rite, Drama, Festival, Spectacle: Rehearsals toward a Theory of Cultural Performance* (Philadelphia, 1984), 42–57; Edward P. Thompson, "'Rough Music': Le charivari anglais," *Annales: Economies, sociétés, civilisations,* XXVII (1972), 285–312; Martin Ingram, "Ridings, Rough Music, and the 'Reform of Popular Culture' in Early Modern England," *Past and Present,* No. 105 (Nov. 1984), 79–113; Bryan D. Palmer, "Discordant Music: Charivari and Whitecapping in North America," *Labour / Le travailleur,* I (1978), 5–62; Young, "English Plebeian Culture," in Jacob and Jacob, eds., *Origins of Anglo-American Radicalism,* 186–212.

Elizabeth, New Jersey, "regulators" practiced a form of "charivari" on wife beaters.[37]

Elements of the ritual, however, can be discerned in other forms of popular disorder within the city. Both the charivari and the Pope Day processions often featured effigies, parades through the streets, and raucous noisemaking. The clamor accompanying other public holidays and New Year's bore similarities to rough music. More suggestive were the overtones of the actions of Oliver De Lancey and his friends. Their efforts paralleled the behavior of those charivaris aimed at disrupting marriages objected to by the community. (The physical comparison of the Jewish wife to Governor Clinton's wife is instructive in this context.) Moreover, after 1765, aspects of the charivari again surfaced in the demonstrations against violators of nonimportation agreements and in the rail riding of suspected tories.

The second form of plebeian ritual detected in New York crowd action is the ritual of misrule. Here the normal rules of society were suspended and, as in the European carnival, all kinds of outrageous and fantastic behavior tolerated. New York crowds did not go to the extremes of southern European and Latin Mardi Gras celebrants. Nor were their symbols as loaded with class meaning as the symbols in the carnival of sixteenth-century Romans.[38] But on popular holidays such as the King's Birthday, and especially on the plebeian celebrations of Pope Day, New Year's Eve, and Pinkster Day, they did follow set patterns of behavior which purposely deviated from the accepted behavior of the rest of the year. Thus the pageantry of earlier lords of misrule in England, with "their pipers piping, their drummers thundering, their stumps dancing, their bells jingling, their handkerchiefs swinging about their heads like madmen, their hobbyhorses and other monsters skirmishing amongst the rout," resembles much of the ceremonial discord of the Pope Day processions and even the parade and burning of a royal barge in an anti-impressment riot in 1764.[39]

37. *Gazette: Post-Boy,* Dec. 13, 1752; *Documents Relating to the Colonial History of the State of New Jersey, Archives of the State of New Jersey,* 1st Ser., XIX (Paterson, N.J., 1897), 225–226, 326–327; Young, "English Plebeian Culture," in Jacob and Jacob, eds., *Origins of Anglo-American Radicalism,* 189–190.

38. Emmanuel Le Roy Ladurie, *Carnival in Romans,* trans. Mary Feeney (New York, 1979). See also Peter Burke, *Popular Culture in Early Modern Europe* (New York, 1978), 178–204.

39. Quoted in John R. Gillis, *Youth and History: Tradition and Change in European Age Relations, 1777–Present* (New York, 1974), 27; see also 26–34; and Davis, "Reasons of Misrule," in Davis, *Society and Culture,* 97–123.

Closely allied to misrule was the ritual of role reversal, in which the crowd purposefully took on the attributes of its social betters. This mimesis was intended both to ridicule the patrician and to remind him of his duties. The lords of misrule in England, for example, chose one individual as a mock king, who would then act as the centerpiece of the ritual. In New York, Pinkster Day included such role reversal. During the Pope Day pageant, revelers carted effigies about town in the same manner as officials had criminals carted through the streets, they enforced a general illumination by smashing unlit windows, and they collected money to support their efforts in a kind of unofficial tax. Role reversal was evident also in other mob activity. Little is known about the behavior of the coinage rioters of January 1754 except that they paraded the streets with a drummer at their head "armed with Clubs and Staves." The presence of that drummer suggests an attempt to copy the forms of militia organization and, perhaps, the processions of officials on holidays. Role reversal appeared in the harassment of the Jewish burial as well, where the rioters mimicked Catholic last rites to parody a Jewish ceremony.[40]

The final ritual evident in New York mob activity was closely tied to the first three—the rite of passage. Anthropologists argue that this ritual can take many forms, including misrule and role reversal, and enabled people to deal with the awkward moments of passing from one status to another.[41] Thus, as a mode of collective behavior, it could follow any of the three rituals outlined above, or it might appear as mere rowdyism. It is treated here as a separate category because of its special association with the passage from adolescence to adulthood. The ritual misbehavior on New Year's, for instance, could be dismissed as "one of the disorderly riotous Frolicks, that most unreasonably are practiced annually," largely because the perpetrators were thought to be young men and other dependents. A similar attitude appeared whenever there was rowdy behavior connected to public celebrations. The window and shutter smashers during the celebration of the victory at Louisbourg in 1745 were "*young* Gentlemen-Rakes." To put it simply, eighteenth-century New Yorkers often tolerated the disorder

40. On ritual role reversal, see John Brewer, *Party Ideology and Popular Politics at the Accession of George III* (Cambridge, 1976), 163–200; Ladurie, *Carnival in Romans,* 109, 190–192, 202, 206–208, 301–324; Burke, *Popular Culture,* 188–192. See also Turner, *The Ritual Process,* 177–178.

41. Turner, *The Ritual Process;* Max Gluckman, "Les Rites de Passage," in Gluckman, ed., *Essays on the Ritual of Social Relations,* 24–40.

of young men because they assumed that those young men needed occasionally to misbehave.[42]

These rituals did not provide a formula that every crowd then followed without variance. For the plebs, any tumult was fun, and the suspension of the normal rules of social behavior in riots and annual plebeian rituals alike made for grand entertainment. The participants acted out fantasies, behaved uproariously, enjoyed the pleasures of shattering glass, contributed to a blazing bonfire, and shouted as loudly as possible in the streets. For the great crowds who watched this rowdyism—and in this type of street theater the boundary between participant and audience was never sharply defined—the carnival atmosphere of mob action was enough in itself. Men and boys were running through the streets, coats turned inside out, some faces blackened, noise and disorder all around. For a brief moment the normal routine was reversed, and those on the bottom of society—be they day laborers, seamen, apprentices, journeymen, or even master craftsmen— could temporarily enjoy the pleasures of disorder. Within this turbulent festivity, however, certain patterns emerged. The people in the street knew what should and should not be done.

This emphasis on set patterns of ceremony and behavior (however honored in the breach), with the belief that the mob generally acted to protect the community's single interest, tended to minimize violence in a riot. In the 1754 coinage riot, the members of the mob did not use their clubs and staves to beat those merchants who supported the new valuation. Instead, the mob merely marched behind the drummer to demonstrate anger. In an anti-impressment riot in July 1764, New Yorkers seized a barge belonging to a British man-of-war, then paraded through the city streets carrying it to the Common, where they fed it to a devouring bonfire. Although the captain of the British warship was in the city, the crowd "offered no Injury" to him. The theme of limited violence was repeated over and over again in the anti-Jewish disturbances in the 1740s, in the rowdiness on holidays, and on almost every occasion a tumultuous crowd met.

There were, however, exceptions. Rioting evokes passions, and although those passions were ordinarily channeled along relatively peaceful lines, occasionally the rioters pushed too far and too hard. Violence be-

42. *Mercury,* Jan. 7, 1765; *Weekly Post-Boy,* July 15, 1745 (emphasis added); Davis, "Reasons of Misrule," in Davis, *Society and Culture,* 97–123; Gillis, *Youth and History,* 26–34; Bernard Capp, "English Youth Groups and *The Pinder of Wakefield," Past and Present,* No. 76 (Aug. 1977), 127–133.

came most pronounced in opposition to impressment when sailors confronted the press-gang face to face. At such times the stakes were high. In
1758 and 1760, sailors, who knew that impressment into His Majesty's
navy meant, in effect, forfeiting their lives to a repressive and often deadly
service, turned to violence that itself led to death. In the 1758 incident
several members of a merchant ship were impressed, but four of the crew
resisted and barricaded themselves in their ship's roundhouse. Armed
with blunderbusses, they fired at the press-gang, mortally wounding one
man, and surrendered only when some regulars appeared and fired a volley at them.[43] The 1760 affair occurred in the harbor, when the crew of a
ship just arrived from Lisbon refused to be boarded from a longboat sent
by a British man-of-war. The sailors seized the ship's small arms and fired
at the navy longboat. Reinforcements were called up and more shots exchanged, damaging the ship, wounding one sailor, and killing another.[44]
Both of these cases were the actions of desperate men faced with a hopeless
situation and represent the exception rather than the rule.

Brutally assailing an individual or engaging in extensive destruction of
property threatened to wreak havoc in the community. Consequently,
Anglo-American mobs concentrated their efforts on the symbols of their
grievances as a means of limiting violence. More typical of colonial riots
was the 1764 impressment disturbance, in which the rioters burned the
barge of the British press-gang. Destruction of the barge prevented the
immediate departure of the press-gang and their forced recruits. The action was effective and pointed. At the same time, the crowd surely knew
that the barge was easily replaceable. It served best as a symbol of British
authority. Likewise, when a mob assailed a bawdyhouse, it first destroyed
the furniture and bedding, and then if the populace was really irate, it
might pull the building down. The idea was to do away with the indispensable tools of the trade. The prostitutes themselves were left un-
touched. Mobs in Boston prevented the exportation of grain by unrigging
the ship and dismantling its rudder. There was no permanent damage, but
the ship was prevented temporarily from leaving port.[45] Property, rather
than persons, was almost always the object of the mob's wrath. There were
few deaths in colonial riots.

43. Stokes, *Iconography,* IV, 698.
44. *Mercury,* Aug. 11, 1760.
45. Maier, *Resistance,* 4–5; Carl Bridenbaugh, *Cities in the Wilderness: The
First Century of Urban Life in America, 1625–1742* (New York, 1938), 70,
223–224, 382–384, 388–389.

The deemphasis of violence worked in two ways. Rioters understood what they could and could not do. But so, too, did the officials. As long as the mob kept within certain traditional bounds, magistrates did not react with violence to repress disturbances. Instead, they attempted to exert influence over the mob to persuade it to disperse.

Ultimately, of course, the local elite could also wield the full force of the state behind their requests. The magistracy could call on a posse comitatus, the militia, and even the army to coerce a crowd. But patricians were generally loath to do so.[46] They did not want to see bloodshed shatter the peace and unity of their community. They did not want their neighbors, even socially inferior neighbors, injured. Most important, they did not want to admit that they could not control their community even during a riot. To resort to force was to concede that the traditional bonds of deference and patronage had failed. Successfully limiting a disturbance by using personal influence over the mob reinforced the social authority of the elite.[47] Interestingly, the English Riot Act of 1715, which was copied by several American colonies, was so constructed as to aid the magistrates in their informal control over the crowd. The Riot Act allowed officials to call upon the military without fear of later civil suits from individuals in the mob. But no action could be taken until the mob had been granted an hour to disperse. This grace period often allowed the mob to achieve limited goals; and, in turn, the power reposed in the magistrates strengthened their hands in dealing with the mob. The community's needs were met by the action of the mob; the larger challenge to social authority was avoided.[48]

Pope Day

Insight into the complexities of eighteenth-century mob ritual can be gleaned from New York's Pope Day. This holiday commemorated the failed plot of the Catholic Guy Fawkes to blow up the Houses of Parliament in 1605 and was marked in England by bonfires, effigy processions, and some rowdyism.[49] In early New York City, Pope Day was just another

46. Maier, *Resistance,* 16–20.

47. Thompson, "Patrician Society, Plebeian Culture," *Jour. Soc. Hist.,* VII (1973–1974), 403–405.

48. Max Beloff, *Public Order and Popular Disturbances, 1660–1714* (London, 1938), 136–137; Maier, *Resistance,* 24–26; New York, *The Colonial Laws of New York,* V, 532–533.

49. Robert W. Malcolmson, *Popular Recreations in English Society, 1700–1850* (Cambridge, 1973), 25–26, 54, 79–80.

of the officially sponsored patriotic ceremonies, and until 1748 the holiday had been celebrated largely under official auspices. For example, in 1737 one newspaper reported that the "Gentlemen of his Majesty's Council, the Assembly and Corporation [city officials], and the other principal Gentlemen and Merchants of this City waited upon" the lieutenant governor at Fort George, "where the Royal Healths were drank, as usual, under the Discharge of the Cannon and at Night the City was illuminated."[50] This celebration mirrored activities on other great patriotic anniversaries. But from 1748 on, New Yorkers in the street, borrowing and building upon the Boston practice, began celebrating the holiday with their own ritual by parading and then by burning effigies of the pope, the Pretender, and the devil.[51] This new ceremony, which later served as a model for Revolutionary mob action, not ony reveals some of the functions of mob ritual but also suggests some of the inner tensions evident in eighteenth-century crowd action.[52]

In 1755 the Pope Day effigies were carried about the city on a bier at night "hideously formed, and as humourously contrived, the Devil standing close behind the Pope, seemingly paying his compliments to him, with a three prong'd Pitchfork . . . on the Back . . . [was] the young Pretender standing before the Pope, waiting his commands." The procession halted before the lodgings of the captured French general, Baron Dieskau, to reinforce the anti-Catholic message. The baron knew how to defuse a potentially dangerous situation and paid homage to the celebrants by sending down some silver. The crowd recognized the traditional concession, returned the favor with three huzzahs, and then "march'd off to a proper Place," where they "set Fire to the Devil's Tail, burning the Three to Cinders."[53]

50. Quoted in Stokes, *Iconography*, IV, 554.

51. Newspaper reports clearly state that 1748 was the first year the effigy procession appeared in New York. *Weekly Journal*, Nov. 7, 1748; *Gazette: Post-Boy*, Nov. 7, 1748.

52. Young, "English Plebeian Culture," in Jacob and Jacob, eds., *Origins of Anglo-American Radicalism*, 186–212; Peter Shaw, *American Patriots and the Rituals of Revolution* (Cambridge, Mass., 1981), 17–18, 71–73, 177–182, 197–217.

53. Although there is no direct evidence of Pope Day processions' occurring every year in New York City, the scattered references in 1748, 1755, 1757, and 1765 suggest that there was an annual celebration of Pope Day starting in 1748 and running to 1764. *Weekly Journal*, Nov. 7, 1748; *Gazette: Post-Boy*, Nov. 7, 1748, Nov. 10, 1755, Nov. 7, 1757; Stokes, *Iconography*, IV, 673, 675; *Mercury*,

PLATE 1. Anti-Catholic, anti-Pretender, and anti-Devil Silver Beaker.

Made by Hughes Lossieux in Saint-Malo, 1707–1708, and engraved by Joseph Leddel in New York City, 1750. Courtesy of the Museum of the City of New York.

In images probably similar to those of the Pope Day effigy celebrations, the devil leads the pope and the Pretender into the mouth of Hell. Text reads: "Three mortal enemies Remember. The Devil Pope and the Pretender. / Most wicked damnable and evil. The Pope Pretender and the Devil. / I wish they were all hang'd in a rope. The Pretender Devil and the Pope."

The meaning of this ritual is complex: it expressed faith in the standing order and simultaneously questioned it. On the surface, Pope Day was a patriotic holiday, celebrating the Protestant succession. All levels of society shared this patriotism, which was of particular importance to New York's disparate Protestants, who were united only in their ardent anti-Catholicism. But there are deeper meanings behind the ritual—meanings that suggest that the Pope Day ceremony after 1748 also acted as an implicit challenge to the social hierarchy. In other words, patriotic ritual served as a screen to hide the more subtle shadows of social conflict.[54]

The intricacies of the symbolic meaning of the Pope Day ritual are evident when we examine the New York crowd's selection of effigies. Although the procession occurred on the anniversary of Guy Fawkes's attempted misdeed, that Catholic fanatic held little significance for New Yorkers in the mid-eighteenth century. The crowd, instead, chose its own anti-Catholic symbols. The patriotic message of all three effigies is clear. The pope naturally represented the hated Romanism, and after the failed invasions of 1715 and 1745, the Pretender epitomized the popular fear of the arbitrary and Catholic monarch in the Stuart mold. The devil, leading, whispering, or hovering about the scene, was a common motif representing evil in eighteenth-century iconography.[55]

The submerged challenge to social authority is less evident. The attack on popery may have represented, in the popular mind, a criticism of all church hierarchy. More important is the central role of the Pretender's effigy. It is granted, of course, that its desecration represented an explicit statement of loyalty to the current regime. But there may have been other, even contradictory meanings to the effigy. The Pretender, despite all his faults, was also a member of the aristocracy. Engraved silver beakers of the

---

Nov. 7, 1757; G. D. Scull, ed., *The Montresor Journals* (New-York Historical Society, *Collections,* XIV [New York, 1881]), 338–339.

54. Much of the following analysis builds upon the discussion of symbols and ritual by anthropologists Max Gluckman and Victor Turner. See Gluckman, ed., *Essays on the Ritual of Social Relations;* Gluckman, *Order and Rebellion in Tribal Africa;* Turner, *The Ritual Process;* and Turner, *Dramas, Fields, and Metaphors.*

55. Shaw, *American Patriots,* 17–18. For the prominence of the devil in 18th-century iconography, see U.S., Library of Congress, *The American Revolution in Drawings and Prints: A Checklist of 1765–1790 Graphics in the Library of Congress,* comp. David H. Cresswell (Washington, D.C., 1975), 240, 244–247, 249, 257, 260, 271–272, 275, 278, 280, 283, 296, 304, 354, 357.

New York Pope Day effigies portray the Pretender as a Scottish lord.[56] With sword at his side, the effigy may have stood as a muted symbol of the aristocracy. Under the guise of patriotism, the common folk could denigrate and humiliate this effigy, which represented an individual ordinarily untouchable. Moreover, there is another possible meaning to the ritual which almost negates the loyalism of the holiday. The prominence of the effigy of the Pretender—who lost his claim to the throne because of the perfidy of James II—may have acted also as a reminder to the monarchy of what might become of the Hanoverian dynasty if it behaved too arbitrarily, if it got too close to the Catholics, or if it betrayed the people.

The evidence that these effigies served as a type of challenge to authority is tenuous, but this interpretation becomes more compelling when placed in the context of the commencement of the Pope Day parades. The political and economic conditions of the 1740s and 1750s certainly were conducive to a New York plebeian challenge to the standing order. During these years a bitter factional rivalry divided the provincial elite. In the process, New York's leadership began to compete for political support from the electorate. Asked to cast their ballots under the watchful eyes of patricians, the common folk witnessed a divided elite who charged one another with failing to protect the welfare of all. Furthermore, the Treaty of Aix-la-Chapelle with France left many New Yorkers feeling betrayed in the fall of 1748. The French remained encamped upon their frontiers, and hostile Indians continued to lurk in the forests. Negotiators in Europe had surrendered the fortress of Louisbourg on Cape Breton and thereby nullified the one great colonial triumph.[57] Economic developments supported these political recriminations. New York merchants scrambled to maximize profits in a mercurial economy in which fortunes were easily won and lost. At times, as in the fall of 1748, such men ignored the moral economy and exported flour to the French West Indies, violating both local customs to protect the price of bread and imperial regulations by trading with a long-

56. Alfred Young kindly informed me of these engravings and provided me with copies of pictures of them. One goblet is in the Winterthur Museum (accession no. 56.521). The other is in the Museum of the City of New York (Museum Purchase, 76.79). See also Jerry E. Patterson, *The City of New York: A History Illustrated from the Collections of the Museum of the City of New York* (New York, 1978), 53.

57. Patricia U. Bonomi, *A Factious People: Politics and Society in Colonial New York* (New York, 1971), 103–178; Nash, *Urban Crucible*, 198–204, 227–229,

time enemy. But even beyond 1748, these decades, frequently marred by war with France, experienced an inflation which created hardship for the poor despite general prosperity and near-full employment.[58]

Thus, as New York filled with men returning from war in 1748, the Pope Day effigy procession, long practiced in Boston, offered itself as a means to express contrasting emotions—clearly hatred for French papists was dominant, but perhaps also this new ritual expressed dissatisfaction with the colonial leadership, the peace, and, subliminally, the king. Class antagonism, confused factional politics, the rise of a market economy, and lower-class national pride, then, combined to transform Pope Day from a conventional and official celebration to a special plebeian holiday from 1748 to at least 1765.

Membership of the Mob

The Pope Day processions that began in 1748, the New Year's frolics practiced throughout the century, the less regular rowdyism accompanying official celebrations, and the sporadic rioting against impressment and over issues like the coinage controversy of 1754—all were plebeian activities. Youths, seamen, mechanics, laborers, and black slaves were the main participants. The patrician might stroll across the plebeian stage and might even participate in the drama. He too, after all, was a member of the community and shared, to some degree, in the popular culture.[59] But if he did join in or lead the tumult, he was only temporarily entering a world in which he might exert some influence, but a world he could never completely control. His presence did not alter the basic plebeian character of rioting.

There are problems in identifying the participants in eighteenth-century mobs. Officials rarely made arrests, and even if they did, they did not record much information on the individuals arrested. Impressionistic evidence about the character of the rioters is unreliable. Magistrates ordinarily denied that those higher up in society participated in disturbances. Instead, they usually insisted (thus implying another connection

232. For an expression of New York dissatisfaction with the peace, see *Gazette: Post-Boy,* July 25, 1748.

58. *Gazette: Post-Boy,* Sept. 12, 1748, July 17, 1749; *Evening Post,* Jan. 9, 1749; White, ed., *Beekman Papers,* I, 61–62; Nash, *Urban Crucible,* 176–178, 180, 227–229.

59. Malcolmson, *Popular Recreations,* 68–71.

with the more traditional rites of passage) that rioters were young men, boys, and other dependents. In 1768, for example, Governor Henry Moore referred to a group of rioters, many of whom were probably white adults, as "a Rabble of Negroes and Children."[60]

Similarly, the identification of the 1754 coinage rioters as the dregs of society cannot be trusted. One articulate spokesman published a defense of the poorer New Yorkers' position, but not of the riot, in a newspaper. There is no indication that this spokesman joined in the riot, but his willingness to speak out against the devaluation demonstrates that not all literate New Yorkers agreed with the merchants. Moreover, the grand jury itself half admitted that its generally pejorative description of the character of the rioters was misleading when it declared that "*almost* every Inhabitant of Reputation" had not participated in the riot. Perhaps, then, not all of those who armed themselves with clubs or staves and fell in behind the shrill beat of a drum on a wintry January morning were so "extremely low" that they "seemed to be Inhabitants of the World, assembled here by mere Chance."[61]

Compounding the problems of identification is the fact that not all eighteenth-century mobs were the same. Although most rioters believed that they acted for the true interests of the community, the effect of the disturbance varied. The devaluation crisis of the winter of 1753–1754 divided the community, and that division probably had some effect on the mix of the aroused crowd. The anti-Semitic mobs of the 1740s certainly marked a division within the community. But in these cases there were clearly some of the gentry involved. During the interruption of the Jewish funeral, the leader was identified by his dress and his command of Latin as a gentleman. Likewise, in all probability the friends accompanying Oliver De Lancey in his attack on the Jewish family were from his level in society and shared not only De Lancey's anti-Semitism but also his perverse sense of humor.[62]

If the degree of communal agreement could affect the composition of the mob, so, too, could the special relevance of the issue triggering the tumult. Seamen and day laborers, no doubt, dominated impressment disturbances, because it was their lives that were most immediately at stake.[63] Merchants

60. *Gazette,* Nov. 28, 1768.
61. *Gazette: Post-Boy,* Jan. 14, 21, 1754 (emphasis added); *Mercury,* Jan. 7, 14, 21, 1754.
62. O'Callaghan, ed., *Docs. Col. Hist. N.Y.,* VI, 471.
63. On one night in May 1757, the British army swept through the city, collect-

and even artisans may have sympathized with the goals of the rioters, but they themselves were relatively immune to the coercive tactics of the press-gang. Moreover, there was probably a difference between the composition of those impressment mobs that used less violence and the composition of those that produced bloodshed. In the 1758 and 1760 incidents, the men who fired shots and whose lives were threatened by impressment were identified as seamen. On the other hand, the crowd accompanying the burning of the barge no doubt represented a broad spectrum of the community. Such demonstrations tended to attract all sorts of people.[64]

Because of the paucity of evidence and this variety in rioting, little can be said *conclusively* about the composition of the eighteenth-century mob. There were mobs predominantly made up of the lowest levels of society, and there was a rare mob almost entirely made up of the elite. But, in general, most mobs had a mixture of lower and middling elements with, on occasion, a few patricians thrown in. Government officials were probably correct, then, when they asserted that "Negroes and Children" and sailors participated in the disorder of 1768. Attracted by the sheer spirit of saturnalia and by real grievances, blacks, adolescents, and jack-tars probably joined most tumultuous crowds. But so, too, did many others. Day laborers and journeymen took part in the joys of the mob, as did some shopkeepers and artisans. Occupying the middle stratum of society, many of these men were careful not to step too far beyond the bounds of accepted behavior. They were also small property owners who did not want to see the mob become wantonly destructive. Often the leaders in the workshop, they were leaders in the mob. Magistrates, merchants, and others from the higher levels of society occasionally joined in.[65] In short, the entire community might be represented in a riot. If the members of the local gentry did not participate themselves, they often condoned the mob's action. Yet, however broad the range of participants, nothing could change the essentially plebeian character of the mob.

---

ing about 800 men. Half, mostly tradesmen, were released quickly. The aim was to take in deserting sailors who wanted to sign up on the more profitable and comfortable privateers commissioned in New York. Stokes, *Iconography,* IV, 690–691.

64. *Ibid.,* 698; *Mercury,* Aug. 11, 1760.

65. Jesse Lemisch, "The American Revolution Seen from the Bottom Up," in Barton J. Bernstein, ed., *Towards a New Past: Dissenting Essays in American History* (New York, 1968), 3–45; Lemisch, "Jack Tar," *WMQ,* 3d Ser., XXV (1968), 371–409; Pauline Maier, "The Charleston Mob and the Evolution of Popular Politics in Revolutionary South Carolina, 1765–1784," *Persp. Am. Hist.,* IV

Although there was a level of tolerance toward rioting in New York in the middle of the eighteenth century, attitudes remained mixed. In every mob action the fear persisted that the cure was worse than the disease. Too much rioting or public disorder led to mob rule; and, mob rule, while not as threatening as a tyrannical monarch in the minds of some, was still very dangerous.

Members of the New York elite especially were aware of the dangers of rioting. Many owned vast tracts of land in New York's patroonships, feared agrarian unrest, and remained suspicious of mob activity. New Yorkers did not have to look far to see examples of riotous crowds seizing the initiative, ignoring law, threatening property, and pushing toward anarchy. Across the Hudson, in nearby New Jersey, land rioters opposed quitrents and challenges to their land titles by freeing imprisoned compatriots, tearing down houses, and attacking officials during the 1740s and 1750s. New York's great landlords faced similar difficulties in the 1760s, reaching a dramatic peak with the great tenant uprising of 1766, which had to be put down, in part, with British regulars. Such troubles continued into the Revolutionary war. Moreover, the problem with land rioters extended to newly settled areas in the 1770s, when New York attempted to exert control over the area that later became Vermont.[66] In fact, the province in 1774 passed its only riot act of the eighteenth century to deal specifically with the turmoil and tumult caused by the Green Mountain Boys.[67]

Thus, for the men who controlled New York, the riot was a measure of

---

(1970), 173–196; Dirk Hoerder, *People and Mobs: Crowd Action in Massachusetts during the American Revolution, 1765–1780* (Berlin, 1971); Wood, "Note on Mobs," *WMQ*, 3d Ser., XXIII (1966), 635–642.

66. For an overview of this land rioting, see Edward Countryman, "'Out of the Bounds of the Law': Northern Land Rioters in the Eighteenth Century," in Alfred F. Young, ed., *The American Revolution: Explorations in the History of American Radicalism* (DeKalb, Ill., 1976), 37–69. See also Thomas L. Purvis, "Origins and Patterns of Agrarian Unrest in New Jersey, 1735 to 1754," *WMQ*, 3d Ser., XXXIX (1982), 600–627; Gary S. Horowitz, "New Jersey Land Riots, 1745–1755" (Ph.D. diss., Ohio State University, 1966); Irving Mark, *Agrarian Conflicts in Colonial New York, 1711–1775* (New York, 1940); Oscar Handlin, "The Eastern Frontier of New York," *NY Hist.*, XVIII (1937), 50–75; Bonomi, *A Factious People,* 179–228; Sung Bok Kim, *Landlord and Tenant in Colonial New York: Manorial Society, 1664–1775* (Chapel Hill, N.C., 1978), 281–415; Staughton Craig Lynd, "The Revolution and the Common Man: Farm Tenants and Artisans in New York Politics, 1777–1778" (Ph.D. diss., Columbia University, 1962).

67. New York, *The Colonial Laws of New York,* V, 647–655.

last resort. Only after all other means of redress failed or proved inadequate could reliance on the mob be condoned. Moments of public license were to be limited. Once the demonstration was over, the celebrants were to go home. For no matter how important the grievance triggering the disturbance, the irrational passions sometimes released in a riot could lead to the destruction of more property and question directly the accepted channels of authority. Even if the rioters committed no serious damage, members of the elite knew that their role as the guardians of society was being challenged, and they therefore wanted to limit the moment of disorder.[68]

Moreover, although the belief in the homogeneous interest of society pervaded all levels of a community, it increasingly failed to reflect reality in both England and America. Vast distinctions of wealth existed in Great Britain, and, as English historians have chronicled, the clash between patrician and plebeian cultures intensified.[69] These developments are less clear in colonial America. But there can be no doubt that the increasing distinctions of wealth, ethnicity, and religion were becoming much more important and thus affected patterns of rioting.[70] Slowly, too, a new ideal emphasizing individual gain and personal satisfaction arose and increasingly challenged the ideal of communal solidarity. Yet the ideal of the single-interest community remained viable; and the elite, unable to explain the changing world around it and unwilling to embrace fully a new ethos of individualism, contemptuously dismissed any disturbance that divided the community as the work of the rabble.

Most Anglo-American riots in the mid-eighteenth century, however, aimed at preserving the world as it was. Rioters wanted to protect their community, to regain lost rights, and to guard the moral welfare. How-

68. Paul A. Gilje, "The Baltimore Riots of 1812 and the Breakdown of the Anglo-American Mob Tradition," *Jour. Soc. Hist.*, XIII (1979–1980), 547–564; Thompson, "Moral Economy," *Past and Present*, No. 50 (Feb. 1971), 98, 120–126; Thompson, "Patrician Society, Plebeian Culture," *Jour. Soc. Hist.*, VII (1973–1974), 397; Thompson, "Eighteenth-Century English Society," *Soc. Hist.*, III (1978), 145; Burke, *Popular Culture*, 200–204.

69. Thompson, "Patrician Society, Plebeian Culture," *Jour. Soc. Hist.*, VII (1973–1974), 382–405; Thompson, "Eighteenth-Century English Society," *Soc. Hist.*, III (1978), 133–165; Douglas Hay *et al.*, *Albion's Fatal Tree: Crime and Society in Eighteenth-Century England* (New York, 1975).

70. Henretta, *Evolution of American Society;* Henretta, "Economic Development and Social Structure in Colonial Boston," *WMQ*, 3d Ser., XXII (1965), 75–92; Jackson Turner Main, *The Social Structure of Revolutionary America* (Princeton, N.J., 1965); Nash, *Urban Crucible;* Allan Kulikoff, "The Progress of Inequality in Revolutionary Boston," *WMQ*, 3d Ser., XXVIII (1971), 375–412.

ever, the temporary suspension of the elite's guardianship of the community, the role reversal of plebeian rituals, and the symbolism of popular ceremonies all presented covert challenges to the social structure. These challenges did not make for the development of class consciousness. Mobs were too oriented toward tradition and too backward-looking for that. But they do reveal social strain. The extremity of Fisher Ames's vitriolic denunciation of mob government at the end of the eighteenth century, then, may have reflected the context in which it was written, but the basic fear of mobs that he expressed was rooted in a long-standing apprehension among the elite. Even in the eighteenth century, too many riots might unravel the delicate social and political fabric. Too many riots led to discord, anarchy, and mobocracy.

Rioting in the Revolution

Last Night a Gallows with the figures of 3 Men suspended by the Neck, said to be intended to represent Lord North, Governor Hutchinson, and Solicitor Wedderburn, with another Figure representing the Devil, were carried thro' the principal Streets of the City, attended by several Thousand People, and at last burnt before the Coffee-House Door. It is said they were decorated with suitable Emblems, Devices and Inscriptions.

New-York Journal, 1774

Effigy processions, such as the one described by John Holt's *New-York Journal,* became standard practice for colonial Americans in their resistance to British imperial measures. Time and again, Americans relied upon the ritual and forms of earlier plebeian crowds and paraded with such mock figures to demonstrate their opposition to the Stamp Act, the Townshend duties, and other regulations passed by Great Britain during the 1760s and 1770s. This crowd activity brought more and more people into the political arena and increased popular confidence that the mob acted for the common good. To many patrician observers, however, this development was not wholly welcome. Viewing these frequent processions with suspicion, both whig and tory leaders feared that street politics might bring on the increased discord, anarchy, and mobocracy said to accompany rampant popular disorder. The tories merely bemoaned these developments and cited them to help explain their loyalty to the king. Whigs divided into two competing camps, with both the conservative and the more radical leadership struggling to control, or at least influence, the newly emergent vox populi.

Despite outcries by loyalists and many whigs, popular processions, especially with effigies, remained one of the most potent weapons in the American arsenal of resistance in the 1760s and 1770s. In an era when the public spectacle still carried far greater impact than the written word, the customary, plebeian practice of ad hoc parades with effigies or other symbols brought the message of resistance most effectively to the people in the street.[1] Mock figures, like those in June 1774 representing the unpopular government officials "most active" in setting up the Coercive Acts against Boston and Massachusetts, allowed the mob to register symbolically its displeasure and anger while committing no personal violence. But the significance of these popular demonstrations goes much deeper than simply channeling the energies of the mob along a safe path and transcends the immediate issues of the imperial crisis. Evident on the night of June 15, 1774, and evident in every effigy displayed and in every popular demonstration in these years in New York and elsewhere, an adherence to plebeian forms and culture infused the nascent Revolutionary movement with a special meaning for the lower classes.

Obviously, the procession of June 15, with effigies of North, Hutchinson, and Alexander Wedderburn, was modeled after the earlier Pope Day

1. Rhys Isaac calls these public rituals the oral dramaturgical process. See his "Dramatizing the Ideology of Revolution: Popular Mobilization in Virginia, 1774 to 1776," *William and Mary Quarterly,* 3d Ser., XXXII (1976), 357–385.

celebrations that displayed the pope and the Pretender in like proximity to the devil. Both sets of figures ended their tour of the city in "sulpherous Flames." More important, the accompanying street theater for both the Pope Day and later anti-British activities harked back to even older forms of pageantry evident in the charivari and rites of passage. Rough music, similar to the drumming and huzzahing accompanying pre-Revolutionary demonstrations, aimed at singling out a violator of local custom and often used an effigy as a means of symbolizing the victim. Ceremonial destruction or desecration of the effigy, either through physical abuse or by fire, was also part of the charivari.[2] So, too, the ritualistic mocking and destruction of those in authority, albeit for political reasons, resembles the role reversal of the European lords of misrule and the puberty ceremonies of primitive societies.[3] The "Thousands" of New Yorkers who either joined the June 15 parade or who merely watched the gallows and effigies disappear into flames before the Coffee House were participating in a familiar communal activity. Such an activity, despite all the high-sounding rhetoric uttered by orators and pamphleteers, was a plebeian affair. The Coffee House, where merchants met and where resistance might be planned, was the province of the elite. The streets and the plaza in front of the Coffee House, especially on nights like June 15, were the province of the plebs.

Yet, during the 1760s and early 1770s, this plebeian activity became charged with the political rhetoric of American whigs. The republican emphasis on virtue, which included an attack on ostentation that came dangerously close to an attack on wealth, fitted neatly into the plebeian sense of fair play and had a certain resonance for the artisan, day laborer, and sailor. Mobs in the Anglo-American world had long rushed into the street against the selfish, deceitful, and vicious man who might raise the price of bread or beat his wife. Now, in New York, they rushed into the street to condemn men who, with "their diabolical Machinations," acted "against the Rights of this Country." Thus on the backs of the effigies displayed on June 15 were signs labeling the crimes of each victim. Thomas Hutchinson, like the grain merchant who charged more than the just price, betrayed his community for personal gain and was an "arch Hypo-

2. Edward P. Thompson, "Rough Music: Le charivari anglais," *Annales: Économies, sociétés, civilisations,* XXVII (1972), 285–312; Violet Alford, "Rough Music or Charivari," *Folklore,* LXX (1959), 505–518.
3. Natalie Zemon Davis, "The Reasons of Misrule," in Davis, *Society and Culture in Early Modern France: Eight Essays* (Stanford, Calif., 1975), 97–103; Max Gluckman, ed., *Essays on the Ritual of Social Relations* (Manchester, 1962).

crite and Traitor . . . who to aggrandize himself, has by the most artful, base and false Representations involved his native Country in the greatest Calamity and Distress." Lord North, although an English minister, was seen in a similar light and was called "an insidious and implacable Enemy to the Liberties of America" who was "a Slave of Power and Betrayer of his Country." And the English solicitor general was referred to as the "mercenary and indefeasibly infamous Wedderburne," a "traitorous wretch" whom "Treachery itself cannot trust."[4]

These placards represented a whig rhetoric less formalized than the pamphlet literature and appealed to the lower orders to act for the public good and combat the corruption, decay, and dissipation that threatened to engulf the New World. The American Revolution was more than a colonial rebellion. It was more than a reaction to the new imperial regulations of Great Britain. It was more than a contest against corruption imposed from without. The Revolution was a movement to purge the colonies of corruption from within. The various British attempts at reordering the colonial empire appeared so ominous because they threatened to heighten the corruption that already existed in the colonies.

This corruption violated plebeian sensibilities about what was fair and equitable and even offered a partial explanation for the maldistribution of wealth. Men saw evidence of corruption in the divisive contentiousness of colonial politics, in the willingness of many colonials to take offices of place and patronage, and in the increasing divisions within society. Republican ideology was highly complex: increasingly it represented a crosscurrent of older values reaffirming the organic ideal of society and newer values extolling the independence of the individual. Yet the tools of American resistance continued to reflect the reassertion of the corporate society.[5] Whig rhetoric emphasized the need for virtue and unity. Virtue became the

4. *Journal,* June 16, 23, 1774; Isaac Q. Leake, *Memoir of the Life and Times of John Lamb, an Officer of the Revolution, Who Commanded the Post at West Point at the Time of Arnold's Defection* . . . (Albany, N.Y., 1857), 86–87; A Freeman, *To the Public* (New York, 1774), broadside; A Citizen, *To the People of New-York* [New York, 1774], broadside.

5. Bernard Bailyn, *The Ideological Origins of the American Revolution* (Cambridge, Mass., 1967); Gordon S. Wood, *The Creation of the American Republic, 1776–1787* (Chapel Hill, N.C., 1969), 3–124; Kenneth A. Lockridge, "Social Change and the Meaning of the American Revolution," *Journal of Social History,* VI (1972–1973), 403–439. Of course, during the Revolution, republicanism was transformed into something else and adapted more to a noncorporate image of society (Wood, *Creation of the American Republic*).

yardstick that measured the individual's willingness to sacrifice for the commonwealth, and the very term *republic—res publica—*implied a unity of interests. Rioting was a way of asserting commitment to that common good.[6] Before the 1760s, as suggested in the antidevaluation riot of 1754 and the anti-Semitic antics of Oliver De Lancey and others during the 1740s, popular disorder at times threatened social unity. But now the resistance movement submerged many of the emerging class, ethnic, and religious differences. This shift was no simple elite trick. The corporate view of society touched all social levels; the common folk wanted to believe, and did believe, that opposition to Great Britain would lead to a reformation of American society.

But the people in the street had their own ideas about what direction that reformation was to take. The repeated use of crowd politics, expressed in traditional plebeian ritual, had some unexpected consequences as the innate sense of fair play implicit in that ritual gave way to incipient egalitarianism. This politicization of the common man, clearly linked to the heavy dependence on crowd activity from 1765 to 1776, pushed the Revolutionary leaders to reformulate their own conception of good government and to include more and more people in the decision making. By 1774, laborers, seamen, and mechanics assumed that they had a voice in the affairs of the province, and the local congresses, committees, and conventions could do little without gaining the assent of the newly sovereign people. Although this active political role was increasingly formalized in the years leading up to Independence through the activities of the Mechanics' Committee, through broadening the membership of New York's other Revolutionary committees, and through open meetings and continual referendums, it was the persistent use of mobs and street politics that propelled the common man into the political arena.

Crucial in this development was the transformation of traditional forms of crowd behavior into tools of resistance and revolution. The Revolutionary mob retained some elements typical of all eighteenth-century rioting. It generally limited its activity to attacks on property symbolic of its grievances or to public assertions of communal unity, and frequently a wide spectrum of society participated in the disorder. But, under the influence of whig ideology, the Revolutionary crowd remodeled many of the tradi-

6. Pauline Maier, *From Resistance to Revolution: Colonial Radicals and the Development of American Opposition to Britain, 1765–1776* (New York, 1972), 3–48; John Phillip Reid, "In a Defensive Rage: The Uses of the Mob, the Justification in Law, and the Coming of the American Revolution," *New York University Law Review,* XLIX (1974), 1043–1091.

tional symbols of earlier crowds into a more overtly political form. This metamorphosis is evident in the Revolutionary crowd's heavy reliance on effigy processions, bonfires, rail riding, night serenading, tar and feathers, liberty poles, and disguises like blackened faces and Indian garb.[7] All of these practices had antecedents in the activities of Anglo-American plebeian rituals and riots, such as the Pope Day celebrations, the charivari, and fertility and maypole festivities. Although New Yorkers did not practice all of these plebeian rituals in the years immediately before 1765, they remained in the collective conscious to be drawn on when the need arose.[8] There had been occasions in which this traditional activity had a political content, but now in New York it became even more evident. In other words, active participation of crowds to oppose British imperial regulations not only transformed plebeian ritual but also contributed to a growing political awareness among common men and confirmed popular belief in the value of politics out-of-doors to protect the interests of the community.

Not everyone was sanguine about the more overtly political mob. Gouverneur Morris's famous comment in May 1774, that "the mob begin to think and to reason," expressed the anxieties of many of New York's "patricians" (a term Morris used). This man, who later signed the Declaration of Independence, prophesied "with fear and trembling, that if the disputes with *Great Britain* continue, we shall be under the worst of all possible dominions; we shall be under the domination of a riotous mob." The leadership of the resistance movement, then, feared an excess of disorder and persistently argued for limiting mob action.[9]

Morris and other whig patricians had good reason to be apprehensive. The whig orientation of mobs in the 1760s and 1770s was not automatic. Divisions within the community ran deep, and personal, parochial, and class interests could challenge the fragile fabric of society.[10] For the patrician, mobs not only jeopardized his hegemony by introducing greater

7. Peter Shaw, *American Patriots and the Rituals of Revolution* (Cambridge, Mass., 1981), 183–188, 207–215.

8. Alfred F. Young, "English Plebeian Culture and Eighteenth-Century American Radicalism," in Margaret C. Jacob and James R. Jacob, eds., *The Origins of Anglo-American Radicalism* (London, 1984), 185–212.

9. Peter Force, *American Archives* (Washington, D.C., 1837–1843), 4th Ser., I, 342–343.

10. The best discussions of these developing tensions in 18th-century America are James Henretta, *The Evolution of American Society, 1750–1815: An Interdisciplinary Analysis* (Lexington, Mass., 1973); and Gary B. Nash, *The Urban Crucible: Social Change, Political Consciousness, and the Origins of the American Revolution* (Cambridge, Mass., 1979).

numbers of people to street politics but also threatened the community by destroying its sense of solidarity. Even in the heat of the imperial debate, and with the obvious need for mob action to enforce compliance with the resistance movement's goals, tumult still threatened to engender mobocracy.

Yet under that threat, not all of New York's patricians rejected the mob. Although some whig leaders feared crowd politics, others recognized that a balance was necessary: these more radical whigs believed that the people in the street could be an effective and constitutional means of resistance if they were limited and guided along a nonviolent and nondestructive path.[11] To this end, groups like the Sons of Liberty in the 1760s and the Committees of Safety and Correspondence in the 1770s struggled to keep the American mob within traditional modes of behavior by assuming leadership in the street and reinforcing plebeian crowd behavior with whig forms and ideology.

The Stamp Act, the Crowd, and the Whig Leaders

The efforts of whig leaders to guide the people in the street and the plebeian orientation of Revolutionary crowd action can be seen as early as 1765. As whig leaders appealed to the mob and then struggled to control the ensuing popular disorder, the lower orders practiced and expressed, through crowd action, their own interpretation of whig ideology. The whig attack on virtue could become, at the hands of the mob, an attack on wealth and ostentation. The combination of whig ideology and plebeian ritual continued throughout the months of resistance to the Stamp Act and persisted even after the law was repealed. The expression of plebeian animosity toward symbols of wealth during some of the crowd activity threatened to magnify class distinctions. Yet the ability of whig leaders to restrain the mob and place its activity within a whig context muted this challenge. The final result was to strengthen both the resistance movement and the popular faith in mob action.

11. Several historians emphasize the conflict within the whig leadership. See Carl Lotus Becker, *The History of Political Parties in the Province of New York, 1760–1776* (Madison, Wis., 1909); Staughton Lynd, "The Mechanics in New York Politics, 1774–1788," *Labor History,* V (1964), 225–246; Alfred F. Young, *The Democratic Republicans of New York: The Origins, 1763–1797* (Chapel Hill, N.C., 1967), 3–32; Edward Countryman, *A People in Revolution: The American Revolution and Political Society in New York, 1760–1790* (Baltimore, 1981).

Plebeian patterns of crowd behavior appeared almost as soon as New Yorkers began to resist the Stamp Act on the eve the law was to take effect. While merchants met on the night of October 31 to agree not to import goods from England, a crowd in the street mimicked a formal public funeral (such as might occur when a government official died) and held a "serious" ceremony to inter "liberty." Then, just as at countless official celebrations, some of the demonstrators broke away and "proceeded thro' the streets in a mobbish manner whistling and Huzzaing," breaking lamps and windows, and threatening to pull down houses.[12]

On the following night there was an even larger demonstration, displaying popular opposition to the Stamp Act, plebeian ceremonial activity, and a degree of restraint. Two separate processions formed. Both had parallels to Pope Day: each paraded with effigies, featuring most prominently Lieutenant Governor Cadwallader Colden. One party, in mock ceremony, marched through the streets with its effigy of Colden seated in a chair and was accompanied by a growing crowd carrying lights. Raiding Colden's coach house outside Fort George, this group strengthened the message of the farce by transferring the effigy to the governor's own carriage. Then the crowd headed uptown toward the Fields (New York Common).

The second party, which had been gathering at the Fields, even more clearly followed the ritual of Pope Day. Colden's effigy was placed in a movable gallows with stamped paper in one hand and a boot, symbolizing George III's unpopular adviser the earl of Bute, in the other. Just as in the 1755 New York Pope Day celebration, the devil, "the grand Deceiver of Mankind," was positioned in such a manner as to seem to urge Colden "to Perseverance in the Cause of Slavery." The parallel in symbolism did not end there. Hanging on the effigy's back was a drum which, as a label on the chest indicated, was "supposed to allude to some former circumstance of his Life" when Colden had served in the Pretender's army as a drummer.[13]

Joining forces, the two groups vowed not to break any windows and together moved down to Fort George, where Colden had sought safety. The mob taunted the soldiers stationed inside by throwing bricks and stones at the fort and daring the guards to fire. Placing their hands on the top of the ramparts and knocking at the gate, the New Yorkers grew

12. R. R. Livingston to [former Gov. Monckton], Nov. 8, 1765, Livingston Family Papers, box 3, transcripts, NYPL; G. D. Scull, ed., *The Montresor Journals* (New-York Historical Society, *Collections,* XIV [New York, 1881]), 331 (hereafter cited as *Montresor Journals*); *Gazette: Post-Boy,* Nov. 7, 1765.

13. *Gazette: Post-Boy,* Nov. 7, 1765.

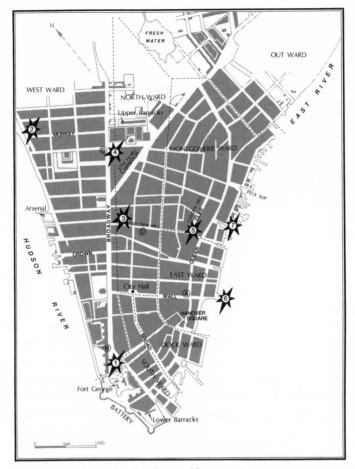

1. Stamp Act riot outside Fort George, Nov. 1, 1765
2. Stamp Act riot at Major James's residence, Nov. 1, 1765
3. John Street theater riot, May 5, 1766
4. Liberty pole disturbances, 1766–1770
5. Golden Hill riot, Jan. 19, 1770
6. New York tea party, Apr. 22, 1774
7. Tarring-and-feathering of shoemaker Tweedy, Aug. 22, 1775

A. Merchant's Coffee House
B. Burn's City Arms Tavern
C. Montagne's Tavern
D. Methodist meetinghouse

- - - - Ward Boundary

MAP 1. Revolutionary Rioting, 1765–1775.
After Lester J. Cappon et al., eds., Atlas of Early American History: The
Revolutionary Era, 1760–1790 *(Princeton, N.J., 1976)*

bolder. One effigy "was brought up within 8 or 10 feet of the Fort Gate with the grossest ribaldry from the Mob." Then the crowd took the effigies, the carriage, and two sleighs also commandeered from Colden's coach house to Bowling Green. With wood from some recently dismantled palisades, they burned the effigies and vehicles in a tremendous bonfire before thousands of people and within sight of Fort George.[14]

Besides demonstrating a strident antiauthoritarianism by derisive treatment of the Colden effigies and the taunting behavior at the fort, some New Yorkers also gave vent to an odd combination of feelings. A group of rioters expressed their dislike of the local commandant, Major Thomas James, and a resentment of his wealth by marching to his house and ransacking it, destroying furniture and private belongings. Then they proceeded to several nearby bawdyhouses and attacked them. Here the crowd expressed its own sense of morality. Although houses of prostitution ordinarily were tolerated, these dens of corruption, no doubt patronized heavily by British soldiers, now appeared to sully American virtue.[15]

Passions remained high the next few days as Pope Day approached. Colden began to work out a compromise, and whig leaders attempted to avoid further conflict. On November 2, people "were the whole Day collected in Bodies throughout the Town which seemd to be in the greatest Confusion and Tumult," and there were rumors of a planned assault on the fort.[16] By night the mob became increasingly riotous, and Colden, in consultation with government officials and several of the city's leading gentlemen, decided that he would not distribute the stamps until Sir Henry Moore, the new governor, arrived. Armed with this concession, whig leaders went into the street to pass the word. Eager to restrain the mob, these men enlisted the aid of several ship captains to exert influence over any "Sons of Neptune" who might riot.[17]

The next day was a little quieter, but notices and broadsides appeared threatening more violence unless trade were resumed without stamped clearances from the Customs House. More ominous, and revealing the

14. *The Colden Letter Books* (New-York Historical Society, *Collections,* IX–X [New York, 1877–1878]), Pt. I, 55–56 (hereafter cited as *Colden Letter Books*).

15. The above account of the Nov. 1, 1765, disturbances is a composite drawn from *Gazette: Post-Boy,* Nov. 7, 1765; *Montresor Journals,* 336–337; *Colden Letter Books,* Pt. II, 54–63, 74–75, 78–82, 89–93, 97–100, 103–107, 461; R. R. Livingston to [Monckton], Nov. 8, 1765, Livingston Family Papers, box 3, transcripts, NYPL.

16. *Colden Letter Books,* Pt. II, 103–107.

17. R. R. Livingston to [Monckton], Nov. 8, 1765, Livingston Family Papers, box 3, transcripts, NYPL; *Colden Letter Books,* Pt. II, 103–107, 461.

continued influence of plebeian ritual on the forms of resistance, were the "advertisements and many papers placarded throughout this city declaring the storming of the Fort" on November 5 "under cover of burning the Pope and pretender unless the Stamps were delivered."[18] Again, whig merchants sought the help of sea captains to prevent—or at least mitigate—violence. November 4 thus passed with little more than the gathering of a large crowd at the Common at night. By the following day, the traditional Pope Day, Colden relented and surrendered seven boxes of stamps to the city magistrates, who placed them in City Hall. The threat of an assault on the fort was never carried out.[19]

The potential confrontation with British troops at Fort George, the destruction of Major James's property, the attacks on bawdyhouses, and the presence of bold mobs came a bit too close to mobocracy for many whig leaders. This fear forced men like Robert R. Livingston, one of the whig merchants who went out into the streets to persuade mobs to disperse, to speak out in the early days of November to control the passions of the crowd—even though, as Livingston later claimed, it left him in jeopardy from the "Vox Populi." More effective than the "Men of greatest Property" in influencing the crowd were the sea captains, who knew the "Sons of Neptune" and others in the street personally.[20]

Soon middling merchants (including ex–sea captains) and leading mechanics organized the Sons of Liberty to guide resistance to the Stamp Act. This organization, in response to the threatened anarchy, attempted to restrain the crowd and issued statements urging less misconduct. To limit mob action, the Sons of Liberty asserted its leadership of the whig cause in the coming months and began supervising noncompliance with the Stamp Act by inspecting ships suspected of harboring stamp paper. The merchants and mechanics who dominated the Sons of Liberty were concerned as much with protecting property as with opposing the Stamp Act. They organized popular demonstrations to intimidate anyone who did not adhere to the ban on stamps and to assert a communal unity in support of stamp resistance.[21] The Sons of Liberty were thus willing to

18. *Montresor Journals,* 338–339.

19. *Ibid.; Gazette: Post-Boy,* Nov. 7, 1765; *Colden Letter Books,* Pt. II, 58–63, 74–75, 78–82, 103–107, 461; and R. R. Livingston to [Monckton], Nov. 8, 1765, Livingston Family Papers, box 3, transcripts, NYPL.

20. R. R. Livingston to [Monckton], Nov. 8, 1765, Livingston Family Papers, box 3, transcripts, NYPL.

21. For New York Sons of Liberty, see Roger J. Champagne, "The Sons of Liberty and the Aristocracy in New York Politics, 1765–1790" (Ph.D. diss., Univer-

PLATE 2. Effigy Demonstration.
Wood engraving from J. W. Barber, Interesting Events in the History of the
United States *(New Haven, Conn., 1829). Courtesy of the Metropolitan Museum
of Art, Bequest of Charles Allen Munn, 1924.*
*This stoning of a stamp-master in effigy in New Hampshire shows a plebeian crowd
activity repeated frequently in New York City between 1765 and 1776.*

flirt with the use of the mob both as a tool of coercion and as a traditional
means of representing communal support. But they carefully tried not to
let the mob get beyond control.

Although the tensions within the city relaxed appreciably after the surrender of the stamps to city officials, the streets remained far from quiet.
Several demonstrations took place in November and December. On November 28, three hundred New Yorkers crossed over to Long Island
to intimidate the Maryland stamp distributor into resigning. In mid-
December, a crowd paraded with the effigies of Lord Colville, George
Grenville, and General William Murray hanging from a gallows. Toward
the end of December one crowd boarded a ship to search for stamps con-

sity of Wisconsin, 1960); Henry B. Dawson, *The Sons of Liberty in New York*
(Poughkeepsie, N.Y., 1859); Maier, *Resistance,* 69, 78–112, 277–278, 302–
303; Maier, *The Old Revolutionaries: Political Lives in the Age of Samuel Adams*
(New York, 1980), 51–100; Herbert M. Morais, "The Sons of Liberty in New
York," in Richard B. Morris, ed., *The Era of the American Revolution: Studies In-
scribed to Evarts Boutell Greene* (New York, 1939), 269–289.

signed to Connecticut, and another threatened to destroy the house of the
naval officer Captain Archibald Kennedy.[22] Despite the efforts of the Sons
of Liberty, mobs became a constant presence in New York. By January and February, the British journal keeper John Montresor reported,
"Children nightly trampouze the Streets with lanthorns upon Poles and
hallowing."[23]

Plebeian ritual had left a deep imprint on this crowd activity. The influence of Pope Day persisted in the parading of effigies singling out specific
targets. But other plebeian practices surfaced as well. With mobs marching in the streets nearly every night, it was as if the Stamp Act crisis
allowed some New Yorkers to partake in ceremonial misrule without end.
Youth groups, in particular, took to the streets not only to intimidate
would-be compliers with the Stamp Act but also to act out the rituals of
symbolic inversion. Previously, "lanthorns upon Poles" and candles had
been symbols of loyalty to the crown. Now those symbols became inverted
and represented the new resistance.[24]

The emphasis on plebeian forms meant that plebeian ideas about what
was good for the community also became important. At times the crowd
wanted to take action that exceeded the bounds set by the Sons of Liberty.
Such conflict was potentially explosive. In mid-February the Sons of Liberty castigated two merchants for using stamped paper. In an action typical of the resistance movement, John Lamb, Isaac Sears, and Joseph Allicote held a ceremony, publicly burning the stamps before thousands of
New Yorkers. Here the Sons of Liberty consciously played up to the
crowd, trying to guide and control it. They were not entirely successful.
The language of whig resistance, emphasizing virtue over corruption,
worked upon plebeian sensibilities. By using stamped paper the two merchants revealed their own corruption. The devil had enticed them, and
they, for personal gain, had willingly sinned. For many of the people in the
street, the surrender and burning of stamped paper was not punishment
enough. That evening, "tho' the Sons of Liberty exerted themselves to the
utmost" to "prevent the gathering of the Multitude," a mob formed and
burst into the house of one of the offending merchants. The rioters began
to destroy the furniture—a symbol of wealth and ill-gotten gains. At that
point several members of the Sons of Liberty arrived and prevailed upon
the mob to leave the house. They assured the mob that the two merchants

22. *Montresor Journals,* 340, 342–344; *Gazette: Post-Boy,* Dec. 19, 26, 1765.
23. *Montresor Journals,* 346, 349.
24. Shaw, *American Patriots,* 186.

would appear in the Fields to atone for their misdeeds. The next morning, reminiscent of older forms of Anglo-American collective action and directly calling to mind religious and judicial rituals of absolution, this dramatic rite of public confession took place. But even this humiliation did not satisfy everyone. A great throng escorted the merchants afterwards to their respective houses and forced the offenders to repeat the confessions before their own doors. In this case, as in others, the Sons of Liberty barely managed to control the situation.[25]

The tension in the relationship between whig leaders and the lower orders manifested itself yet again in a riot in the spring of 1766. At that time, the city theater, which had been closed throughout the Stamp Act controversy, reopened. The theater proprietors had miscalculated. On opening night a mob arrived, huzzahed, shouted "Liberty, Liberty," and drove the theater patrons helter-skelter into the street, often with the loss of "their Caps, Hats, Wigs, Cardinals, and Cloaks . . . torn off (thro' Mistake) in the Hurray." The building was "Torn to Pieces" and the debris dragged to the Common, where it was burned in a public spectacle.[26]

This disturbance again revealed a combination of whig and plebeian ideals. The impact of whig rhetoric appeared in the shouts of "Liberty, Liberty." Of more significance, however, were the plebeian elements. The building was torn down, taken to the Common, and burned just as the barge in the impressment disturbance of 1764 and many of the effigies in the preceding months had been. The plebeian content also included a distinct resentment of wealth. The items of clothing lost "thro' Mistake" were obvious symbols of ostentation, and Weyman's *Gazette* commented that the bonfire in the Common, a typical plebeian action in the eighteenth century, was "much to the Satisfaction of Many at this distressed Time and the Great Grievance of those less inclined for the Public Good." Those New Yorkers who stood in the dancing shadows of the raging bonfire that night were participating in a public theater far more meaningful than the stage show planned by New York's would-be entertainers.[27]

Whig leaders saw the threat to social authority of this mob activity. Yet, regardless of the dangers, the mob remained a necessary weapon for American whigs: it ensured compliance with the ban on stamp paper

25. *Montresor Journals,* 349–350; Edmund S. Morgan and Helen M. Morgan, *The Stamp Act Crisis: Prologue to Revolution,* rev. ed. (New York, 1962), 250–251.

26. Weyman's *Gazette,* May 12, 1766; *Gazette: Post-Boy,* May 8, 1766.

27. *Ibid.; Montresor Journals,* 364.

while serving its traditional function of asserting communal unity. Without the mob, without some effective vehicle of coercion, any resolve by a Stamp Act Congress, a meeting of merchants, or action by the Sons of Liberty was meaningless. Clearly the Sons of Liberty knew this. Repeatedly, whenever the Sons of Liberty stepped in to search a ship for stamps, intimidate would-be compliers, or harass uncompromising officials, they made sure that a noisy and threatening crowd was nearby. And just as clearly, whenever the Sons of Liberty called upon a crowd, that crowd might have a mind of its own.

The Liberty Pole

In the years after 1766 the mixture of whig and plebeian elements continued in a series of street confrontations between New Yorkers and British soldiers over another crucial symbol of the emerging Revolution—the liberty pole. In gamelike behavior, typical of youth groups in traditional societies, civilians and servicemen competed to protect or to destroy this fertility symbol, which, at first, was more maypole than liberty pole. This contest was not just mere adolescent frolicking. The liberty pole riots revealed a community protecting common laborers from outside competition; they served as a means of defending American liberty as defined by whig rhetoric. The joining of these two issues in what might otherwise have been a frivolous contest strengthened, with ideological content, the plebeian struggle to be guaranteed a fair and livable wage while it widened popular support for the whig cause. Together, the whole process of the conflict further legitimized direct popular action and politics out-of-doors.

Had there been no opposition to the imperial regulation of the 1760s, the presence alone of British armed forces on the American continent would have provoked conflict. Soldier and civilian had a natural antipathy toward each other that reached beyond any ideological argument against standing armies.[28] The presence of the military always intruded upon and disrupted a community. Soldiers drank, brawled, and visited brothels. A port like New York could absorb such behavior, but the addition of hundreds of unattached males in red coats tested the limits of that toleration. Moreover, off-duty servicemen unfairly competed with civilian laborers for jobs. The British soldiers, who were provided food and shelter and probably did not have families to support, worked for lower wages. It is little

28. See Fred Anderson, *A People's Army: Massachusetts Soldiers and Society in the Seven Years' War* (Chapel Hill, N.C., 1984), 115–116, 119–120.

wonder, then, that there was conflict. During the 1750s a few civilian-military disturbances had occurred.[29] This antagonism worsened in the declining economic conditions of the 1760s. The arrival of two full regiments of reinforcements in the spring of 1766 only aggravated New Yorkers' complaints that British military personnel in the city unfairly took jobs for less pay.[30]

Soon after the strengthening of the British garrison, New Yorkers held a ceremony to honor the King's Birthday and to celebrate the news of the Stamp Act repeal. In typical eighteenth-century fashion, grand festivities were planned on New York Common, including the serving of two roasted oxen and "25 Barrels of strong Beer, a Hogshead of Rum, Sugar and Water, to make Punch, Bread, &c." This public treat centered on two poles: one was a tall mast surrounded by a pile of twenty cords of wood, "to the Head of which was hoisted 12 Tar and Pitch Barrels"; the other was a flagstaff with colors displayed.[31] Both poles revealed odd mixtures of symbolism. The mast with the tar and pitch barrels probably represented the triumph of American maritime interests now that trade was renewed. But the appearance of those barrels suspended from the top of the pole, much like the streamers of the maypole, also enhanced the resemblance of the pole to that traditional symbol of English folk celebrations of rebirth. This similarity, it might be noted, is not surprising, for the King's Birthday, after all, was in the spring. The other flagstaff also mixed symbols. Although a band played "God Save the King" and there was a standard of George III, the inscriptions on the pole exposed the true sympathies of the crowd; Pitt's name and the word "liberty" were in larger letters and displayed more prominently than the king's name. In short, New York whigs organized the festivities in apparent jubilation over the repeal of the Stamp Act and in recognition of a traditional springtime fertility rite—not from loyalty to the Hanoverian dynasty.[32]

Within days of the King's Birthday, the colonial assembly, to the plaudits of many New Yorkers, refused to comply with the new Quartering Act to provision the army. Quickly the flagstaff, erected on ground often used for military exercise and parade, became an irksome symbol of

29. George William Edwards, *New York as an Eighteenth Century Municipality: 1731–1776* (1917; rpt., Port Washington, N.Y., 1967), 109; Stanley McCrory Pargellis, *Lord Loudoun in North America* (New Haven, Conn., 1933), 129.

30. *Montresor Journals,* 346.

31. *Mercury,* June 9, 1766.

32. *Ibid.; Montresor Journals,* 370; Leake, *Memoir of Lamb,* 28; *Journal,* Mar. 26, 1767.

American opposition to His Majesty's troops stationed in the city. For two months the soldiers contained their seething anger until the night of August 10, when a party of redcoats tore the pole down. Then began the great game of down-again, up-again confrontations. The following day the soldiers and citizens clashed more directly. Two thousand to three thousand persons attended a public meeting called by the Sons of Liberty to demand an explanation why their "Tree of Liberty" was cut down. A party of soldiers also appeared on the Common, and tempers rose as both sides exchanged hard words. A volley of brickbats from the whigs forced the soldiers to draw their bayonets, and with them they beat back any attempt to replace the pole. A few days later the New Yorkers were more successful, as British officers restrained their men from interfering. But on September 23, soldiers acting at night again knocked down the pole. Two days later the pole was restored without violence.[33]

Throughout this period tension remained high between civilian and soldier as each accused the other of provoking incidents. Within a few days of the initial destruction of the liberty pole it became unsafe for soldiers to walk about town, since they were "daily insulted in the Streets without the least provocation." To show popular ill will toward the army, the Sons of Liberty proposed "for the Innholders and Inhabitants not to have any Intercourse with the military or even admit them in their houses." By the fall it was the British regulars who seized the initiative and started to attack New Yorkers in the street and even in their own homes.[34]

While these conflicts surfaced throughout the city, the liberty pole remained the centerpiece of the antagonism between soldier and civilian, and this attention added to its importance. For Americans it became much more than a plebeian fertility symbol; it now increasingly represented American virtue and liberty and became a focal point for patriotic festivities. On March 18, 1767, for instance, New Yorkers organized their celebration of the anniversary of the repeal of the Stamp Act around the liberty pole. But the land surrounding this symbol of American whig principles also became a battleground where civilian and soldier could vent their long-festering mutual antagonisms. The liberty pole now became an easily assailable target for the British soldier to insult colonial pride. On the night after the celebration of the anniversary of the Stamp Act repeal,

33. *Montresor Journals,* 382–384; Leake, *Memoir of Lamb,* 32–33; *Gazette: Post-Boy,* Aug. 21, 1766.

34. *Montresor Journals,* 383–384; Leake, *Memoir of Lamb,* 33; *Journal,* Oct. 23, Nov. 6, 1766; Weyman's *Gazette,* Oct. 27, 1766.

some redcoats retaliated by once again knocking down the liberty pole. Up it went the next day, reinforced this time with iron bands. On the night of the twentieth a few ambitious soldiers attempted to blow the pole up with gunpowder. They failed, and the whigs placed a guard to protect it. Confrontations ensued the next two nights, but the British efforts were to no avail.

The liberty pole stood unmolested for nearly three years, until January 1770, when antagonism between soldiers and civilians flared once again. Opposition to Great Britain intensified at this time with the anonymous publication of a pamphlet by Alexander McDougall. In it McDougall denounced the New York Assembly for finally buckling under to imperial pressure and complying fully with the Quartering Act.[35] Frustration began to build on both sides. Faced with continued popular opposition and growing hostility in the street, the enlisted men eagerly looked for opportunities to insult New Yorkers. For their part, the Sons of Liberty became increasingly hard-pressed to maintain a nonimportation agreement passed two years earlier in response to the Townshend duties, and they felt their political power draining away. The laborer in the street, meanwhile, faced several problems. Every winter made work more difficult to obtain as trade and business slackened with the rhythms of the seasons. Years of limiting trade with England, in accordance with the resistance movement, only exacerbated the situation. Moreover, there were far too many merchants and employers willing to hire off-duty soldiers at half the pay of the normal day laborer. As both soldier and civilian eyed one another in early January, mutual suspicion, distrust, and dislike mounted.[36] Starting on the night of the thirteenth, soldiers and civilians again began to clash around the liberty pole.[37]

Irate over the attacks on this pole "*sacred to Constitutional Liberty*," New York whigs on January 16 issued handbills throughout the city that decried the presence of the British army. These broadsides emphasized the ill effects of the employment of off-duty soldiers. One resolution high-

35. A Son of Liberty [Alexander McDougall], *To the Betrayed Inhabitants of the City and Colony of New-York* (New York, 1769); Roger J. Champagne, *Alexander McDougall and the American Revolution in New York* (Schenectady, N.Y., 1975), 17–40.

36. A Merchant, *The Times, Mankind Is Highly Concerned to Support That, Wherein Their Own Safety Is Concerned, and to Destroy Those Arts by Which Their Ruin Is Consulted* (New York, Jan. 27, 1770), broadside; Leake, *Memoir of Lamb*, 54.

37. *Journal*, Jan. 18, Feb. 8, Mar. 1, 1770; Leake, *Memoir of Lamb*, 54–55.

PLATE 3. New York Liberty Pole.
Drawing by Pierre Eugène Du Simitière. Courtesy of the Library Company of
Philadelphia.
On the right on the "Road to Liberty" is "Libel Hall" (Montagne's Tavern); in
background are Upper Barracks.

lighted the themes of moral economy and communal solidarity so dear to
plebeians: "Whoever seriously considers the improverished state of this
city, especially of many of the poor Inhabitants of it, must be greatly surprised at the conduct of such as employ the soldiers, when there are a number of the former that want employment to support their distressed families." The impoverishment of the lower orders might be avoided, the
resolution continued, "if the employers of labourers would attend to it
with that care and benevolence that a citizen owes to his neighbour, by
employing him."[38] By this time, then, the liberty pole had come to represent both the resistance to Great Britain and the local plebeian concerns of
employment and communal obligations.

The conflict intensified when, that night, the soldiers blew up the pole.
The next day thousands attended a great meeting on the Common in protest. Despite demands for immediate action, the whig leaders again emphasized the need for restraint, and the meeting limited itself to passing resolu-

38. *Journal,* Feb. 8, Mar. 1, 1770.

tions against British soldiers and for reerecting the pole.[39] To counter this action, the soldiers printed a derisive handbill of their own and posted it throughout the city. On January 18, Isaac Sears, a merchant and leader in the Sons of Liberty, and Walter Quakenbos, a baker, seized two soldiers distributing this handbill and held them in custody for the civil authorities. An attempted rescue led to a massive riot, popularly called the Battle of Golden Hill, in which scores of British soldiers fought in hand-to-hand combat with hundreds of civilians. There were several injuries, but no fatalities. Tensions persisted, and violence flared up again on January 19, when American sailors and some soldiers engaged in a brawl.[40]

Each clash between soldier and civilian made the liberty pole standing in New York Common ever more important. Yet this significance emerged almost accidentally. Even New York whigs admitted that the pole "in it self" was a "Trifle," serving at first a "temporary Purpose," and would perhaps have been little thought of "till it had fallen by natural Decay; but being destroyed by Way of Insult, we could not but consider it a Declaration of War against our Freedom and Property, and resent it accordingly."[41] The liberty pole thus became a symbol of American virtue and an emblem of the Sons of Liberty.

But it was much more than that. Labor competition remained the source of much of the agitation. A loyalist report declared that after the riot on the seventeenth, "a Set of lawless Men" patrolled "the Streets, with great Clubs in their Hands, entering Houses and Vessels, and forcibly" turned out and drove away "all of the Soldiers whom they found at work." They also threatened "vengeance against any Inhabitants, who should presume to employ" British soldiers.[42]

The protection of the community against all outsiders was at the heart of these popular disturbances. The aim was not only to prevent soldiers from working. Suggested in the calls for "care and benevolence" owed by neighbors to use local workers even at a higher wage was the attempt to

39. *Ibid.,* Jan. 18, Mar. 1, 1770; Leake, *Memoir of Lamb,* 55.

40. *Journal,* Jan. 18, Feb. 8, Mar. 1, 1770; Leake, *Memoir of Lamb,* 55–59; William Smith, *Historical Memoirs of William Smith, Historian of the Province of New York, Member of the Governor's Council, and Last Chief Justice of That Province under the Crown, Chief Justice of Quebec,* ed. William H. W. Sabine, 2 vols. (New York, 1956–1958), I, 72–73; *Colden Letter Books,* Pt. II, 211, 216–219; Whitehead Hicks, *To the Inhabitants of This City* (New York, Jan. 22, 1770), broadside.

41. *Journal,* Feb. 8, 1770.

42. A Merchant, *The Times, Mankind.*

persuade employers to pay a just price for labor. But the context and significance of this typical eighteenth-century protest was enlarged by the resistance movement against Great Britain. By rallying around and defending the liberty pole, the New York laborer found a symbol and a language to represent his grievances. The Sons of Liberty, on the other hand, were provided an audience ready to listen to their rhetoric and willing to defend the whig cause against the British imperial policy.

The Committees and the Mob

The joining of patrician whig and plebeian communal interests in New York would not always work as smoothly as in January 1770. After 1773, elite concern over popular disorder heightened as the imperial crisis intensified, as the royal government disintegrated, and as the people out-of-doors became more vocal. The man in the street asserted his own political awareness more forcefully than ever before. Frightening loyalist and elite whig alike, he joined committees and crowds to demand allegiance to the Revolutionary cause.[43] The whig leadership needed the popular base, but it strove to control the "poor reptiles" who had just reached their "vernal morning" and who, according to Gouverneur Morris, were in May 1774 "struggling to cast off their winter's slough."[44] Without the support of the plebs, there could be no resistance movement. With that support, the resistance movement became a revolution.

The strain of controlling the people in the street, evident since November 1765, appeared again in the resistance to the Tea Act of 1773. The response of New Yorkers and other Americans to this measure followed the patterns of earlier resistance: a series of semisupervised crowd activities ensured that the law could never be carried out. New Yorkers planned to imitate the Boston Indians and their Tea Party, but when the long-

43. The story of New York's experience in the years before Independence has been recounted several times. Carl Becker's account still stands out for its completeness (*Political Parties*). See also Countryman, *A People in Revolution;* Leopold S. Launitz-Schürer, Jr., *Loyal Whigs and Revolutionaries in New York, 1765–1776* (New York, 1980); Bernard Mason, *The Road to Independence: The Revolutionary Movement in New York, 1773–1777* (Lexington, Ky., 1966); Thomas Jefferson Wertenbaker, *Father Knickerbocker Rebels: New York City during the Revolution* (New York, 1948); Bruce Bliven, Jr., *Under the Guns: New York, 1775–1776* (New York, 1972).

44. Force, *American Archives,* 4th Ser., I, 342–343.

awaited tea ship *London* arrived in New York on April 22, 1774, New York's Mohawks moved too slowly. The "body of the people" collected on the wharf "were so impatient" that, before the intended raid could occur, they boarded the ship and began to dispose of the tea. Several "persons of reputation" hastily posted themselves as a guard about the companionway and hold to ensure that this crowd dispensed with only the detested beverage. With the tea dumped into the murky waters of New York harbor, the crowd dispersed, to meet in a massive rally around the liberty pole the next day. At this well-attended meeting, with banners flying and amidst the strains of "God Save the King," the people of New York affirmed their support of the previous night's activities.[45] Such tea parties, then, exemplified the whig reliance on organized but limited collective activity; and their widespread community support demonstrated their adherence to traditional forms of crowd behavior. But New York's tea party reveals also a whig leadership scrambling to restrain the mob.

During the next two years the effort to control the resistance movement confronted demands for more radical action from a new Mechanics' Committee and from popular meetings. The whig leadership was divided, and some men fled into the loyalist camp. Radicals like Alexander McDougall, Isaac Sears, and Abraham Lott fought the conservatives over the delegates to the Continental Congress and the commitment to nonimportation. Despite temporary victories by the conservatives, the momentum of events allowed them only to delay acts of resistance. By the fall of 1774, the Committee of Fifty-one (the near-official resistance committee) complied with the Continental Congress, adopted the Suffolk Resolves and the Association, and reorganized itself as a new and larger Committee of Inspection (the Committee of Sixty).[46]

As the whig leadership—struggling among themselves and with the crowds in the street—strove to control the popular movement, a complex relationship emerged between the formal political activity of committees and the informal political activity of the people out-of-doors. For example, despite the conservative orientation of the Committee of Fifty-one, within

45. *Ibid.*, 248–258; *Journal*, Apr. 28, 1774; *Rivington's Gazetteer*, Apr. 28, 1774; *Gazette*, Apr. 25, 1774; Smith, *Historical Memoirs*, I, 184–185; Leake, *Memoir of Lamb*, 83–84; *To the Public* (New York, Apr. 19, 1774), broadside (Evans no. 13671); *To the Public* (New York, Apr. 19, 1774), broadside (Evans no. 13672).

46. Becker, *Political Parties*, 142–173; Countryman, *A People in Revolution*, 137–143; Force, *American Archives*, 4th Ser., I, 309–330, 372.

three days of its organization in May 1774 it felt compelled to ratify its position with a meeting of "the inhabitants of the city and county," which included those persons not ordinarily enfranchised.[47] Similar meetings were held throughout the summer and fall, at times called by the Committee of Fifty-one, at times by the Mechanics' Committee, and at times by ad hoc committees.[48] Suddenly, the people out-of-doors wielded new power as the whig leadership sought sanction for the actions of its committees.

Crowd politics, however, expanded beyond public meetings on New York Common. Moderate "men of property" may have taken a lead in the committee work "to protect the city from the ravages of the mob"; yet as Colden reminded Lord Dartmouth, "the spirit of mobbing" remained "much abroad."[49] Throughout the fall and winter, the riotous crowd continued to be a tool of coercion. Likewise, the interaction between crowd and committee remained tense yet interdependent.[50]

This peculiar relationship can be seen in February 1775, when the captain of the *James* attempted to unload his cargo contrary to the orders of the Committee of Inspection. The committee was supposed to watch the wharves to ensure that no contraband was unloaded, but before it could act, "the banditti" hired to unload the ship were "suppressed by the inhabitants, who are for supporting the Association, and who began to assemble in great numbers." The size of the crowd so intimidated the captain that he set sail and anchored four miles away. The committee then sent a delegation to guarantee the ship would not approach the wharves a second time. But when the vessel attempted to dock a few days later, a

47. Becker, *Political Parties,* 114–115; Force, *American Archives,* 4th Ser., I, 293–294.

48. A Citizen, *To the Inhabitants of the City and Colony of New-York* ([New York], 1774), broadside; Another Citizen, *To the Inhabitants of the City and County of New-York* ([New York], June 5, 1774), broadside; An Honest American, *To the Respectable Public* (New York, 1774), broadside; Isaac Low *et al., To the Respectable Publick* (New York, 1774), broadside; *To the Public* (New York, May 17, 1774), broadside; *To the Public* (May 18, 1774), broadside.

49. Force, *American Archives,* 4th Ser., I, 1030.

50. E. B. O'Callaghan, ed., *Documents relative to the Colonial History of the State of New York; Procured in Holland, England, and France,* VIII (Albany, N.Y., 1857), 493; *Journal,* Oct. 6, Nov. 10, 1774; *Rivington's Gazetteer,* Oct. 13, 1774; Force, *American Archives,* 4th Ser., I, 1030, 1070–1072; A Citizen, *To the Public: Stop Him! Stop Him! Stop Him!* (New York, 1774), broadside; The Free Citizens, *To the Public* (New York, 1774), broadside; Legion, *To the Publick* (New York, 1774), broadside; *To the Public* (New York, Sept. 28, 1774), broadside; *To the Public,* affidavit of Thomas Mesnard ([New York], Dec. 30, 1774), broadside; Plain English, *To the Inhabitants of New-York* ([New York, 1774]), broadside.

mob again swung into action. An "exasperated" crowd went to the captain's lodgings, seized him, paraded him "through the principal streets," and sent him in a rowboat to meet his ship with orders to prevent its arrival. The committee then decided to leave a delegation aboard the *James* until it left port. But when the captain of the British man-of-war refused to allow the controversial ship to depart because it did not have the proper clearance papers, again the people in the street acted on their own. A tumultuous mob visited the lodgings of the captain of the British warship and persuaded him to allow the *James* to sail.[51]

By early April the whig leaders were losing their hold on the crowd, and the boundary between formal and informal political activity became ever more hazy. The "sway of the mob," as one loyalist put it, "which includes despotism, the most cruel and severe of all others," appeared on the verge of dominating. City officials as well as conservative and radical whigs futilely strained to control the situation. Great public meetings were held, resolutions were passed against England, and supplies of the British army at Boston were visited by tumultuous mobs.[52]

Although there were moments when they could barely control the crowds they thought they led, a few of the most radical whigs, like Isaac Sears, Alexander McDougall, John Lamb, and Marinus Willett, continued to ally themselves with the people in the street. Under their influence and driven by the intensifying imperial crisis, much of New York's crowd activity began to shade into a form of warfare and militia action. When news of Lexington and Concord arrived on April 23, all regular government disappeared, the committee temporarily lost its power, and the people in the street briefly ruled supreme. John Lamb and Isaac Sears wasted little time organizing a militialike mob to seize guns and ammunition.[53] A few days later, on April 28, they even took over the Customs House.[54] For a week radical whigs armed themselves, paraded through the

51. Force, *American Archives*, 4th Ser., I, 1243–1244.

52. *Ibid.*, II, 347–349; *Journal*, Mar. 9, 23, Apr. 13, 1775; *Rivington's Gazetteer*, Mar. 9, 1775; Ralph Thurman, *To the Inhabitants of the City and County of New-York* ([New York], 1775), broadside; Smith, *Historical Memoirs*, I, 219–220; Leake, *Memoir of Lamb*, 101; Plain English, *To the Inhabitants of New-York*.

53. *Journal*, Apr. 13, 1774; Thurman, *To the Inhabitants;* Smith, *Historical Memoirs*, I, 219–222; Leake, *Memoir of Lamb*, 101–102; William M. Willett, ed., *A Narrative of the Military Actions of Colonel Marinus Willett* . . . (New York, 1831), 30–31; Force, *American Archives*, 4th Ser., II, 347–349, 364.

54. Smith, *Historical Memoirs*, I, 222; O'Callaghan, ed., *Docs. Col. Hist. N.Y.*, VIII, 571–572; R. R. Livingston to his wife, May 3, 1775, Livingston Family Papers, box 3, transcripts, NYPL.

streets, and made preparations for war. All was "continual confusion," with Sears and Lamb "calling out the People almost every Day to the Liberty Pole."[55] Whig leaders scrambled to reassert control. The Committee of Sixty perceived "with great anxiety the disorder and confusion into which this City has been unfortunately involved," and it asked for a new, expanded committee of one hundred to deal with the crisis. In short order, the members of the new Committee of One Hundred were chosen, and a Provincial Congress was organized.[56]

Even with these extralegal institutions in place, creating a semblance of government, the mob continued to push toward more open rebellion. In early May rioters drove the arch-defender of the British, Thomas Cooper, from King's College to the safety of the Royal Navy. Printer James Rivington, on the same night, barely escaped a mob as he too fled the city.[57] In early June, "a body of people" led by Marinus Willett, a member of the Provincial Congress and the committee, stripped some evacuating British troops of their arms and baggage. Soon afterwards, popular whigs raided the royal storehouse at Turtle Bay.[58] In August, New Yorkers led by Isaac Sears fought a brief engagement with the British ship *Asia* over the control of the cannons at the Battery.[59] The mob and the militia were becoming indistinguishable. This trend became even more evident in November 1775, when Sears headed a band of Connecticut Liberty Boys on a raid to New York, which included the destruction of the press of tory printer James Rivington.[60] For popular whigs, patriotism increasingly became identified with a willingness to countenance or join this kind of activity.

The whig leadership in the Provincial Congress, on the other hand, strove to limit this mobbing. While pursuing measures of opposition, the

55. R. R. Livingston to his wife, May 3, 1775, Livingston Family Papers, box 3, transcripts, NYPL; Smith, *Historical Memoirs*, I, 221–222.

56. Becker, *Political Parties*, 193–199; Force, *American Archives*, 4th Ser., II, 400, 427, 448–449.

57. Force, *American Archives*, 4th Ser., II, 547–548; R. R. Livingston to R. Livingston, Apr. 22, 24, 1775, R. R. Livingston MSS, box 2, NYHS; *Colden Letter Books*, Pt. II, 421–422.

58. *Colden Letter Books*, Pt. II, 426–428; Force, *American Archives*, 4th Ser., II, 2, 1285, 1290.

59. *The Letters and Papers of Cadwallader Colden* (New-York Historical Society, *Collections*, LVI [New York, 1917–1923]), VII, 300–301; *Rivington's Gazetteer*, Aug. 31, 1775; *Gazette*, Aug. 28, Sept. 5, 1775; Leake, *Memoir of Lamb*, 166–168.

60. O'Callaghan, ed., *Docs. Col. Hist. N.Y.*, VIII, 568.

new Provincial Congress trod a delicate line in an effort to avoid a complete break with the loyalists in the colony and with the British government. No doubt the ominous presence of His Majesty's warships stationed in New York harbor contributed to this circumspect course. But the Provincial Congress also wanted to guarantee its own control of events and discountenanced undirected rioting. The Provincial Congress condemned the seizing of arms and baggage from the evacuating British and ordered some of its members to intervene personally to stop the looting of the stores at Turtle Bay.[61] On June 7 they warned that individuals should not interpret the recommendations and resolutions of the Continental Congress for themselves and asserted "that any attempts to raise tumults, riots, or mobs" on the basis of such personal interpretations "is a high infraction of the General Association, and tends directly to the dissolution of this Congress."[62] After the exchange of fire accompanying the removal of some of the guns on the Battery in August, the Congress decreed that "no more Cannon or Stores be removed . . . until further orders from this Congress," and allowed supplies from the city to flow to the British fleet uninterrupted.[63]

Despite its efforts, the problems of the Provincial Congress with the mob's militialike activity continued. For example, in July 1775 a crowd burned a supply barge belonging to the *Asia*. The Provincial Congress moved to correct this affront to authority by ordering the construction of a replacement. When that, too, was destroyed, the Provincial Congress passed a resolution condemning the depredation and dispatched a guard to the carpenter's shop where the boat was being built.[64]

One reason for the inability of the Provincial Congress to control this popular disorder was the lenient attitude of many prominent whigs. Young Alexander Hamilton wrote to John Jay at the Continental Congress after the Sears raid, exclaimed his distaste for the mob, and declared that "while the passions of men are worked up to an uncommon pitch there is great danger of fatal extremes." But Hamilton also admitted, "Irregularities I know are to be expected." A similar theme appeared in the reaction of the Provincial Congress to the raid. It sent an official complaint to Gover-

---

61. *Ibid.,* 646; Force, *American Archives,* 4th Ser., III, 1626–1627.

62. Force, *American Archives,* 4th Ser., II, 1282.

63. *Ibid.,* III, 550, 555, 558. See also Becker, *Political Parties,* 224–225.

64. Force, *American Archives,* 4th Ser., II, 1785–1786, 1792, 1811–1812, 1818–1820, III, 15, 139, 259–263, 526–527, 533, 535, 555.

nor Jonathan Trumbull of Connecticut, but basically admitted that the attack resulted from misplaced zeal.[65] Moreover, firebrands like Sears and Willett, who led some of the tumultuous crowds themselves, sat on the committees and in the Provincial Congress.

Whig leaders also knew, as they became increasingly engaged in outright rebellion, that they had to base their rationale for resistance on the legitimacy of extralegal activity. As the Monitor No. XII essay explained: "Magistracy is essential to civil society" and should be "revered" as long as "it operates consistent with its own nature; and according to the great principles of the social compact, on which it depends." But by itself it conveys "no inherent indefeasible sacredness to the persons of those, who are invested with it." They have authority and respect only "if they act in all things mindful of the end for which they received it." If not, and they deviate from or pervert that end, "they are to be only considered, as *men*;— men who have betrayed the most sacred trust, who have trampled upon all the bonds of fidelity and duty; and who have depreciated the most valuable jewel of society, by dedicating it to the vilest purposes."[66] That was the rationale of the resistance of the committees and congresses; that, too, was the rationale of the actions of the mob.

Armed with this reasoning, a group like the Mechanics' Committee, organized in 1774 by shopkeepers and artisans as a radical counterweight to the Committee of Fifty-one, began to act almost as a government unto itself. It persistently pushed for open support of a declaration of independence in the spring of 1776, and it moved to stifle all opposition.[67] For example, when Samuel Loudoun announced his intention to publish a rebuttal to Tom Paine's *Common Sense,* they hauled him before their tribunal. When Loudoun appeared to persist in his efforts, about forty members of the Mechanics' Committee broke into his shop, seized the controversial pamphlets, carried them to the Common, and publicly burned them. Efforts by Loudoun, a good whig, to get redress from the Provincial Congress were fruitless.[68]

65. Hamilton to John Jay, Nov. 26, 1775, in Harold C. Syrett and Jacob E. Cooke, eds., *The Papers of Alexander Hamilton,* I (New York, 1961), 176–178; Force, *American Archives,* 4th Ser., IV, 400–401, VI, 1398–1399.

66. *Journal,* Jan. 25, 1776.

67. Force, *American Archives,* 4th Ser., VI, 614–615, 895–898.

68. *Ibid.,* V, 438–440, 1389, 1441–1442, VI, 1348, 1363, 1393.

Tar and Feathers and the Revolution

The public burning of Loudoun's pamphlets in the Common emphasizes the persistence of plebeian practices as New Yorkers approached revolution. The various committees and congresses might maneuver to influence events, and some mob activity might take on the guise of the militia, but the people in the street continued to follow ritual behavior borrowed from plebeian ceremonies. Common folk had burned the pope, the Pretender, and the devil in effigy, had likewise kindled a royal barge in 1764, and had ignited countless effigies of political figures since 1765. A bonfire, then, may not seem like a unique act, but taking place within the same arena, and given the special history of such conflagrations, the Mechanics' Committee would appear to be extending a long-rehearsed ritual to a highly political purpose.

The development of mob practices from older plebeian ritual appeared also in the use of tar and feathers. This lower-class activity emerged first in coastal Massachusetts in 1768 and 1769. Shortly after it appeared in New England, New Yorkers tarred and feathered a customs informant. The tarring-and-feathering in both New England and New York represented a combination of popular, official, and traditional maritime punishments. The parading of the victim through town to public opprobrium recalled the practices of the charivari (or skimmington) and the decrees of magisterial tribunals. In addition, the coating of tar and feathers long had been used by seamen to single out offenders of custom and morality. Moreover, these tarring-and-featherings came amidst several public ceremonies orchestrated by whig leaders to single out violators of nonimportation. The ritual organized by the local committees emphasized public confession, not physical violence. However, tar and feathers was at least one step beyond what the whig leaders wanted, though generally applied only by and to members of the lower orders.[69]

During the heightening tensions in 1775, tar and feathers reappeared in New York. The victim was from the lower class—a shoemaker named Tweedy who had spoken out against the congresses and committees. On

---

69. Young, "English Plebeian Culture," in Jacob and Jacob, eds., *Origins of Anglo-American Radicalism*, 189–194. See also Shaw, *American Patriots*, 21, 185–188; Reid, "In a Defensive Rage," *N.Y.U. Law Rev.*, XLIX (1974), 1075–1083; Frank W. C. Hersey, "Tar and Feathers: The Adventures of Captain John Malcom," Colonial Society of Massachusetts, *Publications, Transactions*, XXXIV (1941), 429–473.

PLATE 4. Destruction of the Royal Statue.
La destruction de la statue royale à Nouvelle Yorck, *engraving by Francis
Haberman. Courtesy of the Library Company of Philadelphia.
This contemporary French depiction may resemble Paris more than New York.*

the night of August 22, "the Populace" seized Tweedy on a dock near
Beekman's Slip. Finding himself "in the Power of the People," he revealed
his own awareness of Revolutionary mob ritual by quickly begging for-
giveness and making "the most abject Submissions, and lavish Promises
of Reformation and Amendment." Although the crowd wanted to treat
Tweedy more severely, some of the whig leaders interceded. The mob,
therefore, contented itself "with causing him to strip" and coating him
amply with "Tar, plentifully decorated with feathers." The agonizing ritual, however, was not yet over; for then Tweedy had to fall to his knees and
repeat his ritualistic confession, "praying for Success to General Washington, and the American Arms, and Destruction to General Gage and his
Crew of Traitors."[70]

By late spring 1776, plebeian crowd actions flourished almost unchecked as the situation in New York City worsened. The British forces
began to gather for the summer's campaign against the city. Fear of bom-
bardment and invasion drove thousands into the countryside, including
many of the more affluent. The Continental army filled the empty houses

70. *Gazette,* Aug. 28, 1775.

and streets and brought with it the noise and disorder typical of armies occupying cities. Soldiers disrupted Anglican services in an odd inversion of the English church-and-king mob tradition.[71] On June 10 and 11, in a ceremony reminiscent of the charivari, several tories were stripped and ridden through town on rails. Others, who were more contrite, were merely forced to parade the streets with candles held high in the air.[72] This new ritual, like the use of lights and candles during the Stamp Act crisis, parodied traditional demonstrations of loyalty to the monarch.[73] A month after the rail-riding episode, plebeians expressed their antimonarchical sentiments further. When the news of the Declaration of Independence became official, a mob toppled the statue of George III in Bowling Green and desecrated royal symbols throughout the city.[74]

For many conservatives the increased mob activity and the overt challenge to government promised the very dissolution of society. In April 1775 a public meeting called by radicals condemned Ralph Thurman, who had been a member of the Committee of Inspection organized to enforce the nonimportation in 1769 and had been a member of the Committee of Fifty-one, for sending supplies to the British in Boston. His reaction was typical of conservative attitudes. Thurman asserted that these public meetings "are a Reproach to the Community, and an Insult to the present Committees." Although fearing that the civil authorities could do nothing against the mob, Thurman declared, "Those Enemies to Peace and good Order shall not rule over me; I despise their Threats," and he expressed his determination "to do Justice to Liberty."[75] Many of those who became loyalists agreed with Thurman. As early as the fall of 1774 Samuel Seabury, in a pamphlet attacking the Continental Congress, exclaimed: "Tell me not of Delegates, Congresses, Committees, Riots, Mobs, Insurrections,

71. I. N. Phelps Stokes, *The Iconography of Manhattan Island, 1498–1909* . . . , IV (New York, 1922), 913–932; O'Callaghan, *Docs. Col. Hist. N.Y.,* III, 641.

72. "Diary of Ensign Caleb Clap, of Colonel Baldwin's Regiment, Massachusetts Line, Continental Army, March 29 until October 23, 1776," *Historical Magazine,* 3d Ser., III (1874), 135; "Diary of Rev. Mr. Shewkirk, Pastor of the Moravian Church, New York," in Harry P. Johnson, ed., *The Campaign of 1776 around New York and Brooklyn (Memoirs of the Long Island Historical Society,* III [Brooklyn, N.Y., 1878]), 108.

73. For examples of such illuminations before the resistance movement, see Stokes, *Iconography,* IV, 537, 554, 585, 591, 600.

74. *Gazette,* July 15, 22, 1776; *Journal,* July 11, 1776; *Pennsylvania Evening Post* (Philadelphia), July 13, 1776; Force, *American Archives,* 5th Ser., I, 144.

Associations—a plague on them all.—Give me the steady, uniform, un-biassed influence of the Courts of Justice."[76] It was the "Sons of Discord," not the king, who threatened liberty, and during the long months of mob activity and resistance in 1774, 1775, and 1776, many New Yorkers be-came convinced that only attachment to George III could maintain the so-cial order. Others, who supported the Revolution, openly pondered how to curb the "mobility" and how to limit the "tribunal powers" of mobs and extralegal committees. The dangers of seemingly unchecked mobs ap-peared greater than ever before: they threatened the social system and might lead to mobocracy.

The Revolution, however, did not lead to mob government. From the confusion of mobs, extralegal committees, congresses, and conventions, new state governments emerged.[77] In some ways, this successful revolu-tion ratified and further legitimized rioting. On the other hand, conser-vatives maintained and in some ways even extended their reservations about tumultuous crowds. But from the perspective of the people in the street, mobs, because of their use of plebeian ritual, their role in politiciz-ing the common man, and their significance in propelling Americans into revolution, appeared after 1776 more potent than ever before.

75. Thurman, *To the Inhabitants.* See also Benjamin H. Hall, ed., "Extracts from the Letter Books of John Thurman, Junior," *Historical Magazine,* 2d Ser., IV (1868), 283–297.

76. [Samuel Seabury], *Free Thoughts on the Proceedings of the Continental Congress Held at Philadelphia, Sept. 5, 1774* . . . ([New York], 1774) (Evans no. 13602), 16. See also [Seabury], *The Congress Canvassed; or, An Examination into the Conduct of the Delegates at Their Grand Convention, Held in Philadelphia, Sept. 2, 1774: Addressed to the Merchants of New-York* ([New York], 1774).

77. For this process, see Countryman, *A People in Revolution;* and Wood, *Creation of the American Republic,* 306–343.

THREE

Popular Disorder in Wartime and the Post-Revolutionary Period

A little rebellion now and then is a good thing, and as necessary in the political world as storms in the physical.

Thomas Jefferson, 1787

When Thomas Jefferson wrote James Madison that "a little rebellion now and then is a good thing," he was thinking about Shays's Rebellion. But his comments represented an important strain of thought emerging from the Revolutionary experience. During the Revolution the whig idea that "the people are the only censors of their governors" joined with the plebeian belief that crowd action represented the true interests of the community to strengthen the sense of legitimacy held by rioters.[1] In New York after 1776, the persistent faith in rioting is manifest in a diversity of areas. It appeared in mob actions by British soldiers and loyalists during their occupation of New York City. It appeared when whig crowds harassed tories during and immediately after the war. And it appeared in four great riots of communal regulation, in 1788, 1792, 1793, and 1799.

If the mob seemed triumphant in the American Revolution, however, many whig leaders were determined that the triumph would be short-lived. The tension between whig leaders and the people in the street, evident in the efforts to guide and limit the mob since the 1760s, grew more marked. After 1776, conservative whigs built their arguments against direct popular action on a stronger foundation. Much of the rationale for rioting in the Anglo-American world stemmed from the belief that there was a disparity between natural law and civil law. The people out-of-doors were justified in violating the normal bounds of the civil law in order to ensure the maintenance of natural law. Because the new republican form of government theoretically narrowed the difference between the two types of law, the legitimacy of rioting could be called into question. From this viewpoint, the new apparatus of state legislatures and institutional procedures made more immediate forms of redress unnecessary. Mobocracy, which appeared so threatening to tories and conservatives during the Revolution, could be avoided.[2]

The impact of the Revolution on rioting, then, was mixed. On the one

1. Thomas Jefferson to James Madison, Jan. 30, 1787, to Edward Carrington, Jan. 16, 1787, in Merrill D. Peterson, ed., *The Portable Thomas Jefferson* (New York, 1975), 414–418.

2. For a discussion of this idea, see Gordon S. Wood, *The Creation of the American Republic, 1776–1789* (Chapel Hill, N.C., 1969), 319–343; Pauline Maier, "Freedom, Revolution, and Resistance to Authority, 1776–1976," in Norman A. Graebner, ed., *Freedom in America: A Two-Hundred-Year Perspective* (University Park, Pa., 1977), 25–43; and Maier, *The Old Revolutionaries: Political Lives in the Age of Samuel Adams* (New York, 1980), 26–32.

hand, continual practice had strengthened the popular faith in the people out-of-doors. On the other hand, the new republican government, according to the arguments of many whig leaders, rendered irregular public assemblies unnecessary. The strain between these two opposing currents existed before 1776. After Independence, and as regularly organized governments fell into place, that strain increased.

British Soldiers, Loyalists, and the New York Fire

Rioting by loyalists and British soldiers during the Revolutionary war demonstrated the strength of popular faith in mob action. These riots may be surprising, at first, because so many loyalist spokesmen had decried tumultuous whig mobs. But when it is remembered that British soldiers had long taken to the streets to oppose the liberty pole and that many loyalists came from the same plebeian background as their whig counterparts, such activity appears less unusual.

British servicemen, for example, participated in church-and-king riots by harassing the John Street Methodist Church. This evangelical sect not only represented a challenge to the king's Anglican church but also was reputed to harbor many of the city's remaining whigs. In one incident several English soldiers struck up the anthem "God Save the King," which the Methodists countered by singing one of their own hymns with the same music but different words. On New Year's Eve 1777, the Methodists found their watch night disturbed by a party of English officers. The officers had been acting in a play that evening, *The Devil to Pay in the West Indies,* after which they got drunk and went "reeling and yelling through the streets." Coming to the Methodist chapel, they stormed in still dressed in the costumes of the evening's performance. The officer who had played the devil "had a cow's hide fastened to his shoulders, with the horns painted red, while the tail dragged on the floor." As he walked up to the preacher, the women screamed, and the services were stopped until the male parishioners managed to drag the disturbers out. To prevent such intrusions, General Howe eventually had to order out a guard to protect the Methodists.[3]

Loyalist New Yorkers joined with British soldiers in violently punish-

3. Samuel Seaman, *Annals of New York Methodism: Being a History of the Methodist Episcopal Church in the City of New York, from A.D. 1766 to A.D. 1890* (New York, 1892), 74–76.

PLATE 5. Fire in New York City.
Representation du feu terrible à Nouvelle Yorck, 19 Septembre 1776. *Engraving from Augsburg. Courtesy of the New-York Historical Society. In the foreground soldiers and citizens attack supposed incendiaries.*

ing suspected arsonists during the great fire of September 1776, which destroyed nearly one-fifth of the city. The brutality of their behavior was unusual for eighteenth-century rioting and reflected wartime passions and anxieties. Rumor had it that the evacuating Americans had sent spies to set the city ablaze, and the tories and British troops, who struggled to get the conflagration under control, were thus very suspicious. William Wright, a carpenter and a loyalist, chose that night for a spree, and, drunk, he chose to hinder the fire fighters. A crowd of soldiers and civilians seized him and hanged him by his neck from a nearby signpost. A loyalist mob stabbed another man, strung him up by his heels, and left him hanging for several days as an object lesson to any would-be whigs. Capturing still another man with matches in his pocket, riotous fire fighters tossed the supposed arsonist into the flames and burned him alive. General James Robertson, the British commander, ordered the lynchings to stop and even rescued two men as they were about to be thrown into the fire.[4] In these actions both the British soldier and the tory civilian acted together, if somewhat

4. John C. Travis, ed., "The Memoirs of Stephen Allen (1767–1852): Sometime Mayor of New York City, Chairman of the (Croton) Water Commissioners, etc., etc.," 15–17, typescript, NYHS; Thomas Jefferson Wertenbaker, *Father Knickerbocker Rebels: New York City during the Revolution* (New York, 1948), 100; *American,* Apr. 6, 1820.

hysterically, to protect the loyalist New York community from possible annihilation at the hands of imagined whig incendiaries.

Most loyalist crowd activity was more moderate than these vicious attacks caused by the unique condition of a city afire during a war. Even in the last months of British occupation, when assaults on whigs in the city intensified, tory mobs, while sometimes violent, avoided bloodshed. Thus tories attacked one boat from Connecticut bringing cheese, onions, and other goods for sale. Tying the crew to posts on the wharf, the loyalists beat the Connecticut boatmen with hoop poles and destroyed both their boat and their cargo. In another instance, a patriot returning to the city in early September 1783 was roughly treated by the citizens, the military, and the army officers. When he complained, he was told to go to hell "and by a speedy embarkation narrowly escaped a good pelting with stones, with a volley or two of which he was complimented with after the boat left the wharf." [5]

The British Evacuation

Although the British occupied New York City from September 1776 to November 1783, the experience of New Yorkers with mob action in the rest of the province reinforced the popular belief that rioting protected the common welfare. Supporters of the king remained a prime target. Whig rioters harassed tories in many of the areas unoccupied by the British. They seized loyalist-owned goods, ordered loyalists off their property, and in at least one case pulled down a tory's house. Whig mobs extended their activity to economic issues, destroying the hated tea, stopping wagons to search for food in times of shortages, and even setting prices. If New York mobs were not more numerous, it was only because the extralegal committees took over much of this activity. Even when the new state government was instituted, committees and mobs remained as twin agents of the Revolution. Only when the government in 1779 and 1780 started to respond to public demands did direct popular action begin to decrease. [6] The lesson for New Yorkers was obvious: extralegal activity worked.

Leading New York whigs, like the popular George Clinton, the first

5. Travis, ed., "Memoirs of Stephen Allen," 32–33; *Pennsylvania Packet* (Philadelphia), Sept. 18, 1783; Wertenbaker, *Father Knickerbocker Rebels*, 266.

6. Edward Countryman, *A People in Revolution: The American Revolution and Political Society in New York, 1760–1790* (Baltimore, 1981), 169–175, 182–183, 185–186.

governor of New York State, stood up against this rioting. In 1777 and 1778, with Vermont in open rebellion and with tenants rising against whig landowners on the great Hudson River estates, Clinton's reactions to mob activity turned increasingly hostile. His wish for more executions of tory tenants who had rebelled against landlords was to be expected from a hard-pressed wartime governor. But he also objected to whig mob violence. In early March 1778 a group of whigs at Cambridge, New York, rounded up some local tories and whipped several of them. The Albany Committee quickly passed a resolution against "the inflicting of any Corporal punishment or the depriving of any of the Subjects of this State of their property"; it declared such practices "an infringement of the Priviledges of the People contrary to sound Policy and in direct Violation of all Law and Justice." Clinton concurred, declaring to the committee, "It is highly prudent and commendable in the most public Manner to discountenance their Riotous Proceedings and to give the well disposed and peaceable Inhabitants all the Protection in your Power."[7]

The same concern for maintaining law and protecting all New Yorkers appeared during the British evacuation of Manhattan on November 25, 1783. Because of reports that the "Whig Refugees" planned "to plunder some people to the bone," officials on both sides had worried, in the months before the British surrendered the city, about possible chaos.[8] Careful preparation prevented disaster: but on evacuation day, while the British troops embarked for their ships and the Continental army paraded through the streets to the cheers of the crowd, some whigs could not resist the opportunity of striking, at long last, a blow against the tory sympathizers in the city.

Two separate disturbances occurred. One became almost festive, similar to many mid-eighteenth-century riots. The other disturbance threatened death. In the former, a good-natured mob composed largely of sailors en-

7. William Smith, *Historical Memoirs of William Smith, Historian of the Province of New York, Member of the Governor's Council, and Last Chief Justice of That Province under the Crown, Chief Justice of Quebec,* ed. William H. W. Sabine, 2 vols. (New York, 1956–1958), II, 127–128, 132–134, 136, 280, 306; George Clinton, *Public Papers of George Clinton, First Governor of New York, 1777–1795–1801–1804,* II (New York, 1900), 848–859, 876–879. For Clinton and the whig leadership's general attitudes toward tenant rioting, see Alfred F. Young, *The Democratic Republicans of New York: The Origins, 1763–1797* (Chapel Hill, N.C., 1967), 13, 26, 206.

8. Clinton, *Public Papers,* VIII, 236–237, 244–245, 284–285, 287–289, 291–306.

gaged in activity resonant of New Year's and holiday celebrations. The jack-tars romped through the city pulling down the signs of taverns that had served the British forces so well for the seven long years of occupation. Arriving at one notorious inn, the sailors noticed a hastily improvised change: the ship adorning the sign over the door had a new flag. The wily proprietor had quickly painted the Stars and Stripes on top of the British ensign. With a gratis libation, everyone laughed and toasted the new nation. Here, a prank and the traditional practice of "treating" were enough to defuse the crowd's wrath.

The other mob, led by women returning to the city, was much less indulgent. It focused its rage on William Cunningham, the British jailer, who reportedly had been especially cruel to the American prisoners entrusted to his care. It was rumored that, under Cunningham's supervision, several Americans had been dragged from their cells in the dead of night and hanged from the prison gallows. The mob sought to repay Cunningham for this butchery. He had delayed his departure until he had turned his keys over to American officials. He then headed for the wharf, where a waiting boat was to ferry him to the British fleet. The mob of women intercepted him and ordered him back to the jail, where they intended to hang him. Fortunately for Cunningham, some "of the more considerable citizens, and finally Washington himself" intervened and prevailed upon the mob to release the jailer.[9]

The whig leadership continued its efforts to restrain the people out-of-doors after evacuation day. In early November, state officials were wary of potential disorder after the British departure, and they issued an order empowering the commander in chief and his officers to apprehend and confine "all persons who shall commit any felony, riot, breach of the peace, or any other misdemeanor whatsoever."[10] While Washington and the Continental army remained in New York, these fears were not realized. However, as soon as the American troops left the city, more antitory violence broke out. James Rivington, the royal printer in New York City during the war, attempted to operate his paper under the new American regime. For many New Yorkers, however, Rivington's royalist transgressions could not be easily forgiven. Rival patriotic newspapers, struggling to get established in this new American market, cautioned "that a number of whigs, from the *rebel country* mean very shortly to handle a brother typographer 'without mittens.'" Rivington refused to take the hint and failed to close

9. Travis, ed., "Memoirs of Stephen Allen," 35–37.
10. *Independent Journal,* Nov. 24, 1783.

his shop. The threats against his "disgustful paper" became more ominous and warned that the "Mohawks" might soon be expected in town. A few nocturnal visits from a mob finally persuaded Rivington to stop publication on December 31, 1783.[11]

The antitory campaign opened up a debate over the propriety of riots in the new republic. Those who harassed Rivington believed that they were protecting American virtue: they were asserting the values of the American patriotic community. (In 1776 Isaac Sears had led a group of Liberty Boys in an attack on Rivington's press before the British occupation. Other newspapers had suffered similar fates during the Revolution.)[12] Thus the mob attacks on Rivington in December 1783 fitted into a well-established pattern of behavior. Yet so strong was the chorus in support of more lenient treatment for tories that the patriotic *Gazetteer* sadly lamented in early January that even uttering "a single word to the prejudice of the Tories, is," according to conservative whigs, "to *clamor against government, and disturb the public* peace." A month later, the same paper published a long defense of limited rioting. Mobs arise, so the argument ran, when a government uses arbitrary power, violates the law, or institutes an unreasonable law. In such situations, if no other redress is possible, "nature will defend the people, though they use violent means to defend themselves." It is the government that has caused the riot. If, however, after the people "are relieved, they still continue seditious, then they are blamable, and should be punished according to the law."[13]

Whig politicians, like Governor Clinton, could not now accept this argument. Their position became particularly clear after a New York mob assaulted visiting British officers in March 1784. Although those who raised the disturbance acted in good patriotic spirit, a group of "Whig Mechanics" sent a letter to Clinton apologizing for the mob's behavior. After asserting their own patriotism, they declared their "entire disapprobation of proceedings that can bear any construction of opposition to our *own* Laws and the Constitution we have been so instrumental in establishing"

11. *Gazetteer,* Dec. 24, 31, 1783; *New-York Journal,* May 6, 1784.

12. For the Rivington incident, see chap. 2, above. In Baltimore in 1777 a whig mob attacked fellow whig William Goddard because he published an article on Howe's peace proposal that was generally misinterpreted. J. Thomas Scharf, *History of Baltimore City and County, from the Earliest Period to the Present Day: Including Biographical Sketches of Their Representative Men* (Philadelphia, 1881), 778–779.

13. *Gazetteer,* Jan. 7, 14, Feb. 23, 1784.

and confidently declared "that no *real Friend* to his Country, would or ought on any pretense, to commit a breach of the peace."[14]

Governor Clinton, an arch-republican, wholeheartedly agreed with this condemnation of rioting. Indeed, he had acted to suppress popular disorder during the Revolutionary war. (Later, in 1787, he would speak out against Shays's Rebellion, pursuing any rebels escaping from Massachusetts.)[15] For Clinton and those like him, any popular collective action threatened the new legitimate government. Clinton reaffirmed this position in 1784. He personally helped to quell the attack on the British, and he believed that the Whig Mechanics' letter firmly proved "that men who have made so many sacrifices to establish a free Government, will never suffer that Government to be subverted, or their laws violated with impunity."[16]

Riots of Communal Regulation in the 1780s and 1790s

Yet many of the men who made those sacrifices remained convinced that an occasional mob was one of the best ways to maintain a free government. In the closing years of the eighteenth century there were four great riots in New York City. They had widespread community support, and they reveal the persistence of Anglo-American patterns of popular disorder after the Revolution. Each of the disturbances lasted more than one day; two of them (according to eyewitness estimates) included more than one thousand participants. Official reactions to these riots were mixed. In at least one case the authorities made some attempt to accommodate the mob. But in all four cases the magistrates tried to assert informal controls over the crowd. When these efforts failed, officials invoked the more formal mechanisms of government. Clearly, despite the communal orientation of these riots, toleration for popular disorder had decreased.

The Doctors' Riot of April 1788 best exemplifies those diverging tendencies. The New York medical profession had long violated the moral

14. *Independent Journal,* Mar. 31, 1784.

15. New York, *Messages from the Governors,* II, *1777–1822,* ed. Charles Z. Lincoln (Albany, N.Y., 1909), 269n, 271. For reference to the disorder throughout the nation, see L. Marx Renzulli, Jr., *Maryland: The Federalist Years* (Teaneck, N.J., 1972), 35, 37–39, 48; *Daily Advertiser,* Oct. 3, 1786; Robert J. Taylor, *Western Massachusetts in the Revolution* (Providence, R.I., 1954).

16. *Independent Journal,* Mar. 31, Apr. 3, 1784; *Gazetteer,* Mar. 31, Apr. 2, June 25, 1784.

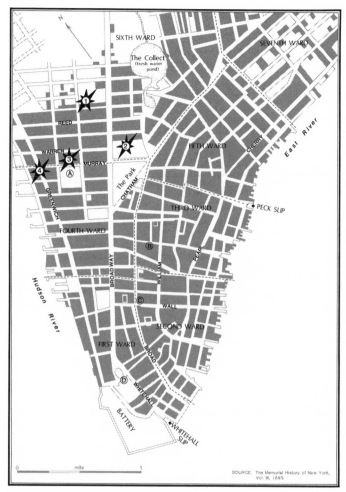

1. Hospital. Doctors' Riot, 1788
2. Jail. Doctors' Riot, 1788; anti-Duer riot, 1792
3. Bawdyhouse. Riot, 1793
4. Bawdyhouse. Riot, 1799

A. Columbia College
B. Methodist Church
C. Federal Hall
D. Government House

- - - - Ward Boundary

MAP 2. Riots of Communal Regulation, 1788–1799.
After James Grant Wilson, ed., The Memorial History of the City of New York:
From Its Settlement to the Year 1892 *(New York, 1892–1893), III*

sense of the community by indiscriminate grave robbing to gain corpses for dissection. On April 13, a small boy thought he recognized his mother's body among the medical school's cadavers. The boy told his father, a mason working nearby, who then led his fellow laborers and a gathering crowd in an attack on the hospital. In their depredations the mob showed, like most other eighteenth-century rioters, a high degree of discrimination. They occupied the medical college and wrecked or robbed the various instruments and scientific preparations used to dissect bodies. Exhibiting a practical concern with the immediate issue of grave robbing, the mob removed bodies and gave them a respectable burial.[17]

Throughout, the rioters maintained a sense of purpose and limited their violence against both persons and property. Because the building itself was not associated directly with the affront to public morality, it was not damaged seriously. Moreover, although the rioters captured and abused several medical students, they surrendered their prisoners to government officials on the promise that there would be legal action instituted against the doctors. By negotiating with the mob and taking custody of the medical students, the city magistrates exhibited a toleration, almost a sympathy, for the crowd. The rioters, content with the jailing of the medical students, deferred to the magistrates, and the disturbance soon broke up.

The next morning, however, brought renewed disorder. Again, the authorities attempted to avoid force; but when serious violence threatened, their tolerance for rioting began to wear thin. The mob at first demanded only to reexamine the medical school. The governor, mayor, and other officials acquiesced. Then the rioters wanted to tour the city to search the

17. Discussion of Doctors' Riot based on the following sources: William Alexander Duer, *New-York as It Was during the Latter Part of the Last Century: An Anniversary Address Delivered before the St. Nicholas Society of the City of New York, December First, 1848* (New York, 1849), 20–22; *New-York Journal,* Apr. 15–17, 19, 1788; *Packet,* Apr. 15, 18, 25, May 13, 1788; *Daily Advertiser,* Apr. 23, 26, May 10, 1788; *Massachusetts Centinel* (Boston), Apr. 23, 26, 1788; *Boston Gazette,* Apr. 28, May 5, 1788; *MCC,* I, 363–364, 393, 623; Alexander Anderson, "Diarium," Jan. 28, 1793, microfilm, Columbia University. For secondary accounts, see Joel Tyler Headley, *The Great Riots of New York, 1712–1873* . . . (Indianapolis, Ind., 1970 [orig. publ. New York, 1873]), 55–65; Jules Calvin Ladenheim, "'The Doctor's Mob' of 1788," *Journal of the History of Medicine and Allied Sciences,* V (1950), 23–43; Sidney I. Pomerantz, *New York, an American City, 1783–1803: A Study of Urban Life,* 2d ed. (Port Washington, N.Y., 1965), 401–402; Isaac Q. Leake, *Memoir of the Life and Times of General John Lamb, an Officer of the Revolution, Who Commanded the Post at West Point at the Time of Arnold's Defection* . . . (Albany, N.Y., 1850), 332–336; Young, *Democratic Republicans,* 120–121.

houses of physicians for stolen bodies. Here, too, the authorities complied and even accompanied and guided the mob on their inspection in order to minimize the damage to private property. Satisfied with this search, many of the mob dispersed. That afternoon crowds again collected, and some soon insisted on attacking the medical students in jail. When the authorities refused to surrender the prisoners, the situation became tense. Fearing a mob assault on the jail, the magistrates ordered out the militia. As in many similar circumstances when a mob seemed to be protecting community values, few troops reported for duty. The mob intimidated one militia patrol by surrounding it and seizing and breaking its weapons. A short while later, the mob harassed the rest of the militia and several prominent citizens defending doctors at the jail. This small corps, which included Governor Clinton, General von Steuben, and John Jay, was bombarded with rocks and brickbats, and in a frenzy the harried officials ordered the militia to fire. In a running battle between the militia and the mob, three rioters were killed, and the mob dispersed. By the next day, when the militia from the countryside was called in, all threats of further disorder had subsided.

Although the death of three rioters was unusual in eighteenth-century American riots, this *type* of violence was not atypical in Anglo-American popular disorder. In both England and America casualties were ordinarily caused by the military, not the rioters, as in the Boston Massacre. But fatalities in America were few because armed confrontation between the military and the mob was rare. The situation was different in England, where casualties, as in the Gordon Riots of 1780, could run into the hundreds. George Rudé asserts, after cataloging the relative bloodlessness of English mobs, that the rioters' own violence against persons "contrasts sharply with the toll of life exacted among the rioters by the military and the law courts."[18]

While the New York rioters in 1788 obviously believed that they represented the general will of the community, exactly how much of the community actually participated in the Doctors' Riot remains unclear. Estimates of the size of the mob range from four hundred to five thousand.[19]

18. George Rudé, *The Crowd in History: A Study of Popular Disturbances in France and England, 1730–1848* (New York, 1964), 255.
19. Sources do not indicate how much of this large crowd was actively involved in the violence. But the legal practice of the day labeled all the people in the street as rioters and equally culpable. Both the larger and smaller estimates appeared in letters from "gentlemen" in New York published in the *Massachusetts Centinel* (Boston), Apr. 23, 26, 1788.

Since New York City's population in 1790 was approximately thirty-three thousand, the smaller number represents about 1 percent of the urban population, the larger number about 15 percent. If we assume the proportion was somewhat between the two extremes, then perhaps one in twenty, or as many as one in fifteen, urban residents took part in these riots—a surprisingly high rate of participation. Like many eighteenth-century riots, this one was essentially plebeian. There is no indication that any member of the elite was directly concerned in the riot, but artisans, like the mason who led the attack on the hospital on April 13, did play a prominent role. Alexander Anderson, an apprentice who took a piece of mica from a science laboratory in the hospital on the first day of rioting, was the son of a skilled carver and later became a doctor himself. The descriptions of the three casualties of the riot—identified only as a cartman, a "servant of Mr. Livingston's," and "a young man"—suggest a plebeian composition that was typical of an eighteenth-century mob. Only three persons were arrested for riot that April, and they cannot be positively identified.[20] In short, the rioters seem to have come from the same middle to lower sections of society that composed most eighteenth-century Anglo-American mobs.

The fear of grave robbing and the desecration of the dead was important to nearly everyone in the community. Plebeian traditions, especially, held that a proper burial and an inviolate grave were requisite for the soul's ascension into heaven. If graves were disturbed, so it was believed, ghosts would remain to haunt family and friends. Thus in England these apprehensions, reinforced by other popular traditions, led to persistent rioting during the eighteenth century at Tyburn between the relatives of criminals and the authorities who wanted to surrender corpses of the executed to doctors for dissection.[21] In New York City the concern was with robbing ordinary graves. The elite, too, was interested in the question. Before the riot, newspapers had discussed the issue, and a motion against grave robbing had been put before the Common Council.[22]

20. Anderson, "Diarium," Jan. 28, 1793; *Massachusetts Centinel* (Boston), Apr. 23, 1788. The names of the arrested are found in NYC Courts, "A General List of All Persons Indicted and Convicted in the City and County of New York from the End of the American Revolution to the Year 1820," 20, MS, microfilm, Historical Documents Collection, Queens College, CUNY.

21. See Peter Linebaugh, "The Tyburn Riot against the Surgeons," in Douglas Hay *et al., Albion's Fatal Tree: Crime and Society in Eighteenth-Century England* (New York, 1975), 65–117.

22. Ladenheim, "'The Doctor's Mob,'" *Jour. Hist. Medicine and Allied Sciences,* V (1950), 23–43.

Some of the postriot commentary, moreover, suggests tacit support for the mob action. The *New-York Journal* devoted fully half of its coverage on the riots to outlining the outrageousness of the doctors' offense. After condemning both the rioters and the doctors, the editor declared, "It is no wonder the spirit of the citizens is aroused, it is not only the vulgar, but all ranks [who] join in condemning these scandalous enormities [the grave robbings]." The article continued, "There is little doubt, but this specimen of the public resentment will fully check the practices of stealing the dead."[23] Even Chief Justice Richard Morris in a charge to the grand jury made some excuses for the earlier phases of the rioting while wholeheartedly condemning the latter: "Though it [the riot] may be palliated in the first stages of it," Morris declared, "yet, after every search was made to satisfy the wishes of the people, the attack upon the jail, and the insults to the Magistrates were altogether inexcusable."[24] Morris's attitude, the article in the *New-York Journal,* and the initial reaction by officials were typical of eighteenth-century patterns of disorder, in which the patrician condoned the riot as long as it did not threaten too much violence or challenge the rule of law too directly. When the rioters threatened the jail, they had gone too far, and the officials had to depend upon force.

In 1792, New Yorkers again turned to mob action to defend communal morality when the financial collapse of a group of speculators threatened widespread economic ruin. This time, however, the disorder remained more limited, and the city officials had less need of force to suppress the disturbance.

During the early months of 1792 a multitude of complex funding and land schemes engulfed all classes in New York. According to one observer, "The merchant, the lawyer, the physician and the mechanic, appear to be equally striving to accumulate large fortunes, by that improbable business" of speculation.[25] Everyone wanted to participate, and many people entrusted their savings to William Duer. The speculating Duer sought to create a "Million Bank," which had as its ultimate object the takeover of the Bank of the United States. Borrowing money at usurious rates and suddenly confronted by a government investigation of his actions during his earlier tenure at the Treasury Department, Duer overextended himself and had to default. When Duer failed to meet his economic obligations in mid-March, the financial balloon he floated suddenly burst, and with it

23. *New-York Journal,* Apr. 15, 19, 1788.
24. *Packet,* Apr. 18, 1788; *Daily Advertiser,* Apr. 17, 1788; *New-York Journal,* Apr. 17, 1788.
25. *Diary,* Mar. 13, 1792.

went the fortunes of many large and small investors. New Yorkers were outraged by the collapse of Duer's financial manipulations. His major creditors threw him into the debtors' jail, his other creditors lost all hope of recovering their money, and a panic seized the city.[26]

Many New Yorkers were not happy about the sanctuary Duer found in the jail. Under lock and key Duer could do little to aid his creditors, and it was an empty consolation to see this once-mighty financier and government officer reduced to penury. On the evening of April 18, 1792, three hundred to five hundred persons gathered outside the jail and clamored to get their hands on Duer, crying, *"We will have Mr. Duer, he has gotten our money."* Unlike the Doctors' Riot, the participants came from a wide spectrum of society. The mob included merchant John Hazard and artisans John Van Pelt and Daniel Tucker as well as Tom, a slave of Joseph Towers—all arrested.[27] The rioters did little damage, limiting themselves to pelting stones at the jailhouse and breaking a few street lamps. In response, the magistrates handled the crowd gently; there were only a few arrests. Similar demonstrations continued for several nights, and, as a precaution, the mayor increased the guard at the jail. The size of the mob, its varied composition, and its persistence indicated widespread community support.[28]

The limited goal of the anti-Duer mob is clear: to pressure Duer and the others who had fallen in his wake to do everything possible to meet all financial obligations. This position can be seen in the trial of John Hazard. The defense argued that, on the night of the eighteenth, while at the scene of the riot, Hazard had expressed only his opinion that the city corporation should make Duer account for his financial wrongdoings. Hazard was, so his lawyers asserted, simply exercising his right of free speech. The *Diary*

26. For an explanation of Duer's financial machinations, see Cathy Mitten, "Private Economic Opportunity during the Revolutionary War to 1792: The Example of a Few True Whigs in New York," paper presented at conference, "New York and the Rise of American Capitalism," May 18–19, 1984, NYHS. See also Robert F. Jones, "William Duer and the Business of Government in the Era of the American Revolution," *William and Mary Quarterly,* 3d Ser., XXXII (1975), 393–416.

27. Names in NYC Courts, "General List," 33; identification in William Duncan, *The New-York Directory, and Register . . . , 1791.*

28. *Daily Advertiser,* Mar. 22, Apr. 13, 18, 19, 26, May 8, 1792; *Diary,* Apr. 20, 23, 1792; *New-York Journal,* Apr. 28, 1792; NYC, Misc. MSS (Apr. 1792), box 14, NYHS; William Livingston to Walter Livingston, Apr. 10, 1792, and Philip H. Livingston to Walter Livingston, Apr. 20, 1792, in Robert R. Livingston MSS, microfilm, NYHS.

supported this position by stating explicitly the aim of the rioting: "It would be a happy thing for him [Duer] if such fearful appearances would compel him to publish a statement of his accounts to show what has become of the immense sums of money which passed through his hands; what profits have accrued to him; what balance and what property remain in his possession."[29]

Despite the mob's restraint, there were public outcries against popular disorder. Some of these critics were still willing to countenance rioting in certain circumstances. "Publicola" advised against such disturbances even though he admitted that the speculators had insulted and deceived the public and were nothing but "crafty swindlers." Instead, he argued, "submit the trial and decision of your cause to the laws of your country." "If upon proper application to them, they refuse to render justice to the injured; you will have a right to be yourselves the avengers of the oppressive injurers—you will then have a right to seek revenge in the way you shall think best." In other words, allow the law to punish Duer; if it should fail, the people in the mob could punish him.[30]

The two other major riots in defense of community mores at the end of the eighteenth century, like the anti-Duer riot, occurred when the laws seemed inadequate or incapable of punishing violators of the public good. These disturbances were the great bawdyhouse riots of 1793 and 1799. Destruction of houses of prostitution by mobs was typical of eighteenth-century traditional rioting. There were several such cases in American communities during the colonial period, and all of these riots tend to fit the same general pattern. Prostitution was uneasily accepted as a part of seaport life. Everyone knew the location of the bawdyhouses, and prostitutes solicited trade openly. This kind of acceptance did not imply public approval of prostitution. Although many poor women sold their bodies out of economic necessity, often on a temporary basis, that conduct met with disapproval even from lower levels of society. But unless some exceptional circumstance occurred, neither the magistrates nor the general public paid much attention to streetwalkers and the houses of ill fame.[31] Antiprostitu-

29. *Daily Advertiser,* Apr. 23, 26, May 8, 1792; *New-York Journal,* Apr. 28, May 9, 1792; *Diary,* Apr. 20, 1792.

30. *Diary,* Apr. 19, 1792.

31. Popular attitudes toward prostitution in the 18th century are difficult to discern. For an insight into popular attitudes, see William Wyche, *Report of the Trial of Henry Bedlow, for Committing a Rape on Lanah Sawyer, and Arguments of the Counsel on Each Side, at the Court of Oyer and Terminer, and Gaol Delivery*

PLATE. 6. Corner of Warren and Greenwich Streets.
Watercolor by Baroness Hyde de Neuville, 1809. Courtesy of the Museum of the City of New York.

tion riots occurred, then, when some incident riveted attention on the bawdyhouses and local officials appeared helpless or unwilling to remedy the problem. Then moral indignation grew heated, and the community united in a riot by attacking the bawdyhouse in question.

The New York riots of 1793 and 1799 followed this pattern. During the 1790s, the most notorious section of the city was in the northwestern corner of the settled area, centering on Warren and Murray streets. This neighborhood, commonly known as the Fields, included the homes and workshops of many artisans as well as several bawdyhouses. Bridging

for the City and County of New-York, Oct. 8, 1793 (New York, 1793); Anderson, "Diarium," Jan. 17, Apr. 9, Oct. 3, 21, 1793. See also Mary Christine Stansell, "Women of the Laboring Poor in New York City, 1820–1860" (Ph.D. diss., Yale University, 1979), 170–199.

both the Third and Fifth wards, it was also, in the 1790s, the poorest section of the city.[32] So blatant was the activity of the prostitutes here that it was almost impossible for a young man to walk the streets without being accosted. Alexander Anderson, then a student at Columbia College, recorded in his diary how he and a friend were returning from school one day, when a prostitute appeared at a window opposite a church near Chapel Street "and displayed her Breast to our view, with a most artful smile" in an attempt to solicit their business.[33] This persistent affront to the moral sensibilities of Bible readers like Anderson was not enough to trigger a riot.

A celebrated seduction case in 1793, however, focused popular rage against Mother Carey's bawdyhouse. Many such houses served also as a rendezvous for illicit lovers. Mother Carey's establishment was the scene of one such supposed assignation: Lanah Sawyer, the seventeen-year-old girl involved, claimed she was tricked into coming into the house and then was raped. The ensuing court case excited much interest. The prosecution stood behind Lanah Sawyer, portraying her as a "modest, prudent and discreet girl," living with her parents, who had been victimized by a smooth-talking and affluent rake. The defense attorneys admitted that the accused, Henry Bedlow, had seduced Lanah, but asserted that seduction was not criminal rape. Moreover, they attacked Lanah's character, claiming that a truly prudent girl would not have gone out with Bedlow in the first place.[34]

The case, however, assumed a larger meaning. The defense extended the assault on Lanah's reputation to all of her neighborhood friends who had attested to her virtue. Referring to these young female witnesses as "of the same condition of life" as Lanah Sawyer, one of the defense attorneys argued, "What they term discretion and prudence, may by people of more mature judgment, be termed the highest indiscretion and the highest imprudence." Another of the defense attorneys echoed these sentiments by asking, "But who are these Witnesses?" and then answering, "An obscure set of people, perhaps of no character themselves." In other words, not only was Lanah Sawyer put on trial for bringing a charge of rape, but

32. NYC, Tax Assessments, First–Tenth wards, 1795, NYCA; Edmund Philip Willis, "Social Origins of Political Leadership in New York City from the Revolution to 1815" (Ph.D. diss., University of California, Berkeley, 1967), 58–59.

33. Anderson, "Diarium," Jan. 17, 1793.

34. Details of Bedlow case and quotations from Wyche, *Trial of Henry Bedlow,* 3–8, 30, 36–37, 40–41, 44–45, 48, 56–59.

so, too, were all girls from her station in life. In an effort to elicit sympathy for Lanah, the prosecution put the issue more baldly when detailing why she had delayed bringing criminal charges. The district attorney explained that Lanah hesitated "to disclose an unfortunate occurrence to the world" because, being "poor and unknown," she feared "to oppose a man of rich family and connections, who might through influence and art, or the quibbles of law, obtain an acquittal."

What made the attack on poor girls from mechanic and working class families—and the contrast in economic background between plaintiff and defendant—even more galling was that much of Bedlow's defense depended upon testimony from Mother Carey and those who lived in her bawdyhouse. These defense witnesses were, in the words of the district attorney, "women of the most infamous occupations, employed in the destruction of the innocent, or in support of themselves by prostitution." When the case ended in acquittal, many New Yorkers believed that the law had failed them. On October 14, six days after the trial, a mob demanded vengeance.[35]

The rioters, as in the doctors' and anti-Duer disturbances, exhibited purposefulness in their action and limited themselves to the destruction of property. They vented their anger against the bawdyhouses rather than Henry Bedlow. Although it is difficult to be sure of their reasoning, the rioters probably were aware that these dens of iniquity were more vulnerable than was the property of the affluent Bedlows. Perhaps, too, many New Yorkers sought to destroy the scene of possible future corruption of their own sisters and daughters. Whatever the thinking, a crowd of several hundred gathered in the early evening to hurl stones at the notorious building before launching a full-scale assault. Despite a pistol shot from Mother Carey's, the mob quickly entered and "showed their dexterity in tumbling out the beds and other Furniture—the Air was instantly filled with Feathers and Fragments—they next mounted the roof which they soon unshingled, working with great industry." By morning, the house was almost completely dismantled. On the following evening, popular rage was transferred to the other bawdyhouses in the neighborhood, and mobs attacked the establishments of Mother Giles and Mother Gibbins. Faced by this spreading disorder, the mayor and the other public officials acted to restrain these attacks, and by the third night the streets were patrolled "by a party of horsemen . . . to prevent the progress of riots."[36]

35. Anderson, "Diarium," Oct. 14, 1793.
36. *Daily Advertiser,* Oct. 16, 17, 1793; *Diary,* Oct. 15, 16, 18, 23–25, 1793; *New-York Journal,* Oct. 16, 19, 1793; Moreau de St. Méry, *Moreau de St. Méry's*

The 1799 bawdyhouse riot followed a similar pattern. The disturbance centered on the same neighborhood, near the corner of Murray and Greenwich streets. This time the mysterious murder of a man on July 4 triggered the rioting. Last seen alive at a bawdyhouse, the man's body was found in the Hudson River. The rioting began on July 17 and continued for four nights, as mobs, eight hundred to one thousand strong, threw stones at the bawdyhouse and threatened its complete destruction. The mayor, magistrates, and several prominent citizens struggled to maintain order. At first they relied heavily upon their positions as social and political leaders to influence the mob. In the eighteenth century, patronage was an important component of this influence, and Mayor Richard Varick revealed how this power was explicitly wielded when he deprived "a cartman of his license on the spot, for attempting to foment the disturbance."[37] Yet this power was not enough, and it was necessary to order out the militia. Fortunately, there was no gun battle with the mob. Many arrests were made, however, and the militia patrolled the streets for the next few nights, as mobs repeatedly threatened to tear the Murray Street bawdyhouse down.[38]

The people who participated in the bawdyhouse riots of 1793 and 1799 tended to come from the middle to lower segments of society. Seven men were arrested for the 1793 bawdyhouse riot, and they represent people whose families were "of the same condition of life" as Lanah Sawyer. Five were artisans: two were carpenters, and three were cartmen. A grocer and a mariner were also involved. Moreover, the student Alexander Anderson, who was not arrested, was a part of the crowd and was close enough to the action to get covered with the feathers from the bawdyhouse bedding.[39]

Although there were more arrests in 1799, the character of the rioters was essentially the same. Forty-five people were taken into custody during the four days of rioting, but only fourteen can be identified. Again tradesmen were prominent. The occupations of those arrested included rigger, boatbuilder, cordwainer, carpenter, stonecutter, blacksmith, wheelwright, and cartman. At least one of the cordwainers, Isaac Carpenter, was a mas-

American Journey (1793–1798), trans. and ed. Kenneth Roberts and Anna M. Roberts (Garden City, N.Y., 1947), 312; *MCC*, II, 46, 51, 85.

37. *Mercantile Advertiser*, July 18, 1799.

38. *Argus*, July 19, 20, 1799; *Commercial Advertiser*, July 18, 1799; *Gazette*, July 18, 20, 1799; *Mercantile Advertiser*, July 18, 20, 1799; *MCC*, II, 560, 563, 567.

39. Anderson, "Diarium," Oct. 14, 1793.

ter craftsman, since he is listed in Longworth's directory for 1800 as having his own shoestore. There were also a grocer and a little boy about ten years old, who was released soon after being brought to the police office. The remaining thirty-one were probably minors, day laborers, younger journeymen, sailors, and transients, since these groups were not ordinarily included in the directory.[40] In short, the rioters in 1793 and 1799 were largely plebeian and typical of eighteenth-century mobs in both England and America.

Although the bawdyhouse riots occurred in a particularly disreputable neighborhood, the identified rioters did not all reside nearby. The sense of community fostered by the mob, then, transcended any one section of the city. Of course, several artisan rioters did live close to these houses of prostitution and might have been particularly interested in closing them down. In the 1793 disturbance three of the rioters lived in that vicinity: Henry Foreman, cartman, lived on Reed Street; Moses Hunt, grocer, resided on Warren Street; and Hugh Smith, also a cartman, is listed in the court records as from the Fifth Ward. Similarly, five of the identified rioters in 1799 lived in the area around Murray Street. But in both 1793 and 1799 the rest of the known addresses were dispersed throughout the city. In 1793, three men came from the Seventh Ward along the East River on the other side of the city, and one of the cartmen resided on Whitehall Dock in the First Ward. The residential pattern for the 1799 mob is even more scattered: two hailed from Cherry Street in the Seventh Ward, one from the Seventh Ward with no address given, another from William Street in either the First or Second Ward, and three from the outskirts of the city in the Sixth Ward.[41] When New Yorkers rioted against bawdyhouses, then, it was anything but a local affair. A sense of community existed that knew no neighborhood boundaries.

Community support, at least for the 1793 riot, can also be seen in a few of the newspapers that expressed sympathy for the rioters' goals. The *New-York Journal,* for example, published a humorous account of the dis-

40. The 1799 rioters are named in NYCMMPO July 18, 19, 21, 27, 1799; NYC Courts, "General List," 78. Occupations not named in these sources are found in NYC, Bonds, July 19, 20, 1799; David Longworth, *The American Almanack, New-York Register, and City Directory . . . 1800* (New York, 1800); NYC, Tax Assessments, First–Tenth wards, 1795.

41. The 1793 rioters are named in NYC, "General List," 42; *People* v. *Clawson,* NYCGS, Nov. 8, 1793; *People* v. *Burr et al.,* NYCGS, Nov. 7, 1793. Identifications not in the above are found in Duncan, *New-York Directory;* NYC, Tax Assessments, First–Tenth Wards, 1795.

turbance under the heading "An Airing." The report declared, in language which suggests agreement with the aims of the rioters, "The night before last *Mother Carey's nest of CHICKENS* . . . was sadly interrupted by about 600 enraged citizens." The editor chose his words carefully. Referring to rioters as citizens was to portray them as respectable, representative New Yorkers. By contrast, the report emphasized the luxurious contents of the brothel, "consisting of petty-coats, smocks, and silks, together with downy couches, or feather beds." When the magistrates attempted to discover who was responsible for the tumult, the editor sarcastically rattled off the fictitious names of rioters—"Nicky Rapevenger, Ichabod Whorehatter, Ebenezer Justicemonger, Ec., Ec., Ec."—and, with tongue in cheek, asserted, "It is hoped, such INDECENT outrages will be prevented in future."[42]

Even more revealing of broad support for the mob is the debate over the riot that appeared in the *Diary* in late October 1793. Under the signature "Justicia," written "from the *hand of a female author*," came the serious charge that the magistrates were so active in quelling the disturbance because some of them patronized these establishments and had passed many "comfortable hours . . . in these peaceful abodes, far from the complaints of a neglectful wife, or the very vexatious cries of hungry children." The author claimed that the outcome of the seduction trial was unfair and that the city magistrates had not done anything to close the bawdyhouses. In an idiom reminiscent of an earlier rationale for rioting, Justicia explained, "Since *law* and *equity* go not together, *equity* should be *suffered* the least." In other words, because the courts did not mete out justice, the mob was right to riot. Since the magistrates were "such advocates of good order," Justicia continued, "it is wished that their own exertions to ensure it, may prevent the *people* in future from taking such business into *their* hands."[43]

These charges brought a response. Defenders of the city officials denied Justicia's claims and accused her of libel. Moreover, one newspaper reply declared that Justicia was only inciting her "*night-errants*" or "midnight mob" to riot. Still, Justicia's comments fell upon receptive ears, and after several newspaper exchanges, one of her supporters warned that, if "this evil [prostitution] is suffered to become too notorious, the *people* also will be busy." If riots were to be avoided, in other words, "those who have the power, should be vigilant in guarding against the causes."[44]

42. *New-York Journal,* Oct. 16, 19, 1793.
43. *Diary,* Oct. 18, 1793.
44. *Ibid.,* Oct. 15, 16, 18, 21, 23–25, 1793.

Instead of a renewed commitment to moral guardianship, however, the magistrates were more likely to direct their vigilance against the people out-of-doors. With the roots of government newly anchored in the popular will, the guardians of social order possessed a new weapon to wield against violators of the community's peace. Acceptance of riots had always been tacit, for mobs were always feared by the elite. Even during the extended opposition to Great Britain, the whig leadership resorted to mob violence only when it had no other recourse; and when it did so, it strove to limit the mob to the immediate objects at hand. Now the community's needs, so the leadership argued, could be met more directly through the normal channels of politics. Riots might still occasionally be tolerated as long as they were not too violent and were on behalf of the whole community; but as indicated by the willingness of city officials to suppress riots with force in 1788, 1793, and 1799, the threshold of toleration had been lowered. Tension was thereby heightened between an elite who abhorred disorder and a populace emboldened by its Revolutionary experiences. The story of rioting in the early national period is the story of how this tension increased as the mob became both more violent and less representative of the greater community.

PART II

Community in Conflict

FOUR

Political Popular Disturbances

FEDERAL INTELLIGENCE. *In consequence of the outrageous behavior of the mock-federal faction of the county of Huntingdon, in publicly tearing the petitions of the inhabitants of the county, which they had signed to the assembly against the proposed constitution; a number of people of the town of Standing Stone collected, and conducted, upon the backs of old* scabby *ponies, the EFFIGIES of the principles of the junto, viz. John Cannon, Esq., member of Council and president of the court, and Benjamin Eliot, Esq., a member of the convention of that county. The effigies passing near the door of the court, his honour, Mr. Cannon, who was then sitting on the bench, thinking his dignity wounded, ordered the officers of the court to assist his partisans in apprehending the effigy-men, which they effected in part (as they were not numerous) and a number of persons were thrown into gaol. Immediately the county took the alarm, assembled and liberated the sons of liberty, so unjustly confined; who passed down the gaol steps, under loud huzzas and repeated acclamations of joy from a large concourse of people; who soon after retired from the town declaring their intention to duck the junto if they repeated their insults.*

New-York Journal, 1788

I n politics, as with communal morality, Americans did not abandon traditional mob tactics with the end of the Revolutionary war. Antifederalists, for example, eagerly turned to effigy parades, like one in Huntingdon County, in mid-March 1788, to register their grievances. They likewise rescued men from jail (a maneuver Americans rehearsed dozens of times in the eighteenth century) and threatened traditional punishments like dunking. Similar disturbances broke out the same year in Carlisle, Pennsylvania, where an Antifederalist demonstration, including another jail rescue, lasted two days, and in Albany on the fourth of July, where Antifederalists and Federalists battled in the street. In the politically charged atmosphere of the 1780s and 1790s, then, Americans continued to rely on politics out-of-doors as a means of political action.[1]

But who condoned this type of outdoor political activity? Obviously John Cannon and Benjamin Eliot, the Federalists whose effigies were paraded in Standing Stone, did not encourage such popular demonstrations. Editor Thomas Greenleaf's sympathies, however, are evident in his glowing report of the procession and jail rescue in his *New-York Journal*. By stating that the "county took the alarm," he implied that the entire community supported the Antifederalists; by calling the prisoners "sons of liberty," he asserted that they had acted in the spirit of the Revolution; and by insisting that the prisoners were "unjustly confined," he suggested that the law of the land did not always reflect justice.

When a mob turned on Greenleaf, his attitude changed. On July 26, 1788, New York City Federalists rioted in celebration of the state convention's ratification of the Constitution. The rioters, just like the Antifederalists of Standing Stone, followed the pattern of eighteenth-century mobs. They confined their actions to the destruction of Greenleaf's printing office and a late-night demonstration outside the homes of prominent Antifederalists, including Governor George Clinton and General John Lamb. The attack on the printing office was reminiscent of similar actions

1. For Albany see Isaac Q. Leake, *Memoir of the Life and Times of General John Lamb, an Officer of the Revolution, Who Commanded the Post at West Point at the Time of Arnold's Defection* . . . (Albany, N.Y., 1850), 331–332; Alfred F. Young, *The Democratic Republicans of New York: The Origins, 1763–1797* (Chapel Hill, N.C., 1967), 119; *New-York Journal*, July 4, 1788. For Carlisle, Pennsylvania, see *Independent Journal*, Apr. 2, 1788; *New-York Journal*, Mar. 8, 21, Apr. 18, 1788. There were also disturbances in Hudson, New York; Baltimore, Maryland; and Dobb County, North Carolina. See Young, *Democratic Republicans*, 120; L. Marx Renzulli, Jr., *Maryland: The Federalist Years* (Teaneck, N.J., 1972), 107–111; *Packet*, Mar. 25, 1788.

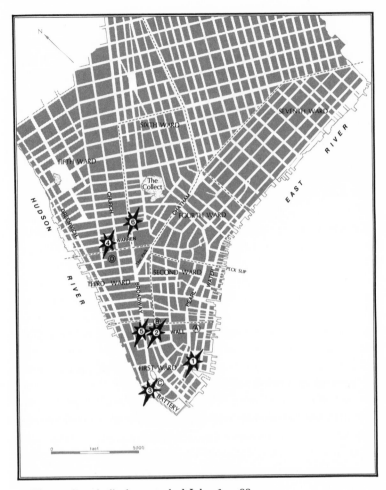

1. Thomas Greenleaf's shop, attacked July 26, 1788
2. Jay Treaty meeting, July 18, 1795
3. Federalist-Republican singing clashes, July 27–28, 1798
4. Knights of the Dagger disturbance, July 31, 1799
5. Trinity Church. Columbia College riot, Aug. 7, 1811
6. Washington Hall riot, June 29, 1814

A. Tontine Coffee House
B. Federal Hall
C. Government House
D. Columbia College

- - - - Ward Boundary

MAP 3. Popular Political Disorder, 1788–1814.
After Charles Burr Todd, The Story of the City of New York *(New York, 1888)*

both during and immediately after the Revolution. Moreover, the anti-Greenleaf mob, led by a member of the elite Livingston family, remained relatively circumspect in its behavior, limiting itself to breaking windows and dumping the printing apparatus into the street. Greenleaf was allowed to escape unharmed. When the mob paraded in front of the homes of Governor Clinton and General Lamb, there was no assault on either house. Clinton was out of town and thus did not know there was any threat. Lamb, expecting trouble, had gathered several supporters ready to defend him and his property. But the rioters outside remained unaware of the armed band inside Lamb's house, and, like the traditional charivari and many of the Revolutionary disturbances, they contented themselves with making noise until one o'clock in the morning.

Although the mob was not violent, was headed by a member of the Livingston clan, and behaved much like crowds during the Revolution, Thomas Greenleaf believed that the attack on his printing office was outrageous, unjustifiable, and threatening to the fabric of society.[2] The incident, he declared, "ought to alarm the citizens of New York, for what dignified character . . . , would willingly reside in a country, where, in violation of all law, the existence of an individual is unsafe, and his property exposed to instant molestations."[3] For Greenleaf the Federalist mob in July was illegitimate, whereas the Antifederalists in March were simply protecting the true interests of the Republic.

Complicating the issue of support for political mobs was the ambiguous status of crowd politics. After years of public meetings, ad hoc committees, and the introduction of new groups into the political arena during the 1760s and 1770s, the exact role of these agents of popular will in the 1780s and early 1790s remained ill defined. The new governments on both the state and federal level encouraged some demonstration of public support, as shown by the famous ratification procession in New York City on July 23, 1788. To what extent more politics out-of-doors ought to be tolerated remained unclear. During the resistance movement the organized political procession could easily become disorganized popular disorder; now, with republican government in place, the boundary between the two had to be more sharply drawn. At first, political partisans, like Greenleaf, bestowed favor on those crowds active in their cause while dis-

2. *New-York Journal*, July 31, Aug. 7, 21, 1788; Leake, *Memoir of Lamb*, 332–336; Mary L. Booth, *History of the City of New York, from Its Earliest Settlement to the Present Time* (New York, 1859), 590–591.

3. *New-York Journal*, Aug. 7, 1788.

approving of crowds opposed to them. Convinced of the righteousness of their own cause and well practiced in the politics of the street, they eagerly used the crowd to coerce opponents.

By the end of the 1790s, however, as elections became more regular and political parties developed to express popular ideas through more peaceful channels, mob action, harassing one's opponents, and coercive crowd tactics were increasingly questioned. The two-party system, after all, and especially the Jeffersonian Republican party, provided a political forum for the common man. Formal political societies, like the Democratic-Republican clubs, replaced ad hoc committees and became an arena for public discussion and a vehicle for selecting party candidates. Peaceful popular demonstrations became integral to the political process in expressing public opinion and in normal electioneering. Against this background, any violence or intimidation threatened to tarnish these new democratic practices. Moreover, the repeated condemnation of opposition mobs made it more and more difficult to defend any political mobs. Drawing on long-standing commonwealth apprehensions of mobocracy and newfound fears of Jacobin France, a language crystallized that decried *all* mobs—whether in defense of the community or in actions driving the community apart.

After 1800, although the two-party system began to disintegrate, the tacit acceptance of partisan popular politics and the antimob rhetoric decreased tolerance for tumultuous crowds even further. By 1811 and 1812, magistrates like De Witt Clinton used the antimob rhetoric of the late 1790s and moved forcefully to restrain political popular disorder. For these later public officials, political riots were simply divisive and destructive.

Partisan Politics and Antimob Rhetoric

This antiriot rhetoric developed during the political controversies of the 1790s. Federalists, fearing too much popular influence, pushed for a stronger national government, and Jeffersonian Republicans, maintaining faith in the common man, wanted power to remain with the states. Beginning in the early 1790s with the introduction of Hamilton's financial program, this debate intensified after 1793, as passions ran high over the course of the French Revolution. This partisanship brought New Yorkers clamoring into the street and forced victims of mob violence on both sides to reassess the function of crowd politics.

Attaching themselves to the cause of France, the Republicans popular-

PLATE 7. A View of Broad Street, Wall Street, and the City Hall.
Painting by George Holland, 1797. Courtesy of the New York Public Library.
This was the scene of the Jay Treaty meeting in 1795.

ized issues by turning to traditional plebeian practices like organized processions. The political content of these public spectacles was evident in the union of symbols from the American and French revolutions. Of course, this activity meant that "the business of the day was often interrupted by tumultuous noises in the streets." In one instance the crew of a French frigate, moored off Peck Slip, "disgorged on shore, and organized to march in file." Many Americans joined them; and "bearing the liberty cap with reverence," together French sailors and American citizens paraded past the French consul's house on Water Street and on to Bowling Green, where they "patriotically" rooted out, "by paving stones thrown in showers, the debris of the old statue of George III," which had been torn down in 1776. "The tri-color was in every hand or affixed to every watch-chain, while from every lip was vociferated the carmagnole."[4]

Political rancor remained intense. Almost daily there were brawls and fights between supporters of the French and the British causes. The Tontine Coffee House, the central meeting place for the city's merchants, be-

4. John W. Francis, *Old New York; or, Reminiscences of the Past Sixty Years*, rev. ed. (New York, 1866), 118–119; Alexander Anderson, "Diarium," June 11–14, July 30, 1793, microfilm, Columbia University.

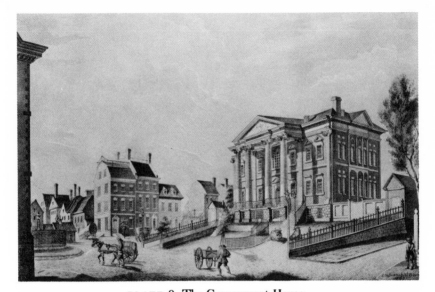

PLATE 8. The Government House.
Drawing by C. Currier, 1847, after drawing by W. J. Condit, 1797. Courtesy of the Metropolitan Museum of Art, Bequest of Charles Allen Munn, 1924.

came the scene of many political debates that seemed to result inevitably in fisticuffs. One observer wrote, "Whenever two or three people are gather'd together it is expected there is a Quarrel and they crowd round, hence other squabbles arise." No major political disturbance broke out among New Yorkers in 1793, but in August there was a riot between English and French sailors on shore leave in the city.[5] In 1794 the appeal of the Republican and French cause was so great that it became unsafe for British officers and men to go ashore when their vessels were in port.[6]

Attitudes toward this politics out-of-doors continued to be partisan. The controversy over a public meeting on the Jay Treaty demonstrates the persistence of a Janus-like approach to political mobs, reveals New Yorkers struggling to define the nature of the new popular politics, and shows the rhetoric developing to condemn this type of street politics. In July

5. Anderson, "Diarium," June 11, Aug. 18, 1793, microfilm, Columbia University; *New-York Journal,* Aug. 21, 1793. There were some unspecified minor disturbances and threats of an attack on a Federalist building; see *Diary,* June 14, July 18, 19, 1793.

6. Arthur Irving Bernstein, "The Rise of the Democratic-Republican Party in New York City, 1789–1800" (Ph.D. diss., Columbia University, 1964), 130–131.

1795, when the details of the treaty became public, the Republicans, fearing quick ratification by the Senate, held a mass rally to protest the abandonment of the French alliance. Considering the background of intensive popular agitation in the previous years and the experience with similar demonstrations in the 1760s and 1770s in resisting Great Britain, a rally was not altogether surprising. What appears unusual, however, was the attempt by the Federalist leadership, including Alexander Hamilton and Rufus King, to take control of the meeting personally and gain public support for their Anglophile policies.

As the crowd gathered in front of City Hall at noon, July 18, 1795, Hamilton mounted a stoop in Broad Street and attempted to harangue them. Jeers greeted him, and Hamilton quickly found himself in a shouting match with two of the Livingstons, Peter R. and Brockhurst. Since some Republican advertisements had declared that there was to be a discussion of the treaty, Hamilton insisted that the merits of the treaty be debated. The Livingstons, on the other hand, claimed that the treaty was universally disliked and that the crowd was there only to voice its disapproval. The general hubbub and calls for points of order drowned out the argument, and Hamilton could scarcely be heard over the "hissing, coughings, and hootings." Stationed on the balcony of the Federal Hall, Colonel William S. Smith, chairman of this informal assembly, was unable to control the situation. No clear decision on any issue emerged amid all this confusion. The Federalists later claimed that protreaty resolutions had been passed, and the Republicans retorted that those resolutions had been shouted down and that a committee, dominated by Republicans, had been organized to draw up a statement reflecting the general sentiments of the people.[7]

Having failed in their attempt to garner popular support for the Jay Treaty, the Federalists tried to minimize the political damage by promptly charging the Republicans with behaving riotously, and claiming that the crowd silenced Hamilton by throwing stones at him.[8] Because of this alleged violence, Federalist publicists, using language inherited from the traditional whig fears of faction and excessive democracy, denied the legit-

7. *American Minerva,* July 20, 1795; *Daily Advertiser,* July 20, 1795; *New-York Journal,* July 18, 22, 1795; *Herald,* July 22, 1795; *Gazette,* July 20, 25, 27, 1795; Anderson, "Diarium," July 18, 20, 1795; Edward to Margaret Beekman Livingston, July 20, 1795, in R. R. Livingston MSS, microfilm, NYHS; J. Beckly to De Witt Clinton, July 24, 1795, Clinton Papers, microfilm, Columbia University.

8. *Gazette,* July 20, 1795.

imacy of popular assemblies. "An Enemy to Confusion" declared that the meeting was "dangerous to peace and good order, and to the due and regular conduct of our public affairs." From this perspective, all popular demonstrations represented nothing more than invidious party spirit and could not possibly reflect a true sense of the people.[9]

Republicans, of course, disagreed with this attack on politics out-of-doors. They pointed with pride to the symbolic action of a splinter group of about five hundred who found the tumult of the "Town Meeting" too disconcerting and, "proceeding to the battery, formed a circle, and there BURNT *the treaty,* opposite the government house." The public burning of the treaty closely resembled the burning of effigies during the Revolutionary opposition to Britain. In both cases the idea was to do no untoward damage, yet still express the intense displeasure of the people. The location of the act was not accidental. The crowd destroyed that treaty yet to be ratified by the Federal government, in front of the Government House— the residence of the treaty's architect, Governor John Jay, the building once intended as the residence for President George Washington when New York was the nation's capital.[10]

But the Republicans, like the Federalists and their common English whig forebears, also disapproved of violent political divisions. The Republicans had great faith in the public and blamed the putative Federalist minority for the tumult. The *New-York Journal* contrasted the discord of the eighteenth, "when *tumult* lifted her *bloated* head, the head of faction," to a controlled Republican meeting a few days later in which "all was harmonious and the citizens unanimously retired" soon after they passed anti-treaty resolutions.[11]

Republicans again defended public demonstrations as a legitimate form of crowd politics in 1796 during a controversy between an obscure state

9. *Daily Advertiser,* July 20, 1795. This position fits the general tone of Federalism. The Federalists opposed the popular thrust of the American Revolution and feared the excesses of the French Revolution. What is surprising is that, despite this rhetorical and ideological condemnation of rioting, the Federalists were willing to use mobs for their own political ends. For an excellent discussion of the Federalist ideological position, see Linda K. Kerber, *Federalists in Dissent: Imagery and Ideology in Jeffersonian America* (Ithaca, N.Y., 1970), 173–215.

10. William Bruce Wheeler, "Urban Politics in Nature's Republic: The Development of Political Parties in the Seaport Cities in the Federalist Era" (Ph.D. diss., University of Virginia, 1967), 97–99, 372. I. N. Phelps Stokes, *The Iconography of Manhattan Island, 1498–1909* . . . (New York, 1915–1928), I, 443.

11. *New-York Journal,* July 22, 1795.

assemblyman, William Keteltas, and the New York State legislature. This Keteltas affair helped galvanize New York politics because the Federalists not only charged the Republicans with using a mob which threatened the Republic but also alienated masses of New York voters by their high-handed manner. The result was to strengthen the Republican appeal and that party's commitment to the man in the street.[12]

The Keteltas case had a striking resemblance to the Wilkesite movement in England during the 1760s and the McDougall affair in New York City in 1769 and 1770. Both John Wilkes and Alexander McDougall had posed as guardians of liberty and pitted themselves against a legislative body. The British government repeatedly denied Wilkes his seat in Parliament for satirizing the ministers of George III, and the New York Assembly arrested McDougall and charged him with libel for a scathing attack on the legislature's passage of a provisioning act for the British army in New York. Both men consciously played up to the crowd while purposefully acting to restrain it. Londoners often paraded Wilkes through the streets to the acclamation of thousands, yet he always made an effort to curb the tumultuous demonstrations on his behalf. McDougall, dubbed "the Wilkes of America," also advised his supporters to behave themselves; and when he was released from jail, six hundred peaceful followers escorted him home. This pattern was repeated in 1796 in the processions that escorted Keteltas to and from prison.[13]

William Keteltas had demanded the dismissal of Mayor Richard Varick and other city officials because of their handling of a minor court case. A magistrate had been insulted by two Irish ferryboatmen who objected to taking him as their passenger across the East River before the scheduled departure time. For this insolence the mayor ordered one of the ferryboatmen whipped, and sentenced both to two-month jail terms. Keteltas and many Republicans viewed Varick's actions as an affront to the people and an abuse of office. But the assembly disagreed and decided that the petition of Keteltas attacked the integrity of all government and that Ket-

12. Young, *Democratic Republicans.*

13. For Wilkes, see George Rudé, *Wilkes and Liberty: A Social Study of 1763 to 1774* (Oxford, 1962); John Brewer, *Party Ideology and Popular Politics at the Accession of George III* (Cambridge, 1976), 163–200; Pauline Maier, *From Resistance to Revolution: Colonial Radicals and the Development of American Opposition to Britain, 1765–1776* (New York, 1972), 162–169. For McDougall, see Maier, *Resistance,* 192–193; Roger J. Champagne, *Alexander McDougall and the American Revolution in New York* (Schenectady, N.Y., 1975), 22–28.

eltas had intended to "create distrust, and destroy that confidence which the good people of this state have, and ought to have of their representatives." A formal apology on the assembly floor was demanded.[14]

On March 8, 1796, Keteltas, escorted by a large throng that filled the galleries and crowded the street outside, appeared before the assembly. When he defiantly refused to apologize, "the hall resounded with the clappings and shoutings" of his supporters, and it seemed unlikely that he could be imprisoned. But Keteltas enjoyed playing the martyr and voluntarily submitted to confinement. His followers, however, insisted on escorting him to jail and, lifting him up on their shoulders, ceremoniously carried him through the city. After lodging Keteltas in jail, the crowd took his advice and dispersed.[15]

A month later, under a writ of habeas corpus, officials released Keteltas. Once again the people gathered to celebrate their hero and met him as he left the jail. And once again Republicans relied upon the people in the street to make a political statement. The symbolism of the action was unmistakable. The crowd purposefully combined "insignias" of both the American and French revolutions around a picture that depicted the harsh treatment of the ferrymen at the hands of the city authorities. They raised Keteltas into a "phaeton" and paraded him in triumph. On the phaeton were the American and French flags, the cap of liberty (which Keteltas held in his hands), and a picture of a man being whipped. Over this picture was a scroll with the inscription, "*What, you rascal, insult your superiors!*" The citizens themselves pulled the phaeton through the streets with drums beating. Like similar demonstrations and parades before the Revolution, the path taken by the procession was also instructive. The Keteltas procession marched in front of the Tontine Coffee House, where merchants transacted much of their daily business, up Wall Street, past Federal Hall and the Old City Hall, where the state assembly and city magistrates met, and down to the Battery and the Government House, which was the scene of the treaty burning the year before. Having thus paraded in front of every major elite institution in the city, the crowd went to

14. Young, *Democratic Republicans,* 483–490; Sidney I. Pomerantz, *New York, an American City, 1763–1803: A Study of Urban Life,* 2d ed. (Port Washington, N.Y., 1965), 264–267; *New-York Journal,* Mar. 15, 1796.

15. *American Minerva,* Mar. 9, 10, 15, 1796; *Herald,* Mar. 12, 19, 1796; *Diary,* Mar. 10, 14, 15, 1796; Thomas F. De Voe, *The Market Book, Containing a Historical Account of the Public Markets in the Cities of New York, Boston, Philadelphia, and Brooklyn . . . ,* I (New York, 1862), 189–192.

Hunter's Hotel, the location of many Republican meetings, and listened to a short speech from their hero. In it he thanked the people for their support, declaring, "Your decorum, combined with all your insignias, evidence to me your attachment to the Constitution and the laws of your country—they are the best supporters of liberty, and I am sure you revere them."[16] Throughout, just as in the Wilkes and McDougall affairs, the crowd exhibited considerable restraint and limited itself to massive demonstrations in the name of republican liberty.

The Federalists viewed things differently. They continued their attack on popular demonstrations and again resorted to standard whig rhetoric against the excesses of democracy. After the imprisonment of Keteltas, one newspaper reported: "A fuss! A mob! William Kettletas mounted on the *Sovereign people* and carried in triumph *to* prison. A pretty figure this: but he is not the first demagogue who has *ridden the people*." The article asserted that the only difference between the man who is carried on the people's shoulders and the monarch is that the one "*coaxes*" while the other "*forces* the people to be his slaves and run about in the mud to wait on him." Similar articles appeared upon Keteltas's release.[17] The authors of these articles feared that this sort of celebration of a popular hero, which the Federalists viewed as demagogic worship, would lead to the corruption of the Republic and a new form of despotism.

By the late 1790s the Federalists had developed strong arguments, rooted in the long-standing whig fears of ochlocracy, against not only mob action but also public demonstrations. With a shift in the winds of popular opinion in 1798 and 1799, however, the Federalists began to take a different tack. American animosity toward the French intensified during the Quasi War crisis, and the Republicans, who had attached themselves to the French cause, lost political ground. The Federalists gained popularity and, despite their rhetorical attacks on public disorder, were ready and willing to rely on street politics for their own ends.

Several battles erupted in the streets between the Federalists and Republicans, centering on their respective patriotic symbols. In April 1798, the Federalists' Society for Free Debate attempted to take down the Liberty Cap in Hunter's Hotel. Some Republicans resisted, and the Federalists did not succeed. At another meeting that same month a "species of

16. *New-York Journal,* Apr. 15, 19, 22, 1796; *American Minerva,* Apr. 13, 1796; *Herald,* Apr. 16, 1796.

17. *American Minerva,* Mar. 10, Apr. 13, 1796; *Herald,* Mar. 12, 13, Apr. 16, 1796.

fracas" occurred when Federalists did not allow the opposing argument to be heard in a debate. In July "a number of *'unjudged would be soldiers'"* frequently paraded through the streets between ten o'clock at night and midnight "vociferating" "God Save the King," "Hail Columbia," and other Federalist tunes while damning Congressman Edward Livingston as a Jacobin, a Frenchman, and a democrat. Although perhaps more melodious than the rough music of the charivari, the Federalist songsters appeared to be relying on a revised plebeian ritual to put their political message across. As with earlier traditional crowds, emblems were prominently displayed. In this case, however, it was the wearing of either the tricolor cockade of France or the Federalist black cockade that led to several fights and brawls.[18]

When large disturbances broke out, they took the form of earlier political brawls, like the liberty pole battles of the late 1760s, in combining traditional competition between youth groups with larger political issues. Meeting at the Battery on the night of July 27, 1798, the Federalists marched up Broadway "with colours flying and martial music," singing their partisan songs. Fearing that the Federalists planned to insult Congressman Edward Livingston's house, a number of young Republicans followed the procession. When both groups returned to the Battery, a singing contest began. The Federalists bellowed forth their political tunes, and the Republicans responded with patriotic refrains borrowed from the French Revolution. A scuffle soon followed that ended in a general melee. The watch arrived on the scene and restored order, but not before several persons received black eyes and severe bruises. Among the walking wounded on the Federalist side were Samuel Malcom, President Adams's personal secretary, and Peter Jay, Governor John Jay's son. Apparently neither side had wielded serious weapons, and the watch refused to make any arrests despite Malcom's insistence that the attack had been aimed at him because of his political position.[19] On the following night, the Federalist "YOUNG MEN, of the city" became more aggressive. Conscious of their greater number on this occasion, the Federalists, again in a charivari ritual, repeatedly sang "Hail Columbia" while marching round and round a group of Republicans. The assembled Federalist host was so large that the

18. *New-York Journal,* May 2, 5, 1798; *Argus,* July 26, 1798; *Spectator,* July 4, 1798; *Time-Piece,* July 27, 1798.

19. *Argus,* July 31, Aug. 1, 1798; *Time-Piece,* July 30, Aug. 1, 1798; *Spectator,* Aug. 1, 1798; Dorothy C. Barck, ed., *Diary of William Dunlap (1766–1839): The Memoirs of a Dramatist, Theatrical Manager, Painter, Critic, Novelist, and Historian* (New York, 1931), I, 318.

Republicans accepted the humiliation and offered no challenge. But in the weeks after this event, crowds of both parties continued to threaten each other.[20]

The Republicans drew a distinction between, on the one hand, their parades, popular meetings, demonstrations, and even the burning of the Jay Treaty and, on the other hand, the crowd intimidation practiced by the Federalists. Distraught over the effects of Federalist mobs, Republican newspapers, despite their own willingness to rely on popular action, attacked the riotous behavior of the Friends of Order with rhetoric similar to the antimob language recently developed by the Federalists. One Republican paper charged the Federalists with introducing "the system of Jacobinism" into the country. Pursuing the same theme, the piece continued by declaring that the Federalist parades in front of Livingston's house were "indecencies, which would have disgraced the sans-culottes of Paris, even in the time of Robespierre."[21] Although Republican support for the French Revolution had weakened by the late 1790s, this was a strange statement from a party organ committed to the general principles of the French Revolution and reveals the lengths to which each political group was willing to go to discredit the use of popular action by its political opponents.

Republicans may have begun to refine their understanding of proper political crowd activity and condemned the Federalist mobs, but they continued to see their own mobs in a different light. While castigating the "sanguinary aristocracy, and a standing army, aided by a wicked and profligate Jacobinical mob," the Republican Brutus urged his partisans to form associations to defend the freedom of the press "AND TO ARM AND DISCIPLINE THEMSELVES WITHOUT DELAY, TO DEFEND THEIR PERSONS AND PROPERTY AGAINST ANY ILLEGAL VIOLENCE WHATEVER."[22] Thus the Republican *Time-Piece* reported with pride that, when "one of the patricians" (a Federalist) struck a "citizen," the Republicans seized the patrician and, despite the best efforts of the Friends of Order, took him to the watchhouse. Rather than labeling this action as mob violence, the article proudly asserted that "the Republicans conducted themselves with singular courage and moderation; from the shew of cockades there could not have been less than two hundred present."[23]

As long as the crisis with France continued, the conflict between the

20. *Spectator,* Aug. 1, 1798; *Time-Piece,* Aug. 3, 1798; Bernstein, "The Rise of the Democratic-Republican Party," 82–283.
21. *Argus,* Aug. 1, 1798.
22. *Ibid.*
23. *Time-Piece,* Aug. 3, 1798.

two parties remained intense. Despite some doubts about the course of the French Revolution, New York Republicans continued to wear the tricolor, sing the "Ça ira" and "La carmagnole," and raise liberty poles—a revolutionary symbol used by both the French and Americans. Yet there was no other outbreak of political violence in the city until the summer of 1799.[24] At that time, another wave of political disturbances occurred, triggered by the presence of the Federalist armed forces. Once again there were political recrimination and charges of mob government by both sides. And once again, Republicans turned to an antimob rhetoric to defend themselves from the Federalist onslaught.

Sometime before July 1799, a group of navy petty officers formed a militant Federalist organization with the chilling title of Knights of the Dagger. Although these young men were not regularly commissioned officers, some of them, like the debtor William Duer's son, had connections to the city elite. These knights would carouse and disturb the quiet of the evening with their hard drinking and occasional harassment of a stray Republican. On the Fourth of July one notorious knight drew his sword and threatened to run a Republican militiaman through.[25] Later that month a riot broke out in Warren Street, where a "sedition pole" had been raised in the spring. The knights apparently enjoyed marching up and down this Republican avenue, forcing all passersby off the walkway and looking for a fight.

On the night of July 31 they did this once too often. Picking on an innocent upholsterer coming home from work about ten o'clock at night, the knights quickly attracted the attention of the neighborhood. A fight followed, and someone called for the watch. The knights declared that they were "man-of-warsmen" and would not be taken by the watch. The watch deputized the assembled Republican crowd, and the battle continued until the navy men were taken into custody. Even so, on the trip to the jailhouse Federalist supporters rescued some of the prisoners, and only three were ever brought to trial. The incident provided great ammunition for the hard-pressed Republican newspapers. Persecuted under the sedition law,

24. For examples of contested liberty poles outside New York City, see description of confrontation in Huntington, Long Island (*Spectator,* Apr. 3, 1799); in Hackensack, New Jersey (*Gazette,* July 11, 1799); and in Dedham, Mass. (Seth Ames, ed., *Works of Fisher Ames . . .* [Boston, 1854], I, 242, 247). For New York City liberty poles, see *Gazette,* Mar. 12, 1799; *Spectator,* Mar. 9, 1799.

25. *New-York Journal,* July 13, Oct. 26, 1799; *Argus,* Aug. 1, 3, 7, 13, 15, 27, Oct. 10, 1799.

they made fun of the Friends of Order and their military, which now became increasingly unnecessary as the crisis with France subsided. When yellow fever struck New York later in August, the military quickly evacuated the city. Their departure left little cause for further political popular disturbances.[26]

The composition of the tumultuous political crowd of the late 1780s and the 1790s probably resembled the composition of the other riotous crowds in the same period, with one significant exception. Members of the elite played a more active role in the political popular disorder. Thus, Thomas Greenleaf tells us that a member of the Livingston clan was at the head of the mob that destroyed his printing press in 1788. Likewise, the Livingstons were leaders in the anti–Jay Treaty demonstration in 1795. Although Keteltas did not come from as high a social stratum as the Livingstons, he was no pauper. His speech to the crowd demonstrating in his behalf indicated the continued influence men like him exerted over New Yorkers in the streets. The Federalist mobs of 1798 and 1799 also included patricians. The presence of the governor's son and the president's secretary in the disturbance the night of July 27 and the role of William Duer, Jr., as a Knight of the Dagger also demonstrate elite participation in street politics. No doubt the vast majority of rioters in these demonstrations and disturbances came from lower in society. One Federalist newspaper eagerly asserted that the crowd singing "Hail Columbia" on the night of July 28 contained sailors and mechanics as well as young gentlemen. All three groups marched "arm in arm . . . like a band of brothers."[27] The Federalist report was overly sanguine about these diverse groups' feeling like brothers, but the limited participation of and partial encouragement from the city's elite suggest the continuance of patterns of popular disorder established in the mid-eighteenth century and the Revolutionary war.

There was an important difference, connected to the heated political rivalry, between the political disorder of the 1790s and earlier rioting. Each party rejected the legitimacy of mobs supported by the other party and called upon a political rhetoric that capitalized on long-standing fears of too much mob action. Republicans successfully worked to legitimize some outdoor political activity—like the procession demonstration and active electioneering. But although they seemed to monopolize popular action

26. *Argus,* Aug. 5, 7, 8, 10, 12, 1799.
27. *Spectator,* Aug. 1, 1798.

for much of this period, they were as vehement as any high Federalist in
their denunciation of mob activity by their political foes. When a Republican called the serenading black cockade mob of the summer of 1798 "jacobinical" and accused it of behaving like the Parisian mobs of the days of
Robespierre, his language could have been taken right out of the mouth of
the most fervent mob-hating Federalist spokesman, Fisher Ames.[28]

Acceptance of rioting had always been conditional in the eighteenth
century. The basis for the antiriot rhetoric of both Federalists and Republicans was in classical whig theory. English commonwealth thinkers, while
asserting the need to safeguard liberty, had cautioned against too much
rule by the people because it would lead to mobocracy. Strengthening this
warning in the 1790s was the frightening image of the Parisian sans-
culottes in the French Revolution.[29] The specter of political factions' using
mobs in America—even though some few mobs still acted to protect true
liberty as defined by Republicans or Federalists—rekindled fears of mob
government among both parties and reinforced the idea that all mobs were
illegitimate.

Authority Competent to Check and Stop Assemblages

After 1800, political rioting reflected a new emphasis on factional politics
and became a means by which small groups registered their dissatisfaction
or manipulated political meetings and elections. The 1790s had witnessed
a polarization between Federalists and Republicans. With the election of
Thomas Jefferson as president, the coalition of factions making up the Republican party evaporated: the Clintonians, the Livingstons, and the Burrites began quarreling among themselves. They broke alliances, split up,
re-formed old alliances, and created a maze of political entanglements. Nor
were the Federalists excluded from the confusion. They often controlled

28. For Ames's position on mobs, see Ames, ed., *Works of Fisher Ames,* II,
92–95, 106–107, 111–112, 386, 399.

29. Gordon S. Wood, *The Creation of the American Republic, 1776–1787*
(Chapel Hill, N.C., 1969), 326–328; Kerber, *Federalists in Dissent,* 173–215;
Caroline Robbins, *The Eighteenth-Century Commonwealthman: Studies in the
Transmission, Development, and Circumstance of English Liberal Thought from the
Restoration of Charles II until the War with the Thirteen Colonies* (Cambridge,
Mass., 1959).

the Common Council and worked with one or another of the Republican factions.[30] In this situation, the larger questions of the destiny of the American republic began to take second place to the day-to-day political infighting. When there was a disrupted meeting, representing divisions within the political structure, the various factions inevitably resorted to the rhetoric of the 1790s to charge each other with improper behavior.

A Republican meeting in 1808 in which two Republican factions, Clintonians and Lewisites, fought to control Martling's Hall and the presidential nomination reveals the factional mob in action and the rhetoric mustered against it. The Lewisites, under the leadership of Tunis Wortman and Maturin Livingston, hoped to nominate James Madison for the presidency and to pass resolutions in favor of the Embargo. The Clintonians, who wanted to nominate George Clinton for president, opposed this plan and attempted to fill the meeting place before the Lewisites appeared. But the Lewisites kept the door locked until enough Madison supporters arrived to counterbalance the assembled Clintonians. As soon as the doors opened, there was a rush to get inside. Both sides strove to control the appointment of a chairman as chaos prevailed. "Such an assemblage of mankind never before met together," one report declared;

---

30. Dixon Ryan Fox, *The Decline of the Aristocracy in the Politics of New York, 1801–1840,* ed. Robert V. Remini (New York, 1965); Jabez D. Hammond, *The History of Political Parties in the State of New-York, from the Ratification of the Federal Constitution to December, 1840 . . . ,* 2 vols. (Albany, N.Y., 1842); Craig R. Hanyon, "De Witt Clinton and Partisanship: The Development of Clintonianism, from 1811 to 1820," *New-York Historical Society Quarterly,* LVI (1972), 109–131; Alvin Kass, *Politics in New York State, 1800–1830* (Syracuse, N.Y., 1965); Howard Lee McBain, *De Witt Clinton and the Origins of the Spoils System in New York* (New York, 1907); Jerome Mushkat, *Tammany: The Evolution of a Political Machine, 1789–1865* (Syracuse, N.Y., 1971); Gustavus Myers, *The History of Tammany Hall,* 2d ed. (New York, 1917); Thomas E. V. Smith, *Political Parties and Their Places of Meeting in New York City* (New York, 1893); M. R. Werner, *Tammany Hall* (Garden City, N.Y., 1929); Richard P. McCormick, *The Second American Party System: Party Formation in the Jacksonian Era* (Chapel Hill, N.C., 1966); Robert V. Remini, *Martin Van Buren and the Making of the Democratic Party* (New York, 1959); Lee Benson, *The Concept of Jacksonian Democracy: New York as a Test Case* (New York, 1969); Michael D'Innocenzo, "The Popularization of Politics in Irving's New York," in Andrew B. Myers, ed., *The Knickerbocker Tradition: Washington Irving's New York* (Tarrytown, N.Y., 1974), 12–35; Edmund Philip Willis, "Social Origins of Political Leadership in New York City from the Revolution to 1815" (Ph.D. diss., University of California, Berkeley, 1967).

there "was such a clatter of tongues, such hedious noises, pulling, haulling, crowding, jostling, and hallowing 'Hustle him—Hustle him—He is a Clintonian.'" After an hour and a half the Lewisites finally drove the outnumbered Clintonians off and nominated Madison.[31]

Although both sides relied upon strong-arm tactics, neither side attempted to justify its actions. Instead, borrowing language from the 1790s, each side blamed the other for the disturbance. The Lewisites charged the Clintonians with being "federalists and tories" who "intruded themselves into the room for the purpose of creating disorder, and assisting the operations of FACTION." The Clintonians, in turn, accused Wortman and Livingston of engineering the "tumult and violence."[32] Both sides claimed that the disorder of the meeting was the act of a minority's usurping the will of the majority.

This same pattern can be seen in the other political disturbances both before and after the 1808 meeting. After a fracas in January 1804, a Burrite newspaper charged the Clintonians with trying to "manipulate" a Republican meeting and subvert the will of the people, and a Federalist newspaper declared that the battle between the Burrites and Clintonians "exhibited the discord, the tumult, the zeal and the fury of a Parisian mob."[33] Political rancor also expressed itself outside the confines of a scheduled meeting. Republicans in 1810 paraded the streets, harassed leading Federalists, and broke the windows of some of their homes at night when the election results were known. The Federalist *Evening Post* used both whig rhetoric and the comparison to revolutionary France to attack the Republican mob. An editorial questioned whether there was an "authority competent to check and stop mob assemblages of this sort." If the answer were no, "then farewell to life, liberty and property," the cornerstones of every good republic. One should be prepared instead "to see the horrid scenes of Revolutionary France enacted in our streets."[34]

By 1810, however, the forces of law and order began to assert them-

31. *Evening Post,* Sept. 16, 1808; *American Citizen,* Sept. 15–17, 19–20, 22, Oct. 3, 1808; *Public Advertiser,* Sept. 20–21, 1808.

32. *Public Advertiser,* Sept. 20, 1808; *American Citizen,* Sept. 15, 17, 19–20, 1808.

33. *Spectator,* Feb. 4, 8, 1804; *American Citizen,* Jan. 31, Feb. 2–4, 1804; *Morning Chronicle,* Jan. 12, 31, Feb. 2, 1804.

34. *Evening Post,* Apr. 27–30, May 12, 1810; *American Citizen,* Apr. 23, 30, May 1, 1810; *Commercial Advertiser,* Apr. 26, 28, 30, 1810; *Republican Watch-Tower,* May 1, 1810; *Columbian Centinel* (Boston), May 2, 1810.

selves. The city magistrates, who had acted to quell the great popular mobs of the 1780s and 1790s but had done little to control political rioting, became increasingly hostile to all mob action. In the years immediately after 1810, the public authorities led by Mayor De Witt Clinton (whose supporters had participated in more than one political mob) reacted swiftly to stifle any possible mob activity in New York.

City magistrates exhibited a new approach to political rioting in the summer of 1811 in their reaction to the disturbance at Columbia College, caused by the refusal to grant a graduating student, John B. Stevenson, his diploma.[35] Stevenson, a Republican, had denied the authority of the Federalist faculty to censor his address on the right of the people to instruct their representatives. Had he been contrite, he could have picked up his diploma later that day. Instead, Stevenson, at the urging of his friends, attempted to speak to the audience at Trinity Church during the commencement exercises. A number of others leaped to the stage to support him, and the crowd began hissing, booing, stamping their feet, and clapping their hands when the faculty refused to change its mind.[36]

Beyond the jostling of a few professors, this was not much of a riot. But it created great interest at the time, and the city papers reported the ensuing trial. Apparently the most offensive thing about the incident, to both the Columbia faculty and the city officials, was that several respectable young lawyers and the sons of the elite had behaved so insolently. De Witt

35. For other discussions of early student riots, see David F. Allmendinger, Jr., "The Dangers of Ante-Bellum Student Life," *Journal of Social History*, VII (1973–1974), 75–85; Morris Bishop, "The Lower Depths of Higher Education," *American Heritage*, XXI (Dec. 1969), 26–31, 58–64; Lowell H. Harrison, "Rowdies, Riots, and Rebellions," *American History Illustrated*, VII (June 1972), 18–29; Steven J. Novak, *The Rights of Youth: American Colleges and Student Revolt, 1798–1815* (Cambridge, Mass., 1977); Herbert T. Wade, "The Riotous Commencement of 1811," *Columbia University Quarterly*, III (1901), 229–238, 354–366.

36. De Witt Clinton, "Minutes of Cases, Court of Session, NYC," 465–492, MS, NYHS; *The Trial of Gulian C. Verplank, Hugh Maxwell, and Others, for a Riot in Trinity Church at the Commencement of Columbia College, in August 1811* (New York, 1821); *People v. Edward Ferris et al.,* Aug. 10, 1811, NYCGS; *Commercial Advertiser,* Aug. 8, 12, 16, 20, 21, 1811; *Morning Post,* Aug. 10, 19–23, 26, 1811; *Gazette,* Aug. 8–10, 16, 19, 21, 1811; Hammond, *Political Parties,* I, 397–398; Fox, *Decline of Aristocracy,* 160–166; Robert William July, *The Essential New Yorker: Gulian Crommelin Verplanck* (Durham, N.C., 1951), 32–39; Charles P. Daly, *Gulian C. Verplanck: His Ancestry, Life, and Character* (New York, 1870), 21–30.

Clinton, who as mayor presided over the subsequent criminal trial, declared the disturbance "the most disgraceful, the most unprecedented, the most unjustifiable, the most outrageous that has ever come within the knowledge of the court." Such a statement was obvious hyperbole. However, Clinton claimed—and may have believed—that the "solemnity of the occasion, the importance of the parties involved, the respectability of the professors," and the fact that it occurred in a church all contributed to the seriousness of the offense.[37] To make matters worse, those involved attempted to justify their actions before the public in the newspapers and in the courtroom. Rather than admit guilt, these men capitalized upon their positions in society to continue to challenge the authority of the faculty. To Clinton this intransigence was unpardonable, and after forcing the arrested rioters to abandon an appeal, he fined them according to their willingness to submit to authority. The fines ranged from two hundred dollars, for those like Gulian Verplanck and Hugh Maxwell who were well-known lawyers and who had most persistently pushed for an appeal, to ten dollars, given to John B. Stevenson because he had admitted guilt and did not contest the court's opinion.[38]

One year later, when rioting threatened the peace of the city as the United States entered the War of 1812, Clinton further demonstrated his hostility to all such disturbances in his ringing charge to the grand jury of the court of general sessions. Expanding upon eighteenth-century whig theory and the antimob polemics of the 1790s and early 1800s, Clinton articulated a new belief in "freedoms of opinion and enquiry" and argued that all mobs were bad. He asserted that "there can be no state of things more deplorable—no condition of society more detestable than to subject law to the fury of the mob." For Clinton, "the triumph of the mob over the majesty of the laws would inflict a deadly wound upon the character and the interests of the city—would render the property of everyman insecure—and would disgrace and degrade republican Govt. in the eyes of all mankind."[39] Thus, "tumultuous and riotous assemblies" had no legitimacy in a republican government, and Clinton turned his back on the politics out-of-doors of the colonial era, the Revolution, and the first thirty years the nation. Since several cities faced a similar dilemma that sum-

37. *Commercial Advertiser,* Aug. 21, 1811.

38. *Trial of Verplank,* 29.

39. De Witt Clinton, "Charge to the Grand Jury," July 1812, Clinton MSS, NYHS (printed in many New York newspapers, including *Gazette,* July 13, 1812; *Columbian,* July 13, 1812).

mer—riots broke out in Boston, Providence, Philadelphia, and Savannah as well as in Baltimore and other places—this message struck a responsive chord, and newspapers throughout the land reprinted it.[40]

Because of the new desire to maintain urban order, officials opposed even those mobs raised in the spirit of American patriotism at the height of the war with Great Britain. On the night of June 29, 1814, hundreds of New Yorkers gathered outside the Washington Benevolent Society's dinner celebrating the defeat of Napoleon. Fearing that British armies in Europe would be freed for the war in America, and angered by the apparent affront to patriotism, the crowd broke some windows and filled the air with cries of "tory—tory." David Tricedale, one of the rioters, declared that the hall ought to be burned, since a "Damned set of Tories" occupied it. But there was no serious damage. The watch and other police officers quickly appeared, arrested twenty of the rioters, and dispersed the rest.[41]

The disturbance reveals the clash between rioters persistently clinging to their faith in politics out-of-doors and repeating much the same rhetoric used by mobs since the Revolution, and magistrates concerned with maintaining order and protecting a political minority. Men like David Tricedale who came from the lower strata of society were loath to give up their right to express themselves politically in a riot.[42] Tricedale and his companions had only shattered a few windows, uttered threats, and acted in a manner no more violent than the Republican-Federalist fights of 1798 and 1799 or the window smashing of 1810. Moreover, these rioters acted against a background of widespread dissatisfaction with the Federalists. Yet the offi-

40. For other riots in the summer of 1812: In Boston, *Columbian,* Aug. 9, 1812; Henry Adams, *History of the United States of America . . . ,* VI (New York, 1890), 400, 409. In Providence, *Evening Post,* July 31, Aug. 4, 1812; *Columbian,* July 29, Aug. 4, 1812. In Philadelphia, *Columbian,* July 14, 1812. In Savannah, *Evening Post,* June 17, 1812. Also see Donald R. Hickey, "The Darker Side of Democracy: The Baltimore Riots of 1812," *Maryland Historian,* VIII (Fall 1976), 4, 14. For a sample of newspapers outside New York that reprinted Clinton's charge, see *Poulson's American Daily Advertiser* (Philadelphia), July 14, 1812; *Maryland Gazette* (Annapolis), July 23, 1812. Clinton's hard stand against rioting helped to make him attractive to Federalists as a presidential candidate in 1812 (Fox, *Decline of Aristocracy,* 165–166).

41. *People* v. *Tricedale et al.,* July 11, 1814, NYCGS; *Evening Post,* July 30, 1814; *Commercial Advertiser,* June 30, 1814; *Gazette,* July 1, 1814; Rocellus Sheridan Guernsey, *New York City and Vicinity during the War of 1812–1815 . . .* (New York, 1889–1895), II, 103–107.

42. *People* v. *Tricedale et al.,* July 11, 1814, NYCGS; Bail Bond, June 30, 1814, box 7847 (1814–1815), NYCSCPC Bonds.

cial reaction was harsh and nonpartisan. The number of arrests was unusually high, and complaints were heard that the watch had maltreated
some of the crowd.[43] Significantly, the willingness of city magistrates
to suppress the Washington Hall rioters reveals a new attitude toward political opposition, which found reprehensible any popular action against
the Federalists, even when they were celebrating the victory of the national enemy.

The response of the city officials in 1814 and the reaction of De Witt
Clinton in 1811 and 1812 seem out of proportion to the danger posed by
New York's political riots. Neither the Republican nor the Federalist mobs
of the 1790s and early 1800s were very destructive. The key to understanding the increased hostility to mob action in the beginning of the nineteenth century is in the antimob rhetoric developed by all political groups.
Throughout most of the eighteenth century, mobs theoretically represented a united community acting to protect agreed-upon morals and customs. The political riots of the 1790s and early 1800s, however, revealed
sharp divisions within the community. The English commonwealth whig
thinkers had always feared such a factious spirit and warned against it.
They also cautioned that a republican government was susceptible to corruption from an excess of democracy, which led to a mobocracy. In the
1790s both Republicans and Federalists seized upon these warnings and
used them as political propaganda when they were, in turn, assailed by
mobs. The bloody example of the French Revolution only enhanced the
effectiveness of the antimob sentiment. Confronted by violent political divisions, party leaders recoiled from the use of mobs, even those whose aims
coincided with their own.
But the intense divisions evident in the factionalism of New York politics were not by themselves sufficient to make every mob illegitimate. In
1812 De Witt Clinton assailed all mobs representing violent divisions
within the community. He did so because in the opening years of the nineteenth century there were many nonpolitical riots that revealed ethnic,
racial, and religious conflict and presented an even more frightening specter of an unordered society. Confronted by these increasingly stark divisions in society, New York magistrates, like Clinton, sought a means to
maintain order amid what threatened to turn into violent chaos. Gradually, these officials abandoned the corporate ideal of community espoused

43. *People* v. *Tricedale et al.,* July 11, 1814, NYCGS.

by eighteenth-century whig thinkers and grew to accept a pluralistic society in which people with diverse interests and backgrounds handled disputes through peaceful and democratic channels. In such a divided society,
any mob action was anathema because it threatened to loosen the bonds
that held the disparate elements of society together and break out in
greater destruction and bloody attacks on persons.

FIVE

Emergence of Ethnic Conflict

There is a portagues let us kill him, let's mob him.

Charles Morrison to a group of sailors,
1812

We should get along well enough if it was not for the Irish.

Whig politician at the Sixth Ward poll,
1834

When Mayor De Witt Clinton issued his denunciation of all rioting in June 1812, he had in mind more than the political disturbances of that month in which young Republicans serenaded prominent Federalists with fife and drum.[1] For Clinton, political clashes formed only a part of the problem. Other rifts had appeared in New York City by 1812—along ethnic lines. In the years before 1812 the Irish already had participated in several violent disturbances, two of which had led to fatalities. Of more immediate concern at the moment Clinton penned his antiriot comments were the disturbances in late June arising from ethnic tensions between American sailors and resident Hispanics.

On the night of Tuesday, June 23, 1812, three sailors were "on a cruise" of the town going from one grog shop to another. About midnight, while they walked along James Street on their way to their Batavia Lane boardinghouse, they passed Stephen Melo's tavern. Hearing some fiddling and dancing, they decided to go in for a drink. Melo, however, told them it was a private party and refused to allow them in. A short scuffle ensued, and the outnumbered sailors retreated from the scene, their pride dented and their thirst unquenched. Continuing home, they met seven or eight of their shipmates. Now reinforced, the sailors were intent on securing a drink and returned to James Street. Again Melo refused to serve them; indeed, he bolted the door in their faces. This time the sailors showed more determination by voicing their displeasure and breaking a few windows. Soon about six men charged out from Melo's tavern and drove the sailors off. In the process, one man stabbed a sailor, Edward A. Burnham.[2]

Incidents like this were commonplace in seaports. Generally, nobody gave them another thought. However, in this case, the sailors were not inclined to forget their defeat. Melo was Hispanic—he was alternately called Spanish and Portuguese—and the rowdy sailors all had Anglo-American names. Since both Spain and Portugal were considered allies of Great Britain against Napoleon, many Americans labeled natives of those countries the enemies of the United States. More important, Americans had long held prejudices against the Catholic Spanish. Throughout the colonial period Spain stood as a threat to the English in America, and after the Revolution, battles erupted periodically between American and Spanish

1. Rocellus Sheridan Guernsey, *New York City and Vicinity during the War of 1812–1815* . . . (New York, 1889–1895), I, 24–28.

2. *People* v. *Adam Western*, July 13, 1812, NYCGS; *Columbian*, July 4, 1812; *Evening Post*, June 30, 1812.

seamen in Atlantic ports.[3] Given the war fever of June 1812 and this long-standing animosity, the Anglo-American sailors were set on revenge.

For the next few days tension mounted. On Saturday, June 27, Burnham died of his wounds, and the American seamen became even more belligerent. On Monday a large crowd of sailors gathered on James Street, demanded that Melo name the man who stabbed Burnham, and threatened to pull Melo's house down. Fearing for his life, Melo called the magistrates, who in turn ordered the watch and military units to disperse the tumultuous sailors. Officials took more than thirty men into custody, although they arraigned only four on charges of riot. Attacks on Hispanics continued the next day. While peacefully talking to a Mr. John Fulkerson on James Street, John Silva, a literate ship joiner, heard Charles Morrison call out to a group of men dressed in sailors' garb, "There is a portagues let us kill him, let's mob him." Some of the sailors immediately assaulted Silva, who ran for his life into a nearby house. On the same day a mob of about forty men led by Morrison "paraded about the street with the announced purpose of beating Portegus and Spaniards" and attacked at least one other Hispanic.[4]

City officials continued their efforts to quell these mobbings, arresting Morrison and others. The magistrates wanted to protect property and prevent bloodshed. This attitude astonished the sailors, who had assumed that there would be no interference with an attack that could be construed as patriotic. One seaman, Samuel Bills, declared that "the magistrates ought to be damned for not suffering the mob or rioters to take the Spaniard [Melo] and his boarders out of the house and do with them what they please."[5]

3. Ships bound for Iberia and Cuba were dismantled during the Baltimore riots of that summer. Paul A. Gilje, "The Baltimore Riots of 1812 and the Breakdown of the Anglo-American Mob Tradition," *Journal of Social History,* XIII (1979–1980), 551. There were other anti-Hispanic riots: Savannah, 1798; Philadelphia, 1802, 1804, 1812; Charleston, 1802, 1811; New Orleans, 1808. See *Time-Piece,* Aug. 30, 1798; *Evening Post,* Apr. 9, Oct. 2, 1802, Sept. 16, 1811, Jan. 13, 1812; J. Thomas Scharf and Thompson Westcott, *History of Philadelphia, 1609–1884* (New York, 1884), I, 519; George Austin Ketcham, "Municipal Police Reform: A Comparative Study of Law Enforcement in Cincinnati, Chicago, New Orleans, New York, and St. Louis, 1844–1877" (Ph.D. diss., University of Missouri, Columbia, 1967), 48; *Gazette,* Sept. 16, 1811.

4. In NYCGS: *People* v. *Swann et al.,* July 13, 1812; *People* v. *Charles Joseph et al.,* July 8, 1812.

5. In NYCGS: *People* v. *John Barry,* July 8, 1812; *People* v. *Charles Swann et al.,* July 13, 1812. *MCC,* VII, 192; *Columbian,* June 30, July 1, 13, Aug. 1, 1812; *Morning Post,* July 1, 2, 9, 1812; *Evening Post,* June 30, 1812.

The ethnic tensions brought into the open by the disturbances of June 1812 were not easily erased, despite De Witt Clinton's active police measures. In March 1813 officials found thirty or forty sailors "cruelly beating a Spaniard of the name Manuel Prede" at the corner of East George and Henry streets, and in June of that year a Hispanic crowd of equal size rioted on Walnut Street.[6] Thus, De Witt Clinton's firm stand against rioting in the summer of 1812 was not simply an attack against political rioting; it was a warning against violent divisions within society.

Irish Catholics, Paddy Processions, and Highbinders

New York City had always been an ethnically diverse community. At the end of the seventeenth century, that diversity violently surfaced in Leisler's Rebellion, when many of the New York Dutch revolted against the increasing power of the newly arrived English. The bitterness of the aftermath of that rebellion lingered on into the eighteenth century, but did not manifest itself in any violent form.[7] In fact, except for a few rare instances, like the occasional harassment of Jews, the city was remarkably free from overt ethnic conflict. The Dutch, English, Scotch-Irish, French Huguenots, and other groups that made up the polyglot city may have retained some elements of their ethnic origins (evident largely in the churches they attended), but for most of the eighteenth century, they interacted peacefully with one another and shared in the cultural hegemony of white Protestantism.

By the beginning of the nineteenth century, however, new ethnic groups, including many Roman Catholics, began to enter the city and awakened centuries-old fears and prejudices. Statistics detailing the magnitude of this new immigration are hard to come by because no record of the new arrivals was kept until 1819. By that time, New York's Catholic population already had increased dramatically. At the end of the Revolutionary war, there were at most a few hundred Roman Catholics in the city and no Roman Catholic church. By 1829, approximately one in eight New York-

6. *Wm. Bryson* v. *Wm. McPherson et al.*, Mar. 14, 1813, box 7433 (1811–1814), NYCSCPCC; *People* v. *Lewis Manuel et al.*, June 15, 1813, NYCGS.

7. Thomas Archdeacon, *New York City, 1664–1710: Conquest and Change* (Ithaca, N.Y., 1975); Patricia U. Bonomi, *A Factious People: Politics and Society in Colonial New York* (New York, 1971), 18–102; Michael Kammen, *Colonial New York: A History* (New York, 1975), 73–190; Milton M. Klein, "The Cultural Tyros of Colonial New York," *South Atlantic Quarterly*, LXVI (1967), 218–232.

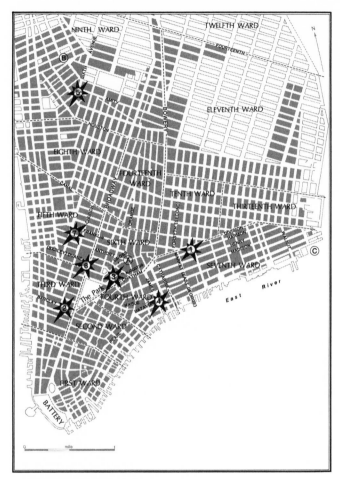

1. Paddy procession riot, Mar. 18, 1799
2. Saint Peter's Catholic Church disturbed by Highbinders, Dec. 24, 1806
3. Augustus Street riot, Dec. 25, 1806
4. Melo's house, rioting, June 1812
5. Battle of the Boyne riot, July 24, 1824
6. Masonic Hall, center of election rioting, April 1834
7. Arsenal, threatened by Whigs in election rioting, April 1834

A. Five Points   - - - - Ward Boundary
B. Greenwich Village
C. Corlear's Hook

MAP 4. Ethnic Disturbances, 1799–1834.
After James Hardie, The Description of the City of New York . . .
(New York, 1827)

ers was Roman Catholic, with a choice of four churches. Of this Roman Catholic total of about twenty-five thousand, only a handful were Hispanic like Stephen Melo. A much larger group, and the focus of most of the ethnic hatred in the early Republic, was the Irish.[8]

The Irish who came to America after the Revolution were besieged by prejudice. In New York City they enjoyed only limited economic opportunities; most Irishmen became day laborers, cartmen, or weavers. They also were segregated into special neighborhoods. When an Irishman attempted to move into a house on Harlem Common in 1825, an angry mob surrounded his home, stoned the doors and windows, and tore off part of the roof.[9] Instead of risking loss of property, the Irish congregated in the cheaper and slum housing on the outskirts of the city along the upper East Side docks, in the Sixth Ward just north of the City Hall, and in Greenwich Village.[10] Living conditions in such areas were not always pleasant. In 1811 Timothy Dwight described the East River waterfront as being "a very great collection of miserable temporary buildings." The 1819 census reveals a disproportionate number of foreigners, most of whom were Irish, living in the Fourth and Seventh wards, which made up this waterfront district. Yet it was the Sixth Ward which had the highest percentage of immigrants. Almost one-fourth of the Sixth Ward's population is listed as aliens in 1819.[11] In the 1820s even more immigrants moved into this area, clustering around Cross, Orange, and Anthony streets. The intersection of these three streets created five distinct corners; as a result, by the mid-1820s, the whole district was called the Five Points. It was a crowded and dangerous place to live, with few wealthy persons residing there. The houses, constructed mostly of wood, were one or two stories high, with

8. William Forbes Adams, *Ireland and Irish Emigration to the New World from 1815 to the Famine* (1932; New York, 1967); William Harper Bennett, *Catholic Footsteps in Old New York: A Chronicle of Catholicity in the City of New York from 1524 to 1808* (1909; New York, 1973); Jay P. Dolan, *The Immigrant Church: New York's Irish and German Catholics, 1815–1865* (Baltimore, 1975); Robert Ernst, *Immigrant Life in New York City, 1825–1863* (New York, 1949); John Dawson Gilmary Shea, ed., *The Catholic Churches of New York City, with Sketches of Their History and Lives of the Present Pastors* . . . (New York, 1878).

9. *P. Sauler v. Daniel Wiseburn et al.,* Sept. 29, 1825, box 7438 (1824–1825), NYCSCPCC.

10. Elizabeth Strother Blackmar, "Housing and Property Relations in New York City, 1785–1850" (Ph.D. diss., Harvard University, 1981), 314–315.

11. Timothy Dwight, *Travels in New England and New York,* III (New Haven, 1822), 449; NYC, Census in 1819, NYCA.

anywhere from two to five families living in them. But some buildings, like 122 Anthony Street, had almost one hundred residents.[12]

Not all Irishmen living in these areas were poor. Greenwich Village, for instance, had many immigrant weavers, and the Sixth Ward had so many cartmen that it was often called the cartmen's ward. But whether they struggled for daily existence or had a trade, most of the Irish lived close to their countrymen. In these neighborhoods they formed subcommunities within the city and maintained strong cultural ties focused on the Catholic church, local groceries, and taverns.

The form and occasion of much of the ethnic conflict centered on the cultural values and institutions most vital to the Irish community. The Irish rioted to defend the Catholic church, invisible neighborhood boundaries, and the few occupations that they dominated. Cultural holidays, such as Saint Patrick's Day, Christmas, and the anniversary of the Battle of the Boyne, provided the occasion for the largest ethnic disturbances. The fact that religious and Irish holidays played such a significant role here highlights the cultural roots of ethnic conflict.

Riots pitting Irishmen against each other and against Protestant Americans injected a more virulent strain of violence into the popular disorder of New York City. This violence had two major sources. One was the violent tradition of resistance that Irishmen brought with them. Coming from a land where resistance to English rule was endemic and where antagonism between Protestant and Catholic was deep-rooted, the Irishman seemed all too ready to pick up his shillelagh and brutally assault his opponent.[13] But the new degree of violence cannot be blamed solely on the Irish. Brought up to view all Catholics as agents of the devil, an attitude revealed in colonial Pope Day celebrations, many Protestant Americans eagerly

12. NYC, Census in 1819, NYCA. For a general discussion of conditions in the Five Points and other poor neighborhoods in New York City, see Raymond A. Mohl, *Poverty in New York, 1783–1825* (New York, 1971), 14–34; Carol Groneman Pernicone, "The 'Bloody Ould Sixth': A Social Analysis of a New York City Working-Class Community in the Mid Nineteenth Century" (Ph.D. diss., University of Rochester, 1973).

13. T. Desmond Williams, ed., *Secret Societies in Ireland* (Dublin, 1973); Maurice J. Bric, "Priests, Parsons, and Politics: The Rightboy Protest in County Cork, 1785–1788," *Past and Present,* No. 100 (Aug. 1983), 100–123; Galen Broeker, *Rural Disorder and Police Reform in Ireland, 1812–36* (London, 1970); W.E.H. Lecky, *A History of Ireland in the Eighteenth Century,* ed. and abr. L. P. Curtis (Chicago, 1972); Maurice R. O'Connell, *Irish Politics and Social Conflict in the Age of the American Revolution* (Philadelphia, 1965); Hereward Senior, *Orangeism in Ireland and Britain, 1795–1836* (London, 1966).

took up cudgels against Catholic intruders. Confronted by intensified violence and divisive conflicts emphasizing cultural distinctions in society, New York magistrates took measures to curtail the opportunities for riot and thereby imposed restrictions on all popular activity.

The first serious and violent battle in New York City between the Irish and Americans occurred on the celebration of Saint Patrick's Day, March 18, 1799.[14] The year was significant. Not only had there just been a rebellion in Ireland, supported by the French, but also the Federalists were riding high on a wave of popularity that included an appeal to nativist sentiment. The Alien Act, aimed at controlling the political influence of immigrants, was in force, and Federalists like Harrison Gray Otis bewailed the "hordes of wild Irishmen" coming to the United States to disturb American tranquillity.[15]

The form of the riot was also important. New Yorkers before the Revolution had a long history of parading with effigies in Pope Day celebrations and in popular demonstrations against British imperial measures. In the 1790s "riotous cavalcades of blackguard boys" copied an English practice, which, like the earlier Pope Day processions, was anti-Catholic: on Saint Patrick's Day they paraded the streets with effigies called Paddies. The practice was intended as a deliberate insult to the Irish because a Paddy was a mock image of Saint Patrick, usually stuffed with straw and made to look ridiculous. In 1799, when the Paddy procession marched along Harmon Street, a rough area near the East River docks, indignant Irishmen attacked it. The ensuing fight resulted in the death of one man and the arrest of several others.[16]

Saint Patrick's Day served as the occasion for other violent disturbances. On March 17, 1802, a number of Irishmen collected about sunset on East George Street, not far from where the Harmon Street riot had occurred three years before; and armed with clubs and stones, they beat nearly everyone who walked by, all the while "Hallowing, Huzza for Dublin, we'll shew the Americans Freedom." The seven men arrested for this disturbance all came from the Seventh Ward: two were grocers, and the rest were laborers.[17] The following year, the Common Council passed an ordinance making it illegal to "carry or drag through or along any

14. Saint Patrick's Day fell on a Sunday that year, and the celebration of the holiday was held on Mar. 18. *Argus,* Mar. 25, 1799.

15. James Morton Smith, *Freedom's Fetters: The Alien and Sedition Laws and American Civil Liberties* (Ithaca, N.Y., 1956), 23–24.

16. *Argus,* Mar. 20, 1799.

17. *People* v. *Peter O'Brien et al.,* Apr. 16, 1802, NYCGS.

street . . . an effigy of St. Patrick . . . disguised to ridicule" him. Although the magistrates designed the law to curb disorder on Saint Patrick's Day, they drafted it broadly to prohibit effigy processions of "any other titular saint, or of any person or persons" on March 17 or any other day.[18] In other words, Paddy processions, and the conflict they evoked, persuaded city officials to repudiate an eighteenth-century popular tradition and outlaw all effigy processions and displays.

The intensity of ethnic hatred and the violence it bred also appeared in a riot on Christmas 1806, when a group of Americans took advantage of another holiday to insult the Irish and their church. Catholic Christmas Eve services, "attending with pomp and splendor," as the *Herald* put it, generally were not held in New York City, "lest the novelty, by attracting crowds at an untimely hour of the night, and a festive season of the year, might terminate in broils and riots."[19] On Christmas Eve 1806, about fifty men, calling themselves Highbinders, gathered outside the Catholic church on Barclay Street and demanded entrance. These Highbinders, labeled by one newspaper "a desperate association of lawless and unprincipled vagabonds," were mostly apprentices and propertyless journeymen living near the Irish in the area between the Sixth Ward and the East River. Three of the Highbinders worked in the shipyards, one was a sailor, another was an oysterman, and two others were tradesmen (see table 1). The group had already gained disrepute in several riotous actions committed under the pretext of closing houses of ill fame. On Christmas Eve, they intended to insult the Catholic church and its parishioners. It took the entreaties of a magistrate, who was a Catholic, to dissuade them from entering the building. Still, despite the stationing of watchmen to guard the church, the Highbinders returned a second time that evening and behaved in an even more disorderly way, abused the watchmen, and did not retire until a very late hour.[20]

These insults struck at Irish pride. All of Christmas Day, "the lower class of Irishmen, residing principally in Augustus, Cross and Barclay street" (in and about the Sixth Ward), heard rumors that the Highbinders

18. *MCC*, III, 228; *Evening Post*, Mar. 15, 1804; John D. Crimmins, *St. Patricks Day: Its Celebration in New York and Other American Places, 1737–1845 . . .* (New York, 1902), 298–303.

19. *Herald*, Dec. 27, 1806.

20. *Ibid.; The American Register; or, The General Repository of History, Politics, and Science* (Philadelphia), I (1807), 14–16; *Mercantile Advertiser*, Dec. 27, 1806; *Public Advertiser*, Jan. 24, 1807; *People* v. *George Little et al.*, Jan. 13, 1807, NYCOT.

TABLE 1

Highbinder Rioters in December 1806

Name	Occupation	Address
John Bailyard	shipwright	Corlear's Hook
Thomas Bowne	aumistat[a]	Catharine Slip
Adam Fash	shipwright	82 Bedlow
Samuel Haviland	boatbuilder	Second and Division
John McDermot	oysterman	29 George
Joseph Rice	gunsmith	51 Church
James Trawbridge	shoemaker	94 Chatham
Joseph Wismik	sailor	79 Wall

Note: The tables list only participants whose address and occupation were identified.
[a] Perhaps clerk or accountant.
Sources: NYCGS; NYCSCPC Bonds; city directories; NYC Tax Assessment Records.

had planned to pull down their church. In the evening, it was reported that the Highbinders were coming to Augustus Street "to demolish their houses."[21] That night, hearing a noise in the street, the Irish responded quickly. Rushing out of their homes armed with cudgels, they prepared to meet the Highbinders head-on. Alerted to the danger, eighteen watchmen under Captain Van Orden went to Augustus Street, where they ran into one hundred armed Irishmen. The watch attempted to persuade the crowd to disperse.

Watchman Isaac Anderson approached John M'Cosker to ask him to give up his club. Not only did M'Cosker refuse to surrender his weapon, but he and his friends then attacked Anderson and "beat him very much." A general melee broke out. Exhibiting a ferocity unknown in most riots of the previous century, the club-wielding Irishmen charged at the watch while other Irishmen threw stones and brickbats. Arthur Donelly, an Irish rioter, later bragged how he ran into the street with a bayonet and there "played away with it" until it was batted out of his hands during the fight.[22] Christopher Newslanger, a watchman, chased an Irishman down the street. He overtook him and knocked him down, but then another Irishman attacked Newslanger, stabbing him in the chest with a stiletto.

21. *Mercantile Advertiser,* Dec. 27, 1806; *Public Advertiser,* Jan. 24, 1807.
22. *People* v. *John M'Cosker,* Jan. 8, 1807, NYCOT; *People* v. *Arthur Donnelly,* Jan. 12, 1807, NYCOT.

TABLE 2
Irish Rioters in December 1806

Name	Occupation	Address	Assessment
John Brown	grocer	Barclay and Cross	
Michael Conner	mariner	31 Augustus	
Patrick Curran	laborer	1 Hague	
Michael Dunn	laborer	31 Augustus	
John Hanley	mason	Anthony	$100
Thomas Henry	cordwainer	Barclay	100
John McCosker	grocer[a]	3 Augustus	
John McGown	laborer	4 Catherine Lane	
Patrick Waters	grocer	27 Augustus	250
Luke Whim	laborer	14 Augustus	100

[a]Bond for John McCosker, dated Oct. 31, 1806, lists same address, but occupation as cordwainer.

Sources: NYCGS; NYCSCPC Bonds; city directories; NYC Assessment Records

The watchman fell to the ground "and expired without a struggle" in a pool of blood.[23]

Word of the murder spread, and an anti-Irish mob formed to revenge the death of the American watchman (Newslanger had been born in Pennsylvania). Native-born rioters, led by Highbinder William Noah, attacked George Coburn's Augustus Street grocery. After stoning Coburn's house and breaking his windows, several men "came into his house and spilled his liquors."[24] The mayor, some magistrates, and more police officers then arrived. By arresting several Irishmen and a few of the American mob, they managed to restore order.[25]

The Augustus Street riot stands as one of the most violent riots of

23. *Herald,* Dec. 27, 1806; *American Register,* I (1807), 14–16; *Mercantile Advertiser,* Dec. 27, 1806; *Morning Chronicle,* Dec. 27, 1806; *Spectator,* Dec. 26, 1806.

24. *People* v. *John McDermot et al.,* Jan. 15, 1807, NYCOT.

25. Besides the sources listed above, see also the following. In NYCOT: *People* v. *John Hanley et al.,* Jan. 7, 1807; *People* v. *Patrick Curran,* Jan. 8, 1807; *People* v. *Thomas Henry,* Jan. 8, 1807; *People* v. *Michael Cannon,* Jan. 8, 1807; *People* v. *Patrick Waters,* Jan. 8, 1807; *People* v. *John Brown,* Jan. 12, 1807; *People* v. *John McGowan et al.,* Jan. 13, 1807. *Commercial Advertiser,* Dec. 26, 27, 1806; *MCC,* IV, 324, 343, 410, 411, V, 250; Clinton Letterbook, Dec. 26, 1806, De Witt Clinton Papers, microfilm, Columbia University.

the early national period. A watchman was killed, and dozens of Irishmen and watchmen were severely wounded. More important, the intense ethnic tensions, evident in the earlier Saint Patrick's Day disturbances, were starkly exposed. The Irish rioters were generally poor and lived in and around Augustus Street. Of the ten identified Irish rioters, four were day laborers, three were grocers with little or no assessed property, one was a mariner, and two were tradesmen worth one hundred dollars each (see table 2). These Irishmen of the Sixth Ward were defensive about their community and believed that both the watch and the Highbinders were their enemies. The native-born Americans, for their part, lived nearby and came from almost the same socioeconomic stratum as the Irish. There were more mechanics among the Highbinders, but one suspects that their trades were under challenge from Irish immigrant competitors.

The goals of the Augustus Street rioters also marked a departure from past disturbances. Now people as much as property were the object of vicious attack. The Irish indiscriminately assaulted all the watchmen. The Americans were equally callous. When a gentleman attempted to restrain the Highbinder William Noah from throwing stones at Coburn's house by telling him that he might kill someone inside, Noah glibly replied, "Damned if I care."[26] Thus the Augustus Street riot revealed a community divided against itself, with rioters turning away from traditional limited mob action and toward increased violence arising from bitter ethnic hatred. New York magistrates recognized the danger posed by such tumults. After the Augustus Street riot, one city official declared, "Mobs, if not checked, and the promoters and stimulaters of them punished will have a tendency finally to subvert all law and government, which are the only bulwark to keep us a happy and virtuous people."[27]

Irish Catholics and the Orangemen

Irish immigrants were not always united. Building upon a heritage of bitterness and opposition that reached back centuries, religious divisions intensified in both Ireland and America in the early nineteenth century.[28] As Protestant and Catholic Irish entered the city in the decades after 1800,

26. *People* v. *McDermot et al.*, Jan. 15, 1807, NYCOT.
27. *Morning Chronicle*, Dec. 30, 1806.
28. On increased tensions in Ireland, see Hereward Senior, "The Early Orange Order, 1795–1870," in Williams, ed., *Secret Societies;* Senior, *Orangeism in Ireland and Britain.*

these religious rivals turned to rioting to settle their differences. In New York City during the 1820s at least two confrontations erupted, revealing not only the intensity of violence in ethnic conflict but also the increasingly hardened attitude of public officials toward rioting. On July 12, 1824, the celebration in Greenwich Village by Protestant Irishmen (or Orangemen) of the Battle of the Boyne precipitated a riot. Greenwich was then a settlement on the outer limits of the built-up portion of the city. Populated mostly by Irish Catholic weavers, some Protestant Irish lived there as well. Both groups were aware fully that July 12 was the anniversary of William of Orange's seventeenth-century victory over the Catholics in Ireland. By eight o'clock in the morning Catholics defiantly had displayed a large green banner on a building on the corner of Amity Street and Sixth Avenue. Across the street Protestants erected a pole decorated with orange lilies.[29] The Catholic weavers worked at their looms most of the day while the local Orangemen paraded the street, accompanied by fife and drum, under orange flags and purple flags (the purple representing the secret Orange Society of the Purple Marksmen).[30] The Orangemen visited one grog shop after another. Each side exchanged insults and later claimed that the other side had issued a challenge for a fight.

No violence broke out until early evening, when several Catholics approached the Orangemen who were leaving one tavern and, with banners waving, were on their way down Sixth Avenue to another. James Cassidy, who was at the head of the Irish Catholics, demanded that John Moore put away the Orange flag he was carrying. Moore refused, and "a furious fight ensued, which resulted in sundry broken heads and bloody noses, together with violent and revengeful expressions." At least fifty Protestant and Catholic Irishmen locked in combat, flailing out at one another with billets of wood, stones, and even, in one case, a hammer. Women, too, joined in the brawl. The pregnant wife of one Irishman was knocked down, and another woman charged into the melee swinging a stick at all who stood in her way. The two sides parted, and shortly thereafter the watch arrived and arrested thirty-three Irish Catholics and not one Orange-

29. Jacob D. Wheeler, *Trial of John Moore, John Mullen, John Lowry, and Henry Bush, on an Indictment for an Assault and Battery on James Murney, on the Twelfth of July, 1824, before the General Sessions of New York on Monday and Tuesday, the Thirteenth and Fourteenth Days of Sept., 1824* (New York, 1824), 8–9, 14.

30. For the Irish background of the Purple Marksmen, see Senior, "The Early Orange Order," in Williams, ed., *Secret Societies,* 39; Senior, *Orangeism in Ireland and Britain,* 78–79.

man.[31] This blatant one-sidedness led to a celebrated trial, in which lawyer Thomas Addis Emmet successfully defended his fellow Catholic Irishmen by reciting the long history of anti-Irish feeling in England and America.[32]

The 1824 Battle of the Boyne riot was not an isolated affair. Less than a year later another Orange-Catholic confrontation erupted as the two groups attempted to settle a dispute over a lottery in an "Irish shillelagh frolic"—a riot—in an empty lot in the northern part of the city. The police tried to part the two combating forces, only to find themselves attacked by several hundred "sons of Erin" involved in the affray. One police officer was severely wounded, and several arrests were made before order could again be restored.[33]

The reaction of city officials and most of the commercial newspapers to these Irish disturbances in the 1820s reveals their changing attitude toward the rioting. During the 1790s both the detractors and defenders of mob action grounded their opposition to or support for mob action in republican ideology. After the first decade of the nineteenth century, there were few outright defenders of rioting. New York magistrates, aghast over the violent rifts within the community, ignored the republican belief that mobs could protect liberty and capitalized upon the republican fear of excessive popular disorder. Moreover, as they came to espouse an ideology that viewed political parties, interest groups, and economic competition as the best means of achieving the public good, city officials came to regard violent confrontations between competitors as a threat to the workings of both the political apparatus and the marketplace. All disorder became anathema. The city elite even came to deny that riots ever had had a place among America's hallowed traditions. The ethnic disturbances of the

31. Wheeler, *Trial of John Moore; Henry Bush* v. *James Cassidy et al.,* July 13, 1824, box 7438 (1824–1825), NYCSCPCC; *National Advocate,* July 15, 23, 1824; *Evening Post,* Aug. 19, Sept. 18, 1824.

32. Thomas Addis Emmet, *Incidents of My Life: Professional, Literary, Social, with Services in the Cause of Ireland* (New York, 1911), 257; Emmet, *Memoir of Thomas Addis and Robert Emmet with Their Ancestors and Immediate Family* (New York, 1915), I, 464–465. (The author of these two books is the namesake and grandson of the Thomas Addis Emmet in the text.) See also An Unbiased Irishman, *Orangism Exposed, with a Refutation of the Charges &c. &c. Brought against the Irish Nation, by Lawyer David Graham, of New-York, in His Defense of the Orangemen, Tried in This City, on the Thirteenth and Fourteenth Days of September, 1824, for Assault and Battery on a Poor Irishman, on the Twelfth Day of July, 1824 . . .* (New York, 1824).

33. *People* v. *Owen Daley et al.,* Apr. 7, 1825, NYCGS; *Gazette,* Apr. 1, 1825; *American,* Mar. 31, Apr. 18, 1825; *Commercial Advertiser,* Apr. 17, 1825.

1820s were portrayed as completely alien to the American experience. "What?" asked the *National Advocate* after the riot of July 12, 1824, "in our happy country where the jew and the gentile are equally protected by our institutions; where all men are free in their persons, their property, their religious rights, shall a body of emigrants be permitted to celebrate the bloody conflicts of European despotism and create riot and confusion among us?" The *National Advocate* answered its own query with a resounding "Never." For, "What have the Irishmen to do with the sanguinary battles of the old world? They have turned their backs upon such scenes, and in our free and happy climes they seek liberty, peace and happiness."[34]

In April 1825 the city recorder, who was then the presiding judge of the court of general sessions, expressed similar sentiments. When he sentenced the convicted rioters of the "Irish shillelagh frolic," he asserted, "Conduct like this cannot be allowed." He claimed that America was a "country of freedom" where "all pursue their lawful business, protected alike by the laws in person and property" and that "the stranger and the citizen are alike secure beneath the protecting influence of the law." Echoing the *National Advocate* of the year before, the recorder reminded the Irishmen that in America they had religious freedom. But he warned them that "the riot, the outrage and violence so long practiced in your native land, must not be introduced" to America, for it would lay "the foundations for the form of government from which you have fled" and would persuade the authorities to create a standing army to, as the recorder baldly stated, "protect ourselves from your outrages."[35]

What the recorder and the *National Advocate* failed to realize was that the Irish knew better than to believe this rhetoric. The Irish knew that they were often treated like second-class citizens and that they were not "protected alike by the laws in person and property." The thirty-three Irishmen arrested on July 12, 1824, could hardly have failed to notice that all Orangemen had escaped scot-free.[36] The vicious attacks on police officers in the Augustus Street riot and in the incident of March 31, 1825, indicate that the Irish had little faith in the authorities' fairness.

34. *National Advocate*, July 15, 1824.
35. *American*, Apr. 18, 1825.
36. Let it be said on behalf of the city officials that all of the Irishmen were acquitted in the subsequent trial. This, however, was due largely to the timely intercession of Thomas Addis Emmet, who just happened to be in the courthouse on another case on the day of the trial. Seeing his fellow countrymen about to be quickly dispensed with by judge and jury, Emmet dropped his other client and

Irish suspicions of Protestant Americans were amply demonstrated in a riot in Greenwich reminiscent of the Doctors' Riot of 1788. An Irishman died of tetanus in a boardinghouse in March 1828. The attending doctor, who obtained what he thought was the proper authorization from the landlord, began to dissect the dead patient, when another Irishman entered the room and insisted that the doctor refrain from cutting up his countryman. The doctor tried to reason with the intruder but failed to convince him that he had opened the "body for the purpose of surgical inspection." The Irishman knew only that a countryman's body, and possibly his soul, was being violated. Excited by the gruesome scene, the Irishman spread the word around Greenwich "that a Protestant physician was cutting up a Catholic for the mere gratification of sectarian animosity, or of vampyre taste." A mob quickly collected, and the doctor barely managed to escape their hands alive. Moreover, the Irish continued to harass the doctor, threatened his life, and forced him to retire temporarily to the country.[37] By the late 1820s the siege mentality of the Irish was such that they were apparently all too ready to react aggressively to any threat, real or imagined, posed by the larger Protestant society.

This same defensiveness can also be seen in Irish attempts to protect those few jobs that they controlled. In May 1825, Irish cartmen attacked their Connecticut counterparts for carrying larger loads than the Irish.[38] The next year a similar incident occurred at a construction project at Dandy Point, when cartmen were employed to remove the excavated dirt. Most of those hired were Irishmen who wanted the job to last as long as possible. They became upset with Isaac Anderson because he loaded his cart too quickly. At first, they approached Anderson in a roundabout fashion, asking him if he was an Orangeman and telling him that only Roman Catholics were allowed to work there. Failing to take the hint, Anderson kept diligently at his work. One of the other laborers decided to address the issue more directly and cautioned that Anderson had better "work easier," that is, "should work slower, like the rest, and not load his cart so

---

took over the defense of the Irishmen. Not only did he get them an acquittal, but, a few months later, four of the Orangemen were tried and convicted. Emmet joined the prosecution in the latter case. The second trial was the court case reported in Wheeler, *Trial of John Moore,* and in An Unbiased Irishman, *Orangeism Exposed.* See also Emmet, *Incidents of My Life,* 257; Emmet, *Memoir,* I, 464–465.

37. *Statesman,* Apr. 4, 1825; *Gazette,* Mar. 29, Apr. 1, 1825.

38. *American,* May 4, 16, 1825.

fast," for there had been talk that otherwise "it would be the worse" for him. Anderson ignored the advice and paid the penalty. The Irish cartmen assaulted him and drove him off the job.[39]

Irish cartmen did not always have to rely on such tactics of intimidation, because they did not remain entirely out of the political system. One way New York politicians solidified electoral support from the Irish was by granting them licenses as cartmen. Through this type of assistance and through other effective organizational techniques, early in the nineteenth century the Irish became a part of the city's Democratic political machine. But the integration of this alien group into the mainstream of politics was not smooth, and the same type of group violence evident in 1799, 1806, and the 1820s appears in the Irish involvement in politics. The Irish defended their church, their neighborhood, their jobs; so, too, they defended their political party.

The Irish and the Democratic Party

By the 1820s and 1830s the Sixth Ward was an Irish bastion and intimately connected to the Democratic party, which allied itself to the immigrant group. Any attempt at changing the Democratic orientation of the Sixth Ward challenged the Irish in the neighborhood. In an effort to sweep the city in the April 1834 election, the Whigs stationed some of their supporters at the Sixth Ward poll. They offered bribes, and when that means was not sufficient, they traded insults. On April 8 Whigs and Democrats exchanged harsh words as they debated a "scurrilous article" in the Whig news organ, the *Courier and Enquirer*. The Democrats claimed that Whigs were there to intimidate and "overawe the laboring classes of the community." They further held that the Whigs had intended "to plant a guard at the polls to spy into the ballots of men dependent on the merchants for their bread." The Whigs asserted that they were only there to organize their supporters: "We should get along well enough if it was not for the Irish." Words led to blows, and the Irish Democrats drove the Whigs out of the Sixth Ward.[40]

Such confrontations, while not welcome, were not unusual during

39. *People* v. *John O'Neil et al.*, Apr. 7, 1826, NYCGS.
40. *Evening Post*, Apr. 9, 11, 1834; "Philip Hone Diary," VIII, Apr. 8, 9, 1834, microfilm, NYHS; *Courier and Enquirer*, Apr. 9, 1834; *Commercial Advertiser*, Apr. 9, 1834.

heated political contests. But the rioting did not stop there. The next day Whigs again crossed over into the Sixth Ward. This time, however, it was with a political procession centered on a mock ship, the *Constitution,* and escorted by hundreds of partisans. A battle quickly erupted between the Whigs and the Irish Democrats. The mayor and the watch, however, restored order and arrested about thirty rioters. Although no further violence occurred that day, the situation remained tense. At a meeting that evening hundreds of Whigs volunteered to aid the mayor in his peacekeeping efforts. But the mayor had not solicited this action and was not overly excited about such a self-appointed partisan posse.[41] The third day brought even more violence.

Again the Whigs paraded through the city with their mock ship, passing through the Sixth Ward along Duane Street to Broadway and the Masonic Hall. There the procession halted. Both Whigs and Democrats crowded the street. A few men began a scuffle, and an Irishman ran back up Duane Street into the Sixth Ward to get reinforcements. Soon hundreds of Irishmen charged down Duane Street armed with clubs and brickbats. Scores of men on both sides clashed amid the tumult. Whigs poured out of the Masonic Hall; a few shots rang out. The mayor ordered the men of the watch to the scene, but they, too, were attacked. A rioter struck the mayor, and several watchmen were severely wounded. The Whigs decided that they needed more weapons, and a large group broke into a nearby arsenal. More people, including Democrats, arrived outside the arsenal, but, fortunately, the mayor persuaded the Whigs to return the weapons. With a bloodbath averted, the rioting soon died down. By the evening, there were only a few instances of disorder.[42]

Although only one person, a watchman, died in the riots, dozens suf-

41. *Evening Post,* Apr. 10, 11, 1834; *Courier and Enquirer,* Apr. 10, 1834; *Commercial Advertiser,* Apr. 11, 1834; "Hone Diary," VIII, Apr. 9, 1834. In NYCGS, box CC-6: *People* v. *John Sheahan et al.,* May 7, 1834; *People* v. *Patrick Burke et al.,* May 17, 1834; *People* v. *Michael McMahon,* May 17, 1834. In NYCSCPCC, box 7446 (1833–1834): *Oliver Kilburn* v. *Thomas Gore et al.,* Apr. 19, 1834; *John Smith* v. *Michael Hunter et al.,* Apr. 9, 1834.

42. *Evening Post,* Apr. 11, 12, 16, 19, 1834; *Courier and Enquirer,* Apr. 12, 1834; *Commercial Advertiser,* Apr. 11, 17, 28, May 1, 1834; "Hone Diary," VIII, Apr. 10, 1834. In NYCGS, box CC-5: *People* v. *John Waters,* May 16, 1834; *People* v. *Patrick McLaughlin et al.,* May 16, 1834; *People* v. *Francis McGowan,* May 17, 1834. In NYCSCPCC, box 7446 (1833–1834): *William Collins* v. *James Narre,* Apr. 10, 1834; *Simon P. Smith* v. *John Smith,* Apr. 10, 1834; *People* v. *George D. Strong,* Apr. 1834.

PLATE 9. Seventh Ward Promenades.
"Not very like a whale but very like a fish," lithograph. Courtesy of the New-York
Historical Society.
New York politics of the 1830s are caricatured in the rabble on right supporting
Lawrence and the assembly on left supporting Verplanck.

fered injury. The extent and violence of the disturbance went well beyond any riot of the eighteenth century and far exceeded any previous political tumult in New York. Even more ominous was the Whig mob poised at the gate of the arsenal ready to spill the blood of Democratic Irishmen.

The city election of April 1834 demonstrated the dangers of a divided society's seeking redress in the streets. Political disturbances were certainly not new: a mob hustled an election official in 1816; there were frequent irregularities at the polls during the 1810s and 1820s; partisans occasionally turned to blows to settle political debate; and not a few voters found their tickets challenged and themselves "knocked down and dragged out."[43] But never before had an election pushed the city so near the brink. Never before had there been such anarchy. Political passions ran high in

43. *People* v. *Jasper Blair et al., New York City-Hall Recorder,* I (1816), 97–98; *National Advocate,* May 1, 1816; *Evening Post,* Apr. 26, 1817; *Columbian,* Apr. 25, 26, 28–30, May 1, 6, 7, 1817; *National Advocate,* Apr. 30, May 1, 1817; William Graham to William P. Van Ness, Apr. 28, 1817, Van Ness MSS, NYPL; *Statesman,* Nov. 5, 1828; *Evening Post,* Nov. 8, 1832. In NYCSCPCC, box 7445 (1832–1833): *People* v. *Michael McDermott et al.,* Nov. 8, 1832; *John E. Walker* v.

the 1830s, as Jackson men squared off against the new Whig political party. But partisan fervor cannot explain the vehemence of the animosities exposed in the three days of election rioting in 1834. Using the language developed in the 1790s to condemn mobs, one newspaper referred to the disturbance as the "SIXTH WARD–REIGN OF TERROR" in which "the *Whigs* have been assailed, trampled upon, and beaten to the earth by the TORIES and HESSIAN mercenaries" who were driven by "a blood thirsty spirit which could have disgraced Paris in its most revolutionary days."[44] The language, however, did not expose the core of the problem in April 1834 and in the other Irish and American or Hispanic and American confrontations—ethnic animosity and a community divided against itself.

The increased violence accompanying these divisions affected the composition of the mob. In almost all of these ethnic disturbances, the rioters, unlike those of the eighteenth century, tended to come exclusively from the bottom of society. The Saint Patrick's Day rowdies of 1802, the Highbinders, the Augustus Street rioters, and the anti-Hispanic mobs as well as those involved in the conflicts of the 1820s all came from the lower classes: laborers, grocers, a few tradesmen among the Irish; journeymen, apprentices, and laborers among their opponents. The April 1834 election riot, however, was different, since, as in the other political disturbances, there were also some individuals from higher in society. Alderman George D. Strong was indicted for leading the Irish, and Philip Hone in his diary blamed the whole tumult on several Jacksonian politicians: Abraham Le Foy, D. Rhinelander, and Preserved Fish as well as Strong. The Democratic newspapers claimed that the downtown merchants along Pearl Street gave their clerks time off during the election to intimidate the Irish; and the Whig mob at the arsenal, according to its keeper, included several prominent citizens. But the men who were most violent in the riots, attacking the watch and the mayor as well as their political opponents, were

---

Wm. Harrington et al., Nov. 9, 1832; *E. Wm. Brown v. Wm. Harrington,* Nov. 9, 1832; *John Cox v. Wm. Harrington,* Nov. 10, 1832; *Abraham Florentine et al. v. Daniel Gilmartin et al.,* Apr. 10, 1833. "Hone Diary," VIII, Nov. 1, 1833; *Evening Post,* Feb. 8, 10, 1834; *Courier and Enquirer,* Feb. 8, 10, 1834; Paul O. Weinbaum, *Mobs and Demagogues: The New York Response to Collective Violence in the Early Nineteenth Century* (Ann Arbor, Mich., 1979), 12, 43–44.
44. *Courier and Enquirer,* Apr. 9, 1834.

most likely from the bottom of society. Examination of all of the ethnic riots from 1799 to 1834 suggests that as the violence intensified between new immigrant groups and native-born Americans, fewer members of the middle and upper levels of society were active in the mob. The April 1834 disturbances stand out as an exception to this trend largely because of the political nature of the riots. The main issue, however, remained ethnicity and the place of the Irish within New York society.

The Irish viewed themselves as a community within the larger New York community, with interests and values that were often set apart from the mainstream of American society. The Irish were more than willing to resort to violence in defense of their ethos, from the beating of the overly industrious non-Irish cartman to the murderous attack on the watchman invading an Irish neighborhood in the Augustus Street riot of 1806. The city authorities rejected the Irish appeal to force and never condoned any of the Irish riots. In fact, the violence of those riots further convinced the magistrates that every mob was to be condemned. In the first decade of the nineteenth century, the effort to stop Paddy processions led inexorably to the banning of all effigy processions, and the ferocity of the Augustus Street riot showed how terrifying unrestrained tumult could be. The repeated outbreaks of Irish rioting during the 1820s and 1830s only confirmed the magistrates in their opposition to all disorder.

SIX

Racial Rioting

The fury of demons seems to have entered the breasts of our misguided populace. Like those ferocious animals which, having once tasted blood, are seized with an insatiable thirst for gore, they have an appetite awakened for outrage, which nothing but the most extensive and indiscriminate destruction seems capable of appeasing. The cabin of the poor Negro, and the temples dedicated to the living God, are alike the objects of their blind fury. The rights of private and public property, the obligations of law, the authority of its ministers, and even the power of the military, are all equally spurned by these audacious sons of riot and disorder. What will be the next mark of their licentious wrath it is impossible to conjecture.

New-York Evening Post, 1834

A few months after the election riots of April 1834, another wave of rioting swept the city, as whites expressed their intense hatred of blacks in an attack on their persons, their homes, and their institutions. To understand this racism and the violence it fostered, it is necessary to go beyond white perceptions of blacks and examine how and why blacks came to identify themselves as a conscious group. More than race separated white from black. In the years following the Revolutionary war, as more slaves gained their freedom, the city's blacks created a distinct subculture, molded around separate black institutions and a common group identity.

A black subculture existed in embryo during the colonial period. The ritual role reversal of Pinkster Day was one expression of this subculture. Moments of black assertiveness, like the slave conspiracies of 1712 and 1741, were another. And the organization of black thieves into a criminal gang known as the Geneva Club, terrorizing the waterfront at mid-century, was yet another. Slaves were an important component of New York's labor force throughout the eighteenth century, constituting as much as one-sixth of the city's population. Employed in a variety of occupations, from house servants to skilled craftsmen, blacks lived scattered among the white population. Although the possibilities for companionship may have been greater in the urban environment than in the countryside, this residence pattern tended to limit expressions of a distinct Afro-American culture. A harsh slave code, enforced more rigorously after 1741, also had the same tendency. Not until the Revolutionary war brought new opportunities for freedom did blacks act to define their own culture and community more openly.[1]

The New York black subcommunity matured in the years after the Revolutionary war. By the end of that conflict both sides offered manumission to black slaves willing to fight for them. More important, the rhetoric about liberty was contagious, and many men, particularly in the North,

---

1. Joel Tyler Headley, *The Great Riots of New York, 1712–1873* . . . (Indianapolis, Ind., 1970 [orig. publ. New York, 1873]), 24–25; Daniel Horsemanden, *The New York Conspiracy,* ed. Thomas J. Davis (Boston, 1971 [orig. publ. New York, 1744]); Edgar J. McManus, *A History of Negro Slavery in New York* (Syracuse, N.Y., 1966), 105–106, 134; Gary B. Nash, "Forging Freedom: The Emancipation Experience of Northern Seaport Cities, 1775–1820," in Ira Berlin and Ronald Hoffman, eds., *Slavery and Freedom in the Age of the American Revolution* (Charlottesville, Va., 1983), 21–22; Alice Morse Earle, *Colonial Days in Old New York,* 2d ed. (Port Washington, N.Y., 1965), 195–201.

talked openly in the 1780s and 1790s of freeing black slaves. In 1785, Revolutionary leaders like John Jay and Alexander Hamilton formed the New York Manumission Society to push for abolition. Although the opponents of slavery did not get the state legislature to pass a gradual emancipation law until 1799, New York's free black population began to expand as some whites manumitted their slaves and as freed blacks from the countryside gravitated to the relatively open social and economic environment of the city. In the years after 1800, the state legislature passed other laws protecting the remaining slaves and extending certain rights to them and finally, in 1817, enacted a full emancipation law, granting freedom by July 4, 1827.

These developments were the genesis of the most important black community in America. But they also put the city's blacks in an odd situation. Black identity was strengthened by an increasing percentage of freemen and by a gain in their total number. In 1790 three-quarters (72.6 percent) of New York's blacks were slaves. By 1810 that proportion dwindled to less than one-fifth (17.2 percent).[2] But, simultaneously, the overall proportion of blacks in the city dropped. In 1800, more than 6,000 blacks made up 10.5 percent of New Yorkers; in 1820, the 10,886 blacks were only 8.8 percent; and by 1840, the 16,358 blacks constituted a mere 5.2 percent of the total population.[3] Despite the gains in absolute numbers, the black community found itself on the defensive.

Although surrounded by a growing population of whites, blacks continued to take the antislavery movement seriously. At times, they even exhibited an assertiveness that frightened and disturbed whites. For example, on at least four occasions before 1834, New York blacks, taking to heart the new antislavery doctrine, rioted against attempts to challenge the freedom of ex-slaves. These incidents are important for three reasons.

2. McManus, *Negro Slavery in New York,* 154–173; Leo H. Hirsch, Jr., "The Negro and New York, 1783 to 1865," *Journal of Negro History,* XVI (1931), 382–473. For the impact of the American Revolution on black Americans, see Ira Berlin, "The Revolution in Black Life," in Alfred F. Young, ed., *The American Revolution: Explorations in the History of American Radicalism* (DeKalb, Ill., 1976), 349–382; and the essays in Berlin and Hoffman, eds., *Slavery and Freedom.* For a general discussion of the impact of social change on slavery, see Ira Berlin, "Time, Space, and the Evolution of Afro-American Society on British Mainland North America," *American Historical Review,* LXXXV (1980), 44–78.

3. See table in Hirsch, "Negro and New York," *Jour. Negro Hist.,* XVI (1931), 415.

First, they helped to define the emerging black subcommunity. Second, they antagonized lower-class whites. Finally, in the minds of the city's leadership, they contributed to the image of a disordered and violent world.

Riots by Blacks, 1801–1832

The first of the black antislavery riots occurred in 1801, a time when the revolution of blacks in the French colony of Saint Domingue came to a climax. The success of Toussaint L'Ouverture's rebellion, marked by his unification of the island of Hispaniola in 1801, helped to shape New York City's black community in the early Republic. News of the racial warfare filtered into New York City from several sources: newspaper reports, however biased, failed to hide the triumph of West Indian blacks; the many black seamen who had traveled to the region brought back firsthand accounts; and, most important, émigrés from the West Indies, both white and black, arrived in the city with all kinds of stories. Indeed, many black émigrés felt a sense of pride in the overthrow of the white man's regime.[4]

Against this distant background of racial warfare in Saint Domingue, 250 blacks rioted on August 10, 1801, to liberate the slaves of Madame Jeanne Mathusine Droibillan Volunbrun. An émigré from the West Indies, Madame Volunbrun possessed an estate of little more than the twenty slaves she had brought with her some five years earlier. The status of those slaves, however, remained ambiguous in the opening years of the nineteenth century. Not only were their offspring guaranteed liberty at some future date by the gradual emancipation law of 1799, but the Manumission Society argued that, since émigrés like Volunbrun left the West Indies after 1794, when the French Revolutionary Convention outlawed slavery in all the French colonies, their slaves were legally free.[5]

Confronted by the prospect of total ruin, Madame Volunbrun decided,

4. Roi Ottley and William J. Weatherby, eds., *The Negro in New York: An Informal Social History* (New York, 1967), 47–53; Frances Sergeant Childs, *French Refugee Life in the United States, 1790–1800: An American Chapter of the French Revolution* (Baltimore, 1940), 56–57.

5. *Gazette*, Aug. 4, 6, 24, 28, 29, Sept. 1, 2, 4, 5, 8, 13, 1801; Minutes of Aug. 28, 1801, "Records of the New York City Manumission Society," microfilm, NYHS. For a discussion of the French emancipation, see David Brion Davis, *The Problem of Slavery in the Age of Revolution, 1770–1823* (Ithaca, N.Y., 1975), 137–148.

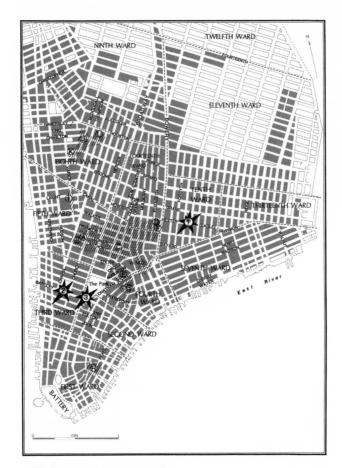

1. Eagle Street riot, Aug. 10, 1801
2. Barclay Street riot, June 19, 1819
3. City Hall. Rioting, Sept. 19, 1826; Nov. 10, 1832

A. African Methodist Episcopal Zion Church   I. Rev. Samuel H. Cox's church
B. Abyssinian Baptist Church   J. Rev. Samuel H. Cox's house
C. Saint Philip's African Episcopal Church   K. Rev. Henry G. Ludlow's church
D. African Ebenezer Church   L. Rev. Henry G. Ludlow's house
E. Chatham Street Chapel
F. Bowery Theater   - - - - Ward Boundary
G. Lewis Tappan's house
H. Tappan's store   ▨ Racial Rioting, July 7–11, 1834

MAP 5. Racial Rioting, 1801–1834.
After James Hardie, The Description of the City of New York . . .
(New York, 1827)

in violation of state law, to send her slaves to Norfolk, Virginia. She claimed that she never planned to sell her slaves and that she intended to join them there and live off their earnings as she had done in New York. Neither the Manumission Society nor the city's blacks believed her. The Manumission Society began legal maneuvers to stop Volunbrun from shipping her slaves out of state. Some of the city's blacks, eager to demonstrate their own commitment to freedom and their sense of solidarity with enslaved members of their race, decided upon more immediate action.[6]

About ten o'clock in the morning of August 10, approximately twenty "French Negroes," with names like "Marcelle Sam," "Isaac Pierre," and "Ceneall," "collected in a body armed with clubs" near Volunbrun's home and threatened "to burn the house, murder all the white people in it and take away a number of black slaves." They remained there all that day, and at night hundreds of others, who appeared "ready to commit the worst of crimes," joined them. A neighbor, John Marie Garvaize, ran for help and returned just in time with fifty watchmen. As the blacks closed in on the house, they managed to destroy only a little of Volunbrun's property before the watch interceded. The blacks resisted the watch, and a furious fight ensued. Many of the rioters escaped during the battle, but officials arrested twenty-three blacks, who were then tried, convicted of riot, and sentenced to sixty days in jail.[7]

Whites, even those in the Manumission Society, were distressed by this riot. The Manumission Society continued efforts on the legal front and gained a temporary release of Volunbrun's slaves. But the society denounced the riot, and one member confessed that, although he believed that all men, black or white, had to be protected by the law, he feared the release of slaves would contribute to the city's disorder.[8] Perhaps for this reason the Manumission Society dropped the case, and Volunbrun once again took custody of her slaves. For its part, the city government vigorously pursued prosecution of the arrested rioters. If the law protected blacks, it also punished them. Whatever the justice of their cause, the twenty-three arrested rioters received unusually harsh penalties for par-

6. *Gazette,* Aug. 24, 28, 29, Sept. 1, 2, 4, 5, 1801.

7. *People* v. *Marcelle Sam et al.,* Oct. 9, 1801, NYCGS; *Gazette,* Aug. 24, Oct. 15, 1801; *American Citizen,* Oct. 15, 1801.

8. *Gazette,* Aug. 24, 28, Oct. 8, Dec. 22, 1801, Jan. 18, Mar. 8, May 17, 1802; Minutes of Aug. 28, Oct. 8, Dec. 8, 1801, "Records of the New York City Manumission Society."

PLATE 10. City Hall from North Side.
Watercolor by Arthur J. Stansbury, circa 1825. Courtesy of the Museum of the City of New York.

ticipating in the riot. Most rioters before 1810 were either acquitted or given light fines. Few had to serve as long as two months in prison.[9]

New York blacks again revealed their community in action by rioting in 1819, 1826, and 1832 to prevent the reenslavement of a few of the runaways living in the city. New York in the early nineteenth century became a dangerous place for blacks, as gangs of men, called "blackbirders," earned their living recapturing supposedly escaped slaves. The city proved to be a magnet for runaway slaves, providing a place where they could meld into the anonymity of the urban scene.[10] Thomas Hartlett, for instance, came to New York after escaping from his master in upstate Montgomery County. But in June 1819 slave catcher John Hall recognized Hartlett and seized him. When Hall, accompanied by a city marshal, attempted to take his captive to a Hudson River dock and an awaiting steamboat, he ran into a group of about forty blacks on Barclay Street, near where

9. *People* v. *Marcelle Sam et al.,* Oct. 9, 1801, NYCGS; *Gazette,* Oct. 15, 1801; *American Citizen,* Oct. 15, 1801.
10. Ottley and Weatherby, eds., *Negro in New York,* 80; McManus, *Negro Slavery in New York,* 176.

many blacks lived. When the trio attempted to retreat to City Hall, the crowd tried to rescue the runaway. They did not succeed, and, after a brief scuffle, the marshal and the slave catcher reached the safety of the City Hall, where they deposited their captive and one arrested rioter.[11]

The riots in 1826 and 1832 were larger than the Barclay Street disturbance and involved more of the black community. As a result, they were more frightening to New York City whites. Black passions, too, were more intense because in these cases the captured blacks were to be returned to Virginia and perpetual slavery. We also have more evidence on the connection between the runaways and the New York black community for the later cases. In 1826 the slave catchers wanted to return an entire family to slavery; in 1832, the New York wife of one of the escaped slaves led the black mob protesting the return of the runaways. In both events, City Hall Park overflowed with blacks distraught at the wresting of runaways from their community and their return to the detested slavery of the South.

The 1826 disturbance was the more serious of the two. While a New York court heard a runaway case in City Hall, a large concourse of blacks waited anxiously outside for the result. Fearing that the blacks might become unruly, the mayor ordered the constables to disperse the crowd at about one o'clock. The police officers managed this maneuver with some difficulty, but by four o'clock the blacks had regathered in added numbers. The crowd was restless. One woman swaggered "about the park with a stick in her hands crying out where are the Virginians." A short time later, after winning his court case, the slavecatcher and some of his witnesses left the City Hall. The assembled blacks bombarded them with bricks, sticks, and stones. The police attempted to intercede.[12]

This riot was a passionate affair, revealing the extent of antislavery feeling among New York City blacks as well as their willingness to challenge the authorities. These blacks were prepared to meet force with force. One black member of the crowd hurled a brick that hit one officer in the face, breaking "the bridge of his nose, and disfigur[ing] him in a frightful man-

11. *People* v. *John Dyos,* July 16, 1819, NYCGS.

12. Discussion of 1826 disturbance based on *People* v. *Wm. Sockum,* Oct. 9, 1826, NYCGS; *Zebulen Harmon* v. *Martha Collins,* Sept. 19, 1826, box 7439 (1826–1827), NYCSCPCC; *American,* Sept. 20, 1826; *Gazette,* Sept. 20, 22, Oct. 17, 1826; *Evening Post,* Sept. 16, 17, 20, 21, 1826; *Statesman,* Sept. 22, 1826; Minutes of Sept. 18, 1826, "Records of the New York City Manumission Society."

PLATE 11. Broadway and City Hall in New York.
Watercolor by Baron Axel Klinckowstrom, 1819. Courtesy of the Museum of the City of New York.

ner." The constables and the watch arrested several of the more active rioters, including one man with a knife, and restored order in the park. But the disturbance continued elsewhere. In nearby Ann Street a mob of blacks chased a white man, shouting "kill him, kill him." The police also had to stop an attack on the slavecatcher's house.

New York's magistrates took the disturbance seriously; the court meted out some of the most severe sentences for rioting in the early nineteenth century. One man was sentenced to prison for nine months, two others were sentenced for one year, and a third (supposedly the ringleader) received three years' hard labor. Even taking into account increased penalties for rioting in the 1820s and 1830s, these black rioters were treated harshly. These punishments were intended as examples to other rioters and the black community in general.

Although less violent, the 1832 riot was similar to the 1826 riot. Two blacks were seized as runaways on November 10. The day their case was to be heard, so many blacks gathered outside City Hall that officials decided to postpone the examination until the next day. Again "blacks of all ages and both sexes" filled the park, awaiting the results of the hearing. Around eleven o'clock in the morning the court delayed its decision further, this time on a legal technicality. As officials brought the two black prisoners from City Hall to be returned to the jail, the crowd attempted to rescue them. Constables Boudinot and Davis were struck and pushed aside; but aided by several other officers who rushed to their assistance, they repulsed their assailants and arrested four of the rioters.[13]

This riot did not contain the prolonged violence of the 1826 disturbance, and the court even dropped the case against the rioters before it came to trial.[14] Yet the overall pattern remains the same. Blacks united to prevent the enforced bondage of members of their own community. However, as far as New York whites were concerned, the resulting disturbances were not to be tolerated. As one antislavery newspaper declared after the September 1826 riot, "These violent interferences with the course of the law (for the proceedings in question were strictly legal) should not be permitted, though it is not surprising that considerable feeling should be excited by an occurance of this kind."[15] The riots against the return of runaway slaves stand as a testament to the emergent sense of community shared by blacks—a sense of community that contrasted and conflicted with white society and the ideal of order and propriety espoused by the self-proclaimed leaders of New York's larger community.

Riots against Black Institutions

Less violent developments also helped to shape the black community after the Revolutionary war. The riots in defense of runaways or to prevent the exportation of slaves stand out as the exception. Although these incidents were important because of the negative image they cast and because of the race solidarity they expressed, such disturbances were not everyday occurrences. Much more significant for the city's black community was the creation of distinct black institutions. Institutions that were a source of pride for blacks were the focal point for attacks by racist whites.

Perhaps the most significant of all these institutions were the new African churches. In the 1790s, as one religious group after another attempted to confine the black members of its congregation to "Negro

13. *Tobias Boudinot v. William Turpin et al.,* Nov. 15, 1832, box 7445 (1832–1833), NYCSCPCC; *Evening Post,* Nov. 14, 1832; Minutes of Nov. 13, 1832, "Records of the New York City Manumission Society."

14. *Tobias Boudinot v. William Turpin et al.,* Nov. 15, 1832, box 7445 (1832–1833), NYCSCPCC.

15. *Statesman,* Sept. 27, 1826.

pews," some blacks objected. Tobacconist Peter Williams, onetime sexton of the John Street Methodist Church, joined with other black Methodists in 1796 to establish a separate church. They erected a building on the corner of Church and Leonard streets and drew up a charter as the African Methodist Episcopal Zion Church in 1801. Blacks in other religious denominations soon followed suit, founding the Abyssinian Baptist Church on Anthony Street in 1808, the Saint Philip's African Episcopal Church in 1818, and the Negro Presbyterian Church in 1821. These churches fostered a sense of community among blacks, helped to establish a black leadership, cared for the poor, and created a forum for the antislavery struggle.[16] No wonder, then, that mobs in July 1834 attacked black churches.

Harassment of African churches, however, began long before the 1834 riots. As early as 1807 the trustees of the African Methodist Church complained to the Common Council that disorderly boys disturbed their services, and they requested that a watchman be posted to protect them. City authorities complied with the request, but it made little difference. A year later the trustees sent another memorial to the council, "complaining of riots before their place of worship" and asserting that the watch failed to protect them. Two years later city officials were still discussing the possibility of building a watchbox at the church. The problem persisted, and crowds of whites continued to disrupt the services of black churches.[17]

Of course, African churches were not the only religious assemblies disturbed by mobs. But the disruption of black religious services had racial undertones, best demonstrated by the plight of Jacob Sands in a disturbance at the African Ebenezer Church in 1829. Two sailors from a crowd of whites outside the church entered the building during services and went among the congregation "making a great noise, cursing and using indecent and profane language." Enraged by this behavior, Jacob Sands, a member of the congregation, attempted to get some of those outside "away from the church in a peaceful manner." He ran into real trouble. Sands must have pushed or touched a white man in the crowd. In retaliation one of the rioters hit Sands with a stick. George Bontacue, who lived next door to the church, joined in the assault. He beat Sands, damned him, and asked "what right he had to put his hands on a white man." Apparently the court thought that Sands had no right, because it acquitted Bontacue

16. Ottley and Weatherby, eds., *Negro in New York,* 53–60; Hirsch, "Negro and New York," *Jour. Negro Hist.,* XVI (1931), 441.

17. *MCC,* IV, 389, 407, V, 272, 278, VI, 446.

TABLE 3
Rioters Harassing Black Churches, 1808–1830

Name	Occupation	Date	Other
Duncan McDonald	watchman	1808	
Burr Berrian	—	1819	
Peter Crawback	—[a]	1819	young man
Dunham Jones	—	1827	young man
Timothy Duffy	—	1829	boy
Michael Sweeny	cartman[b]	1829	
George Bontacue	—	1829	
Alexander Rennie	weaver	1830	immigrant

Note: Excludes rioters disturbing black churches on New Year's Eve 1828.

[a]Peter Crawback listed in David Longworth, *The American Almanack, New-York Register, and City Directory* in 1819 as a butcher, living at 174 Bowery. But court deposition indicates that the Peter Crawback arrested here was young and that his father interceded in his behalf to obtain a more lenient hearing at court. In all likelihood the Peter Crawford listed in the directory is the rioter's father.

[b]Based on description of Sweeny in the court records as having a cart ring in his hand.
Sources: *MCC;* NYCSCPCC; city directories.

of a charge of assault and battery.[18] In short, when a riotous crowd stood outside a black church or even violated its inner sanctum, blacks could do little to protect themselves other than appeal to unsympathetic magistrates.

Why did crowds single out black churches? It was almost as if whites understood the strength and solace blacks received from their participation in their own religious exercises. More than that, it was as if whites feared the sense of moral equality, even superiority, enjoyed by blacks through regular religious worship.[19] Southerners certainly were aware of the implied challenge to white supremacy in a slave religion controlled by the blacks themselves and therefore strove to supply black congregations with white preachers.[20] Northern mobs may have acted from a similar impulse.

Only a handful of these rioters can be identified, but their socioeconomic

18. *People* v. *George Bontacue,* Oct. 13, 1829, NYCGS.

19. Ottley and Weatherby, eds., *Negro in New York,* 56; Nash, "Forging Freedom," in Berlin and Hoffman, eds., *Slavery and Freedom,* 43–48.

20. See Eugene D. Genovese, *Roll, Jordan, Roll: The World the Slaves Made* (New York, 1972), 159–284.

status reinforces the idea that resentment of the achievements of black religion lay behind their actions. Almost all of the identified rioters were young, and several appear to have been immigrants (see table 3). Alexander Rennie, a weaver arrested for breaking in the door at the African Methodist Union Church in October 1830, was born in Scotland and had lived in the United States for three years. Despite having a trade, he was still a transient. Rennie arrived in New York, from New Hartford, only the week before his arrest.[21] Timothy Duffy, described as a boy in a court deposition, and Michael Sweeny, probably a cartman, were taken into custody at a disturbance at the African Church on Sixth Avenue in 1829.[22] Although there is no absolute confirmation of their nationality, their names strongly suggest an Irish heritage. Along with the few other identified rioters at black churches, none of these men had much property. Thus, the young, poor rioter who disturbed an African church might have been jealous of the modest property and social standing of some of the black congregation while also envying the sense of identity the black community attained through religious services.

In the late eighteenth and early nineteenth centuries blacks created other institutions that, like their churches, helped to define the boundaries of their subcommunity. Several blacks organized the New York African Society for Mutual Relief in 1808 to take care of the widows and orphans of its members. By 1820 the association had purchased a lot and erected a building to hold its meetings. The First African Free School was established even earlier, in 1786. A new, larger building was erected in 1814 that could hold two hundred students. A second school opened in 1820 on Mulberry Street. The first black newspaper, *Freedom's Journal,* began publishing in 1827, and throughout most of the 1820s there was a black theater, called the African Grove, near Bleecker and Mercer streets.[23]

Some of these institutions escaped harassment by mobs. Others did not. During the 1820s the black theater attracted attention from rowdies bent on creating a disturbance. In August 1822, for example, "a gang of fifteen or twenty ruffians" bought tickets at the "African Theater" and attempted to "break it up root and branch" by dismantling the lighting, breaking the benches, tearing the curtains, destroying the scenery, stripping the actors

21. *African Methodist Union Church* v. *Alexander Rennie,* Oct. 18, 1830, box 7442 (1830), NYCSCPCC.

22. *People* v. *Timothy Duffy et al.,* July 14, 1829, NYCGS.

23. Ottley and Weatherby, eds., *Negro in New York,* 60–73, 89; Hirsch, "Negro and New York," *Jour. Negro Hist.,* XVI (1931), 466.

TABLE 4

Rioters Arrested at the African Grove, August 10, 1822

Name	Occupation	Address
James Bellomont	—	—
James Carnes	equestrian	Broadway off Grand[c]
Peter Hector	black at circus	Broadway[c]
David C. Hick	constable	375 Broome
Christopher Hughs	sailor[a]	317 Water
William Lawson	equestrian	455 Broadway[c]
Charles Lee	gevoman (?)	43 Howard
David B. Mitchel	pilot	42 Frankfort
Robert J. Mitchel	—[b]	Fulton
Alexander Smith	barkeeper	Broadway and Grand[c]

[a]Lived at a boardinghouse along the waterfront, thus probably a sailor.
[b]No occupation, but did own more than $10,000 worth of property on Fulton Street.
[c]Probably the same address.
Sources: NYCSCPCC; NYCSCPC Bonds; Tax Assessment Records; city directories.

and actresses, and beating the proprietor. They did more than two hundred dollars worth of damage.[24] The men who committed these atrocities were an odd assemblage. Almost all of the rioters were white except Peter Hector, who worked at the Broadway Circus. Apparently, the people involved in that other low theater disliked the competition the African Grove presented, for two other rioters were equestrian performers at the circus, and a third was a barkeep living at the same address as the horseback riders (see table 4). The participation of some of the other rioters, however, is harder to explain. The two seamen might just have been out for a good time, but the mob also included a constable, who was supposed to keep order, and an affluent property holder. Presumably, racism knew no class lines. Mobs continued to disrupt performances until city officials closed the African Grove in 1829.[25]

Blacks confronted violent racial hostility every day. In February 1830 the "very respectable instructor" of the African Free School complained

24. *Allen Royce et al. v. Robert Mitchell et al.,* Aug. 11, 1822, box 7437 (1822–1823), NYCSCPCC; *Spectator,* Aug. 20, 1822; George C. D. Odell, *Annals of the New York Stage* (New York, 1927–1928), III, 34–37.
25. Ottley and Weatherby, eds., *Negro in New York,* 72–73.

that butcher boys from the Centre Street Market frequently set their dogs on his students. On one occasion they had the dogs attack the instructor's son. Another time they seized a black girl and held her fast until the dogs had almost torn all her clothes off. Even the racist *Commercial Advertiser* saw this as an outrage and suggested that these butcher boys be sent to jail for thirty days.[26] White mobs harassed blacks owning small businesses, like oyster or cook shops, and sometimes assaulted blacks in the street. As in the disruption of religious meetings, there was not much blacks could do to prevent these attacks.[27]

Criminality and Politics among Blacks

Racial hostility was not limited to the lower class. If poorer whites viewed blacks as competition in the labor market and a threat to racial purity, their more affluent counterparts believed that the black community was idle, unruly, and criminal. The combined effect of these attitudes was to push the black community ever further to the periphery of society.

Black actions reinforced these attitudes. Black assertiveness in the marketplace and in the creation of their own institutions antagonized lower-class whites, and black willingness to riot in 1801, 1819, 1826, and 1832 fulfilled the negative expectations of the white elite. Moreover, as an increasing number of blacks found it difficult to find any regular employment, some blacks turned toward criminal activity. The police blotter reveals a disproportionately high percentage of black women arrested for prostitution and of black men and women sentenced to prison as criminals.[28] There is no doubt that blacks were more liable to arrest and conviction than their white criminal counterparts, but some New York blacks were indeed turning to illicit activities to earn a living.

Many other blacks, while not felons, participated in rowdy behavior that disturbed their white neighbors as well as the magistrates' sense of order. For example, in February 1809, watchman John Shepard com-

26. *Commercial Advertiser,* Feb. 27, 1830.

27. For examples of this type of harassment, see *Gazette,* Dec. 10–13, 1811; *Joseph Webb* v. *Thos. Manofield et al.,* July 5, 1813, box 7433 (1811–1814), NYCSCPCC. In NYCGS: *People* v. *John Dickerson et al.,* June 11, 1816; *People* v. *Terrence Cosgrove et al.,* July 15, 1819; *People* v. *William Perrigo et al.,* Mar. 9, 1827.

28. See the arrest records in NYCMMPO, 1799–1830.

plained of a group of blacks who often collected in the Fifth Ward at a house in Barclay Street, called the "tobacco box," and disturbed the peace. Shepard declared "that frequently after they quit their dancing and frolicking they leave the house in gangs and go through the streets and make a noise by their laughing, cussing and swearing." When Shepard and the other watchmen attempted to quiet the blacks, they "blackguard and Damn the watch." On the morning of February 3, 1809, a group of eighteen men and women were arrested for their disorderly behavior, and they were subsequently tried and convicted of riot.[29]

The result was that city magistrates were very biased whenever a black stood before them. Despite their prejudice, the magistrates recognized that racial violence contributed to the growing disorder of the city and therefore had to be controlled. When there were white witnesses to the harassment of blacks, the treatment of the rioters by the courts could be severe. During the Fourth of July celebration in 1819, white rioters attacked the temporary refreshment booths run by black street vendors. Shouting, "Kill the negroe, kill him," Terrence Cosgrove led a mob in beating Luke Peterson, a black. In the face of testimony by white witnesses, Cosgrove and another rioter were convicted and heavily penalized: the court fined Cosgrove twenty dollars and sentenced the other man to six months in prison.[30] When there were only black witnesses, it was much more difficult to get a conviction, even though an act of 1813 explicitly allowed blacks to testify against whites.[31] Still, the police made arrests, and the magistrates initiated prosecutions. Typical was the plight of three blacks attacked in front of the Darby and Jones tavern in February 1827. Although the district attorney drew up an indictment, the court dismissed the case before it ever came to trial. The record does not indicate why the case was dropped, but in all likelihood the reason was that it, like several similar cases, rested solely on the word of black men.[32]

Paradoxically, as the black community assumed a more distinct form, as many blacks achieved freedom, and as some managed to obtain modest property, blacks retained and, in some ways, increased their legal invisi-

---

29. *People* v. *Thomas Sanders et al.,* Feb. 9, 1809, NYCGS.

30. *People* v. *Terrence Cosgrove et al.,* July 15, 1819, box 7435 (1818–1819), NYCSCPCC; New York City Courts, "A General List of All Persons Indicted and Convicted in . . . New York . . . to the Year 1820," 500, microfilm, Historical Documents Collection, Queens College, CUNY.

31. McManus, *Negro Slavery in New York,* 177–178.

32. *James Crawford* v. *Michael O'Brien et al.,* Feb. 11, 1827, NYCGS.

bility. In no area was this development more evident than in politics. A part of this process was the move to disenfranchise blacks in New York. After the Revolution, any black meeting the freehold qualification could vote. Blacks did participate in elections in the 1790s and early 1800s and generally supported Federalist candidates. After all, the founders of the Manumission Society were Federalists, and blacks knew where their true interests lay. The Democratic-Republicans, who dominated the state after 1801, strove therefore to limit black political participation by challenging the qualifications of black voters at the polls. In 1821, when the new state constitution removed the property requirement for whites, the property qualification for blacks was increased.[33]

The presence of immigrant groups, especially the Irish, made the plight of the black community even more difficult. Hostility between the city's Irish and blacks was intense and frequently erupted into violence. The Darby and Jones incident—the defendant was a Michael O'Brien, who signaled the attack on the three blacks by calling "Kelly, Kelly"—was one of many confrontations between the Irish and blacks. Both groups competed for the same less-skilled jobs. One report in the 1790s indicates that blacks were "servants, labourers, sailors, [and] mechanics"; a few were even "small traders" with some property.[34] Although prejudice thereafter increasingly limited job opportunities, some blacks still worked at a variety of trades in 1830, as sailmakers, shoemakers, tin workers, tailors, carpenters, and blacksmiths. By far the vast majority of blacks were forced into more menial occupations as porters, coachmen, cooks, and laborers or were relegated to the worst of the city's jobs, such as cleaning out the necessary tubs, or privies, at night. The Irish guarded their own jobs against intrusions, and in the 1820s one of New York's mayors admitted denying a black man's application to be a cartman for fear of the Irish reaction.[35]

The residential proximity of Irish and blacks also created grounds for conflict. Some of the heaviest concentrations of both groups were in the Sixth Ward. In 1819 blacks constituted more than 12 percent of the population of this district, and aliens (many of whom were undoubtedly Irish) made up almost 25 percent. In no other ward were there so many aliens

33. Dixon Ryan Fox, "The Negro Vote in Old New York," *Political Science Quarterly,* XXXII (1917), 252–275; McManus, *Negro Slavery in New York,* 187.

34. American Convention of Abolition Societies, Reports, *Journal of Negro History,* VI (1921), 318–320.

35. Hirsch, "Negro and New York," *Jour. Negro Hist.,* XVI (1931), 433–436; Ottley and Weatherby, eds., *Negro in New York,* 65.

and blacks living together; in most other wards, blacks were only about 4–8 percent of the population.[36] In the Five Points neighborhood of the Sixth Ward the concentration of blacks and Irish was even greater. Despite the overall dominance of the Irish in the area, all along Anthony, Augustus, Cross, Orange, and Mulberry streets stood clusters of houses jammed full of blacks. Of the 211 people living near the junction of Orange and Frank streets, 161 were black. Along Cross Street between Augustus and Duane streets, the very heart of the Irish Five Points, lived more than 200 blacks, or about one-quarter of the street's population.[37] When the city expanded northwards toward Greenwich Village in the 1820s and the 1830s, both the Irish and blacks flocked to the new area as well.

The political impotency of the blacks and the intimate proximity and mutual hostility of the Irish and blacks were revealed in a disturbance on moving day, May 1, 1816. William Edwards, a black who ran an oyster cellar and owned some property, attempted to evict his tenant Andrew Mickle, an Irish merchant tailor, on the day that leases traditionally expired in the city, the first of May. But because city officials were busy supervising the crowded streets and attending to a local election, Edwards could not call upon the assistance of a marshal. Late in the afternoon, Edwards, with the aid of several blacks, tried to take possession of his property and rent it to Lewis Thiery, a Frenchman. Mickle and his journeyman friends, armed with shillelaghs and an old blunderbuss, stood ready to resist this indignity. Edwards and company broke into the apartment and started throwing the furniture out of the room. A scuffle followed, and Mickle ran for the police. Finding the police occupied, Mickle rallied a crowd of two hundred to three hundred and attacked the blacks and the Frenchman. Mickle shouted "Huzza! now I've the strongest party" as the mob cried, "Kill the Frenchman and negroes." By the time the mayor and police officers arrived, the Mickles were once again installed in their apartment. Despite the legal correctness of Edwards's case, the

36. Second, Fourth–Tenth wards, NYC, 1819 Census Wards, microfilm, Historical Documents Collection, Queens College; and First Ward, NYC, 1819 Census, NYCA.

37. Sixth Ward, NYC, 1819 Census, Historical Documents Collection, Queens College. For general comments on black residential patterns, see Nash, "Forging Freedom," in Berlin and Hoffman, eds., *Slavery and Freedom*, 40–43. For a more detailed discussion of black residence patterns, see Shane White, "'We Dwell in Safety and Pursue Our Honest Callings': The Blacks in New York City, 1783–1810," MS.

mayor ruled, for reasons which may have been connected with the political power of the Irish, that the Mickles had a right to continue their occupancy. The subsequent trial sustained his judgment.[38] It was, after all, very difficult for blacks to obtain justice in the legal system.

The Riot of 1834

The tension between black and white New Yorkers, apparent in the harassment of black institutions before 1834, became glaring in the race riot in July of that year. The disturbances began on July 7 at the Chatham Street Chapel with a brawl between the New York Sacred Music Society and blacks celebrating the anniversary of the New York emancipation law. By an oversight both groups had been scheduled to use the chapel the same night. The following evening another small disturbance occurred when a mob disrupted a meeting of the Moral Lyceum called to discuss abolition. These relatively innocuous and limited actions gave way on July 9 to far more violent rioting. For the next three days thousands of tumultuous New Yorkers focused their rage on a variety of objects: sacking the homes and stores of the rich and abolitionist Tappan brothers, disrupting the Bowery Theater because of the anti-American attitude of the British performer, attacking the homes and churches of ministers who supported abolition, desecrating the black churches in the city, pulling down and destroying the homes and property of blacks, and assaulting and beating blacks. To those in New York who cherished good order, these riots were not only an affront to their sense of propriety but also the sign of a society gone wild. The riots were the work of "demons," bloodthirsty and "ferocious animals" who had an "insatiable thirst for gore."[39]

The rioters in July 1834 were not demons. They were enraged white New Yorkers from the lower and middling classes who detested abolitionists and blacks.[40] Moreover, although the riots began as an attempt to disrupt meetings of blacks and abolitionists, it was racism—the hatred of blacks—that drove New York mobs night after night to attack black people, their institutions, and their supporters. Fears of amalgamation and

38. *People* v. *Andrew Mickle et al., New York City-Hall Recorder,* I (1816), 96–97.

39. *Evening Post,* July 12, 1834.

40. Leonard L. Richards, *"Gentlemen of Property and Standing": Anti-Abolition Mobs in Jacksonian America* (New York, 1970), 150–155.

miscegenation, as some historians have argued, were an important part of this racism. So, too, was the worry about labor competition from recently freed slaves.[41] Overshadowing and subsuming both issues, however, was the concern over the development of a black subcommunity within New York.

Fear of amalgamation, for example, was an important backdrop to the rioting that July, but there was little in the behavior of the rioters explicitly demonstrating this fear. In the months before the rioting two New York City papers, the *Courier and Enquirer* and the *Commercial Advertiser,* took a lead in the antiabolition cause and sounded the tocsin against the antislavery forces, labeled the abolitionists as amalgamationists, and allowed their own imagination to run wild. One report went as far as to declare that the Reverend Samuel H. Cox had characterized Christ as "colored." Concentrating on white concern over racial mixing, these papers capitalized on the slightest whisper that there were cases of miscegenation among the abolitionists. Rumor held that Arthur Tappan divorced his wife to marry a black, that abolitionists asked their daughters to wed blacks, and that abolitionist ministers frequently joined whites and blacks in holy matrimony.[42]

But any evidence for the impact of these slanderous news articles remains inferential. The fear of amalgamation might explain the animosity toward racially mixed abolition meetings because many whites suspected that the social and political interaction of the races would lead to sexual interaction.[43] Similar reasoning may have lain behind the attacks on the homes and churches of leading abolitionists. Reverend Samuel H. Cox and Reverend Henry G. Ludlow as well as the abolitionist merchant Tappan brothers suffered serious property damage.[44] Yet the connection of the mob's behavior to fears of amalgamation is inconclusive.

41. *Ibid.,* 47–81; Linda K. Kerber, "Abolitionists and Amalgamators: The New York City Race Riots of 1834," *New York History,* XLVIII (1967), 28–39; Paul O. Weinbaum, *Mobs and Demagogues: The New York Response to Collective Violence in the Early Nineteenth Century* (Ann Arbor, Mich., 1979), 23–27.

42. Richards, *"Gentlemen of Property and Standing,"* 114–115; Weinbaum, *Mobs and Demagogues,* 23–27, 56, 95.

43. Lewis Tappan, *The Life of Arthur Tappan* (New York, 1870; rpt., New York, 1970), 203–224; *Commercial Advertiser,* July 9, 1834; *Courier and Enquirer,* July 7, 8, 1834.

44. *Evening Post,* July 10–12, 15, 1834; *Commercial Advertiser,* July 10–12, 1834; *Courier and Enquirer,* July 10–12, 15, 1834; Milo Osborne to Mr. Lawrence, n.d., in "Riots, New York City, 1834," Miscellaneous Microfilm, reel 34,

TABLE 5

Rioters in the July 1834 Race Riot

Name	Occupational Status	Address	Other
Theodore S. Baldwin	—	65½ Bowery	young man
Wm. Brookington	hatter	186 Orchard	
James Burrows	—	—	young man
William Campbell	dock laborer	none	
John Cappan	—	430 Greenwich	
Henry Clarrot	shoemaker	57 Chapel	apprentice
Thomas Combs	shoemaker	22 Hammersly	age 27
Alex Crawford	butcher	—	age 19
Timothy Donovan	—	none	
John Edwards	sailor	333 Water	
Adolphus Eliot	—	Elizabeth	young lad
Daniel Fitzgerald	mechanic	29 Mulberry	journeyman
George Galbright	—	22 Grand	
Samuel Goodwin	stevedore	186 Broome	
Stephen Gordon	thief	—	
Peter Guyon	—	157 Madison	
Benjamin Halsey	tavernkeeper	202 Spring	
Daniel Holden	—	37 Christopher	young man
Chs. Holliday	lastmaker	50 Anthony	
Stephen Lane	mason	48 Ridge	age 24
Thomas Lee	seaman	Water and Cherry	
William Lee	—	51 Henry	
Abraham Levy	clerk	Water	age 17
Charles Logan	shoemaker	241 Division	
James McDermot	junk store	40 Elm	
John McGovern	—	90 King	
Horace Macy	blacksmith	Depyster	
Kelly Murdock	laborer	Walnut	
John Nixon	merchant	209 Pearl	
George Parmley	shoemaker	69 Hammersly	
Arthur Pitsworth	—	94 Fulton	
Edward Pitsworth	—	94 Fulton	
Patrick Riley	laborer	59 Orange	single
Andrew Rourk	vagrant	—	

Table 5. *continued*
Rioters in the July 1834 Race Riot

Name	Occupational Status	Address	Other
George Spream	—	Christopher	
Levi Tabor	—	Orchard	age 18
Ezekiel Thatcher	—	319 Hudson	
John Vanderbogart	—	166 Christopher	
Robert D. Walker	—	561 Greenwich	
Cornelius White	—	185 Charlton	
Jacob Young	—	—	age 17

Note: Rioters in this table include only those persons for whom some information is available.
Sources: NYCGS; NYCSCPCC; Tax Assessment Records; city directories; newspapers.

The composition of the mob and some of the riot activity more clearly suggest white apprehension over competition of black labor. Although several rioters were tradesmen, they tended to be journeymen and mechanics sliding down the economic scale or young workers whose hold on an occupation was tenuous. Of the seventy-five arrested men named in the court records and newspapers, the occupations of only twenty-two can be identified. Only eight of these can be found in the directories. The rest were either too young to be heads of households or were poor mechanics, apprentices, and day laborers who would not ordinarily be listed. Typical were the four shoemakers (see table 5). Charles Logan and George Parmley appeared in the directory, but the German apprentice Henry Clarrot and journeyman Thomas Combs did not. All four worked in an occupation that experienced a marked decline in status in the early nineteenth century. Although not directly challenged by black laborers, these men were threatened by unskilled workers. The archetypal unskilled worker, in their eyes, was the black man.[45] In the case of sailors, laborers, and less-

NYHS; Isiah Emory to His Honor the Mayor, July 14, 1834, in "Riots, New York City, 1834"; "Philip Hone Diary," VIII, July 10, 12, 1834, microfilm, NYHS; *A. D. Romaine* v. *Jacob Young et al.,* July 11, 1834, box CC-88 (1834), NYCGS; *William Springer et al.* v. *Wm. Campbell,* July 10, 1834, box CC-30 (1834–1835), NYCGS.

45. For a fuller discussion about the impact of economic change on labor, see chap. 7.

skilled workers, who constituted most of the arrested rioters, the direct threat of blacks was much more real. Moreover, both tradesmen and day laborers lived close to blacks and could well imagine that abolition in the South might swell the ranks of this alien mass in their neighborhoods.[46]

White concern with labor competition became most apparent on the second and third days of disorder. As the rioting reached a fever pitch and thousands of riotous white New Yorkers streamed into the streets, attacks on blacks and their property increased. For example, a mob seized a trunk carried by a black porter working for a steamboat company and thereby denied him his livelihood.[47] No doubt similar motivations lay behind the threats and attacks on the property of more affluent blacks. Isiah Emory, for example, received a threatening note stating that he had better shut his shop or be mobbed. Storekeeper E. Davis feared that two brick houses he owned, 121 Broome and 123 Forsyth Street, were to be attacked. Likewise, on the night of the eleventh, a mob destroyed a barbershop at Bayard and Orange streets owned by a black man.[48]

But the real focus of white rage remained the black subcommunity. Both poor and more affluent blacks suffered depredations from the mob as rioters ransacked many black homes in the Five Points area, especially along Orange and Mulberry streets between Anthony and Walker streets. Apparently whites found it difficult to distinguish black from white homes in this impoverished neighborhood, and the mob had to resort to a special signal. All whites were told to place candles in their windows; any house with unlighted windows was liable to attack.[49] During the 1760s and 1770s, parading the streets with candles was a symbol of support for the resistance movement, borrowed and parodied from royalist celebrations.[50] Candles in the night came to stand as a hallowed symbol of a united community. In July 1834 it was a community violently committed to excluding blacks.

46. For a contrasting interpretation, see Richards, "*Gentlemen of Property and Standing,*" 150–155.

47. *Evening Post,* July 12, 1834.

48. Emory to the Mayor, July 14, 1834, in "Riots, New York City, 1834," Miscellaneous Microfilm, reel 34, NYHS; H. A. Averill to Mayor, July 12, 1834, in "Riots, New York City, 1834"; *Evening Post,* July 12, 1834.

49. *Evening Post,* July 12, 1834; *People* v. *Benjamin C. Halsey et al.,* July 18, 1834, box CC-88 (1834), NYCGS; *People* v. *Edward James et al.,* July 12, 1834, box CC-88 (1834), NYCGS.

50. Peter Shaw, *American Patriots and the Rituals of Revolution* (Cambridge, Mass., 1981), 186.

The attempt to root out blacks as an alien group is evident from the persistent attacks on their community institutions. Black churches and black schools were primary targets. On the night of July 11, rioters demolished Saint Philip's African Episcopal Church in Centre Street, taking the furniture out into the street and burning it. The African schoolhouse, in Orange Street, which was used also as a Methodist meetinghouse, was destroyed totally. The Anthony Street Abyssinian Baptist Church fared better. A mob merely pelted rocks at its windows, leaving them "broken to atoms." By the next day, officials feared that all of the black churches were in jeopardy.[51]

The 1834 riot was strikingly different from its eighteenth-century predecessors. Riots in the previous century tended to be limited. The destruction of property in the eighteenth century ordinarily focused on a specific grievance. In July 1834 the rioters displayed a modicum of discretion in picking and choosing targets which were related to their grievance—hatred of blacks—but the activity was much more indiscriminate and wide-ranging than eighteenth-century mob behavior. The intensity of the attack against the black community revealed not just a willingness to demonstrate discontent with blacks and their abolitionist defenders but also a desire to purge the city of them. The assaults on blacks and the destruction of black institutions both attest to this goal. Thus the violence of the riots fits into the new pattern of nineteenth-century popular disturbances and represents a community divided and warring against itself.

Not only did the action of the rioters take on a new character, more extensive and violent, but the intellectual context of the disturbances—that is, how others in the community perceived the riot—also changed. In the eighteenth century, riots frequently were condoned by the rest of society. By the 1830s, however, the corporate notions of community were outdated, and the mob, as it pushed toward new levels of violence, found itself opposed by much of the rest of the city. Even the so-called demagogue and antiabolitionist editor, James Watson Webb, who had all but openly encouraged mob action against abolitionists, abandoned the mob and declared, "The populace must never be the *executive* power of the country,"

---

51. *Evening Post,* July 12, 1834; *Courier and Enquirer,* July 12, 1834. In "Riots, New York City, 1834," Miscellaneous Microfilm, reel 34, NYHS: Osborne to Lawrence, n.d.; "A Nigh Neighbor" to Cor. Lawrence, July 13, 1834; "List of Contemplated Attacks by Mob," n.d. In NYCGS, box CC-88 (1834): *People v. Jas. D. Allen et al.,* July 12, 1834; *People v. Edward James et al.,* July 12, 1834. "Hone Diary," VIII, microfilm, NYHS.

even if its motives were, as Webb believed in this instance, laudable. Webb asserted that rioting, no matter what its cause, was "destructive of all social order and will if permitted to go unpunished, unsettle everything like Government. Mobs must be suppressed!"[52]

The attitude of city officials was even more severe. Magistrates, dreading the violence of the riot, repeatedly ordered the watch and other police officers to quell the tumult. When it became apparent that the civil authorities were not strong enough to control the mob, the militia was called upon. In the eighteenth century the militia regularly failed to suppress riots, largely because so many militiamen were already in the mob. In 1834 the circumstances were different, and enough New Yorkers opposed the rioting to swell the ranks of the militia. More than one thousand men reported for duty prepared to do battle with the rioters. At one point mobs erected barricades in the street and stood poised to fight it out with the militia. Fortunately, a pitched battle was avoided. Both rioters and magistrates showed some restraint, and order was again restored. But city officials left little doubt of their next course of action. They had been prepared to authorize volleys of gunfire directed at the crowd. Judge Richard Riker later reminded some of the convicted rioters that the militia had been ready to use the live cartridges issued them. Had they done so, Riker asserted, the military would have been completely protected by the law: "If a magistrate, when directing the public force[,] acts to the best of his judgement, he cannot be called to an account for his conduct, nor can the military for acting under his orders."[53]

Exactly how far apart the magistrates and the people in the street had drifted in their willingness to countenance rioting can be seen by some of Riker's other comments on sentencing day. Pointing to the standard eighteenth-century fears of demagoguery, he told the court, "All who reflected on the character of a mob, knew that it was a mere brute force which any bold and bad man might direct as an engine to gratify private revenge, and for the worst purposes." Riker's greatest apprehensions, however, did not lie with the potential demagogue's misleading the mob. Instead, like many in the nineteenth century, Riker feared that no one could control the mob. In this view, mobs were capricious and attacked all sorts of objects. The judge believed that the mob "was devoid of discrimi-

52. *Courier and Enquirer,* July 16, 1834. For a different view of Webb, see Weinbaum, *Mobs and Demagogues,* 25.
53. *Evening Post,* July 23, 1834.

nation and reflection; so that no matter how innocent or excellent a man might be, he is liable to become its victim." Its evils were impossible to describe: "Hurried on by a blind fury, everything became subject to its force, and the rights of property and personal security were lost and swept away, as it were, in an ocean of madness." This sort of mob was intolerable: "No man—no friend of liberty and law, could, under any circumstances, countenance" it. The magistracy had been defied, "private property destroyed, the domestic retreat invaded, and the temples of our religious worship desecrated by an infuriated multitude."

In contrast to the rioters, Riker asserted a conception of society that respected the rights of minorities. The judge saw blacks as separate from the mainstream of the New York community, relegating them to the lowest social level, yet decried the general attack made upon them. "Poor as they were," Riker "thanked God" the city's blacks "were entitled to the protection of the laws."[54] In this view, the purpose of the law, and the task of the magistracy, was not to maintain uniformity, as it had been in the eighteenth century, but to protect individual right amid diversity.

Although many July rioters wanted to expel the blacks and destroy their community, most New Yorkers—magistrates and common men—shared the belief that blacks filled a special niche at the bottom of New York society. This perception reflected a very real development.

The most outstanding feature of racial relations in post-Revolutionary New York was the emergence of a distinct black subcommunity. The feeling of solidarity behind this sense of community is revealed in the few occasions when blacks rose up together to prevent the return of runaways to their owners. Whites viewed these disturbances as more proof of the disorder from this underclass. For blacks, like the "French Negroes" of 1801, the mob on Barclay Street in 1819, and the crowds in City Hall Park in 1826 and 1832, these riots were merely attempts to protect members of their community from a fate perhaps worse than death—reenslavement.

But these violent manifestations of black opposition to slavery were only one means by which the black subcommunity began to define itself. Institutions like the African churches, the African Mutual Relief Society, the African free schools, and the African Grove Theater also fostered a sense of identity among New York's blacks. Although most of these institutions were respectable, they were focal points of racist harassment and thereby

54. *Commercial Advertiser*, July 23, 1834; *Evening Post*, July 23, 1834.

contributed to the image of a disordered society. Both the black opposition to slavery and the African institutions created by the black community came under attack in early July 1834. The vehemence of this riot can be comprehended only in the light of the longer development of the black subcommunity. All of these racial disturbances—both against blacks and by blacks to protect other blacks—indicate clearly the intensifying divisions in society; they contributed to the increasing illegitimacy of the mob in the early nineteenth century.

PART III

Class

SEVEN

Labor Action

Boss nox
   Sir
I tak the chnc to let you no
Either Quit the Business
Oi else pay the price
you ought to fo if you
dont you will be fixed
We will neither
lave you house nor
house stade you mind
the Black Cat

An anonymous weaver threw the semiliterate threatening note of the "Black Cat" into the shop of Alexander Knox in late June 1828.[1] With New York weavers on strike, the message was clear. Knox had better pay the demanded wage (or "price") to his employees, or he and his family would be harassed and possibly attacked. Obviously, the weavers of 1828 had come to view "Boss nox" as an antagonist. Gone was any pretense of an identity of interest. The man who owned the shop, who doled out the work, and who paid substandard wages was looking out for his own benefit. What was good for "Boss nox" was not necessarily good for the weavers. Even his title of "Boss" separated him from his working-men. Gone, too, was the deference that had permeated labor relations in the eighteenth century. This anonymous threatening note, like the hundreds of such notes penned in England during the same period, may have represented the weavers' desire for Knox to fulfill his function as a fair employer, but the Black Cat made no requests, did not bow, and was not obsequious. Rather, he was hostile and demanding.[2]

Finding several weavers continuing to work for Knox at the lower wage, the strikers took more forceful action. On July 1, 1828, forty to fifty angry journeymen stormed into Knox's shop and demanded that the remaining workers join them in their turnout. Knox's journeymen refused to comply. In response, the strikers cut at least three webs off the looms in the shop to prevent work from going forward. Although the weavers, like many earlier rioters, were selective in their destruction of property, they did not eschew physical violence. When Knox's son and partner, who had run off to the police office at the first sign of trouble, confronted the strikers in the street, he was hit by a web thrown at him.[3]

Because New York's young and growing textile industry was decentralized, violence flared up elsewhere as well. Weavers labored either in shops like Knox's or as outworkers in their own homes. The continual influx of immigrant weavers from Great Britain in the 1820s and their dispersion

1. The original note is in the Court Records: *People* v. *Hamilton Radcliff et al.*, July 1, 1828, NYCGS. It was also published in some newspapers: *Statesman*, July 5, 1828; *Gazette*, July 2, 1828.

2. See E. P. Thompson, "The Crime of Anonymity," in Douglas Hay *et al.*, *Albion's Fatal Tree: Crime and Society in Eighteenth-Century England* (New York, 1975), 255–344; and Sean Wilentz, *Chants Democratic: New York City and the Rise of the American Working Class, 1788–1850* (New York, 1984), 169–170.

3. *People* v. *Radcliff et al.*, July 14, 1828, NYCGS; *Statesman*, July 5, 1828; *Gazette*, July 2, 1828.

throughout Greenwich Village made it difficult for the weavers to act in concert against their employers. The strikers in 1828 not only had to intimidate physically the bosses and their shopworkers but also had to patrol Eighth Avenue, where many weavers lived, and visit the homes and apartments of individual workers to ensure compliance with their strike. If the strikers discovered some of Knox's webs in these homes, they destroyed them. If there was any resistance, they turned to blows. During these searches the strikers assaulted at least one nonstriking weaver and beat and abused a weaver's wife, tearing the clothes off her back, when she attempted to save Knox's property.[4]

Such violence, which became so much a part of rioting in the 1820s and 1830s, contributed to the growing specter of disorder in New York City. It had its origin in the burgeoning market economy, which extended the distances between employer and employee. Master craftsmen became entrepreneurs whose values and attitude differed from their workers'. These new businessmen joined forces with merchants and lawyers to form a new middle class that adhered to an individualistic and democratic ideal. Basing their beliefs in the republicanism of the American Revolution, the middle class viewed virtue less and less as self-sacrifice for the community, and increasingly as material reward for hard work, temperate living, and austerity. Somehow, an individual's profit would mystically lead to the greater good of the commonwealth. Thus the democracy of this middle class was not necessarily egalitarian. It advocated laissez faire and an open competition that naturally created distinctions in wealth. While still clinging to the hope that those below them would remain deferential, the middle class began to abandon paternalistic obligations as hindrances to the pursuit of profit.[5]

Workers, especially tradesmen, also adhered to the republican values of the Revolutionary era. But, for them, the key to republicanism was an artisan independence based on competent workmanship and a fair reward

---

4. *Ibid.*

5. For general discussions of this development, see Rowland Berthoff, "Independence and Attachment, Virtue and Interest: From Republican Citizen to Free Enterpriser, 1787–1837," in Richard L. Bushman *et al.*, eds., *Uprooted Americans: Essays to Honor Oscar Handlin* (Boston, 1979), 97–124; Howard B. Rock, *Artisans of the New Republic: The Tradesmen of New York City in the Age of Jefferson* (New York, 1979), 151–182; Joyce Appleby, *Capitalism and a New Social Order: The Republican Vision of the 1790s* (New York, 1984); Paul E. Johnson, *A Shopkeeper's Millennium: Society and Revivals in Rochester, New York, 1815–1837* (New York, 1978); Mary P. Ryan, *Cradle of the Middle Class: The*

for an honest day's work. These workers still believed in corporate responsibilities and clung to the rough egalitarianism implicit in the plebeian culture of the mid-eighteenth century.[6]

In reaction to the growing distinction between laborer and boss and to the divergent interpretations of republicanism, both skilled and unskilled workers struggled to gain control over the workplace. In these efforts, workers at first turned to peaceful collective action, based on patterns of crowd behavior practiced in the eighteenth century. When these methods failed, workers had to rely on coercive violence.

The resulting conflict between employers and employees is central to the history of American popular disorder in the years after the Revolutionary war. The violence and tumult accompanying some of the labor agitation frightened the new middle class by threatening open class warfare. Even the nonviolent strikes stood as a constant reminder that there were

---

Family in Oneida County, New York, 1790–1865 (New York, 1981); Karen Halttunen, *Confidence Men and Painted Women: A Study of Middle-Class Culture in America, 1830–1870* (New Haven, Conn., 1982); Paul Boyer, *Urban Masses and Moral Order in America, 1820–1920* (Cambridge, Mass., 1978); Anthony F. C. Wallace, *Rockdale: The Growth of an American Village in the Early Industrial Revolution* (New York, 1972). For a somewhat different view of the middle class, see Stuart M. Blumin, "The Hypothesis of Middle-Class Formation in Nineteenth-Century America: A Critique and Some Proposals," *American Historical Review,* XC (1985), 299–338.

6. Wilentz, *Chants Democratic,* 61–103; Wilentz, "Artisan Republican Festivals and the Rise of Class Conflict in New York City, 1788–1837," in Michael H. Frisch and Daniel J. Walkowitz, eds., *Working-Class America: Essays on Labor, Community, and American Society* (Urbana, Ill., 1983), 37–77; Rock, *Artisans,* 19–44, 123–147. See also Bruce Laurie, *Working People of Philadelphia, 1800–1850* (Philadelphia, 1980); Paul Faler, "Cultural Aspects of the Industrial Revolution: Lynn, Massachusetts, Shoemakers and Industrial Morality, 1826–1860," *Labor History,* XV (1974), 367–394; Alan Dawley, *Class and Community: The Industrial Revolution in Lynn* (Cambridge, Mass., 1976); Alan Dawley and Paul Faler, "Working-Class Culture and Politics in the Industrial Revolution: Sources of Loyalism and Rebellion," *Journal of Social History,* IX (1975–1976), 466–480; Herbert G. Gutman, "Work, Culture, and Society in Industrializing America, 1815–1919," *AHR,* LXXVIII (1973), 531–588; Susan E. Hirsch, *Roots of the American Working Class: The Industrialization of Crafts in Newark, 1800–1860* (Philadelphia, 1978); Jonathan Prude, *The Coming of Industrial Order: Town and Factory Life in Rural Massachusetts, 1810–1860* (Cambridge, 1983); Sharon V. Salinger, "Artisans, Journeymen, and the Transformation of Labor in Late Eighteenth-Century Philadelphia," *William and Mary Quarterly,* 3d Ser., XL (1983), 62–84.

distinct economic interests in society, thereby undermining any lingering adherence to the eighteenth-century corporate ideal. As workers increasingly struck to settle wage disputes and as some of those strikers relied upon violence to intimidate strikebreakers and employers, the divisions and disorder of early nineteenth-century society became ever more apparent.

Although skilled journeymen were the first laborers to organize and turn out for wages, it was the unskilled workers who relied most heavily upon eighteenth-century traditions of collective action to coerce compliance with their strikes. These dockworkers, sailors, and day laborers had to depend upon force because they could not rely on a monopoly of skill; any strike by them was easily undercut by hiring other unskilled workers. This weak bargaining position, coupled with an increasing divergence of interest between the employers and employed, led the unskilled workers to ever greater measures of violence when more peaceful tactics, like massive demonstrations or limited destruction of property, failed. This development is particularly significant for understanding changes in rioting and in perceptions of rioting in the early nineteenth century. The shift from the limited collective activity of unskilled workers, based in earlier, deferential patterns of crowd behavior, to a coercive violence tantamount to collective bargaining by riot, marks a major change in relations between different socioeconomic groups and in patterns of popular disorder.

Labor Unrest among Seamen and Dockworkers

Traditions of collective action among unskilled workers hark back to the colonial period. Anti-impressment mobs, often composed of sailors and dockworkers, were a form of labor action. The men on the waterfront rejected en masse work in the British navy. They were supported in this effort by the merchants and the community that needed their labor to move goods in and out of the city. Anti-impressment riots generally were limited, and the mob ordinarily acted with discrimination.[7] The patterns of mob behavior, evident in the anti-impressment riots, also appeared in the liberty pole disputes of the 1760s and 1770s. A major issue in those disturbances was the off-duty labor of British servicemen.[8] Thus, un-

7. See discussion in chap. 1.

8. Many of the British servicemen were employed on the docks and the shipyards. See discussion in chap. 2.

skilled workers had experience during the colonial and Revolutionary periods in acting together in labor-related issues.

The opposition to impressment continued after the American Revolution. The British inspection of American ships and forced recruitment of seamen during the French Revolutionary and Napoleonic wars proved highly unpopular among all levels of society in America and occasionally led to mob action. The merchants needed to keep the sailors out of the British navy if they were to operate their own ships and hold down wages that were sure to rise if the labor supply dried up. The sailors naturally wanted to retain their freedom and earn the relatively high salaries aboard American ships. This concern with sailors' rights can be seen in the reaction to the accidental killing of an American seaman by a British warship in 1806. A crowd seized British supplies in New York City in a limited action typical of Anglo-American mobs in the previous century. Support for the capture of the skiff loaded with provisions for the British fleet was widespread, and there can be little doubt that the men involved in the capture were American mariners.[9]

Distaste for forced service in the British navy is also evident in crowd support for English deserters. On September 5, 1807, at a time when Americans were agitated over the *Chesapeake* affair (four American sailors had been forcefully taken by a British warship), a New York dockside crowd gathered as a British longboat, manned by a crew of eight under the command of a lieutenant, approached the New York pier. At a given signal six of the British seamen bolted from the boat to the cheers of a supportive American crowd, probably dockworkers and seamen. The British officer drew his pistols, ordered the men to return, and then attempted to follow them. A "mob immediately assembled, protected the men, abused the Lieutenant, and handled him roughly." Captain Isaac Chauncy of the United States Navy had to rescue the British officer from the mob.[10]

Although the opposition of the waterfront community to the British navy received broad patriotic support from most Americans, the seamen

9. *American Citizen,* Apr. 28–30, 1806; *Spectator,* Apr. 30, May 5, 1806; *Boston Gazette,* May 1, 5, 8, 1806; De Witt Clinton to Captain of the *Leander,* May 1, 1806, Clinton Letterbook, De Witt Clinton Papers, microfilm, Columbia University.

10. *American Citizen,* Sept. 7, 1807; *Columbian Centinel* (Boston), Sept. 12, 1807; I. N. Phelps Stokes, *The Iconography of Manhattan Island, 1498–1909* . . . (New York, 1915–1928), V, 1472.

acted from motives of their own. They adopted patriotic rhetoric, but they were concerned mainly with protecting their own liberty. Whenever New York mariners believed that the recruitment of any sailor, even for the American navy, was unjust, they were willing to act together in a mob.[11] On May 9, 1811, for instance, William Vandewater persuaded James Johnson to join the United States Navy. Johnson was paid a bounty of fifty-eight dollars, a large portion of which probably ended up in Vandewater's pocket, and was granted a few days' liberty before having to report for duty. Johnson quickly had a change of heart, and a few of his old shipmates decided to help him. Vandewater, who kept a sharp eye on Johnson to protect a surety he had taken out on the seaman, decided to have the navy put Johnson aboard the USS *Vesuvius*. About dusk Vandewater, a two-man navy guard, and Johnson reached the foot of East George Street, when a large mob headed by Martha Needham appeared. Mrs. Needham ran a boardinghouse and therefore played a prominent role in the waterfront community. Ordinarily, she and others like her made the arrangements for the mariners to sign up on ships in port. Thus, her presence at the head of an angry mob of one hundred seamen is not surprising, especially when the riot concerned the conditions of a sailor's employment. The Needham mob rescued Johnson, who quickly left the city. Following the pattern of collective action in the eighteenth century, the rioters did not harm Vandewater; they were interested only in protecting a shipmate from what they considered an unfair labor agreement.[12]

Also suggested in this type of crowd activity is an ardent sense of camaraderie among sailors. This is only to be expected. Long voyages, visits to strange ports where the only friends were shipmates, shared dangers from nature and from the depredations of foreign nations, and the fear of impressment built strong bonds among maritime workers, which they maintained on shore as well as aboard ship. More than this, sailors shared a special Anglo-American culture expressed in common language, lore, customs, and ritual.[13]

The camaraderie among sailors was apparent when they acted together

11. *People* v. *George Raymond et al.*, Dec. 10, 1804, NYCGS; De Witt Clinton to Gen. Rey, June 9, Oct. 22, 23, 1804, Clinton to James Madison, Nov. 13, 15, 1804, Clinton Letterbook, Clinton Papers, microfilm, Columbia University.

12. *People* v. *Martha Needham*, May 11, 1811, NYCGS.

13. For a discussion of this seamen's world in the early 18th century, see Marcus Rediker, "'Under the Banner of King Death': The Social World of Anglo-American Pirates, 1716 to 1726," *WMQ*, 3d Ser., XXXVIII (1981), 203–227.

against impressment or unfair recruitment, but it also contributed to the sailors' reputation for being disorderly. Frequenting grog shops and bawdyhouses of the dockside areas, many seamen drank, gambled their money away, and ended their evening's carousal in fights. One or two sailors in a tavern brawl was disruptive enough; but, with a call for assistance to one's shipmates, a minor disturbance easily erupted into a riot. In short, although the maritime worker exhibited circumspect behavior in traditional riot activity, he was capable of less decorous behavior and of rowdiness. Fully aware of their habits, city officials always kept a watchful eye on any collective action by sailors.

The nature of the waterfront economy added further to the potential for disorder. Seamen, stevedores, and riggers were recruited from the same labor pool in the rough neighborhoods near the docks and wharves. Any youth in port might sign up as a sailor on one of the thousands of ships that moved in and out of New York annually. Any sailor coming into New York might decide to stay there and work on the docks fitting ships for sea or merely loading and unloading goods. All dockside workers confronted the same economic hardships: casual employment (indeed, underemployment) together with low pay and long hours. The waterfront immediately felt any curtailment of trade. Winter, which was a hard time for every New York workman, was particularly telling upon laborers dependent on the free flow of goods. Maritime laborers were especially vulnerable to seasonal and cyclical economic fluctuations. In the face of such hardships, waterfront laborers had little recourse other than collective action for a redress of grievances.[14]

When sailors and dockworkers in the early nineteenth century turned to collective action, they initially followed the patterns of behavior of crowds in the eighteenth century. Increasing prices convinced New York sailors in October 1802 to strike for a raise from ten dollars to fourteen dollars a month. The turnout lasted several days. Two sailors "who styled themselves *commodores*" sent a letter to all the boardinghouse keepers on the waterfront instructing them not to ship any sailors for less than the fourteen-dollar wage. Fines of ten dollars would be imposed for each offense. Moreover, the "black seamen in the port united in the combination, under the direction of two *black commodores,* who acted in concert with the *white,* they in a subordinate capacity." To strengthen this sense of soli-

14. For an interesting discussion on casual employment and dockworkers in a later period and in another country, see Gareth Stedman Jones, *Outcast London: A Study in the Relationship between Classes in Victorian Society* (Oxford, 1971).

darity, the sailors, following long-standing forms, organized public demonstrations, which drew upon their experience with military processions,
the political activity of the 1790s, the American Revolution, and traditional celebrations like the charivari. The mariners repeatedly paraded
along the wharves "with drums beating and colors flying" under the
leadership of the "commodores," whose hats "were decorated with ribbons
and feathers."[15]

New York City merchants, however, tapping a large labor pool, found a
few sailors willing to work at the old wages. To prevent the collapse of
their strike, the nonworking sailors threatened the crews of ships ready
to sail. When that did not work, they began to take more forceful action.
The strikers boarded at least one schooner "and with great coolness and
order . . . proceeded to dismantle her of her sails and rigging, which they
carefully stowed away in the hold." This was no raging mob. By acting
with restraint, the seamen revealed a respect for property, an unwillingness
to provoke the ire of the civil authority, and a commitment to remaining
within the bounds of traditional popular behavior. All they wanted was to
ensure that no ship would sail with an underpaid crew. To guarantee compliance, the strikers also demanded the vessel's papers from the captain.[16]

Although the sailors did not commit any real violence to persons and
exhibited a sense of discrimination in their attack on property, the dismantling of ships was too much for the city authorities to tolerate. The mayor
summoned the police magistrates and several peace officers and marched
down to the waterfront. They arrived after the strikers had finished their
work and "had retired to a rendezvous house hard by, where they were
regaling themselves after their exploit." The city officials followed the
striking sailors to that "rendezvous house," arrested the ringleaders, and
broke the strike. The sailors, eschewing violence and revealing their continued deference, surrendered without resistance.[17]

The striking mariners were willing to rely on such limited action for
two reasons. First, it was effective tactics; a ship could be prevented from
sailing by dismantling its rigging and seizing its papers. Second, and more
important, the well-behaved and coolheaded sailors' mob held an identity
of interest with the shipowners. They did not want to destroy the rigging,
because they hoped that, once they gained the wage increase, they would

15. *Evening Post,* Oct. 21, 1802; *Spectator,* Oct. 23, 1802.
16. *Ibid.*
17. *Ibid.*

use that rigging to sail the ship. By ordering out the police and arresting the "commodores," the city magistrates denied that identity of interest.[18]

City officials responded differently toward sailors a few years later when the clash of economic interests was less stark. In response to the Embargo Act of 1807, which promised to close down virtually all maritime employment in the middle of the slack winter season, New York seamen decided to gather and publicly demand government assistance. The mere advertisement of this meeting in January 1808 was enough to send Mayor Marinus Willett into a panic. Willett hastily called a special session of the Common Council to consult over "the measures that might be proper to be adopted to prevent any unpleasant consequences" from such an assembly. The mayor ordered the city's newspapers to publish his exhortation against the rally and had handbills distributed with the same message.[19] The sailors held their meeting anyway, but did so in a peaceful manner. They drew up a series of resolutions declaring that the Embargo made it impossible for them to find any employment on or off the sea. Reinforcing their plea for special assistance, the mariners declared that, although they were not yet entirely destitute, the day was not far off when they would be forced to resort to thievery and violence to earn a living. The crowd quietly dispersed after Mayor Willett assured them that they would get some help from the city.

Obviously, both the sailors and the city magistrates were aware of the potential strength and dangers of the crowd, yet for the time being the sailors contented themselves with a brief demonstration and presentation of their grievances to the mayor. Wisely, the Common Council recognized that the entire seaport community suffered under the Embargo, and acted to fulfill its paternal obligations by alleviating the distress of the city's seamen and dockworkers. The city soon instituted a relief program that encouraged some men to join the navy, offered others public works jobs filling in the Collect (a large pond located behind the present-day City Hall on the northern edge of the old Common), and doled out soup four days a week for those who could not get any work at all.[20]

By the mid-1820s, New York's maritime workers began to realize that

18. For a similar labor action as late as 1822, see *American,* Sept. 13, 1822; *Evening Post,* Sept. 14, 1822; *Gazette,* Sept. 14, 1822; *Statesman,* Sept. 16, 1822.

19. *MCC,* IV, 699–700; Stokes, *Iconography,* V, 1483.

20. George Daitsman, "Labor and the 'Welfare State' in Early New York," *Labor History,* IV (1963), 248–256; *MCC,* IV, 700–704, 713–715, 728, 737, 739; Stokes, *Iconography,* V, 1483.

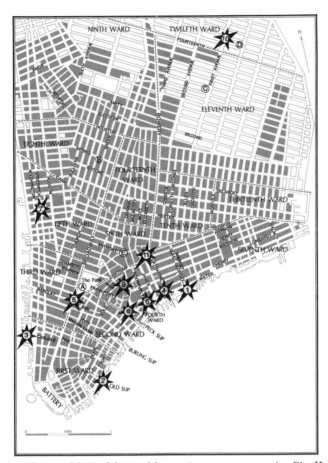

1. Rescue of James Johnson, May 9, 1811
2. Dockworkers' riot, Mar. 14, 1828
3. Dockworkers' riot, Mar. 14, 1828
4. Sacking of Munson's boardinghouse, Apr. 22, 1834
5. Sacking of Farrel's boardinghouse, Feb. 14, 1834
6. Laborers' riot, May 14, 1816
7. Strike, Underhill and Ferris, Mar. 21–23, 1829
8. Stonecutters' disturbance, June 23, 1830
9. Rose Street Church riots, 1809–1817
10. Anti-Stuyvesant riot, Apr. 6, 1828
11. Chatham Square rioting, Nov. 1–6, 1828

A. City Hall, after 1811
B. Johny Edwards's house
C. Nicholas Stuyvesant estate
D. Peter G. Stuyvesant estate
E. Five Points

- - - - Ward Boundary

MAP 6. Labor and Plebeian Disorder, 1809–1834.
After James Hardie, The Description of the City of New York . . .
(New York, 1827)

their economic interests diverged from those of the merchants. Recognizing this class cleavage, these unskilled workers abandoned the more traditional tactics of limited collective action and started to depend upon greater violence to back their demands. Riggers, stevedores, and day laborers all combined to gain a raise in their respective wages in March 1825. Nearly one thousand strong, they marched through the streets and along the wharves chanting, "Leave off work, leave off work."[21] Coming across work crews fitting a ship out for sea or loading or unloading a vessel, the strikers no longer behaved with "great coolness and order." Instead, they intimidated the workmen and compelled a suspension of all work. The nonstrikers were forced to join the mass of strikers. The police again supported the merchants and stepped in; officials arrested the ringleaders and dispersed the rest of the strikers.[22]

Three years later an even more violent and riotous dockworkers' strike took place, with assaults on nonstriking workers as well as destruction of property. In 1828, shipowners reduced wages to cut expenses during a trade slump. The stevedores and riggers opposed this reduction and decided to stand out for the old wage. Moreover, the strikers vowed to force all those willing to work at the lower rate to join them. On the morning of March 14, two hundred to three hundred strikers, including some blacks, assembled in the upper part of the city and began to move down the East River wharves, sweeping all before them. These strikers readily became violent. For instance, at the foot of Old Slip they fought with some men who tried to keep them from boarding a ship docked there.[23] Anyone who stood in their way was knocked down and beaten.

After completing a tour of the East River docks, the marchers crossed over to the Hudson River and began to make their way up the western side of the city. No one resisted the human wave of strikers until they reached the foot of Carlisle Street, where the ship *Sully* was unloading ballast.

21. *People v. Joseph Thompson et al.,* Apr. 11, 1825, NYCGS.

22. *Ibid.* Some details from this case can also be found in *People v. James Thompson,* Apr. 14, 1825, in John Webb, New York City Manuscript Minutes of the Court of General Sessions, NYPL. *Evening Post,* Mar. 22, 1825; *American,* Mar. 22, 1825; *Gazette,* Mar. 22, 1825; *National Advocate,* Mar. 23, 1825; *Statesman,* Mar. 25, 1825; Stokes, *Iconography,* V, 1646; David J. Saposs, "Colonial and Federal Beginnings (to 1827)," in John R. Commons *et al., History of Labour in the United States,* I (New York, 1918), 157; Paul O. Weinbaum, *Mobs and Demagogues: The New York Response to Collective Violence in the Early Nineteenth Century* (Ann Arbor, Mich., 1979), 84–85.

23. *People v. William Denwick et al.,* July 16, 1828, NYCGS.

Then the real battle began. On the refusal of the workmen to leave the
ship, strikers attempted to board the vessel. But Captain Robert J. Macy
expected this; and, supported by captains and mates from several ships
who were on board with him, he ordered the stage to the dock cut, and
prepared for the onslaught of the angered dockworkers. There was to be
no orderly dismantling and stowing of gear here. Nor did these maritime
workers show any deference to Macy and his companions. Instead, "the
signal was then given for a general attack and the rioters immediately
seized on the ballast stones and other missiles which were discharged in
vollies at the persons on deck." Macy and his supporters did fire two
pistols at the crowd of dockworkers, but to no apparent effect; the salvos of
ballast stones, however, damaged the *Sully* and injured Macy and almost
everyone else on deck. Moreover, it took more than a handful of officials to
quell the disturbance. Peace was restored only when the mayor, several
magistrates, scores of peace officers, and a troop of cavalry arrived and arrested a number of the rioting dockworkers.[24]

By the 1830s this same militancy could be found among the seamen.
Obscure men like John Munson, another boardinghouse keeper, spoke
out in defense of seamen's rights. In fact, in the spring of 1834, when
shipowners attempted a reduction in wages, Munson as president of the
Seaman's Friend Society chaired several meetings to discuss the "interests" of the seamen. At one boisterous meeting in February, many of the
sailors wanted to take direct action against Michael Farrel, a boardinghouse
keeper who had signed sailors out at the reduced wage level. Despite ob-
jections by Munson and a few others, the sailors stormed out of the meeting hall and attacked Farrel's Water Street boardinghouse, breaking down
the door and smashing the window and steps. The striking mariners
threatened more destruction if Farrel continued to disregard the sailors'
interests.[25] Two months later, Munson found his own boardinghouse and
bar attacked. Again the issue was wages. After another heated meeting
of the Seaman's Friend Society, a large group of sailors marched toward the
waterfront. On the way a rival boardinghouse keeper persuaded the crowd,
through misrepresentations, to attack Munson's place. They charged in,

24. *Ibid.; People* v. *James Perry et al.,* July 16, 1828, NYCGS; *People* v. *John
Jackson,* July 17, 1828; *People* v. *Lewis Jackson et al.,* July 17, 1828; *Evening Post,*
July 21, 1828; *Gazette,* July 15, 16, 19, 1828; *Statesman,* July 19, 30, 1828;
Weinbaum, *Mobs and Demagogues,* 84.

25. *Michael Farrel et al.* v. *John Rockwood et al.,* Feb. 15, 1834, box 7446
(1833–1834), NYCSCPCC.

destroyed furniture, beat the barkeeper, and tore the place to pieces.[26] In both disturbances, then, these seamen exhibited a willingness to go beyond the limited action of 1802 and turn toward greater destruction of property.

Dockworkers and sailors were not the only ones who became more violent to support their wage demands. In May 1816, when prices were rapidly rising, day laborers stood out for higher wages. Facing many of the same organizational problems that confronted the dockworkers, the striking day laborers stormed from one construction site to another, compelling compliance with their strike. James Teague reported that, while he was working with his shovel at the corner of Pearl Street and Peck Slip, a group of forty or fifty laborers came up to him "and told him that they were turning out for wages and that he must quit working." Teague did not want to leave the job, but the strikers took his shovel away from him and "told him to come along with them, and for peace sake he did follow on and was afraid of getting hurt." The laborers went next to a building in Murray Street, where they grabbed other tools from the workers and beat William Burwick, a mason, when he tried to stop them.[27]

The labor agitation of the lowest class of workers was crucial in establishing patterns of labor protest. The unskilled maritime workers attempted to gain increased wages and job security in the 1802 turnout, and they attempted to replace lost employment in the winter of 1808 by collectively demanding work. In both instances the sailors formed mobs that behaved in the same restrained manner as had the mobs of the previous century. But they met with mixed results. In 1802 the merchants had the city officials put down the strike, while in 1808 a combination of fear and paternalism persuaded the magistrates to act to cushion the depression following the institution of the Embargo. By the 1820s and 1830s, however, the chasm between the merchants, businessmen, and magistrates on one side and the seamen, dockworkers, and laborers on the other had widened. Recognizing this divergence of interests, the unskilled workers realized that greater force and violence were needed if their turnouts were to have any hope of success. They then took a lead in the transformation of traditional crowd behavior into the more violent and aggressive forms evident

26. *Courier and Enquirer,* Apr. 26, 28, 1834.

27. *People* v. *Peter Nowland et al.,* May 17, 1816, NYCGS; *People* v. *Alexander Page,* May 14, 1816, box 7434 (1815–1817), NYCSCPCC; *Columbian,* May 17, 1816. A similar disturbance occurred on Aug. 14, 1832. See *People* v. *Michael O'Brian,* Sept. 10, 1832, box CC-88 (1832), NYCGS.

in the laborers' work stoppage of 1816, the dockworkers' strikes of 1825 and 1828, and the seamen's labor unrest of the 1830s.

Mechanics, Artisans, Journeymen, and Strikes

Changes in the economy and the artisanal work structure also altered labor relations within the more-skilled trades, pitting journeyman against master. Journeyman strikes were rare before 1780, and only in the decades thereafter, when expanding markets and changing modes of production opened the trades to competition from semiskilled or unskilled workers, did this type of strike become integral to the labor scene.[28]

At first, mechanics in the more-skilled trades did not have to rely on the same coercive tactics as the less-skilled workers. Monopoly of skilled production made the tradesman's strike effective without violence; and in an effort to display their devotion to the new political order, most journeymen intentionally avoided violence.[29] Yet even the peaceful turnouts betrayed the growing socioeconomic cleavages in New York in the years after the American Revolution. As a result, both the magistrates and the middle class they represented opposed these labor actions. In the 1820s and 1830s, when a workingman's consciousness developed more distinctly and when some tradesmen found themselves more susceptible to competition and therefore began turning to violence, the opposition to strikes and their disorder became implacable.

In the eighteenth century no great conflict existed between journeymen and master craftsmen. Some trades, like shoemaking, experienced enough change to make it increasingly difficult for the independent craftsmen to eke out a living.[30] In other trades employers shifted to per diem hiring as early as the 1750s rather than depend upon longer, more binding contracts.[31] Yet, many ties continued to unite the interests of all members of

28. In New York City there was a tailors' strike in 1768 and a printers' strike in 1778. On colonial strikes, see Richard B. Morris, *Government and Labor in Early America* (New York, 1946), 196–198.

29. Rock, *Artisans*, 122–147, 279–283.

30. Alfred F. Young, "George Robert Twelves Hewes (1742–1840): A Boston Shoemaker and the Memory of the American Revolution," *WMQ*, 3d Ser., XXXVIII (1981), 570–585.

31. Gary B. Nash, "Urban Wealth and Poverty in Pre-Revolutionary America," *Journal of Interdisciplinary History*, VI (1975–1976), 547–576; Nash, *The Urban Crucible: Social Change, Political Consciousness, and the Origins of the Ameri-*

PLATE 12. Corner of Greenwich and Dey Streets.
Watercolor by Baroness Hyde de Neuville, 1810. Courtesy of the New York Public Library.
This is a typical mechanic neighborhood.

the craft. Both apprentices and journeymen often boarded with the master craftsman and were therefore considered a part of the household. The progression of apprentice to journeyman to master artisan, although an ideal completed by only a few, remained a reality for some. More important, master, journeyman, and apprentice toiled together in the workshop—all wore leather aprons and had calluses on their hands. Their shared experiences may not have forestalled all conflict, but overt rifts, like a strike, were almost nonexistent.

In the years immediately after the Revolutionary war, the increased development of craft traditions also militated against open conflict between artisan and journeyman. Republican ideology extolled the virtues of an honest, hardworking citizenry, and this idea, with the opening up of the political system of the Revolution, gave mechanics a new sense of self-worth. Artisan and journeyman united under traditional craft symbols in new mechanic societies and in public celebrations. This trend reached its apex in the great parade celebrating the ratification of the United States

can Revolution (Cambridge, Mass., 1979), 233–263; Saposs, "Colonial and Federal Beginnings," in Commons *et al., History of Labour,* I, 56–60; Morris, *Government and Labor,* 42, 45, 49, 193–200, 363–389; Bernard Bailyn, *Education in the Forming of American Society: Needs and Opportunities for Study* (Chapel Hill, N.C., 1960), 29–36.

Constitution in 1788. Borrowing English craft symbols and extending the public procession to new purposes, master, journeyman, and apprentice marched together in a new political setting. But the unity of such occasions was short-lived.[32]

The breakdown of the progressive apprentice-journeyman-artisan craft work structure began to accelerate as markets expanded at the end of the eighteenth century. Master craftsmen tried to increase production to meet the demands of the new markets opened up by the improved communications and growing population. Greater capital was thus needed, and it became more difficult for the journeyman to set up his own independent shop. In the meantime the most successful craftsmen, especially in the "conflict trades" of shoemaking, cabinetmaking, tailoring, construction, and printing, moved away from the workshop and branched out into other businesses.[33] These masters concentrated their efforts in entrepreneurial activities: they became wholesalers as well as retailers, served as large contractors, and bought and sold in great quantities. Moreover, the smart master began to exploit his labor force as much as possible. He preferred not to provide bread and board for his workers and relinquished the supervision of laborers' leisure activities. The master craftsman also became less willing to support his journeymen and apprentices during slack production periods, and the practice of paying employees daily, begun in the mid-eighteenth century, increased. Now the ideal was to hire labor for only the time it was needed.[34]

Employment and wages, which had always fluctuated with the seasons and economic conditions, became even more casual. The rhythm of the work year was revealed by the experience of the journeyman house carpenters in 1824. The best wages, $1.25 a day, lasted only during the busy season from March 10 to July 10. Thereafter demand for their labor dropped; even by working longer hours they could not always maintain the $1.25 rate from July to November, and it often fell $.12½–$.37 short. For the remaining months the situation was worse, and if journeyman car-

32. Wilentz, *Chants Democratic,* 87–97; Wilentz, "Artisan Republican Festivals," in Frisch and Walkowitz, eds., *Working-Class America,* 37–77; Alfred Young, "English Plebeian Culture and Eighteenth-Century American Radicalism," in Margaret C. Jacob and James R. Jacob, eds., *The Origins of Anglo-American Radicalism* (London, 1984), 185–212.

33. These conflict trades are identified in Rock, *Artisans,* 236–263.

34. Saposs, "Colonial and Federal Beginnings," in Commons *et al., History of Labour,* I, 50–104; Rock, *Artisans,* 237–263; Wilentz, *Chants Democratic,* 23–48.

penters could get any work at all, they were paid only $.50–$.80 a day. In some ways the house carpenters were lucky; journeyman masons, because of inclement weather, did not work at all for three months of the year.[35]

Masters also tried to cut costs by hiring nonjourneymen to do the least-skilled tasks of the trade. It became more profitable to train apprentices only partially in the craft. Under the old system, no sooner had an apprentice become proficient in one task than he was shifted to learn a new task. This system wasted time and material. In the new, larger workshops many apprentices were hired, and for maximum efficiency each was kept at only one task. Halfway journeymen (workers who had not served full apprenticeships and who were not completely trained), immigrants, and even women often were substituted for the more expensive journeymen. This semiskilled labor depressed the level of wages for the journeymen. But for the youths, halfway journeymen, immigrants, and women laborers, the chance to work at even a substandard wage was a great opportunity. A young man of twenty made far more as a halfway journeyman working for a day wage than he did if he were laboring under the seemingly interminable bond of apprenticeship. Moreover, he was free to do what he chose with his wage. Roaming the city, drinking, and carousing well into the night were more attractive activities than being supervised by a master craftsman.[36]

These challenges to the journeymen's independence and to their sense of integrity for their work made them increasingly militant. In 1809 a controversy over the use of an apprentice led to an unsuccessful strike by journeyman cordwainers. James Britton, an old man who worked as a shoemaker at the shop of Corwin and Aimes, relied almost entirely upon the labor of his apprentice for a living. The other journeyman cordwainers realized that the apprentice was doing a journeyman's work for less than a journeyman's wages and wanted the apprentice dismissed. The shopowners refused the demand because they "thought it a great hardship that the old man should lose the profit of the work of an apprentice he had in-

35. *Evening Post,* May 24, Aug. 24, 1824.

36. Saposs, "Colonial and Federal Beginnings," in Commons *et al., History of Labour,* I, 114–118; Rock, *Artisans,* 237–294. For the breakdown of apprenticeship in nearby Newark, see Hirsch, *Roots of the American Working Class,* 23, 74–75. For development undermining the position of journeymen in another eastern city, see Charles G. Steffen, "Between Revolutions: The Pre-Factory Urban Worker in Baltimore, 1780–1820" (Ph.D. diss., Northwestern University, 1977), 31–109; and Steffen, "Changes in the Organization of Artisan Production in Baltimore, 1790 to 1820," *WMQ,* 3d Ser., XXXVI (1979), 101–117.

structed." The Society of Journeyman Cordwainers therefore decided on a turnout and refused to work in the Corwin and Aimes shop. The journeymen, however, extended the strike to all employers when they discovered that the master shoemakers in other shops secretly were filling orders for Corwin and Aimes.

Although the strike began as a demand for the dismissal of the one apprentice, the journeyman cordwainers also concerned themselves with more general issues. They wanted higher wages and the enforcement of closed shops that would hire only journeymen who belonged to their society. The cordwainers complained as well that the "masters were in the habit of crowding their shops with more apprentices than they could instruct," and insisted that no more than two apprentices be employed by a master at any one time. Thus the journeyman cordwainers decried "the rapacity of the masters" and attempted to maintain wage rates and defend themselves against competition from cheaper labor.[37]

Because the cordwainers were skilled workers, their turnout did put economic pressure on the master shoemakers. The journeymen did not have to resort to physical coercion, and even the prosecution attorneys at the ensuing trial had to admit that "there had been no personal violence, no outrage or disorder" by the strikers.[38] This lack of violence was typical of job actions by skilled journeymen before the 1820s. Strikers threatened and intimidated other workers, but the mainstay of any turnout remained economic coercion and control over skilled production. To combat the strong bargaining position of the journeymen, the masters had to resort to a legal system sympathetic to their cause; based on the idea that strikes restrained trade, the court of general sessions convicted twenty-five members of the Society of Journeyman Cordwainers of conspiracy.[39]

Journeymen had other weapons besides the strike with which to fight for their demands. Although one journeyman had difficulty in raising enough capital on his own to become a master, groups of journeymen, when hard-pressed by uncompromising employers, occasionally attempted to establish cooperative workshops to maintain their status as independent mechanics. A 15 percent wage cut convinced journeyman cabinetmakers

37. John R. Commons *et al.*, eds., *A Documentary History of American Industrial Society*, III (Cleveland, Ohio, 1910), 251–385.

38. *Ibid.*, 377–378.

39. *Ibid.*, 251–385. The judge's attitude was less severe than the jury's. The judge fined the journeyman cordwainers one dollar.

in 1802 to set up their own warehouse to sell furniture to the public. In 1810 the journeyman house carpenters offered to work during their strike under supervision of their own choice at their demanded wage.[40] And in 1819 cabinetmakers again established an independent shop when Duncan Phyfe wanted to lower their wages because of the economic panic. These efforts, along with attempts to get the public to boycott recalcitrant employers, were largely unsuccessful.[41]

The most effective tool for the journeymen to use in labor confrontations remained the turnout. Journeymen lost many strikes, like the cordwainers in the 1809 conspiracy trial, but often they were able to win some concessions, and a successful strike was contagious. In 1810, businessmen believed that, if the wage demands of the house carpenters were met, they would have to be followed up and extended to masons, painters, glaziers, and other tradesmen.[42] This fear was rooted in experience; in the spring of 1809, journeyman bricklayers laid down their tools because they were not given a pay raise, although all of the other workmen in the "mechanical branch" had received one.[43]

The drive for parity among tradesmen helps to explain the clustering of strikes in certain years. Strikes occurred intermittently from the first shoemakers' turnout, in 1785, to 1834 and beyond, but 1809–1810, 1822–1825, and 1829–1834 were especially active years for labor unrest (see table 6).[44] By the last of these periods, many mechanics began to see themselves as a group apart from the rest of society, with interests all their own. In New York City this nascent class awareness led to the ten-hour movement in the spring of 1829, the formation of the Workingman's Party in the same year, and, when the political efforts failed to sustain an inde-

40. Rock, *Artisans*, 275; *American Citizen*, May 23, 1810.

41. Rock, *Artisans*, 273–275.

42. *American Citizen*, June 2, 1810.

43. Rock, *Artisans*, 280–281.

44. *Ibid.*, 273–276, 278, 280–281; *American Citizen*, May 23, 24, 31, June 1, 2, 6, 12, 1820; *Gazette*, Apr. 23, 1810; Commons *et al.*, eds., *Documentary History*, IV, 91; Jacob D. Wheeler, *Reports of Criminal Law Cases, Decided at the City-Hall of the City of New York, with Notes and References* (New York, 1854), I, 142; Saposs, "Colonial and Federal Beginnings," in Commons *et al.*, *History of Labour*, I, 156–157, 164; *William Kemble v. John Walker*, Mar. 18, 1824, box 7438 (1824–1825), NYCSCPCC; *Evening Post*, May 18, 24, Aug. 24, 1824; *Gazette*, Mar. 22, 1825; *Archibald Burgess v. Adam Gervin et al.*, Apr. 15, 1825, box 7438 (1824–1825), NYCSCPCC.

TABLE 6
New York City Strikes and Labor Actions, 1785–1834

Date	Workers	Cause
1785: ca. Mar. 21	jour. shoemakers	decrease of wages
1786: —	jour. printers	—
1790s: —	jour. shoemakers	—
1801: Nov. 3	bakers	against regulation
1802: —	jour. cabinetmakers	decrease of wages
ca. Oct. 20	sailors	demand for increased wages
1805: Apr.	jour. cabinetmakers	demand for increased wages
1809: ca. May	jour. bricklayers	demand for increased wages
ca. Oct. 28	jour. printers	demand for increased wages
Oct.–Dec.	jour. shoemakers	work by competitor laborers; demand for increased wages
Apr. 10	jour. house carpenters	demand for increased wages
1810: May 16–		
June 15	jour. house carpenters	demand for increased wages
ca. May 23	jour. masons	demand for increased wages
1811: ca. June 11	jour. printers	decrease of wages
1814: —	jour. bakers	
1816: ca. May 14	laborers	demand for increased wages
ca. May 17	stonecutters	demand for increased wages
1819: ca. Apr.	jour. tailors	work by competitor laborers; decrease of wages
May	jour. masons	decrease of wages
May	jour. cabinetmakers	decrease of wages
1821: Dec. 17	butchers	for regulation
1822: Sept. 12	sailors	demand for increased wages
Nov. 20	jour. hatters	work by competitor laborers; decrease of wages
1823: —	stonecutters	demand for increased wages
May 15	chairmakers	foreclosure of shop
1824: Mar. 18	machinists	work by competitor laborers (?)
ca. Apr. 24	jour. house painters	demand for increased wages
May	jour. carpenters	demand for increased wages
Aug.	jour. masons	demand for increased wages
1825: Mar.	waterfront workers	demand for increased wages
Mar. or May	stonecutters	demand for increased wages
Apr.	jour. tailors	demand for increased wages
1827: Nov. 1–6	dry goods retailers	for regulation
1828: July 1	jour. weavers	demand for increased wages
July 14	dockworkers	decrease of wages
1829: Mar. 21–23	jour. stonecutters	demand for increased wages
1830: June 22	stonecutters	work by competitor laborers

Table 6. *continued*
New York City Strikes and Labor Actions, 1785–1834

Date	Workers	Cause
1831: May 3	jour. cabinetmakers	work by competitor laborers
ca. May 26	jour. carpenters	demand for increased wages
ca. June 24	jour. printers	demand for increased wages
Dec. 21	jour. cabinetmakers	work by competitor laborers
1832: Aug. 14	laborers	work by competitor laborers
1833: June 17–20	ropemakers	introduction of machinery
ca. May 17	jour. carpenters	demand for increased wages
Nov. 14–16	jour. tailors	decrease of wages
ca. Nov. 20	jour. pianoforte makers	decrease of wages
1834: Feb. 14	sailors	decrease of wages
Apr. 22	sailors	decrease of wages
June 8–23	jour. bakers	demand for increased wages
ca. June 14	jour. shoemakers	decrease of wages
ca. Sept. 6	carpet weavers	decrease of wages
ca. Oct. 4	locksmiths	decrease of wages
ca. Oct. 26	stonecutters	work by competitor laborers
ca. Dec. 20	hatters	decrease of wages

Note: Most dates do not include all of the days workers were on strike.
Sources: NYCGS; NYCSCPCC; newspapers.

pendent party, the organization of the General Trades Union in the summer of 1833. As a backdrop to these labor developments, journeymen in several trades turned out from work.[45]

Changes in economic conditions in New York City are also reflected in

45. The best discussion on the workingman's movement is Wilentz, *Chants Democratic*, 145–296. See also Helen L. Sumner, "Citizenship," in Commons *et al., History of Labour,* I, 236–284; Edward B. Mittleman, "Trade Unionism," in Commons *et al., History of Labour,* I, 354–382. For reference to strikes, also see *Evening Post,* Mar. 23, 1829, June 22, 1830, June 19, 20, 1833, June 9–14, 17, 19, 23, 1834; *Gazette,* Mar. 24, 1829; *Jno H. Ferris* v. *C. Chestnut et al.,* Mar. 23, 1829, box 7441 (1829), NYCSCPCC; *Frs. Olmstead* v. *Patrick Timmins et al.,* June 22, 1830, box 7442 (1830), NYCSCPCC; *Sun,* Oct. 28, 1834; *Transcript,* Oct. 28, 1834; *Commercial Advertiser,* May 5, 1831, Oct. 27, 1834; *Spectator,* May 31, 1831, June 24, 1834; "Philip Hone Diary," VI, May 17, 1833, microfilm, NYHS; *Courier and Enquirer,* May 18, Nov. 16, 21, 1833, June 14, 21, 1834; *Joseph Meeks* v. *Jas Yard et al.,* May [3], 1831, box 7443 (1831), NYCSCPCC; *Benjamin Eastmond* v. *Wm. H. Christopher et al.,* Nov. 21, 1833, box 7446 (1833–1834), NYCSCPCC; *Workingman's Advocate,* June 14, 21, 1834.

this clustering of strikes. Labor agitation tended to intensify during periods of rising prices and recovery from business stagnation. The 1809–1810 strike activity began as the nation started to revive from the trade slump caused by Jefferson's embargo, and the 1823–1825 strikes came at the end of the depression caused by the Panic of 1819. The journeymen saw that the master craftsmen and their employers reaped great profits in the new prosperity, and they wanted to have their fair share of that wealth. In 1810 the carpenters complained that the masters were making plenty of money, as witnessed in their new brick houses and their carriages.[46] A building boom in 1824 created a demand for carpenters and construction workers that enabled them to bargain and then strike from a position of strength. As the journeyman masons put it, in justifying their demands for higher wages in 1824, the "state of the times" could bear giving them their raise.[47]

Economic depression, however, also triggered labor conflict. The Panic of 1819 convinced many masters of the necessity of lowering wages, and some journeymen reacted by striking.[48] Until the early 1830s, however, labor activity was usually quiet during economic hard times; most workers were relieved to receive any form of income in a recession. By 1833 and 1834, as the economy began to wind down from the impact of the Jacksonian bank war, workers were far less complacent. Years of labor agitation and the formation of specific trade organizations convinced many mechanics of the need to bind together for their common interest and prevent any reduction in wages.[49]

Most strikes, in good times or bad, occurred in the spring (see figure 1). This seasonal pattern resulted from the preindustrial nature of New York's economy: with the warmer weather of mid-March, business and trade renewed. Workers recognized that their labor was then in demand and that the time was right for them to act. This trend was true especially of the building trades, because new construction often began in March. But other journeymen and workers—including shoemakers, tailors, weavers, cabinetmakers, printers, ropemakers, bakers, cordwainers, and sailors— all took labor action in the spring. There was also a slight increase in the number of strikes in October and November before winter set in and employment became scarce. Many of these strikes, however, were defensive,

46. *American Citizen,* May 23, 1810.
47. *Evening Post,* Aug. 24, 1824.
48. *Ibid.,* May 27, 1819; Rock, *Artisans,* 276.
49. Wilentz, *Chants Democratic,* 145–296.

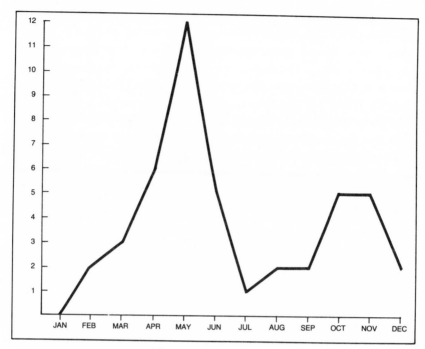

FIGURE 1. New York City Strikes, 1783–1834

attempting to prevent a decrease in wages. There were few strikes in the middle of winter, when jobs were scarce and pay was below standard.[50]

All of these strikes, whether in the springtime or in winter, whether in years of greater labor agitation or in years of solitary turnouts, revealed to New Yorkers the growing social divisions within their midst. By the late 1820s and early 1830s many journeymen became stridently militant, expressing a solidarity with all other mechanics through the General Trades Union and through declarations of support for strikers in other trades. This outburst of class awareness led some journeymen and radical thinkers to extend the republicanism of independent and virtuous workers to a mild critique of capitalism and demand for the redistribution of property.[51]

50. *Packet,* Mar. 21, 1785; Morris, *Government and Labor,* 200–201; *Evening Post,* Apr. 20, July 13, 1819; Saposs, "Colonial and Federal Beginnings," in Commons *et al., History of Labour,* I, 157.

51. For discussion of the variety and shape of this anticapitalistic thought, see Wilentz, *Chants Democratic,* 145–254. For examples of journeyman solidarity and of journeymen's defending their strikes, see *Man,* June 14, 16, 1834; *Workingman's Advocate,* Oct. 4, 1834.

Stonecutters, Ropemakers, and the Rise of Violence

Class conflict became even more apparent when some journeymen began
to rely upon violence to support their labor demands. Of course, there had
been sporadic violence among mechanics before the 1820s. Carpenters reportedly stoned the windows of hostile newspapers and obnoxious employers in 1810. But this activity remained limited; even in later decades
some journeymen prided themselves on their circumspect behavior during
turnouts. For example, the carpenters marched peacefully up and down
the streets, attempting to persuade their nonstriking coworkers to join
them in 1824, 1831, and 1833.[52] In several other trades in the late 1820s
and early 1830s, however, laborers began to rely more heavily on physical
violence and coercion. At times, some of this activity was reminiscent of
earlier crowd behavior, and, at other times, it was more representative of
the new trend of blatant violence.

The weavers who hid behind the anonymity of the ominous "Black Cat"
in 1828 were not the only tradesmen who used force to support their labor
demands. Stonecutters repeatedly resorted to violence in the 1820s and
1830s to protect their trade and livelihood. Strikes in 1823 and 1825 won
wage raises for the stonecutters, but when they tried to repeat this success
in 1829, they ran into difficulties.[53] Many of the journeyman stonecutters
remained on the job during the 1829 strike, and the only way to stop them
from working was by force. Squads of striking stonecutters paraded up
and down Greenwich Street visiting the various stonecutting shops "and
making use of violent and threatening language for the purpose of dissuad-
ing other journeymen from working, and inducing them to join the dis-
contented ranks."

The turnout began on March 19, and for the next few days the strikers,
forming "mobs at the corners of streets," harassed and even beat stonecutters on their way to and from work. On the twentieth these rioters visited
John Simpson, a working stonecutter, at his house and promised to give
him "a hiding" if he continued to work. He quit. So did others who were
intimidated. Strikers "*knocked down and violently abused*" Edward Divine
on his way home from work on the twenty-first. Robert Jolly was attacked

52. *Spectator,* May 31, 1831; "Hone Diary," VI, May 17, 1833, microfilm,
NYHS; *Courier and Enquirer,* May 18, 1833; *Evening Post,* May 18, 24, 1824;
Rock, *Artisans,* 278, 280.
53. Saposs, "Colonial and Federal Beginnings," in Commons *et al., History of
Labour,* I, 157; *Gazette,* Mar. 22, 1825.

several times on the same day, and, that night, strikers came into his house and pulled him out of bed and beat him. Such violence soon brought the police into the dispute, who made nearly twenty arrests.[54]

The arrest of stonecutters in 1829 did not prevent their fellow workers from resorting to violence. In 1830 and in 1834, stonecutters reacted with force to the growing use of marble and granite cut in the state prisons, on the grounds that competition from convict labor was unfair, degraded their profession, and threatened their jobs. On June 22, 1830, about two hundred stonecutters marched to a construction site on Broadway and Ann Street, where they told the contractor "that he and all the others using said marble should be put down." One rioter, resuscitating memories of New York's Revolutionary mobs, declared that the workers on this site "ought to be tarred and feathered and thrown off of the dock." Before such threats could be carried out, however, city officials arrived and arrested the leaders of the disturbance.[55] In 1834, rather than attempting to coerce fellow laborers, the rioters simply vented their pent-up rage against a building being built of prison stone. On the night of October 27, a group of stonecutters assembled and began to attack the new construction with stones and other missiles, breaking windows and doing other damage. "A strong posse of watchmen" arrived and dispersed the rioters, and, showing official support for the builders, the mayor stationed police officers near the building the next night.[56] In short, faced with competition from an inexpensive labor source, these stonecutters in 1829, 1830, and 1834 felt compelled to depend on violence, first to intimidate fellow workmen into supporting their cause, and then merely to express their own frustration.

If stonecutters were particularly vulnerable to labor competition—in their case, from convicts—they were far from alone. As middle-class entrepreneurs sought ways to reduce costs and maximize profits, the livelihood of many skilled craftsmen was threatened. Like the stonecutters, these groups turned to coercion and violence in a largely vain attempt to maintain some control over the workplace. In the spring of 1831, for example, journeyman cabinetmakers harassed Joseph Meek's shop and his employees, many of whom were apparently new arrivals to New York. On

54. *John H. Chestnut et al.* v. *C. Chester et al.*, Mar. 23, 1829, box 7441 (1829), NYCSCPCC; *Gazette,* Mar. 24, 1829; *Morning Post,* Mar. 23, 1829.

55. *Frs. Olmstead* v. *Patrick Timmins et al.*, June 22, 1830, box 7442 (1830), NYCSCPCC; *Evening Post,* June 22, 1830.

56. *Courier and Enquirer,* Oct. 27, 1834; *Sun,* Oct. 28, 1834; *Transcript,* Oct. 28, 1834; *Commercial Advertiser,* Oct. 27, 1834.

May 3 the strikers beat Joseph M. Burgan, telling him "that he should not work in the City."[57] Likewise, in December of the same year, journeyman cabinetmakers disrupted a furniture auction by shouting down the auctioneer and defacing the goods made outside the city. The journeymen explained their rage by asserting that this nonlocally produced furniture "would have the tendency to diminish" their wages. During a strike in November 1833, the leaders of the tailors' organization admitted that it was difficult to avoid violence even at their own meetings. When, in the same month, Benjamin Eastmond refused to join his fellow pianoforte makers in their labor action, the strikers came to his "shop after him, followed and mobbed him in the street."[58]

More reflective of Revolutionary traditions of crowd behavior was the threat of violence in June 1833 by the ropemakers of Brooklyn and New York City when they combined to demonstrate, in Luddite fashion, against the introduction of laborsaving machinery in a Brooklyn ropewalk. Striking in protest, two hundred ropemakers marched to that establishment to demand rope manufactured with the machine. After talking it over with the owner, however, they agreed to buy the "proscribed article." Then, treating the rope much the way mobs of the 1760s and 1770s treated effigies, they paraded it around in a cart and burned it, much to their own delight.[59]

For middle-class entrepreneurs, it was bad enough when laborers joined to demand higher wages, but to offer violence as well was intolerable. Though some of this collective activity had limited violence and even paralleled the behavior of Revolutionary crowds (in the threat of tar and feathers and in the parade and burning of the machine-produced rope), the commercial newspapers and city officials uniformly condemned all of the strikes of the late 1820s and early 1830s. No doubt the intensified violence in some strikes, including the destruction of property and physical assaults on people, contributed to this attitude. But the new middle class also espoused a value system that extolled the virtue of the individual as a solitary economic unit. Collective bargaining and the strike denied that ideal. This

57. *Spectator,* May 10, 1831; *Joseph Meeks* v. *Jas Yard et al.,* May [3], 1831, box 7443 (1831), NYCSCPCC.

58. *Evening Post,* Dec. 21, 24, 1831; *Courier and Enquirer,* Nov. 16, 23, 1833; *Benjamin Eastmond* v. *Wm. H. Christopher et al.,* Nov. 21, 1833, box 7446 (1833–1834), NYCSCPCC.

59. *Evening Post,* June 19, 21, 1833.

conflict led city officials to treat the rioters, not as aggrieved members of the greater community, but as outsiders and criminals who no longer fitted into the mainstream of American culture. One way to emphasize the un-American element of the strikes was to blame them on immigrants. After the 1828 dockworkers' strike, several newspapers reported that the arrested strikers "are all foreigners but one. The ringleader arrived here but three weeks since in a British ship." Such statements ignored the simple fact that, although immigrants participated in these disturbances and brought with them class awareness and knowledge of union activities, it was changes in the American economy and class structure that caused workers to organize and riot.[60]

As the economy changed, so too did the relationship between different groups within society. Merchants and their maritime workers drew further apart when the laborers began to demand higher wages. Master craftsmen moved away from their mechanic roots and took on the trappings of the rising entrepreneur. Gradually the masters merged with the city's elite, leaving their journeymen at the mercy of unskilled and half-skilled workers clamoring for the journeyman's job. Faced with these social and economic changes, workers began to band together in protest. Most journeyman craftsmen, still striving for respect and independence, remained circumspect in their actions. But the journeymen who had the most difficulty enforcing any collective action followed the violent patterns set by the maritime workers and day laborers: they increasingly relied on the coercion of nonstrikers in an attempt to assert not only their economic

60. *Daily Advertiser,* quoted in *Freedom's Journal,* July 18, 1828; *Statesman,* July 30, 1828.

The violence in the strikes in July 1828 was seen against the backdrop of similar labor disturbances in Philadelphia, Pawtucket, and Paterson. The Paterson strike, which occurred among textile factory workers, did give rise to a debate over changing economic conditions in America. But this debate was tainted with politics. The Jacksonians blamed the violence on the American System. The *Evening Post* declared that manufacturing villages would lead to manufacturing cities; and with "the establishment of Manchesters and Birminghams in our country, we shall have Birmingham and Manchester riots, burnings and bloodshed." The *Statesman,* an Adams paper, answered this by pointing to the dockworkers' strike in New York City. This strike was more violent than the Paterson strike and was caused by commerce (the Jacksonian answer to manufacturing). "Thus commerce is a lot more insidious than manufacturing." What both parties failed to point out was that labor relations in all aspects of the economy were becoming increasingly antagonistic and prone to violence. *Evening Post,* July 28, 29, 30, Aug. 1, 5, 14, 23, 1828; *Statesman,* July 30, Aug. 16, 20, 27, 1828.

independence but also a nascent class solidarity. The divisions in society that this incipient class conflict represented also brought greater violence. This trend contributed to the changing character of rioting in the early nineteenth century and helped to reconfirm the belief among the entrepreneurial middle class that rioting was illegitimate.

EIGHT

Middle-Class Culture and Plebeian Mobs

*It is the holy object of Republicanism and of Democracy to reconcile
all men to their condition, and by removing every barrier of birth,
rank, and monopoly, to leave those who suffer nothing to inveigh
against but hard fortune or their own imbecility. . . . There is no*
government *where high handed and illegal violence takes the place of
the slow and sure work of justice and rights are only equal where
they are established, maintained, and if need be, defended according
to the forms of law. If a mob may trample upon a Federalist this year,
next year the Democrat's term may come. If a mob may break into
an abolitionist's dwelling now, they may unhouse a defender of
slavery then.*

New-York Evening Post, 1834

A new value system, based on the sanctity of the individual and his right to make his own choices in politics, economics, and religion, emerged in the early nineteenth century. Equal access to opportunity became the scripture of an ideology that blamed an individual's failure on his own shortcomings. As a growing commercial middle class swore faith in the market economy, private property became sacrosanct and the aggressive entrepreneur a paragon. Rising artisans, shopkeepers, merchants, speculators, investors, and bankers became the agents of this new gospel of hard work and shrewd bargaining. New York's magistrates, too, largely from this same group, made the middle-class morality their own. Although there were limits to the toleration which went with this rise of individualism, city officials now began to see themselves not so much as the guardians of a clearly perceived single-community interest as, instead, referees striving to ensure that all the rights of each individual were secured. Differences were to be settled in the marketplace and at the ballot box through open competition, and not in the street with riots. Violations of an individual's rights, especially by a mob, had to be punished or prevented.

This nineteenth-century middle-class culture contrasted sharply with the eighteenth-century plebeian moral economy. The moral economy held that there must be conformity to maintain a unity of interest; the market economy enforced diversity. The moral economy held that the individual must serve the community; the market economy encouraged individual free rein. In short, the two cultures, middle-class and plebeian, were bound to clash; and given the plebeian penchant for taking grievances into the streets, that clash necessarily involved rioting. In New York City during the opening decades of the nineteenth century, then, violent conflict broke out when rioters, adhering to an ill-defined belief in communal justice embedded in the plebeian culture, confronted a middle class striving to protect individual rights and private property.

What makes this conflict particularly interesting is that, although many New Yorkers rushed into the streets to assert fading ideals of communal unity, it became increasingly difficult to identify any single interest in the community. Divisions and intergroup conflict were rife, and rioting, in turn, became more violent. Adding to this violence was the infusion of new elements into society, like the Irish, who came with their traditions of hostility to authority and to competitive groups. Continually fanning the fires was the rapidly growing market economy, which depersonalized economic relations and exaggerated distances, quantitatively and qualitatively, between levels of society. For city officials, then, each riot became more dangerous to the peace and good order of society. That so many rioters trampled upon the values of the middle class made the opposition of the authorities more adamant.

Riots at Churches and Religious Liberty

The clash between middle-class and plebeian cultures was evident in religious rioting. During the eighteenth century, there was a long Anglo-American history of church-and-king mobs, beginning in England with the Sacheverell riots of 1710 and continuing to the Priestley disturbances of the 1790s. The motivations of the church-and-king rioters, as in other forms of traditional eighteenth-century plebeian crowd activity, were mixed. On one level the rioters acted from a belief in the corporate ideals of community, drawn from the notion that the entire nation had a single interest and a single religion. The rioters thus proclaimed their support not only for the Anglican establishment but also for the monarch as the true head of that church. But the church-and-king rioters were attracted also by the festive atmosphere of the mob, the chance to attack subtly the social order, and the unhampered opportunity to assault an alien group. Although local authorities may have been loath to condone all of the reasons for church-and-king rioting, they often used these disturbances to enforce conformity and to demonstrate public loyalty to the crown. The magistrate and the mob, in other words, frequently worked in concert in the church-and-king riots.[1]

In New York City, even during the colonial period, the situation was a little different because there was no single established church. (Each community in the colony was allowed to choose the denomination—Anglican, Dutch Reformed, or Congregational—that local taxes would support.) Yet the popular spirit of religious intolerance still existed and occasionally

---

1. George Rudé, *The Crowd in History: A Study of Popular Disturbances in France and England, 1730–1848* (New York, 1964), 135–148; R. B. Rose, "The Priestley Riots of 1791," *Past and Present,* No. 18 (Nov. 1960), 68–88; Geoffrey Holmes, "The Sacheverell Riots: The Crowd and the Church in Early Eighteenth-Century London," *Past and Present,* No. 72 (Aug. 1976), 55–85; John Walsh, "Methodism and the Mob in the Eighteenth Century," *Studies in Church History,* VIII, *Popular Belief and Practice,* ed. G. J. Cuming and Derek Baker (Cambridge, 1972), 213–227.

manifested itself in the harassment of Jews and some minority denominations.[2] The Pope Day celebrations were clearly anti-Catholic and were a form of church-and-king mob activity. During the Revolutionary war, British officers broke up services at the John Street Methodist Church. Although royal officials then issued orders to protect the Methodists, the high social rank of the rioters only reinforced the message. Loyalty to the Church of England was loyalty to the king.[3] After the Revolution, religious rioting, though no longer in support of the monarchy, was still a call for uniformity in religion and was partially supported by city officials. The Paddy procession on Saint Patrick's Day during the 1790s, a practice borrowed directly from English church-and-king mobs, is an example of such rioting, because it apparently was tolerated until 1799, when the violence caused unease, and was not outlawed for another four years.[4]

By the early nineteenth century, however, such church-and-king mobs were incompatible with both the new emphasis on religious toleration and the middle-class demand for an orderly society. Particularly frowned upon was the harassment of evangelical workers who had, after all, quickly adopted the hard-work ethos of the rising entrepreneurial middle class. Preaching both industry and temperance, these evangelicals earned the enmity of their traditionalist cousins.[5] Starting in the 1780s and continuing from then on with varying degrees of intensity, Methodist, Baptist, and other evangelical congregations faced a host of indignities, from drunks reeling up and down the church aisle, cursing, and manhandling their womenfolk, to more concerted harassment by larger groups, who rained down on them mud, sticks, and stones as well as nasty epithets (see table

2. See *Weekly Journal*, May 16, 1743; E. B. O'Callaghan, ed., *Documents relative to the Colonial History of the State of New York; Procured in Holland, England, and France*, VI (Albany, N.Y., 1855), 471; Theodore G. Tappert and John W. Doberstein, trans., *The Journals of Henry Melchior Muhlenberg*, I (Philadelphia, 1942), 301.

3. Samuel Seaman, *Annals of New York Methodism: Being a History of the Methodist Episcopal Church in the City of New York, from A.D. 1776 to A.D. 1890* (New York, 1892), 74–76.

4. See chap. 5.

5. For an interesting discussion of evangelical workers, see Sean Wilentz, *Chants Democratic: New York City and the Rise of the American Working Class, 1788–1850* (New York, 1984), 77–87; Bruce Laurie, *Working People of Philadelphia, 1800–1850* (Philadelphia, 1980), 37–52. For a discussion of the rise of evangelicalism and its connection to a democratizing America, see Gordon S. Wood, "Evangelical America and Early Mormonism," *New York History*, LXI (1980), 359–386.

TABLE 7

Mob Harassment of White Churches and Meetings, 1784–1834

Date	Event
1784: Nov. 28	Report that several riots occurred at the door of Methodist meetinghouse.
1807: Apr. 15	Complaints that Methodist services were disrupted by mobs.
Nov.	More complaints about disrupted service.
1808: Sept. 11	Riotous attack on Methodists going to and from church.
1810: Feb. 1	Disorderly crowd harasses religious meeting at house, corner of Hudson and Anthony streets.
1819: ca. May 5	Baptist church on Mulberry Street bothered by mobs on Sundays.
1822: Aug. 1	Riot at Baptist church, corner of Christie and Delancey streets.
Sept. 15	Riot at Baptist church, corner of Christie and Delancey streets.
1823: Jan. 26	Riot at Baptist church between Mott and Elizabeth streets.
1827: Feb. 19	Disturbance at a Christie Street church.
1829: July 16	Religious assembly at Christie Street, between Hester and Walker streets, disrupted.
Nov. 15	Methodist meetinghouse on Twenty-third Street near Third Avenue disturbed.
Dec. 12	Bedford Street Church harassed.
1830: June 7	Meetinghouse for religious services at 245 Spring Street disturbed.
Oct. 3	Stone-throwing disturbances at Mariner's Church on Roosevelt Street.
Dec. 31	Methodist church in Forsyth Street disrupted during evening services.
1831: Jan. 23	Disturbances at Bethel Church.
Feb. 20	Riot at Methodist Church in Allen Street.
Mar. 13	Sullivan Street Methodist Church disturbed.
Sept. 25	Union Society of Christians, 245 Spring Street, disturbed.

Table 7. *continued*
Mob Harassment of White Churches and Meetings, 1784–1834

Date	Event
1833: Jan. 14	Reformed Presbyterian Church in Chambers Street disrupted.
Aug. 19	Church on Second Street harassed.
1834: Feb. 2	Chatham Street Chapel disturbed.

Note: Table excludes the harassment of the religious activities of Amos Broad and Johny Edwards.
Sources: NYCGS; NYCSCPCC; NYCMMPO: newspapers; city directories.

7). The vast majority of these churches were located in working-class neighborhoods and served journeymen and laborers. The deacons and church leaders of the harassed churches tended to be artisans and mechanics living nearby (see table 8).

City officials repeatedly took measures to protect these evangelicals, whose basic attitudes toward work and property they shared. In 1784 Alderman Abraham Lott arrested several of the "bucks begining to beat up a *dust*" at the Methodist service, and in 1807 the Common Council ordered that "on the Application of any Religious Society" a watchman would be stationed "during the hours of such worship" to keep the peace.[6] These efforts found mixed success. The antagonism between evangelicals and traditionalists remained, and when the watchmen attempted to protect a congregation, often the watchmen found themselves confronted by a violent mob bent on rescuing any prisoner that might have been arrested.[7] Many of the riots at evangelical services in the 1820s and 1830s began with the insolence of one or two intruders inside the church, supported by a boisterous crowd outside the church, and then erupted into a larger disturbance when the authorities stepped in to preserve order.

Regardless of the religious orientation of the churches threatened by mobs, the magistrates acted to defend the principle of religious freedom and to demonstrate the reinvigorated desire to maintain public order. The protective umbrella of the law extended even to Irish Catholics and more unconventional revivalists. Thus the Common Council outlawed Paddy

6. *Gazetteer,* Nov. 30, 1784; *MCC,* IV, 407, VI, 446.
7. The distinction between evangelicals and traditionalists is borrowed from Laurie, *Working People,* 37–66.

TABLE 8

Evangelical Complainants against Church Riots, 1807–1833

Year	Name	Occupation	Address
1807	Samuel Stillwell	—	—
	Abraham Russell	—	—
1808	William Mead	—	2 Chatham Square
1810	Charles Gillman	—	—
	Isaiah Lennington	—	—
1822	Renier C. Wortendyke	soda manufacturer	Broome and Sullivan
	Edward Marinar	—	97 Division
	James Pike	—	28 Orchard
1823	Henry Collins	—	364 Broome
1827	James Erving	—	62 Mott
1829	John Owen	gratemaker	534 Pearl
	John Ball	—	—
	Edward Arrowsmith	sailmaker	39 Burling Slip
	William Hall	—	—
	Peter Burt	—	—
	John Allen, Jr.	—	34 Allen
	Griffith Griffiths	shipwright	133 Madison
	Benjam Disbrow	—	Third Ave.
	James Cooper	—	Third Ave.
	David Brown	—	—
1830	John Wilcox	combmaker	86 Bowery
	John Fulkerson	turner	14 Chestnut
	James Lloyd	painter	83 Hester
1831	Renier C. Wortendyke	soda manufacturer	157 Bleecker
	Guy C. Woods	tobacconist	118 Bowery
	John Stewart	painter	466 Broadway
	John Kyster	carpenter	Amos
	James Latourette	merchant	449 Greenwich
1833	Robert Patterson	machinist	193½ Hudson
	William Agnew	tobacconist	264 Front

Note: Excludes complainants in cases involving Johny Edwards, Amos Broad, and black congregations.

Sources: NYCGS; NYCSCPCC; NYCMMPO; *MCC;* newspapers; city directories.

PLATE 13. John Street Methodist Episcopal Church.
Watercolor by Joseph B. Smith. Courtesy of the Museum of the City of New York.

effigy processions in 1803, and authorities protected Saint Peter's Catholic Church on Christmas Eve in 1806.[8] So, too, city officials strove to defend the rights of extremist evangelicals in the early nineteenth century. In fact, it is in the way the magistrates dealt with the latter group that their attachment to the middle-class value of toleration and their rejection of church-and-king rioting can best be seen. For although city authorities at first flirted with accepting some religious rioting against these radical evangelicals and, indeed, curtailed the activities of a few of them, ultimately the officials did not act, like their eighteenth-century English counterparts, in the same spirit as the mob. Instead, and they took great pains to explain this position, they worked to support the growing consensus for religious toleration and moved against both evangelicals and the mob only when they believed there was no other way of protecting the public peace and preventing violence.

One religious enthusiast who presented a problem for New York officials was Johny Edwards, a Welsh scale-beam maker who arrived in New York in 1801. An artisan, Edwards's affluence and occupation placed him a notch below the new middle class, with whom he shared values of temperance and hard work. But he was also a strange character who sought religious controversy. Before he arrived in America, Edwards was suc-

8. See chap. 5.

PLATE 14. Residence of Johny Edwards.
Illustration from D. T. Valentine, Manual of the Corporation of the City of New York *(New York, 1864). Courtesy of Thomas Rosenblum.*

cessively an Anglican, a Methodist, a Baptist, and a Quaker. With each denominational shift Edwards became more radical. By the time he arrived in New York, Edwards provoked fellow religious enthusiasts as well as those not inspired by evangelicalism. For a while he attended the Quaker meetings. But his rantings were too much even for that tolerant sect, and, as Edwards recounted, they were "not willing to hear the truth as it is in Jesus, nor receive it in the love of it," and therefore "they hauled me out of their fine new meeting-house, and bruised me very much by throwing me down the high steps." Edwards refused to leave the Quaker property, claiming that it belonged to the Lord, until one of the Quakers shook him "backwards and forwards" and then shoved him "out of the Meeting-house yard with great violence."[9]

If Edwards could so antagonize pacifist Quakers, he could provoke less tolerant New Yorkers even more. In 1809, mobs assaulted "The Church of Christ" meeting at Edwards's home on Green Street at least twice. One evening in March an angry crowd threw stones and burning "Balls made

9. John Edwards, *Account of the Trial of John Edwards of the City of New-York, Who Was Prosecuted for "Collecting or Promoting an Assembly of Persons, under the Pretence of Public Worship in a Public Street, on Sunday, June 16, 1822," with a Short Account of His Life, an Address to the Mayor and Corporation, and Advice to the Police Magistrates &c.* (New York, 1822), 5–7; David Bruce, "Autobiography of David Bruce; or, Then and Now," 6–7, 15–16, MS, NYHS.

of tow and turpentine" and threatened to set the house ablaze. In September, during a religious service, "his gates were broken open and his yard entered by a number of rude young men who shouted through the windows and made noise and sport." Although Johny Edwards may have aspired to the new middle class and preached the value of temperance and frugality, the eccentricity of his brand of religious fervor made it difficult for the magistrates to take his "Church of Christ" seriously, and in both mob actions the officials abandoned the prosecution of the rioters before they were brought to trial.[10]

The next spring the irrepressible Edwards joined evangelist Dorothy Ripley and took to the streets, once again testing the religious tolerance of New Yorkers. The two evangelists sponsored an outdoor revival, which was greeted with further derision and disorder. Rather than arrest those harassing Edwards and Ripley, however, the authorities tried to prevent Edwards and Ripley from carrying out their evangelical crusade in the streets. On July 2, 1810, the Common Council passed "A law to prevent disorderly assemblies of persons in the City of New York." This ordinance, like the judicial unwillingness to prosecute the anti-Edwards rioters the year before, might be interpreted as support for the mob. But city officials knew they were treading a thin line and explicitly renewed their commitment to "liberty of conscience," although this was "not [to] be construed as an excuse of licentiousness or justify practices inconsistent with peace and good order." Given a choice between order and religious freedom, the officials, in this instance, gave priority to order. After all, the magistrates argued, people "of all descriptions and characters" attended the outdoor meetings, and "such practices" degrade "all religious worship."[11]

The Common Council did not act in concert with the mob by passing this ordinance. No unwritten agreement existed between the authorities and the heckling and tumultuous crowds to censure the evangelicals. The aim was to eliminate an opportunity for plebeian demonstrations by removing the cause for disorder. When Dorothy Ripley defied the law on May 1, 1810, city officials moved to stop her. After she refused to comply with his entreaties, the mayor ordered city marshals to drag Dorothy Ripley from her soapbox pulpit. This task the officers managed despite a note of comic opera. The female evangelist, as the marshals hauled her off,

10. *John Edwards v. Henry Dedrick,* Apr. 1, 1809, box 7432 (1808–1810), NYCSCPCC; *Edwards v. James Robinson,* Sept. 19, 1809, box 7432 (1808–1810), NYCSCPCC.

11. *MCC,* VI, 268–269.

turned her eyes toward heaven and cried, "Lord have mercy upon them; Lord have mercy upon them for Christ's sake." This scene, no doubt, entertained the assembled crowd and might have suggested a complicity of interest between magistrates and those who ridiculed Ripley's religious message. But it also effectively ended both the disorder and the revival.[12]

To remove any doubts over the official position on religious toleration and to show support for other, less radical religious groups, the Common Council revised the law a month later to allow a clergyman of any regular church to preach publicly after obtaining the proper permission from the mayor or an alderman. The amendment also stipulated that Baptists could still practice their open air "rites of baptism" within the city.[13] This action cleared the way for evangelicals to continue to reach out to the poor and the working class with their doctrines of hard work and sobriety.

Even the eccentric ministrations of Johny Edwards were tolerated once the uproar over the 1810 revival ended. Edwards found it difficult to keep quiet, and for years he periodically appeared on street corners and admonished amused onlookers against vice, sin, worldly possessions, and "all manner of wickedness." Only once, in 1822 when he extemporaneously lectured a crowd on temperance (an important topic to the middle class), did officials arrest him under the provisions of the 1810 law. But then it was impossible to convict Edwards. The jury acquitted him in the belief that no great disturbance had accompanied his sermon.[14] In short, the real danger eccentric evangelicals posed was not religious. Rather, it was their habit of provoking unruly mobs that demanded official attention.

The threat to urban tranquillity from such evangelicals and the difficulties they posed for the middle-class magistrates who clung to their belief in religious freedom is even more evident in the series of disturbances surrounding the activities of the self-appointed "minister and missionary to the world," Amos Broad. Again city officials confronted a dilemma: should they limit the religious freedom of a fringe evangelical minority to preserve the public peace?

12. Edwards, *Trial of John Edwards,* 48–49, 52; Bruce, "Autobiography," 15–16.

13. *MCC,* VI, 273, 286, 307, 579, 620.

14. Edwards, *Trial of John Edwards,* 23–44. In his reminiscences of early New York, Thomas F. De Voe referred to "the well-known and eccentric Johnny Edwards" (*The Market Book, Containing a Historical Account of the Public Markets in the Cities of New York, Boston, Philadelphia, and Brooklyn . . .* , I [New York, 1862], 480).

Amos Broad, like Edwards, was a well-to-do artisan. He arrived in New York City from Albany around 1800 and set up an upholstery shop on Maiden Lane. Unlike Edwards, Broad had a nasty streak and was probably the most disliked man in the entire city. Aggressive, contentious, and vindictive, Broad antagonized his neighbors and abused his servants. He frequently appeared in court in both civil and criminal cases. In 1809 the Manumission Society charged him with excessive cruelty to his two slaves. At trial, a jury convicted Broad, even though he had liberated both the slaves. The judge sentenced him to sixty days in jail and fined him a princely five hundred dollars for each offense. Broad, however, soon experienced a religious conversion.[15] After his release from jail, Broad began to attend informal religious services in the upper part of a house on the corner of Anthony and Hudson streets.[16]

Dissatisfied with this makeshift arrangement, Amos Broad soon bought himself a church on Rose Street and set up shop, much to the chagrin of the neighborhood, as a self-proclaimed minister. Although the exact tenets of Broad's doctrine are unclear, he apparently saw himself as a messiah creating a new, democratic church to unite all Protestants. He thereby planned to prevent the decline of religion and hoped to strengthen the new nation.[17]

Whatever else Broad's confused thoughts were, they certainly provoked much opposition. Repeatedly, listeners, whether lowly apprentices or high city officials, became outraged at his sermons.[18] Broad's congregation was often noisy and disorderly; when Broad expounded upon the Scriptures, he encouraged his listeners to give "loud plaudits of huzzaing, clapping of hands and stamping of feet." The only check on the exuberance of these demonstrations was Broad's young son, who patrolled the church with a

15. [Henry C. Southwick], *The Trial of Amos Broad and His Wife, on Three Several Indictments for Assaulting and Beating Betty, a Slave, and Her Little Female Child Sarah, Aged Three Years, Had at the Court of the Special Sessions of the Peace, Held in and for the City and County of New York, at the City-Hall, of the Said City, on Tuesday the Twenty-eighth Day of February, 1809* (New York, 1809).

16. This religious group was harassed by mobs both before and after Broad left them. *People v. Nicholas Lozici*, Feb. 10, 1810, NYCGS; *Charles Gilman et al. v. Cornelius Prince*, Feb. 2, 1810, box 7432 (1808–1810), NYCSCPCC.

17. Amos Broad, *A Discourse, Delivered on the Thirteenth September, 1814, to a Detachment of the United States Army, (Stationed at Brooklyn, Long Island) under the Command of Colonel Berrian* (New York, 1814).

18. *People v. Charles Bunce et al.*, Nov. 9, 1812, box 7433 (1811–1814), NYCSCPCC.

long pole to prod any overenthusiastic member of the congregation. At the end of some services, which often were held three times a week, Broad used the prodding pole to chase the congregation into the street.[19]

Great crowds also gathered outside the church and "reechoed" the noise from the congregation. The people in the street "fired squibs and black-guarded cursed," shouting obscenities like "Amos frig your fist." They often banged at the door and shutters and threw mud, sticks, stones, and occasionally excrement at Broad and his followers.[20]

At first the festivities outside Broad's church seemed harmless enough and, except for the occasional assaults on Broad and his few disciples, followed the limited patterns of plebeian crowd behavior established in the eighteenth century. In 1809 and 1810 the anti-Broad rioters came from a wide spectrum of society, ranging from Broad's abused ex-slave Betty, apprentices, and laborers to skilled mechanics and young gentlemen like Peter Van Zandt, Jr. The earliest disrupters of Broad's religious practices included even a city marshal.

By 1816 and 1817 the situation on Rose Street became more serious as the crowds grew larger and larger, sometimes numbering more than one thousand persons. The upper and middle levels of society retreated from disturbances that no longer appeared so innocent. The majority of the rioters now were dependents, apprentices, and journeymen recruited from all over the city (see table 9). In early February 1817, a mob gutted Broad's church when his intoxicated sexton left the door unlocked after an afternoon service. Some boys discovered this oversight, entered the church, and started the disturbance. The fifty to one hundred rioters in the church, with several hundred looking on, scattered the hymn books and broke several partitions and the organ. One black boy, in an obvious

19. *Gazette,* May 16, 1810.

20. *Ibid.* In NYCGS: *People* v. *John M. Bloodgood,* Apr. 13, 1810; *People* v. *Peter Van Zandt, Jr., et al.,* Apr. 13, 1810; *People* v. *Henry Diedrick,* June 15, 1810; *People* v. *Betty* [Broad's old slave], Oct. 15, 1810; *People* v. *Samuel E. Thompson,* Nov. 12, 1812; *People* v. *Isaac Stevens,* Dec. 18, 1812. In NYCSCPCC, box 7432 (1808–1810): *George Risby et al.* v. *Richard Willson et al.,* May 21, 1810; *John W. Brindsmade* v. *Miln Parker,* Feb. 10, 1810; *Walter Butler* v. *Robt. Stakes et al.,* Feb. 13, 1810; *Amos Broad* v. *Henry Dedrick,* Apr. 4, 1810. In NYCSCPCC, box 7433 (1811–1814): *People* v. *Charles Bunce et al.,* Nov. 9, 1812. In NYCSCPCC, box 7434 (1815–1817): *Amos Broad* v. *John W. Jarvis,* ca. Dec. 1815: *Wm. Slater* v. *Jacob Johnson alias Shourt,* Jan. 4, 1817; *A. Broad et al.* v. *Ch. Rogers et al.,* Mar. 24, 1817; *Luke Purdy et al.* v. *S. Romane et al.,* Nov. 10, 1817. *MCC,* VI, 299, 309, VII, 215, 288, 311, VIII, 173.

reversal of roles typical of eighteenth-century rioting, mounted the pulpit and pretended to preach. This action, in the words of one observer, "completed a scene of mockery and derision to the vile and worthless—of amazement and horror to those who reverence things divine."[21]

Such actions, like the outdoor revival of 1810, seemed derogatory of all religion. And religion was very serious business to the middle class. Many in the city, especially the magistrates, tired of the ceaseless disorder accompanying Amos Broad's ministrations. A month after the February 1817 riot, the *Gazette* reported another incident and asked: "Why are these things suffered to be? Is there no law to reach the case?—if not, there must be a law to reach the fanatic, who is the occasion of these riots." The article reminded readers that these disturbances had been going on for a long time. "It has not happened once or twice, but it has continued for several years; and it is high time that either the pretended preacher receive his quietus, or his *congregation* be made to keep the peace."[22]

It was not until November 1817, when the court dockets became overcrowded with cases of riot initiated by complaints from Broad, that Mayor Jacob Radcliff ordered a grand jury investigation of the Rose Street disturbances. Mayor Radcliff explained his reluctance to take preventive measures against Broad by invoking the doctrine of religious liberty. Radcliff, who disliked Broad, carefully addressed this issue in his charge to the grand jury. They were to see whether Broad "so conducted himself . . . as to be the cause of the riots." If Broad was responsible for the disturbances, "he ought to be amenable to the law, and liable to a public prosecution." But the investigation could not "be considered as infringing the rights of conscience, or the religious privileges secured to every citizen by the constitution." Repeating the sentiments of the law of July 2, 1810, Radcliff asserted that freedom of religion "cannot, under the pretence of religious worship, justify acts of licentiousness or practices inconsistent with the public peace." If Broad was not responsible for the disorder, then "he ought to be protected, and the authority of the law should be exerted in his favour." In other words, the grand jury was to examine only Broad's role in encouraging riot and disorder, and not his religion.[23]

21. *People* v. *John Scott et al., New-York City-Hall Recorder,* II (1817), 1–4; *People* v. *John Scott et al.,* Feb. 12, 1817, NYC, Mayor's Court Minutes, 1816–1817, MS, NYHS.

22. *Gazette,* Mar. 25, 1817.

23. *People* v. *Amos Broad, NYCHR,* III (1818), 7–8.

TABLE 9

Rioters Harassing Amos Broad's Religious Activities, 1809–1817

Year, Name	Address	Probable Status
1809		
Nicholas Lozici	—	marshal
Peter McBoyen	Maiden Lane	apprentice
1810		
John M. Bloodgood	52 Frankfort	currier, dependent
August Brocco	—	—
Henry Dedrick	Frankfort	sailor
James Lorton	382 Pearl	apprentice carver
Peter Parcells	—	laborer
Millen Parker	7 John	coachmaker
State Rockwell	—	—
Robert Stakes	—	—
Peter Van Zandt, Jr.	—	gentleman
Richard Willson	—	—
Betty ———	—	ex-slave[a]
1812		
Charles Bunce	Pearl	apprentice
Henry Field	Chatham	apprentice shoemaker
Robert Mead	Peck Slip	—
Isaac Stevens	—	—
Samuel Thompson	—	—
Cornelius Van Winkle	Pearl	—
George Webster	24 Gardiner	—
1815		
John W. Jarvis	—	—
1816		
Jacob Shourt	387 Water	dependent
1817		
Oliver Bancroft	69 Pine	apprentice or journeyman printer
James Biggs	135 Lombardy	journeyman ship carpenter
Samuel Burrows	—	—
Charles Cromwell	5 James	apprentice baker
Peter Darling	—	—

Table 9. *continued*
Rioters Harassing Amos Broad's Religious Activities, 1809–1817

Year, Name	Address	Probable Status
John Davis	—	—
Edward Frazier	86 Front	apprentice printer
Ritter Hadley	209 Broadway	apprentice clerk
James Harson	Brown	apprentice shoemaker
Harmon Johnson	30 Roosevelt	journeyman shoemaker
Berney Larry	11 Warren	—
Jacob Smith Mills	89 Gold	journeyman carpenter
James Owens	Third	master butcher
———— Peck	135 Lombardy	dependent
Yewitt Prince	17 Rose	apprentice or journeyman printer
Charles Rogers	14 Warren	apprentice
Michael Romene	142 Church	dependent
John Scott	17 Rose	apprentice or journeyman printer
Jacob Shourt	387 Water	dependent
James Tailor	95 Mulberry	carver, dependent
James Thompson	Oliver	apprentice blockmaker
Samuel Wynant	89 Gold	journeyman carpenter

Note: Dependent status inferred when security was offered by a person with the same last name. Apprentice status, in most cases, inferred when security offered by person at same address (most defendants were boys or young men).

[a]Broad's ex-slave.

Sources: NYCGS; NYCSCPCC; NYCMMPO; newspapers; city directories.

Despite the careful language of Radcliff's charge, the net effect of the grand jury investigation, like the anti-Edwards and anti-Ripley actions of 1810, was to close down Amos Broad's church. The evidence gathered by the grand jury led to his arraignment on four counts of being a public nuisance and keeping a "certain disorderly and ill-governed house." Amos Broad, however, never made it to trial. He was affluent enough to hire two very able lawyers, who managed to delay the trial from December to January despite the protest of the prosecutor. In the interim, Broad's counsel convinced him of the hopelessness of his case. To mollify the authorities,

Broad swore out an affidavit that he would no longer preach and promised to sell his Rose Street church as soon as he could get a reasonable price for it. Satisfied with this compromise, the court, not wanting to set a precedent for the persecution of religious practices, dropped the case.[24]

The most striking thing about the Amos Broad disturbances was their continuance for so long. Neither the city officials nor the public they served liked Broad. In the eighteenth century, if both magistrates and mob had agreed, such an obnoxious affront to the community quickly would have been stopped. The magistrates would have prosecuted the offender much sooner, and, if they failed, there would have been no civil protection from the mob. In the early nineteenth century, however, even though the city authorities may have hoped at first that the mob might drive Broad away, they stood committed to the principles of religious freedom. The magistrates refused, until November 1817, to remove the prime cause of the Rose Street mobs. Instead, they invested time, effort, and money in dispatching constables, marshals, and the watch to restrain the rioters. Although magistrates like Mayor Jacob Radcliff detested Broad, and told him so, they did act to protect him. The closing of the Rose Street church, then, should not be viewed as an act by the magistrates in support of prolonged rioting. Rather, it should be seen as a desperate attempt, after seven years of struggle, to restore order to Rose Street without unduly threatening religious liberty.

Public Lands and Trade Agreements

Cultural conflict between plebeian mores and the middle-class sanctity of private property came to trigger riots and threaten public order. One area of this conflict concerned the use of land in the open area on the northern edge of the city in the 1820s and 1830s; another was the resentment of violators of a trade agreement among retailers in November 1827. The resulting disturbances demonstrated not only increasing official condemnation of popular disorder but also the intensifying violence accompanying changes in rioting.

The origins of the first area of conflict lay in the emerging urban landscape of the early nineteenth century. Until 1800 the urban area of New York City was confined to the southern tip of Manhattan Island. Gradually in the first decades of the new century, the built-up area of the city

24. *Ibid.,* 7–9.

moved inexorably northward as new streets extended past present-day City Hall (opened in 1811), along the Bowery, and up Broadway to the rim of Greenwich Village. In the 1820s, 1830s, and 1840s there was an explosion of settlement extending the city to present-day midtown. Previously this area had been more or less free for anyone's use. Many a New Yorker, rich and poor, had fished in ponds and hunted in meadows and forests on this open land. Now real estate values began to increase, and the owners of the land, who were often affluent and established families, started to close it off, either for development or for privacy on large estates. A new urban environment thus appeared. Just as many of the city's richest citizens began to covet property to the north of the city proper, so too did many of the city's poorest begin to occupy nearby land because of its relative cheapness.[25] The fences and hedges erected around the uptown estates, aimed at keeping the poorer neighbors at arm's length, aroused resentment—a resentment often expressed in vandalism and collective violence.

When poorer New Yorkers uprooted hedges and tore down fences, they acted out of a belief that the land should be open to all. Their motivation was similar to that of the eighteenth-century antienclosure rioters in England who objected to the engrossing of the commons for private use.[26] In May 1821, for example, twenty men on Third Avenue, including at least two butchers (who may have previously used the land to graze animals before slaughter), crossed over Stuyvesant ground to Second Avenue. They methodically "fell to work and broke down the Post and rail fence from a dozen to twenty pannels." Several of these vandals declared "that they intended to break down all the fence they could." Afterwards, they went along First Avenue tearing down more fences and destroying a stable belonging to the Stuyvesant family.[27]

Although New York land rioters, like their English counterparts, vented latent resentment against the wealthy in their attacks on fences, hedges, and other property, much of their collective violence fits long-established pat-

25. For a discussion of this development, see Elizabeth Strother Blackmar, "Housing and Property Relations in New York City, 1785–1850" (Ph.D. diss., Harvard University, 1981).

26. E. P. Thompson, *Whigs and Hunters: The Origin of the Black Act* (New York, 1975), 42–46, 133–134, 143, 171, 179.

27. *George Smull* v. *Adam Fisher et al.,* May 14, 1821, box 7436 (1820–1821), NYCSCPCC. This is probably the same George Smull who himself was charged with rioting in the next example cited. He was the son of Ladwich Smull, gardener, and his later actions may also represent some grudge.

terns of popular behavior. The Stuyvesants were popular targets.[28] Late
one Saturday night in August 1826, several men, including George Smull
(whose father worked for the Stuyvesants), ripped off the garden gate of
Nicholas W. Stuyvesant's on First Avenue, broke a tree on the property,
and destroyed a wide section of fences. In February 1828 Nicholas W.
Stuyvesant complained that such fence breaking happened frequently and
that stones were also thrown at his house, shattering its windows.[29] But as
annoying as these acts of vandalism were to the Stuyvesants and to other
large property owners along the city's outskirts, they were limited acts of
destruction or defacement. No persons were assaulted, and no extensive
damage was done to property.

There were times, however, when the rioting became more extensive.
Then city officials stepped in and revealed their commitment to the sanctity of private property in a competitive, individualistic social order. On
Sunday, April 6, 1828, the violence in an anti-Stuyvesant riot increased
when two hundred to five hundred people, many of whom were apparently Irish, joined in a "most outrageous and disgraceful" disturbance.
Moving beyond simple fence breaking, the mob attacked two houses: one
had been the residence of Peter G. Stuyvesant, and the other had just been
sold by Stuyvesant to Denis Guinan. The rioters demolished an entire
wall of Guinan's house, and the shower of stones severely wounded his
wife. Even before the tumult began, city magistrates ordered police to the
scene to put down any potential riot. The mob furiously resisted these
peace officers, and in "their endeavors to quell the mob" the police "were
all more or less injured." One of the marshals "received at least thirty
blows from stones, most of them hitting him on the back," and another
officer was at one time beaten down by the mob, "and had it not been for
speedy relief, he would probably have been killed." Undaunted by the resistance, the police arrested several so-called ringleaders, most of whom
were later convicted of riot.[30]

28. For Stuyvesant legal problems in land development, see Hendrik Hartog,
*Public Property and Private Power: The Corporation of the City of New York in
American Law, 1730–1870* (Chapel Hill, N.C., 1983), 174–175. See also the
case Hartog cites: *Underwood* v. *Stuyvesant*, 19 Johns (N.Y.) 180–187 (1821).

29. *Charles H. North* v. *Roosevelt Van Kranst and George Smull*, Aug. 21, 1826,
box 7439 (1826–1827), NYCSCPCC; *People* v. *Jeremiah Hopper et al.*, Mar. 11,
1828, NYCGS.

30. *People* v. *Nathaniel Cromer et al.*, Apr. 11, 1828, NYCGS; *Statesman*, Apr.
11, 1828; *Evening Post*, Apr. 8, 1828; *Gazette*, Apr. 8, May 10, 14, 1828; *MCC*,
XVII, 200.

Although there is no record of any grand pronouncements condemning these rioters, the willingness of the officials to resort to force suggests that they had little tolerance for this tumultuous behavior. The strident conflict which erupted on April 6, 1828, also suggests that the people in the street still had faith in crowd action as a means of defending perceived community interests. The result of such battles between the police and the people was an increased fear on the part of the magistrates of any gathering and a growing hostility among those in the street toward agents of law enforcement. The explosive clash between a middle class desiring to protect property and a plebeian culture holding to a vague sense of communal justice is repeated in several incidents in the late 1820s and early 1830s.

In early November 1827 a series of riots against two dry goods stores for violating an agreement among retailers again revealed how New Yorkers in the street upheld communal values and how the magistrates and middle class insisted on the sanctity of private property. The clothing-storekeepers had decided to save lighting expenses in the shortening days of winter by closing their shops at five o'clock in the evening. Two retailers on Chatham Square, however, reneged on that agreement and kept their stores open after the appointed hour. In response the other retailers, joined by the store clerks who feared the loss of their newly gained free evenings, demonstrated in the hope of closing the open stores. Like the anti-Stuyvesant riot, here a mob was attempting to dictate how private property should be used. Such coercion ran counter to middle-class market values. As the *American* put it, "Such proceedings" forcing "an individual into an agreement, which ought to be voluntary, are inconsistent with social order and should be severely punished."[31]

Many common New Yorkers disagreed; protesting against the acquisitive values of an overly commercial middle class, thousands from all over the city eagerly joined the crowd. Angered by the mercenary action of the noncomplying retailers, the people in the street quickly began to riot.

31. Discussion of riots against dry goods stores based on these sources. In NYCGS: *People* v. *John Youngerson et al.*, Nov. 9, 1827; *People* v. *John Phalen et al.*, Nov. 9, 1827. In NYCSCPCC, box 7440 (1827–1828): *John G. Horton et al.* v. *Thomas B. Odell et al.*, Nov. 2, 1827; *John Winton* v. *Benjamin C. Bannons et al.*, Nov. 3, 1827; *Azel Conklin* v. *Henry Smith et al.*, Nov. 3, 1827; *Benjamin Fuller* v. *Bailey Hall*, Nov. 3, 1827; *Andrew Van Norton* v. *William Plumb et al.*, Nov. 7, 1827. *American*, Nov. 3, 6, 1827; *Evening Post*, Nov. 6, 1827; *Gazette*, Nov. 5–7, 1827. Paul O. Weinbaum, *Mobs and Demagogues: The New York Response to Collective Violence in the Early Nineteenth Century* (Ann Arbor, Mich., 1979), 53, 55 n.

Chanting "*Shut him up, Shut him up, Shut him up,*" the mob threw eggs, rocks, and other materials that demolished the windows of the offending stores; some rioters, in the spirit of eighteenth-century crowds, even threatened to pull the buildings down.

Night after night the watch and marshals, often led by the mayor, rushed to the scene to restrain the clerks, retailers, shopkeepers, artisans, journeymen, laborers, and apprentices in the street. The police opposition raised the level of violence. When the watch attempted to make an arrest, the mob immediately went to the rescue. Pitched battles were fought over any prisoner taken by the watch, and several rioters managed to escape. Officials arrested dozens of others and on one night dispatched two hundred watchmen to Chatham Square to restore order. After a week the disturbances finally subsided.

Dogs and Hogs in the Street

Although the middle class ordinarily defended individual rights and private property, in their efforts to clear the decks for commercial development these might be cast aside. Such development was usually at the expense of the rights and property of the lower classes. One middle-class reform which curtailed the freedom of choice and threatened long-established plebeian practices was the attempt by municipal authorities to control the unleashed dogs and unpenned hogs that cluttered the city streets. Rioting, which became increasingly violent, erupted when lower-class New Yorkers opposed the licensing and limitation of these animals in the city.

The contrast between middle-class attitudes toward dogs and pigs in the city (based on their ideas of progress, decorum, and order) and the plebeian view could not have been more stark. As the urban community expanded in the first three decades of the nineteenth century, the city magistrates came to see these animals as nuisances. Reformers portrayed dogs as the carriers of disease, especially rabies, and they insisted that hogs, which were once considered efficient street cleaners, disrupted traffic, destroyed pavement, and occasionally attacked helpless children.[32] The market-oriented middle class viewed the free-roaming hogs and dogs as a sym-

32. *MCC,* III, 9, V, 199, 456, VI, 601, VII, 553, 785, VIII, 5, 84, 595, IX, 668, XIV, 674; Sidney I. Pomerantz, *New York, An American City, 1783–1803: A Study of Urban Life,* 2d ed. (Port Washington, N.Y., 1965), 270–271.

bol of an age gone by. The urban presence of these animals stood in the way of progress, hindering growth and commercial development. Yet both types of animals were important to the lower classes. New Yorkers valued dogs mostly as pets, but the hogs supplied crucial protein and income for the city's poor. As long as these animals were not confined to a yard or a pen, their upkeep was inexpensive; both dogs and hogs scavenged for food and fended for themselves, feasting upon the garbage and scraps in the streets and alleys. Any curtailing of the freedom of these animals increased the cost of their upkeep and challenged the right of the poor to own them.[33]

When the people in the street collectively demonstrated their displeasure over these new animal regulations, the authorities at first showed some flexibility. But the basic conflict over what was good for the community remained. As succeeding riots became more violent and as city officials increasingly saw the need to enforce the regulations, toleration of mob action decreased. The result was to limit further the opportunities for plebeian mob behavior.

During the first decade of the nineteenth century the Common Council passed several ineffectual laws to prevent dogs from running at large. In May 1811, however, it issued a comprehensive ordinance which created a special office, the Register and Collector of Dogs, to ensure enforcement. The dog law of 1811 had three main provisions: dogs were not allowed to run loose, every dog owner had to pay a three-dollar tax on each dog he owned, and the dog had to wear a collar with a tag giving the owner's name and address. All unleashed and untagged dogs were to be taken and exterminated. To encourage vigorous enforcement, the city government awarded Register and Collector of Dogs Abner Curtis fifty cents for every dog killed. The law created a real hardship for the poor. Not only would a family's budget be burdened with the cost of the dog's food, but the three-dollar tax was itself extremely oppressive. A common laborer, making one dollar a day, needed three days to earn enough money to pay the tax.[34]

33. For popular attachment to dogs, see *American Citizen,* July 13, 1810. For the importance of hogs to the preindustrial urban poor, see *Evening Post,* Oct. 10, 1816, July 17, 1830; *People* v. *Christian Harriet, New-York Judicial Repository,* I (1819), 264, 266; Alan Dawley, *Class and Community: The Industrial Revolution in Lynn* (Cambridge, Mass., 1976), 52–53; and Hartog, *Public Property,* 139–142.

34. The state passed an ineffective dog tax in 1785 (Pomerantz, *New York,* 270). For the Common Council's efforts at writing a dog law, see *MCC,* III, 93, 214, 406, 477, 483, 732, IV, 7, V, 191, 210, 519, VI, 236, 245, 258, 259, 295, 296,

PLATE 15. Dog Killer and Cart.
*Painting of Water Street between Roosevelt and Dover streets by William Chappell,
1813. Courtesy of the Museum of the City of New York.*

It was little wonder, then, that when the law went into effect in June
1811, some New Yorkers forcibly resisted it. Journeyman tradesmen, apprentices, sailors, and others mobilized in defense of established local customs and attacked the dogcatchers hired by Curtis. Like eighteenth-
century traditional mobs, the rioters limited their violence. On June 6,
1811, for instance, a crowd of nearly one hundred persons followed Gar-
ret C. Van Horne and his dogcart. When he finally stopped, the mob
gathered around him, jostled him slightly, but did no serious harm other
than offering him insults. They freed the dogs he had collected. On the
next day rioters confronted two other dogcatchers. The pattern was much
the same. The two dogcatchers had brought their captive dogs to the old
potter's field to be liquidated. The appearance of these helpless dogs about
to be killed struck a sympathetic chord in the breasts of two nearby blacksmiths. They began to abuse the dogcatchers, and a crowd gathered. A
rioter called one dogcatcher—Thomas Carlock—a "Damned Murdering

311, 573, 596, 603–605, 625, 707, 713, VII, 155, 164, 496, 546, 735, VIII, 28,
270, IX, 712, XI, 103, 104, XV, 217. Curtis was also to pocket 20% of the three-
dollar tax. It was apparently easier to kill the dogs than to collect the tax, even
though Curtis got ten cents more per dog if the tax was collected. Twice as many
dogs were killed as were registered and taxed (*MCC,* VI, 603–605, 719–720).

Bugger" and threatened to throw him into the ditch alongside the dead dogs. Carlock's response was legalistic: he showed his warrant from Abner Curtis. This only infuriated the crowd, who "damned Curtis, the Law, and those who made the Law." The rioters then broke the dogcart and released fifty-three captive dogs.[35]

Neither side in this contest won or lost. More than two thousand dogs were taken and killed. But after a massive roundup of dogs in the summer of 1811, the magistrates no doubt believed that there was no need to antagonize the public further and dismissed the cases against all of the rioters arrested in the dogcart mobs. Moreover, although Abner Curtis remained dog register until 1818, he never again attempted to collect so many dogs in such a short period of time. This outcome suggests that at this point the magistrates were willing to compromise with the mob. Dogs roamed the streets for years to come, the tax was seldom paid, but the law remained on the books.[36] With the appointment of a new dog register in 1818, there was some renewed resistance to the dog law, but the mobs that harassed the dogcatchers in 1818 were much smaller, and the opposition to the dog law was not as widespread and sustained. The magistrates saw no reason to react too harshly, since New Yorkers had come to accept the occasional dogcatcher, who was now allowed to go about his business unmolested.[37]

The dogcart mobs of 1811 and 1818 behaved relatively peacefully, and the magistrates approached their activities after the initial summer of enforcement with conciliation. Despite the plebeian opposition to the law, the issue was marked by compromise between the elite and the mob reminiscent of traditional eighteenth-century social relations. In contrast, there were several hogcart riots in the 1820s and 1830s which were more violent and evoked more determination from the civil authorities to withstand any and all mob activity.

Ordinances aimed at controlling the nuisance of hogs running at large in the city had been passed even in the seventeenth century under the

35. *People* v. *Francis Passman et al.,* June 11, 1811, NYCGS; *People* v. *John Gillespie et al.,* June 11, 1811, NYCGS.

36. *MCC,* VI, 718–720. For the occasional enforcement of the dog law, see *MCC,* VII, 1–2, 256, 257, 261, 262, 644, VIII, 284, 299, 300, 354, 380, 381, 400.

37. *Ibid.,* VIII, 270, IX, 703, 706; *People* v. *Charles Williams,* Sept. 16, 1818, NYCGS; *B[enjamin] Watson* v. *George Lynch,* Sept. 2, 1818, box 7435 (1818–1819), NYCSCPCC; *Stephen McCormick* v. *Michael Sherlock et al.,* June 29, 1819, box 7435 (1818–1819), NYCSCPCC.

Dutch, but they were largely ignored.[38] But in the early nineteenth century hogs became a major urban problem. After 1810 the local newspapers frequently repeated complaints about unpenned hogs. In 1821 the Common Council resolved to enforce the existing law against hogs in the streets. By that time swine were found largely in the poorer districts and the near-rural upper wards of the city. In these areas the poor might raise a few pigs as a margin against poverty. Moreover, along the Bowery, known for its slaughterhouses, there were many roaming pigs owned by butchers.[39]

At first the hogcart mobs, like the early dogcart riots, appeared harmless enough and were not taken seriously. The *Evening Post* in August 1821 humorously reported that a hogcart met with "all the opposition of sticks and hot water, and indeed the female blacks were very ferocious."[40] In 1822 the city government exempted some of the outer wards from the hog law. But when the Common Council repealed that exemption for the Eighth Ward in 1825, the action of the hogcart mobs became more menacing and the authorities' reactions more harsh.[41] On April 5, 1825, a "crowd of men, women and boys of all sizes and colours" in the Eighth Ward rioted, beating the black driver of the cart and assaulting the marshals assigned to protect him. A rioter threw a four-pound weight that struck Marshal Abner Curtis (the same Curtis who had been the register and collector of dogs) on the head. Then, after driving off the marshals and hog collectors, the rioters liberated the captured animals.

The magistrates responded to this disturbance with a new severity. At the trial of the man charged with assaulting a city marshal, the judge viewed the disturbance within the context of a series of riots that spring and declared that it was "high time the number of breaches of the peace

38. Arthur Everett Peterson, *New York as an Eighteenth Century Municipality: Prior to 1731* (1917; rpt., Port Washington, N.Y., 1967), 91–98; Pomerantz, *New York,* 270–271; *MCC,* I, 250, 251, 369, 379, 417, IV, 375, V, 214, 215, 232, 268, VI, 465, 508, 692, VII, 542, VIII, 607, 660, IX, 143, 155, 310, 653, 654, X, 603, XI, 158, 600, 704, XII, 293, XIV, 363, 441, XV, 485, 515, 516. Carl Bridenbaugh, *Cities in the Wilderness: The First Century of Urban Life in America, 1625–1742* (New York, 1938), 167–168, 323; Bridenbaugh, *Cities in Revolt: Urban Life in America, 1743–1776* (New York, 1955), 32–33.

39. *MCC,* XI, 704, 751, XII, 430, 447, 460, 461, XIV, 410, 411, 515, 674, XV, 269, 270, 330.

40. *Evening Post,* Aug. 4, 1821; *MCC,* XI, 722. See also De Voe, *The Market Book,* I, 482.

41. *MCC,* XII, 430, 447, 460, 461, XIV, 410, 411.

with which we are troubled should be lessened" and felt "compelled to use more decisive means" to stop riots. He therefore sentenced the accused Henry Bourden to sixty days in jail, levied a $20 fine (no mean sum for a laborer), and ordered him bound over under a recognizance of $250. The city recorder, the judge in the Bourden case, also seized the opportunity to lecture the court on the illegitimacy of mob action in opposing an unpopular law. Repeating an argument which had emerged in the 1780s and 1790s, the recorder declared that, if "any citizen finds himself aggrieved by any law, can he not but go to the polls, and putting in office individuals of his own opinion, thereby change the law." Democracy, according to the recorder, had made direct popular action superfluous.[42]

New York's commercial press supported the recorder's position. Outraged when a mob of nearly five hundred attacked a hogcart in September 1826, the *Evening Post* addressed its readers: "The question is now at issue whether the laws are to be obeyed, or are we to be ruled by a mob?" The *Statesman* echoed these sentiments by denying the popular base of the hogcart riots and claiming that these disturbances were the work of a special interest. "Things have come to a strange crisis," the *Statesman* reported, "if the removal of a nuisance, which is offensive to almost every citizen, is to be prevented by the riotous assemblage of a few, interested in its continuance."[43]

Bolstering the idea among the middle class that the antihogcart mobs represented special interests was an apparent shift in the character of the rioters. Although the evidence is scanty, the people charged with being in the antidogcart riots of the 1810s included a variety of occupations such as tobacconist, slater, blacksmith, and sailor (see table 10). The hogcart rioters in the 1820s, on the other hand, were either butchers, who had definite economic interests at stake, or were from marginal groups in New York society. Newspapers identified rioters in 1821 as "female blacks" and in 1825 as "men, women, and boys of all sizes and colours." In fact, those arrested in 1825 and in later disturbances in 1830 and 1832 appear to have been Irish. Thus Henry Bourden is referred to as an Irishman, and most of the other names identified in the 1825 and later riots have a Gaelic ring to them (see table 11). Since these rioters were from an alien group, there is little wonder that officials spoke of special and separate interests.

42. *People* v. *Alexander Allaire et al.*, Apr. 9, 1825, NYCGS; *American*, Apr. 6, 18, May 5, 1825; De Voe, *The Market Book*, I, 483.
43. *Evening Post*, Sept. 7, 1826; *Statesman*, Sept. 12, 1826.

TABLE 10

Arrested Dogcart Rioters, 1811, 1818

Name	Occupation	Address
George Creuthers	—	—
Francis Downie	sailor	24 Barclay
John Gillespie	blacksmith	—
William Gillespie	blacksmith	Bowery
James Horne	coachmaker (?)	Old Potter's Field
George Lynch[a]	tobacconist	169 Orange
Francis Passman	tobacconist	196 Washington
Daniel Randall	—	—
William Robinson	—	—
Michael Sherlock	slater	30 Barclay
Charles William	sailor	—

[a]Boy.
Sources: NYCGS; NYCSCPCC; city directories.

Moreover, after the 1830 riot one newspaper complained that all of the people attacking the hogcarts as well as those involved in another riot a few days later were immigrants who seemed not to understand the system of American law.[44] The court records also suggest that the hogcart rioters represented a different interest from the middle-class magistrates'.

From the standpoint of the hogcart rioters, the city officials were attempting to seize property without any good reason. As one rioter, Dennis Dougherty, put it in August 1832, "The corporation, the police and their officers . . . were a damned set of thieves" who "were stealing their hogs."[45]

44. *Courier and Enquirer,* July 6, 1830. See also *Evening Post,* July 2, 1830; *John Nixon et al.* v. ——— *McReady et al.,* July 3, 1830, box 7442 (1830), NYCSCPCC.

45. *John Hall* v. *Dennis Doughterty et al.,* Aug. 15, 1832, box 7444 (1830), NYCSCPCC. For 1832 disturbances, see the following. In NYCSCPCC, box 7444 (1832): *Jonathan D. Stevenson* v. *John McDonald,* Aug. 21, 1832; *Nathl. F. Randolph* v. *John McDonald,* Aug. 22, 1832; *Sidney Roberts* v. *John McDonald,* Aug. 22, 1832; *Benjamin Robinson* v. *John Glancey et al.,* Aug. 22, 1832; *Isaac Kendall* v. *Jas. Carrigan,* Aug. 21, 1832; *Clement Robbins* v. *Jas. Barhytd,* Aug. 22, 1832. In NYCGS, box CC-88 (1832): *People* v. *John Glancey et al.,* Nov. 16, 1832; *People* v. *James Barhytd,* Nov. 16, 1832.

TABLE II
Arrested Hogcart Rioters, 1825, 1830, 1832

Year	Name	Occupation	Address
1825	Alexander Allaire	cartman	Renwick near Spring
	Edwin Allaire	cartman	Renwick near Spring
	Henry Bourden	—	—
1830	James Barhytd	—	—
	Baroth Brown	—	—
	John Davis	—	—
	William Flenders	—	—
	Daniel Harmony	—	—
	Bernard McManus	—	—
	——— McReady	—	—
	George Pessenger	butcher	117 Norfolk
	Jacob Pessenger	butcher	30 Catharine
	Daniel Sembler	—	—
	Asa Ward	—	—
1832	James Corrigan	—	—
	Bridget Dorsey	—	—
	Dennis Dougherty	—	—
	[wife] Dougherty	—	—
	——— Fitzsimmons	—	—
	John Glancey	—	—
	John McDonald	—	131 Greene

Sources: NYCGS; NYCSCPCC; city directories.

This violation of plebeian property compelled the residents of the outer wards to resist the hog collectors. When the common belief that city officials were stealing the animals confronted the determination of the marshals and constables to enforce the law, the violence of the rioting intensified. Time and again, when the hogcart appeared in 1825, 1826, 1830, and in 1832, the mobs had to beat back the guard as well as free the animals. Faced by this opposition, the attitude of the magistrates hardened, and they argued that all such popular demonstrations violated the good order of society. In July 1830 the *Courier and Enquirer,* reflecting views expressed by the magistrates, asserted that in a country where "the laws are made by the authority of the whole body of the people" and where the laws are "for the people's benefit," there is "no excuse, no palliation . . . for resisting the due execution of the law."[46] By denying the right of people collectively to resist laws which they saw as unjust, New York's middle class closed down an important avenue of plebeian popular activity.

46. *Courier and Enquirer,* July 13, 1830.

NINE

A Disordered Society

*A riotous disposition once aroused
knows no Bounds.
As the smell of the Blood arouses
the sleeping Tiger.*

"Philip Hone Diary," 1831

Saturday night in August 1834. The city's grog shops, taverns, oyster cellars, and bawdyhouses were busy. Throughout the mechanic and poorer neighborhoods men and women caroused, drank, and made merry. The streets were far from quiet, not unusual for the metropolis at the end of a work week. Shortly after midnight a group of twenty New Yorkers, frolicking in Canal Street between Elm and Broadway, raised a cry of fire. The noise quickly brought about 150 persons into the street. Here, in the densely populated Sixth Ward and only a few short blocks from the notorious Five Points, it was always easy to gather a crowd. There was no fire, but the shouting and clamor continued as more people joined in the sport. Several men began to pelt stones at houses on Canal Street, breaking windows and knocking down signs. Someone sent for the watch. The disorder built to a fortissimo, and the party of watchmen had to battle with the rioters in order to restrain the tumult. One watchman and a bystander were injured, and the crowd did not completely disperse until three o'clock in the morning.[1]

During the late 1820s and early 1830s such disturbances broke out with great frequency. Even worse, as far as the middle-class magistrates were concerned, many of these riots seemed to have no real cause. After describing the above incident, the *Evening Post* reported, "The rioters appeared to have no definite object, but indulged in wanton mischief apparently for the mere love of it."[2] Of course, such rioting was hardly new, but in the eighteenth century large-scale rowdyism had occasioned little serious apprehension. Magistrates expected the lower classes to blow off a little steam now and then. Indeed, rowdy behavior might even be seen as a form of social insurance. By August 1834 this belief no longer held. The large-scale riots in April and July of that year and the countless other disturbances over a wide variety of political, ethnic, racial, and class differences in the previous decades had undercut the legitimacy of rioting. Moreover, the city's population had passed two hundred thousand by the 1830s. The more people in the city, it seemed, the greater the frequency of disturbances. The more people in the city, the greater the danger that the "sleeping Tiger" would awake.

1. *Evening Post,* Aug. 25, 1834.
2. *Ibid.*

Tavern and Brothel Disturbances

Rowdiness could be triggered in a variety of ways.[3] Age-old urban-rural antagonisms provoked a crowd of nearly three hundred, in January 1813, to harass and chase down the street two men from the country. Intervention in popular recreations might easily lead to violence, so that to break up a fistfight was to court an attack from bystanders. When William Donahue tried to disperse such a group of spectators on his stoop in February 1828, the crowd assaulted him, broke into his house, shattered some of his windows, and gave his wife a black eye. Similarly, in July, cartmen nearly killed an old man who threatened to report their licenses to the civil authorities for racing in the street. Shortly after attacking the old man, the same cartmen started fighting among themselves while arguing over the outcome of a race. During the second affray one cartman had a part of his ear bitten off.[4]

The presence of the military, as during the War of 1812, could also spark disorder. Antimilitary animosity had a long history, and civilian-military clashes were inevitable in the nineteenth century. In February 1813 soldiers and butchers fought on the Bowery because the soldiers had marched down the sidewalk knocking every man, woman, and child out of their way. There was even antagonism between the military services. On July 3, 1814, Stephen Decatur's crew from the frigate *President* rioted. More than two hundred sailors attacked an army lieutenant, an artillery sergeant, and the owners of a tavern on the corner of Market and Broad streets.[5]

For many of the street riots and tavern disruptions it is impossible to determine the cause. In 1806 innkeeper Thomas Rogers complained that

3. The street and tavern riots analyzed here are defined as disturbances involving at least 15–20 persons and for which there is no easily classifiable reason. Because liquor was sold in a variety of grog shops, groceries, oyster shops, and semi-private homes, all disturbances breaking out in any one of these are considered tavern brawls. The riots discussed as street or tavern disturbances exclude political, ethnic, racial, and religious riots, labor disorder, and the plebeian resistance to middle-class culture. Had these been included, the overall trends discussed below would remain the same.

4. In NYCGS: *People* v. *James Van Brauer et al.,* Jan. [7], 1813; *People* v. *John Roach et al.,* Feb. 13, 1828; *People* v. *Cornelius Van Riper et al.,* Aug. 13, 1828. *National Advocate,* Aug. 1, 1828; *Gazette,* Aug. 1, 1828.

5. *Evening Post,* Feb. 10, 1813; *People* v. *John Jones et al.,* July 9, 1814, NYCGS.

PLATE 16. Provost and Chapel Streets.
Interior of New-York, Provost Street and Chapel, *illustration by J. Milbert for*
Picturesque Sketches in America, *1826. Courtesy of the New York Public Library.*
The Chapel Street area was one of the poorer neighborhoods, noted for its
many bawdyhouses.

several men frequently came to his tavern in a "riotous manner," broke
open his doors, and destroyed his furniture while bidding "defiance to the
law."[6] Similarly, in 1828 another tavern owner complained that a "gang of
noisy riotous, disorderly persons have repeatedly come into his place and
have caused a great disturbance with their yelling, hallowing, crying for
the watch, shouting murder, throwing flour about on persons." Women
tavern and brothel keepers were particularly subject to this sort of harassment. Phoebe Dotty of 148 Church Street described for the police magistrates in 1824 how a dozen or so persons forced their way into her house
"hallowing and making a great noise." They threw her furniture about
and broke her glassware and crockery. When she declared her intention of
complaining to the authorities, one of the rioters "told her that if she did he
would have her put on the Steeping Mill [treadmill]." Often, beds were
torn apart and thrown into the street, or some prankster slipped onions
under the bed, and the mob made a quick retreat.[7]

6. *People* v. *William Lewis et al.,* Feb. 7, 1806, NYCGS.
7. *People* v. *John Harris et al.,* Nov. 14, 1828, NYCGS; *Phoebe Dotty* v. *John
Snell et al.,* Nov. 12, 1824, box 7438 (1824–1825), NYCSCPCC. There are
scores of such bed cases in the court records. For typical examples, see *People* v.

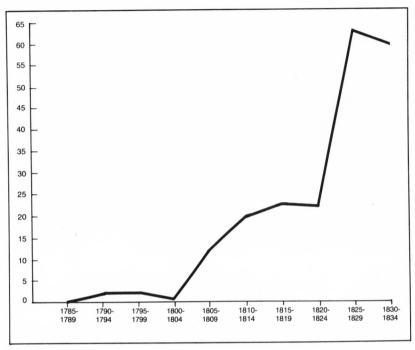

FIGURE 2. Street and Tavern Riots, 1785–1834

These tavern disruptions and attacks on women innkeepers were not repetitions of the great bawdyhouse riots of 1793 and 1799. They did not represent the sentiments of an indignant community giving vent to its moral outrage. Instead, they were more like drunken frolics by a handful or more of men and women who were out for a good time. Such activity was commonplace in the urban environment, especially in the seaports, and it had been tolerated to a limited degree. What had changed by the early nineteenth century was that the middle-class magistrates suddenly began prosecuting more and more of these disturbers as traditional means of social control broke down.

The increase in reported disturbances was dramatic. The court records and newspapers seldom mentioned street rowdiness and tavern brawls before 1805. As a result, there is evidence of only a handful of incidents from

Nicholas Lozier et al., Jan. 12, 1812, NYCGS; *People* v. *Isaac Varian et al.,* Apr. 11, 1812, NYCGS; *People* v. *John Lee et al.,* Dec. 15, 1824, NYCGS; *Letitia Tredwell* v. *John Hanisin et al.,* ca. Dec. 1, 1829, box 7441 (1829), NYCSCPCC; *People* v. *John Day et al.,* July 22, 1813, box 7433 (1811–1814), NYCSCPCC.

1785 to 1804 (figure 2). No doubt there were more barroom disruptions and street brawls in this era, but neither the magistrates nor the commercial press thought them serious enough to prosecute or mention in the newspapers. After 1805 more indictments for riot and reports of these incidents appear. Between 1810 and 1820 the level of such cases remains constant at about twenty per five-year period despite the near doubling of the population. But in 1825–1829 the number of reported incidents jumps to sixty-three, marking a steep increase in both absolute and relative terms.

All of a sudden, the entire city appeared to have succumbed to disorder. On one day in September 1828 the *Gazette* rattled off a report of three different disturbances: "Murray, a black was arrested for being concerned in a riot in Five Points. Penitentiary. About a dozen Irishmen were called up for being concerned in a mob at the foot of Oliver Street. Some had black eyes, others bloody noses—lost hats, shirts. . . . Two of them committed. Thomas Chick, a decent looking fellow, was taken up for promoting a riot in front of the Methodist church in Forsyth St."[8] Exhibited in these court records and newspapers is increasing anxiety over urban disorder and an inability to understand the intensifying violence of the street crowd.

Although the city seemed to be coming apart completely, certain streets and neighborhoods experienced more tavern and street disturbances than others. The Church-Chapel streets area, near Leonard and Anthony streets in the Fifth Ward, had a reputation for tumult reaching back to the eighteenth century, when the neighborhood marked the northern limits of the city. The brothels and taverns in this section remained a problem for city authorities long after the bawdyhouse riots of 1793 and 1799. Between 1805 and 1834 twenty different disturbances can definitely be placed in the neighborhood. Many of these were attacks on women innkeepers, who, in all likelihood, were prostitutes. Another notorious part of the city was the East River waterfront in the Seventh Ward. Eighteen tavern and street disruptions were located in this ward between 1805 and 1834, but much of this activity either centered around Catharine and Bancker (later Madison) streets in the western part of the ward or around Walnut Street at Corlear's Hook. Between Catharine and Market streets, Bancker Street was particularly notorious; full of "rum holes," people there loitered "about the streets and grog shops" day and night. Its inhabitants, according to a reporter in 1820, were "a motley mixture of whites, yellows, and blacks,

8. *Gazette,* Sept. 20, 1828. The Thomas Chick incident has not been included as a street or tavern riot in table 12.

from all ends of the earth." Consequently, the tone of the place was deplorable. "Of *fifty* houses fronting on the block, *thirty-five* are grog shops, the proprietors of which are, with few exceptions, purchasers of stolen goods."[9] Likewise, Corlear's Hook long had a reputation as a locale for prostitutes and a scene of rowdy behavior.

In the 1820s, however, the Five Points in the Sixth Ward began to eclipse both the Church-Chapel streets area and the Seventh Ward as the most infamous section of the city. This district, which retained its reputation throughout the nineteenth century, attracted increasing attention from magistrates and middle-class observers.[10] Six disturbances can be located there between 1820 and 1824, and between 1825 and 1829 the court records and newspapers reveal at least eighteen more. Jammed with poor immigrants, blacks, and native-born Americans, the Five Points was a scene of vice and crime surpassing anything New York had previously known. In 1826 the *American* called the area "the *Alsatia* of New York" and declared, "It is prolific in riots, robberies, and larcenies, and sends larger daily deputations to Bridewell than any other part of the city." A commentator in 1829 asserted that "Five Points" was like a "cancer" which "eats round, and drives honest men away."[11] The slum was full of shops selling liquor: Cross Street, for example, had 103 houses containing "57 grog shops and numerous other buildings of viler condition." Likewise, Anthony Street, between Broadway and Cross Street, had 90 houses with 54 groceries, which sold liquor, with "nearly all the rest" disorderly houses. This area was a wild, wicked, and violent place. Men and women of all ages and races could be found in the numerous "rumholes . . . drinking, swearing, and fighting." As one New Yorker in 1826 put it, "So much indeed is the organ of combativeness developed" in the people of Five Points that "I saw no less than four fights in as many minutes."[12]

The magistrates and commercial classes found the proximity of these disorderly neighborhoods to the city's more affluent citizens particularly disconcerting. Although the homes of affluent New Yorkers lay dispersed throughout the city, the elite still tended to reserve certain streets for themselves. Broadway contained almost one-fourth of the city's rich. Parts

9. May 9, Oct. 25, 1817, in NYCMMPO, XVIII (1816–1818); *Commercial Advertiser,* June 22, 1820.

10. Carol Groneman Pernicone, "The 'Bloody Ould Sixth': A Social Analysis of a New York City Working-Class Community in the Mid Nineteenth Century" (Ph.D. diss., University of Rochester, 1973), 20–34.

11. *American,* Aug. 26, 1826; *Evening Post,* Aug. 21, 1829.

12. *Evening Post,* Sept. 21, 1826.

PLATE 17. Five Points.
Intersection of Cross, Anthony, and Orange Streets, *1827, lithograph by McSpedon and Baker, printed in D. T. Valentine,* Manual of the Corporation of the City of New York *(New York, 1855). Courtesy of the New-York Historical Society.*

of Broadway also bordered both the Five Points and the Church-Chapel street neighborhood. Likewise, the fine houses on Chambers, Reed, Fulton, and Cortlandt streets stood but a few blocks from Phoebe Dotty's house on Church Street. A short walk from the imposing homes on Washington and Greenwich streets were the brothels on Chapel and Church streets.[13] Since the rich lived so close to the poor, their grand homes were not exempt from street disorder. Disturbances occurred at the Battery, the City Hall Park, and Washington Square, all of which were fronted by homes of the elite. So too, as the city expanded north of Canal Street, the newly settled sections, with a mix of population from wealthy merchants to impoverished day laborers, played host to dozens of riots. Increasingly, the middle and upper classes wanted to distance themselves from such rowdy behavior.[14]

13. See Charles Haynes Haswell, *Reminiscences of an Octogenarian of the City of New York (1816 to 1860)* (New York, 1896), 13–14, for earlier location of the rich; and Edward Pessen, *Riches, Class, and Power before the Civil War* (Lexington, Mass., 1973), 172–179. See, especially, Pessen's map and table, pp. 176, 172.

14. For a discussion of middle-class efforts to deal with the problem of disorder, see Paul Boyer, *Urban Masses and Moral Order in America, 1820–1920* (Cambridge, Mass., 1978); Raymond A. Mohl, *Poverty in New York, 1783–1825* (New York, 1971); Robert S. Pickett, *House of Refuge: Origins of Juvenile Reform in*

Class Composition of Street Disorders

Not many rich New Yorkers, or even affluent artisans, participated in this street or tavern disorder. The few who did were either adolescents, perhaps rebelling against their parents, or master craftsmen, perhaps rejecting the new middle-class values. By far the vast majority charged in court were poorer mechanics, day laborers, sailors, and their children. Many of these people lived so close to the margin of poverty that they cannot be traced. They were not rich enough, nor were their residences permanent enough, nor were many old enough to be listed in the city directories, tax records, or even the census.

A handful of rioters who came from affluent families can be identified through bail bonds and tax records. John Wheeler, for instance, a fourteen- or fifteen-year-old boy arrested in a tavern disruption in April 1823, lived with widow Margaret Wheeler, probably his mother, who owned 79 Front Street, assessed at $4,000.[15] Likewise, law student John Lee and his friend Neil A. McKinnon, arrested in a riot in Collect Street on April 8, 1822, both came from substantial homes. Lee lived with tallow chandler William Lee at 61 Reed Street, assessed at $4,700, and McKinnon resided with a Mrs. McKinnon at 73 Fulton, assessed at $6,750. Both addresses lay in affluent neighborhoods.[16] The evidence for both Lee and McKinnon suggests that they, too, were younger men living with their parents. Yet such sons of the rising middle class form but a small percentage of the total number of identified rioters in tavern and street disturbances listed in the court records.

Among the rioters, mechanics far outnumbered those identified as the

---

New York State, 1815–1857 (Syracuse, N.Y., 1969); Carroll Smith Rosenberg, *Religion and the Rise of the American City: The New York City Mission Movement, 1812–1870* (Ithaca, N.Y., 1971); David J. Rothman, *The Discovery of the Asylum: Social Order and Disorder in the New Republic* (Boston, 1971).

15. *People* v. *John Mount et al.*, May 8, 1823, NYCGS; *People* v. *John Mount et al.*, in Jacob D. Wheeler, *Reports of Criminal Law Cases, Decided at the City-Hall of the City of New York, with Notes and References* (New York, 1854), I, 411–412; bond for John Wheeler, Apr. 29, 1823, box 7855, NYCSCPC Bonds; First Ward, Tax Assessment, 1823, NYCA.

16. *People* v. *John Lee et al.*, May 10, 1822, NYCGS; Third, Fifth, Eighth wards, Assessment, 1820; David Longworth, *The American Almanack, New-York Register, and City Directory*, 1820–1821; bond for John Lee, Apr. 16, 1822, box 7854, NYCSCPC Bonds; Third Ward, Tax Assessment, 1822, NYCA.

children of the well-to-do. Some of these mechanics owned enough property to suggest that they were master craftsmen. Thus in a tavern disruption at 487 Pearl Street in 1820, close to Five Points, officials arrested
cooper Bartholomew Skaates and cartman Henry Filender with eight
others. Skaates and Filender each owned property on Wooster Street in
the Eighth Ward worth approximately one thousand dollars. However, the
overwhelming majority of mechanics in these riots were either journeymen
or apprentices. Also arrested in the Pearl Street bar were a fisherman,
painter, tanner, shoemaker, baker, two butchers, and another cartman.
Only two of these other men had assessed property of their own, each owning only one hundred dollars worth of property.[17]

That two of the Pearl Street rioters in 1820 were butchers is instructive.
Of all of the tradesmen represented among the rioters, butchers stand out
as the most numerous and provide an example of the kind of mechanic who
turned his back on middle-class values of order and sobriety. Time and
again, police arrested butchers in disturbances, especially at taverns. Between 1806 and 1824, the years for which the records are best, at least
twenty butchers were arrested in tavern brawls. The evidence after 1824
indicates that this trend continued to 1834 and probably beyond. These
butchers included wealthy master artisans, owning several thousand dollars worth of property, as well as apprentices.

One man, the Bowery Butcher, or Butcher George Messerve, earned a
particularly nasty reputation and became feared throughout all the grog
shops and bawdyhouses of the city. Hardly a year passed from 1808 to
1834 that either Butcher George or a member of the extensive Messerve
clan did not appear in court on charges of assault and riot. Despite his
penchant for violence, Butcher George was a man on the make. Already in
1810 he was a master butcher who owned one thousand dollars worth of
property on the Bowery near Prince Street. By the 1820s he had expanded his holdings in that neighborhood to more than ten thousand dollars worth of property.[18] He could easily afford, therefore, the heavy fines

17. *People* v. *Henry Filender et al.,* Apr. 6, 1820, NYCGS; bonds for William
Beach, Jacob Brewer, Henry Filender, Thomas Fitch, Luke Lave, Bartholomew
Skaates, James Wainwright, Joseph L. Webb, Apr. 10, 1820, and Jacob Pessen-
ger, Apr. 13, 1820, box 7852 (1820), NYCSCPC Bonds; Tax Assessment Records, 1820, NYCA; Longworth's *Directory, 1820–1821.*

18. The names "Butcher George" and the "Bowery Butcher" are in the depositions in the criminal records. Riot cases involving George Messerve include the
following. In NYCGS: *People* v. *Henry Carrier,* Apr. 9, 1811; *People* v. *Frederick
Talbot et al.,* Dec. 7, 1827; *People* v. *Abraham Hall et al.,* Feb. 16, 1828; *People* v.

levied against him for his extracurricular activities. In January 1829, for example, the court of general sessions recognized Butcher George's special notoriety as a troublemaker when it convicted him of three separate counts of riot and assault and fined him three hundred dollars plus costs. This sum was more than the average laborer earned in a year and was ten times the fine levied against Butcher George's codefendant in all three cases, butcher John Harrison.[19] Despite such fines, Butcher George and the other rowdy members of his trade continued to carouse, brawl, and riot in grog shops throughout much of the city.

The exact reason for the involvement of butchers in these disturbances remains obscure. The early nineteenth-century transition from a municipally regulated trade to a business subject to much more competition might have created a certain amount of anxiety among butchers.[20] Was this, perhaps, expressed in tavern brawls? The material success of Butcher George and others involved in these riots as well as the general affluence of butchers belies such a socioeconomic interpretation. Perhaps more germane is the nature of the butchering trade. Butchers frequently began their violent careers as apprentices. More than one unsuspecting passerby found himself pounced upon by butcher boys along the Bowery, where many butchers lived, or in the city markets, where the butchers sold meat. Butchering seems to have recruited individuals who had a particular bent toward violence. Moreover, the constant slaughtering of animals toughened individuals in body and mind. Those exposed to the brutality of the slaughterhouse may have needed an outlet, which was best served by hard drink and rowdy behavior. In any case, in the early nineteenth century a culture of violence emerged among butchers living in and around the Bowery, which was passed on from one generation to another and may

---

James Harris et al., Nov. 14, 1828; *People v. John Harrison et al.,* Dec. 9, 1828. In NYCSCPCC: *James Costigan v. George Messerve,* July 5, 1818, box 7435 (1818–1819); *Letitia Tredwell v. John Harrison et al.,* ca. Dec. 1829, box 7441 (1829). For property evaluation, see Tax Assessment Records, Eighth Ward, 1815–1829, NYCA.

19. *People v. Edward Bull et al.,* Nov. 12, 1825, NYCGS; *Gazette,* Jan. 21, 1829.

20. Howard B. Rock, *Artisans of the New Republic: The Tradesmen of New York City in the Age of Jefferson* (New York, 1979), 205–206, 208–211, 214–218, 223–224; Thomas F. De Voe, *The Market Book, Containing a Historical Account of the Public Markets in the Cities of New York, Boston, Philadelphia, and Brooklyn . . . ,* I (New York, 1862), 223, 489–496.

well be the origins of the infamous mid-nineteenth-century gang, the Bowery Boys.[21]

Although many of these rowdy butchers and even a few of the other tradesmen arrested in street and tavern riots owned enough property to place them among the new middle class, these men were the exception. Most street and tavern rioters had little or no property. In fact, they tended to come from the periphery of society. Many were laborers and sailors, some were grocers who sold liquor, but only a few of the men and women arrested in this type of disturbance can be identified in the city directories that listed established tradesmen. It was precisely this anonymity that the middle class feared. A chasm seemed to be opening up between the respectable and disreputable citizens of the city. That some artisans or alienated well-to-do youths joined in this ignominious rowdyism made little difference. Butchers, after all, were a tough, quarrelsome crew who worked in a violent, dirty, and smelly occupation. As for the other artisans and tradesmen and even the handful of sons of the affluent who caroused and rioted, they obviously were rejecting the new middle-class values of sobriety, temperance, and good order. The gap between the lower levels of society and the middle to upper classes was widening.

The deep wells of antagonism which helped to define this growing cultural divide occasionally came boiling to the surface. On August 5, 1833, for example, a line of dirt carts driven by Irish immigrants slowly worked its way up Third Avenue in the late afternoon. At Nineteenth Street the carts met a series of carriages racing downtown occupied by gentlemen and some ladies. The first carriage came dangerously close to the lead cart and almost caused an accident. William McGlauglin, the driver of the cart, lacked deference and determined not to take this abuse lightly. The democratic rules of the road had been violated, so McGlauglin cursed the gentleman and his female companion. Two other cartmen decided to put the gentleman in his place, grabbed his horse, and forced the gig back onto the sidewalk. The confrontation quickly erupted into a fight as the cartmen, joined by thirty to fifty Irishmen, attacked the gentlemen. The merchants and manufacturers in the carriages, angry at this challenge to their presumed social authority, desperately lashed out with their whips, but at least two were severely beaten. It was some time before peace was restored.

The aftermath of this disturbance further highlighted the differences be-

21. De Voe, *The Market Book,* I, 214, 358.

tween middle-class notions of order and lower-class behavior. Magistrates
took the riot seriously and arrested several of the cartmen. To the surprise
of the city officials, a number of these men openly admitted to drinking
alcohol and appeared to have little remorse over their attack on the merchants and businessmen in the carriages. This candid rejection of temperance values and the blatant disrespect for gentlefolk combined to show
the middle class that these workers seemed to cling to the worst values
of both the new egalitarianism and the Old World traditionalism. The
Irishmen had demonstrated a belief that democratic principles governed
social relations while joining drink with work and readily turning to violence to settle an argument.[22]

Theater Riots

The contrast between middle-class ideas of decorum and the popular disorder of the lower classes became especially evident in the city's theaters.
Until the late 1820s, theater audiences were extremely heterogeneous. By
then, however, the unceasing uproar coming from the less expensive seats
proved to irritate the ever more sophisticated sensibilities of the middle
class.[23] All the world's a stage, and theater disturbances can reveal much
about the middle-class critique of rowdyism, perceptions of increased disorder in society, and a real rise in the level of violence in rioting.

Until the second decade of the nineteenth century, rowdyism in the theater aroused little criticism. Most theatergoers did not object too strenu-
ously to the antics of the sailors and laborers or the misbehavior of young
gentlemen out for an evening. In fact, such activity was almost expected,
having, like the traditional eighteenth-century crowd ritual, cathartic
value. Occasionally a few humorless souls found the hubbub too tumultuous. One patron in 1764, for example, grumbled that "a certain Set of
Males and Females" disturbed the theater with their "laughing and talking very loud, Squawling, overturning the Benches, etc.," and in 1773 another reported that "some mischievous Persons in the Gallery" not only
insulted the stage and the orchestra but also abused the rest of the audi-

22. *People* v. *Martin et al.,* Aug. 14, 1833, NYCGS.

23. On seating arrangements, see David Grimsted, *Melodrama Unveiled: American Theater and Culture, 1800–1850* (Chicago, 1968), 52–56. Grimsted says
that it was only in the 1830s that different theaters were patronized by differing
social classes. These distinctions, however, were emerging in the late 1820s.

ence.[24] After the Revolution minor disturbances continued in New York theaters. Fruit, pies, and plates were hurled occasionally at the stage, and fights erupted on occasion in the audience.[25] But most New Yorkers took such rowdiness in stride. In his Jonathan Oldstyle letter of December 3, 1802, Washington Irving facetiously described the "discharge of apples, nuts, and gingerbread" from the gallery (the cheaper seats) "on the heads of the honest folks in the pit" (the more expensive seats). Irving and other "honest folks" tolerated this misbehavior, believing "that it was useless to threaten or expostulate" with the disturbers and that it was best to "sit down quietly and bend your back to it."[26]

On the night of October 27, 1817, however, a full-scale theater riot erupted because Charles Incledon, a touring British actor, refused to sing the audience's favorite song, "Black-Eyed Susan." The boisterous crowd jeered and bombarded the manager "with all sorts of objects" when he attempted to explain that Incledon was too tired to perform. The other actors unsuccessfully struggled to continue the evening's program, which became "a mere pantomime amidst all the noise and confusion." The manager called for the watch, but its arrival only exacerbated the violence. The rioters revealed a new aggressiveness and refused to succumb to any authority; they attacked the watch, and they even assaulted Justice James Hopson. Only after making several arrests could the police restore order.[27] The violence of the "Black-Eyed Susan" riot was new and disquieting to the emerging middle class. The *National Advocate* claimed that theater riots seldom happened in New York City. Sympathizing with the disappointment of the audience, the editor nevertheless deprecated "anything like a riot." He hoped that such tumult would not be repeated.[28]

Theater riots in New York City and elsewhere became a fixed feature of the American stage in the first half of the nineteenth century. On several occasions riots began in reaction to the performance of a British actor like Incledon. Rooted in more than patriotism, the riots were probably directed at the social pretensions of the middle and upper classes, who

24. George C. D. Odell, *Annals of the New York Stage* (New York, 1927– 1928), I, 97, 162–163.

25. *Ibid.,* 247, 280, 346–348, 380–381, 430–431, II, 29, 162–163, 213, 464.

26. Washington Irving, "Letters of Jonathan Oldstyle," in *Biographies and Miscellanies,* ed. Pierre M. Irving, Vol. XIX of *Irving's Works,* Geoffrey Crayon Edition (New York, 1866), 28–35.

27. *Evening Post,* Oct. 29, 1817; *Columbian,* Oct. 29, 1817; *National Advocate,* Oct. 29, 1817; Odell, *Annals of the New York Stage,* II, 496–499.

28. *National Advocate,* Oct. 29, 1817.

openly mimicked the trappings of English culture and society. Theater patrons like Philip Hone and his friends relished the supposed superior talents of the British actors and purposely courted and cultivated them. British actors were doubly resented; not only were they foreigners competing with American actors, but they were also associated with the commercial middle class. In 1825, for instance, rowdy New Yorkers refused to allow the famous British actor Edmund Kean to perform because he had reportedly insulted a Boston audience during an earlier tour. The rioters drowned out the play and drove Kean from the stage. In the process the audience inside destroyed benches, and a crowd outside battled the watch in an attempt to enter and do further damage.[29]

Similar disturbances occurred in October 1831, March 1832, and July 1834. The 1831 disturbances lasted several days and were larger than previous New York theater riots. Again the ostensible cause was the presence of an English actor, in this case Joshua Anderson. On the first few nights of his appearance, the disorder advanced from prolonged heckling to persistent bombardments of fruit and eggs. By the fourth night, the rioting outside the theater reached a fever pitch as the crowd broke windows and attempted to batter down the door. When the men of the watch appeared, the rioters channeled their animus against them, attacking them with stones and clubs amidst cries of "Knock the leather heads down," "Take care of your clubs," and "Mind how you strike." Finally, in an attempt to appeal to the rioters' patriotism and Anglophobia, the theater manager displayed the American and tricolor flags from the upper windows of the theater. This act, along with more than a score of arrests, seemed to calm the mob. Still, the general din continued for a long time, and as Philip Hone, ensconced in his home several blocks away, reported, the noise made "it hard for anyone in the neighborhood to sleep."[30]

In 1832 the presence of Anderson again led to a riot, and in 1834 William Farren, another British actor, became a target of the July race

29. Evening Post, Nov. 15–17, 1825; American, Nov. 15–18, 1825; National Advocate, Nov. 15, 16, 1825; Statesman, Nov. 18, 1825; I. N. Phelps Stokes, The Iconography of Manhattan Island, 1498–1909 . . . (New York, 1915–1928), V, 1652; Odell, Annals of the New York Stage, III, 178–180; Paul O. Weinbaum, Mobs and Demagogues: The New York Response to Collective Violence in the Early Nineteenth Century (Ann Arbor, Mich., 1979), 37, 42–43.

30. In NYCSCPCC, box 7443 (1831): Hunt et al. v. Theater Rioters, Oct. 18, 1831; Reed v. Theater Rioters, Oct. 16, 1831; Stevens v. Ward, Oct. 17, 1831; Merret v. Brackett, Oct. 17, 1831. Allan Nevins, ed., The Diary of Philip Hone, 1828–1851 (New York, 1927), I, 50; Evening Post, Oct. 14, 18, 1831.

TABLE 12
Theater Riots in New York City, 1816–1834

Date	Location	Cause
1816: Sept. 6	the theater	rowdy prostitutes
1817: Oct. 27	the theater	English actor
1822: ca. Apr.	Circus	rowdyism
Aug. 10	Mercer Street Theater[a]	race
Aug. 12	Circus	rowdyism
1823: Nov. 27	Circus	rowdyism
Nov. 28	Circus	rowdyism
Dec. 1	vampire display	community indignation
1825: Nov. 14	Park Theater	English actor
Dec. 1	—	black actor
Dec. 12	Circus	rowdyism
Dec. 14	Park Theater	rowdyism
1826: Mar. 6	Circus	rowdyism
July 20	Circus	rowdyism
ca. July 31	Circus	rowdyism
1827: ca. July 21	Theater	nonappearance of actress
1828: Nov. 20	Bowery Theater	rowdyism
1830: ca. Feb. 22	Theater	rowdyism
Dec. 20	Chatham Theater	rowdyism
1831: Apr. 12	Chatham Theater	rowdyism
Oct. 13, 15–17	[Bowery] Theater	English actor
Nov. 25	Richmond Hill Theater	rowdyism
1832: Feb. 7	Chatham Garden Theater	rowdyism
ca. Mar. 18	Theater	English actor
Oct. 7	Park Theater	rowdyism
1833: Mar. 11	Park Theater	rowdyism
Nov. 23	Richmond Hill Theater	rowdyism
Dec. 23	Bowery Theater	firing of actor
1834: July	Bowery Theater	English actor

[a]Black theater.
Sources: NYCGS; NYCSCPCC; NYCMMPO; newspapers.

rioters. In the first case, the manager had anticipated trouble and had sought the permission of his patrons to allow Anderson on the stage, but he had not reckoned with the huge crowd assembled outside the theater. They broke in, overran the stage, and destroyed enough property to keep the theater closed the next day.[31] Two years later, there were again com-

31. *Commercial Advertiser*, Mar. 19–20, 1832.

PLATE 18. Park Street Theater.
Interior of the Park Theatre, N.Y.C., Nov. 1822, *watercolor by John Searle.*
Courtesy of the New-York Historical Society.
Prominent New Yorkers are portrayed in the orchestra section; the second-topmost tier
is occupied by prostitutes.

plaints against the performance of a British actor at the Bowery Theater, but the disturbance was also part of the prevailing abolitionist and race rioting. Since middle-class abolitionists like the Tappan brothers were popularly associated with the British abolition movement, the crowd may have focused on Farren in order to express their resentment at British abolitionist intrusion into America.[32]

Besides large-scale rioting triggered by unpopular actors, there were many minor theater disturbances, often with no discernible precipitating action, which violated the middle-class sense of order. The same rowdyism in the streets and taverns, which became so pronounced in the 1820s, also infested the theaters. Of some twenty-nine theater disturbances, nineteen had no ascertainable cause other than sheer rowdyism (see table 12). At times the rioters claimed they were reacting to poor performances, but audiences were only too ready to riot at the slightest provocation. Theaters, for instance, were notorious rendezvous for prostitutes. When watchman Hughes in July 1826 asked one noisy "profligate female" to leave the Lafayette Circus, she refused. When she slipped and accidentally fell down a staircase, much of the audience leaped to her rescue. Threatened by this "enfuriated Mob," Hughes escaped only with the aid of a company of watchmen.[33]

The plight of poor Hughes was not unusual. In the 1820s watchmen and city marshals stationed themselves inside theaters to combat the increasing disruptions. Repeatedly the peace officers met with stiff opposition. A disturbance broke out at the Lafayette Circus, for instance, on the night of December 12, 1825. When two marshals tried to stop the fighting, they were attacked so severely that reinforcements were requested. In this disturbance Marshal William D. Hughes was "beat and kicked by some of the gang," and one of the rioters drew a dagger on him.[34] Such violence stands in marked contrast to the harmless rowdiness and apple throwing described by Washington Irving.

The more sober members of the audience, as well as the middle-class magistrates, reacted with horror to such behavior. They demanded greater decorum in the theaters, stationed police officers inside and out, and prosecuted the offenders more rigorously. Middle-class rectitude is exemplified in the lecture one justice delivered on the rights of patrons in theaters in 1822. "The ticket which you purchase," he told two rioters, "gives you the

32. See chap. 6.
33. *MCC*, XV, 537–538, 557–559.
34. *John M. Lester* v. *John Foyle et al.*, Dec. 13, 1825, box 7438 (1824–1825), NYCSCPCC.

privilege of a seat to witness a performance, and you are at liberty to express your pleasure or disapprobation . . . in the customary way, by ap-
plause or by hissing." He reminded them, however, that this must be done
in "a proper manner" without disturbing the audience and within certain
limits, "or the eccentricities and other whims of individuals may make the
Theatre a scene of riot or confusion" which denies "those who come to be
amused" their gratification.[35]

Most of the people arrested in theater disturbances in the 1820s and
1830s came from the lower classes, and, like the tavern and street rioters,
they were usually laborers and seamen. A few rioters had a higher social
standing. But men like master butcher William Hopkins, who was one of
the rioters the judge lectured in 1822, were the exceptions. For Hopkins
and the other theater rioters the clearly defined rules of behavior, articulated by the justice, held little meaning. Theaters were for amusement,
and as far as these rowdies were concerned, their entertainment could extend beyond the performance on stage to pie throwing, fighting, scream-
ing, hooting, drinking, and rioting.

Unable to quell this disorderly behavior and no longer willing to "sit
down quietly and bend" their backs, many affluent theater patrons faced a
quandary. How were they to enjoy their moments of high culture without
being exposed to the low humor of the poorer classes? The answer, which
began to emerge in the 1820s and 1830s, was the establishment of different theaters catering to different classes. This development, in turn, enhanced the growing divisions in society. The Lafayette Amphitheater (or
Circus) in the 1820s, with its dancing girls and horseback riders as well as
theatrical productions, appealed to cruder tastes. In fact, much of the recorded rowdyism of the mid-1820s took place there. By the end of the
1820s the Lafayette, where "scenes of riot and disgraceful excesses" continually occurred, closed. During the early 1830s the city had three theaters: the Park for the rich, the Bowery for the middle levels of society, and
the Chatham for the poor.[36]

The same popular boisterousness and riotous disposition were evident
at other public exhibitions besides the theater. Dissatisfied spectators at a
balloon ascension in 1828 attempted to break into a private garden, where
the balloon was launched, and had to be beaten back by the watch.[37] A far

35. *National Advocate,* Apr. 15, 1822.

36. *MCC,* XIV, 656; Grimsted, *Melodrama Unveiled,* 52–56, 68–75.

37. *Gazette,* July 22, 1828; *Evening Post,* July 22, 1828. J. Thomas Scharf and
Thompson Westcott, *History of Philadelphia, 1660–1884* (New York, 1884), I,
598, II, 958–959.

more serious incident had occurred two years earlier at the Washington Parade Ground during an exhibition of fireworks sponsored by the city corporation. When the fireworks began, the partial and smoky discharges disappointed the spectators. People started to hiss their displeasure before taking matters into their own hands. A large mob rushed forward, "took violent possession of the stand where the rockets had been projected, and entirely demolished it." They also set fire to the whole mass of fireworks, sending flames soaring into the sky. All of New York City could see the conflagration, and a fire alarm was sounded in the lower part of the town. Using undischarged rockets as clubs, the rioters fought the watch and those citizens who came to their aid. The fire was further fed with boards and lumber taken from a nearby construction site. Finally, the watch managed to secure a few of the rioters and drag them to the watchhouse. The mob then stoned this building and attempted to rescue the captured rioters. Officials arrested seventeen men before they restored order.[38] The "sleeping Tiger" of mob disorder seemed fully aroused.

Callithumpian New Year's Celebrations

The "Tiger" even stalked New Year's celebrations. Traditionally, the New Year was seen as a moment of license and an evening of fun and frolic. Bands of laborers, apprentices, and journeymen ushered it in by parading the streets "'piercing the nights dull air' with kettle drums, trumpets and all sorts of unmeaning noises." Such processions were commonplace in preindustrial societies and served to strengthen the normal lines of authority through temporary inversions of the social order. Occasionally a person might accidentally be injured, as occurred January 1, 1765, when an apprentice broke his arm during the New Year frolics. But most often only mild vandalism accompanied these pranks, extending no further than the dismantling of store signs or the breaking of a few stoops. City officials openly winked at the throwing down of a few casks and empty barrels in the street, considering it mere "TOM AND JERRYISM" and little more than harmless, drunken roistering.[39]

---

38. *David McDermott* v. *William Hagan et al.*, Aug. 16, 1826, box 7439 (1826–1827), NYCSCPCC; *Gazette*, Aug. 17, 1826; *American*, Aug. 16, 1826. For a similar incident on a smaller scale, see *Robert Holliday* v. *Asa Taylor et al.*, May 8, 1821, box 7436 (1820–1821), NYCSCPCC.

39. *Gazette: Post-Boy*, Jan. 3, 1765; *American*, Mar. 25, 1826; *Gazette*, Dec. 27, 1826; *Statesman*, Jan. 5, 1827; *Evening Post*, Jan. 2, 1828; Gabriel Furman,

By the 1820s a special youth cult dominated the New Year's proceedings, calling themselves the Callithumpian Band. These New Year's revelers borrowed their distinctive name from English traditions. The word *Callithumpian* was thought to originate from a combination of the Greek form for "beautiful," *kalli-*, and the English term *thump*. Thus it was beautiful thumping. In England it was a noisy serenade, characterized by beating on tin pans, blowing horns, shouts, groans, catcalls, and such and, like the charivari, was usually performed for persons who had evoked ridicule or hostility.[40] New Yorkers applied the term "Callithumpian" to New Year's celebrants. The connection between the charivari and the Callithumpians is instructive; the Callithumpian parade, no doubt, derived its name, its method, and its meaning from the traditional charivari.[41] One newspaper sarcastically described the composition of the Callithumpian corps as "a number of ill-bred boys, chimney sweeps, and other equally illustrious and aspiring persons" who assembled together on New Year's Eve "to perambulate the streets all night, disturbing the slumbers of the weary and the repose of the sick, by thumping upon tin kettles, sounding penny and other martial trumpets." Such youthful discord parallels other ceremonies of misrule and performed a multitude of functions in a traditional society. Thus, although many people in the city believed that this rough music was unpleasant, it, like the earlier New Year's pranks, was at first "considered as a tolerable joke."[42]

During the 1820s the joke became much less tolerable as the Callithumpian host grew and as more and more people riotously celebrated the New Year. The change in the behavior of New Year's revelers and the

---

"The Customs, Amusements, Style of Living and Manners of the People of the United States, from the First Settlement to the Present Time, ca. 1844," MS, NYHS. For a discussion of a similar practice in Philadelphia, see Susan G. Davis, "'Making Night Hideous': Christmas Revelry and Public Order in Nineteenth-Century Philadelphia," *American Quarterly,* XXXIV (1982), 185–199.

40. *The Century Dictionary and Cyclopedia* (New York, 1889–1911). *Webster's Third New International* traces the word to *gallithumpian* (Devonshire, Dorset), "disturber of order at elections in 18th century."

41. See John Russell Bartlett, *Dictionary of Americanisms: A Glossary of Words and Phrases Usually Regarded as Peculiar to the United States,* 4th ed. (Boston, 1896), 93; *A Dictionary of American English on Historical Principles,* I (Chicago, 1938), 393; Mitford M. Mathews, ed., *A Dictionary of Americanisms on Historical Principles,* I (Chicago, 1951), 471.

42. *Gazette,* Jan. 3, 1828.

changed attitude of the middle class was rather dramatic. It can be traced
to the late 1820s. As late as 1825, for example, the *National Advocate* reported lightheartedly, "Sundry Tom and Jerries have been arraigned for
milling the matches [boxing] but on account of the New Year's frolics,
they were discharged." The next year another newspaper provided more
information on the annual "New Years Spree." The officials this time took
the disturbance a bit more seriously, arresting four men and fining them
for assaulting a watchman, knocking over empty barrels, and breaking
two stoops in the Church-Chapel streets neighborhood of the Fifth Ward.
Still, such behavior was not outrageous, and there were no calls for drastic
action to curb the holiday frolics.[43]

During the celebration greeting the New Year of 1827, however, at least
three separate disturbances broke out. Taken together, they forced city
officials to reassess their tolerant attitude toward the New Year's frolics.
Two were relatively minor affairs. In one riot, the revelers attacked a house
in Frankfort Street. In the other, the established lines of social authority
were challenged. One group of rioters "enacted in front of Mr. Mayor
Hone's house a scene of disgraceful rage." Ordinarily the mayor of the city
opened his home on New Year's Eve, treating all callers, whether rich or
poor. To abuse his hospitality was not just to offer personal insult but to
flout the emerging middle-class sense of decorum.[44]

Meanwhile, in the Five Points there was no pretense of decorum and
order. The final disturbance was more serious, revealing racial tensions as
well as lower-class hostility to the agents of municipal authority. A riot began when a group of Irishmen assaulted a black walking down Anthony
Street. When the watch attempted to rescue the victim, the Irish, armed
with cartrings and cords of wood, fell upon them. Scores of Irishmen
poured into the street, and some erected barricades of carts to confuse the
watch further. The rioters injured several police officers and beat four
watchmen so severely that they had to be taken home. The Irish also revealed their contempt for the police when, in an act of open defiance, they
destroyed their watch caps. Of course, the watch, although hard-pressed,
did manage to knock a few Irish heads and arrested almost one dozen men.
The *Statesman* described the courtroom the next day as "literally, the pic-

43. *National Advocate,* Jan. 4, 1825; *American,* Mar. 25, 1826.
44. *Gazette,* Jan. 4, 5, 1827; "Philip Hone Diary," IX, Jan. 1, 1835, microfilm,
NYHS. For a fuller discussion of the connection between Callithumpian and charivari, see Bryan D. Palmer, "Discordant Music: Charivaris and Whitecapping in
Nineteenth-Century North America," *Labour / Le travailleur,* I (1978), 34–35.

1. Procession begins: pelting tavern with lime etc.
2. African church attacked, battle with watch
3. Reinforcements added
4. Rowdyism
5. Windows smashed
6. City Hotel, confrontation with watch

A. Five Points   E. Park Theater
B. Corlear's Hook   F. Bowery Theater
C. Rowdy waterfront area, Seventh Ward G. Chatham Theater
D. Church-Chapel streets district   H. Lafayette Circus

⇐ Route of Callithumpians   - - - - Ward Boundary

MAP 7. The Callithumpian Procession, 1828.
After James Hardie, The Description of the City of New York . . .
(New York, 1827)

ture of a hospital" because the arrested rioters' "noodles were all embellished with bandages and napkins." Despite the humorous tone of the *Statesman*'s article, city officials took this concerted opposition to the watch seriously. The court of general sessions convicted nine of the arrested Irishmen and then sentenced some of them to three years' hard labor. Several newspapers supported even sterner action, advising that "a few companies of horse be ordered to patrol the streets on New Year's Eve" thereafter so that an end could be made "to a practice, which though it may have originated in innocent amusement, had grown to a formidable evil."[45]

Despite these unusually severe penalties, the New Year of 1828 was greeted with even greater disorder. This time the Callithumpian host was the mainspring of disorder. In 1828 "the *corps*" numbered nearly four thousand strong, and their excesses outstripped all previous behavior. Sometime between eight and nine o'clock at night a large crowd gathered in the Bowery with "drums, tin kettles, rattles, horns, whistles, and a variety of other instruments." They soon began pelting a public house with balls of lime, flour, and other substances "until they had changed its color from red to white." This prank, while disconcerting for the tavern owner, was not too serious. The Callithumpians then procured a large "Pennsylvania Wagon" and, tying ropes to it, dragged it through the streets. Heading downtown, they turned up Hester Street and moved toward Broadway.

Their direction was not capricious. The Bowery, where the Callithumpian procession began, had a long reputation as a seat of rowdyism. No doubt the butcher boys and other Bowery toughs played an important role in this tumult. The quickest way for the Callithumpians to get downtown would have been to continue on the Bowery till they reached Chatham Street, which would then lead them to the Battery via either Pearl Street or Broadway. The Callithumpians, however, took the more circuitous route of cutting eight blocks across town to Broadway. They did this, no doubt, because Broadway contained so many affluent homes and because the refined gentlemen and ladies of the city were all attending a ball at the City Hotel on Broadway just north of City Hall Park. The citizens of misrule were not about to pass up an opportunity to parade their triumphal

45. *People* v. *William Donough et al.,* Jan. 3, 1827, NYCGS; *MCC,* XVI, 50; *Statesman,* Jan. 5, 1827; *American,* Jan. 4, 1827; *Gazette,* Jan. 4, 5, 1827; *Evening Post,* Jan. 4, 15, 1827.

discord past such a gathering. The Callithumpian path also skirted the Five Points, thereby avoiding the gauntlet of the Irish.[46]

If the Callithumpians hoped to sidestep the Irish, they intended to confront another of the city's minorities—the blacks. Their route took them past the African church in Elizabeth Street, where they could not resist disrupting the congregation gathered there for a watch night. The Callithumpians "demolished all the windows, broke the doors, seats," and attempted to pull parts of the building down with ropes. Luckily for the church, the ropes did not prove strong enough; unluckily for the congregation, the mob decided to concentrate their attentions on them. The Callithumpians were whites, particularly apprentices and laborers, and resented the black community. The rowdy youths chased the blacks in all directions, beating them with sticks and pieces of rope.

The violence continued when the watch, soon after the attack on the African church, intercepted the Callithumpian host on Hester Street and secured a number of rioters. The mob quickly raised a call for a rescue, and in the heat of the battle the Callithumpians forced the watch to relinquish their captives and to beat a hasty retreat. The youths then resumed their march "with more tumult than ever," crossing over to Broadway and heading downtown. At Chatham Street another group joined them, and the crowd stretched for three or four blocks.

Despite the open and easy avenue down Broadway to the Battery, the Callithumpians again changed course, turning into Cedar and then Pearl streets. This brought them through the heart of the city's commercial district, where many probably worked. All along their route they smashed crates and barrels and whatever else stood in their way. Pearl Street provided many business signs for souvenirs, but this mob went straight to the source, broke the bow window of a sign shop, and looted it of all of its contents. At the Battery the procession halted while some of the host attempted "to force the iron railing" around the park "in order to make way for the free ingress of the sovereign people," but the fence proved too strong. Instead, the Callithumpians turned over a cart and broke windows

46. Although there is no solid evidence of who composed the Callithumpian host, the fact that no newspaper account identified the Callithumpians with the Irish suggests that few Irish participated in the procession. Given the ethnic bias of the editors of most of the newspapers at the time, and given their derogatory treatment of the Callithumpians in the papers, had the Irish participated in any large numbers, some of the papers would have pointed this out.

in one or two of the houses facing the Battery, which were the homes of the wealthiest people in the city.

The mob then began its slow return up Broadway until it came to the City Hotel. There they stopped, and the street became "blocked . . . with an impenetrable crowd" which obstructed the hackney coaches just then carrying the ladies and gentlemen home from the ball. To remove this "inconvenience" the gentry summoned a large contingent of the watch. The Callithumpians then revealed the extent of their informal organization. Although some of the mob wanted to fight it out immediately, the Callithumpian leaders initiated a five-minute truce to give the watch time to deliberate. The watch, fearing another confrontation, decided to step aside, "and the multitude passed noisily and triumphantly up Broadway." Only toward morning did the uproar gradually diminish and quiet return to the city.[47]

The triumph of the lords of misrule could hardly have been more complete. Twice that night the Callithumpians had faced the watch. The first time, on Hester Street, they had rescued the few prisoners taken and sent the officers of law and order in pell-mell retreat. The second time, at the City Hotel, the watch had refrained from battle and bowed to the will of the mob, an event witnessed by the elite attending the ball. In between, the Callithumpians did what they pleased, be it the harassment of innocent blacks or mere rowdiness in breaking windows and making noise. In reaction, the city's commercial newspapers, speaking for "the sober part of the community," called upon the authorities to put a halt to these New Year's celebrations. If the police force was inadequate, "it is high time its strength and its numbers were increased." The editorials proposed that, the following year, two or three hundred constables should be put on duty supported by a "squadron of horse directed to scour the streets."[48]

Apparently the magistrates agreed. The following year Mayor Walter Bowne issued a proclamation against all riotous proceedings and backed it up by ordering out extra watch and police. No frolic was to be winked at. There was to be no Callithumpian procession. Every time a crowd gathered, the watch appeared in force, dispersed the group, and disarmed

---

47. *Thomas Blakely* v. *Robert Hunter et al.,* Jan. 1, 1828, box 7440 (1827–1828), NYCSCPCC; *Gazette,* Jan. 3, 5, 10, 1828; *Evening Post,* Jan. 2, 1828; Furman, "The Customs, Amusements," MS, NYHS; Weinbaum, *Mobs and Demagogues,* 53, 55 n.

48. *Evening Post,* Jan. 2, 5, 1828.

them of their musical instruments. The operation was a success. The *Statesman* gave the magistrates "liberal praise for the vigorous and complete suppression of every disorder" and declared, with obvious satisfaction, that many "of these musical amateurs spent their 'happy New Year' in the Bridewell."[49]

In New York City the Callithumpian band represented a bridge between the traditional youth group misrule of the English village or town and a more direct challenge to authority typical of the new urbanizing environment. At first these New Year's street celebrations functioned in much the same manner as other public demonstrations and riots in the eighteenth century, by both expressing and easing tensions between plebeian and patrician. The ritual also acted like earlier youth ceremonies and eased anxiety over an awkward stage of social development for males caught between puberty and marriage. But by the early nineteenth century, the status of "youth," roughly defined as those unwed young men ages fifteen to twenty-five, began to change as members of this group found themselves cast out into an aggressive economic environment that provided them little protection yet enabled them to obtain increased independence. As these young men gained greater economic freedom, slipped out from under patriarchal supervision, and lost most signs of dependence, they subtly turned their New Year's misrule into an outright challenge to authority.[50] The path of the procession, the attack on the African church, the battles with the watch, the overall rowdiness, and the demonstration in front of the ball at the City Hotel greeting New Year's in 1828 were all calculated expressions of the peculiar social and economic position of the young men composing the Callithumpian host.

Youth Gangs

While the Callithumpians confined their activities to one night a year, more permanent organizations emerged that served a similar purpose. These gangs also, like the Callithumpian band, were an extension of the

49. *Statesman*, Jan. 7, 1829; Nevins, ed., *The Diary of Philip Hone*, I, 9.

50. Palmer, "Discordant Music," *Labour / Le travailleur*, I (1978), 5–62; Violet Alford, "Rough Music or Charivari," *Folklore*, LXX (1959), 505–518; Natalie Zemon Davis, "The Reasons of Misrule," in Davis, *Society and Culture in Early Modern France: Eight Essays* (Stanford, Calif., 1975), 97–123; Edward P. Thompson, "'Rough Music': Le charivari anglais," *Annales: Économies, sociétés,*

informal youth groups of village life molded into a more regular form. They retained a clannish cast by organizing around specific neighborhoods or streets and often maintained their sense of identity by fighting with competing gangs. In the eighteenth century, gangs, like the early Callithumpian processions, seemed innocuous enough and frequently included the sons of the well-to-do. By the 1820s, however, gangs began to be seen as especially dangerous and representative of an uncontrolled and unsupervised urban youth drawn largely from the laboring classes.[51]

A few observers noted this change. William Duer, for example, recalled that in late eighteenth-century New York City there were originally two gangs: the Smith's Vly Boys, who were recruited from the lower and eastern portions of the city and took their name from the marsh, or lowlands (Dutch *Vly*), extending northwards from the Vly (or Fly) Market; and the Broadway Boys, who came from the western and upper portion of the city. These two gangs fought each other with slings and stones. However, a third and more powerful gang emerged as the city reached north and eastward. These were the Bowery Boys. This "*tiers état*" (the third force) soon outnumbered the other two gangs; "composed of such formidable materials from the slaughter-houses in the neighborhood," they compelled Smith's Vly and Broadway Boys to "form an alliance offensive and defensive against the hardier hordes of the north."[52] The entry of the Bowery Boys onto the scene increased the level of violence between the competing gangs, but the combat still remained relatively tame. "Sometimes *hard battles,* as they were considered by the actors, were fought by throwing stones at one another." When it came to close quarters, "fists and sticks

---

civilisations, XXVII (1972), 285–312; Bernard Capp, "English Youth Groups and *The Pinder of Wakefield," Past and Present,* No. 76 (Aug. 1977), 127–133. On youth cults in general, see John R. Gillis, *Youth and History: Tradition and Change in European Age Relations, 1700–Present* (New York, 1974); and Joseph F. Kett, *Rites of Passage: Adolescence in America, 1790 to the Present* (New York, 1977).

51. Herbert Asbury, *The Gangs of New York: An Informal History of the Underworld* (New York, 1928); David R. Johnson, *Policing the Urban Underworld: The Impact of Crime on the Development of the American Police, 1800–1887* (Philadelphia, 1979), 29–30, 79–89; Bruce Laurie, "Fire Companies and Gangs in Southwark: The 1840s," in Allen F. Davis and Mark H. Haller, eds., *The Peoples of Philadelphia: A History of Ethnic Groups and Lower-Class Life, 1790–1940* (Philadelphia, 1973), 71–82.

52. William Alexander Duer, *New-York as It Was during the Latter Part of the Last Century: An Anniversary Address Delivered before the St. Nicholas Society of the City of New-York, December First, 1848* (New York, 1849), 5–6.

were brought into play," but seldom was anyone gravely injured. The gangs "were generally routed by the dreaded appearance of one or two constables."[53]

In the early nineteenth century, gang violence began to increase, and some gangs, rather than fighting with a rival group, became involved in other riotous and criminal activities. The Highbinders are a good example of this transformation. Although they were an active gang for less than twenty years, they degenerated from a group whose original avowed aim was the suppression of prostitution to a notorious gang known only for its unrestrained violence. By the 1820s, and for the rest of the nineteenth century, the name *Highbinder* became American slang for "street tough."[54]

Other gangs emerged in the early nineteenth century. In 1812 frequent fights broke out near the corner of Beaver and Broad streets between the Whitehallers, who were "outdoor boys and uncultured watermen," and Old Slippers, who "were composed of bookbinders and printers."[55] By the 1820s the Old Slip Rangers lost their "affected style" and became a large and powerful gang which fought with other groups and preyed upon anyone who came into their neighborhood. One Sunday evening in May 1828, thirty or forty members of the gang gathered and, arming themselves with brickbats and stones, began an indiscriminate attack on unsuspecting passersby. The gang shouted: "Old-Slip forever! Old-Slip can protect itself!" Nearly a dozen persons were wounded. This same sense of territoriality led the Old Slip gang to attack Fire Engine No. 3 on its return from a fire and to fight with the crew of a ship docked at the foot of their street. The Old Slip depredations left local businessmen crying for the interposition of "the strong arm of the law," without which, it was feared, it would be "dangerous to walk the streets . . . after dark."[56]

53. De Voe, *The Market Book*, I, 358. See also Frank W. Norcross, *A History of the New York Swamp* (New York, 1901), 5–6.

54. *The Oxford English Dictionary* says that *Highbinder* is United States slang for "a rowdy, one of a gang which commits outrages on persons and property," dating the word from Dec. 1806, or the Augustus Street riot. The court records reveal some references to Highbinders before that: *People v. Jared Smith et al.,* May 30, 1806, NYCOT; *People v. Adam Fash et al.,* Aug. 11, 1806, NYCGS. In the late 1880s and 1890s "Highbinder" was a term used on the West Coast for a Chinese gang member.

55. David Bruce, "Autobiography of David Bruce; or, Then and Now," 19–20, MS, NYHS; *People v. Leonard Emmons et al.,* May 12, 1812, NYCGS.

56. *Gazette,* May 19, 1828; *Abraham V. Vandenburg v. James Bannon et al.,* Mar. 24, 1828, box 7440 (1827–1828), NYCSCPCC; *Gazette,* May 19, 1828. For the fight with the crew of a ship, see *People v. Castle et al.,* June 4, 1828, NYCGS.

In the 1820s and 1830s urban gangs became a serious problem for city officials. The city's youth seemed uncontrollable. Some gangs, like the Holy Gang or Lafayette Gang, which destroyed a gate and bell at the estate of John B. Murray on Eighth Avenue and Thirty-sixth Street, were mere vandals. Others created more formal organizations and attached themselves to fire companies. Many youths were too young to be regular members of a volunteer fire company but acted as auxiliaries. In the 1830s a series of complaints came before the Common Council about "young lads" who were given "night keys" to the firehouses and who stayed there all night carousing. These boys also signaled false alarms "for the purpose of getting the Fire Engines out, and racing through the streets."[57] Worse than this type of behavior, of course, were the gang attacks on fire companies going to and from fires. Such assaults, like the action of the Old Slips in 1828, increased in both intensity and frequency in the 1830s and 1840s. But some gangs hardly bothered with petty competition and became, like the Highbinders or the Forty Thieves of the Five Points, outright criminals.[58]

What shocked the middle class about the youth gangs was the way they flouted authority and willingly turned to violence. The murder in 1825 of Henry Lambert, one of the city's leading businessmen, by the Spring Street Fencibles revealed just how dangerous and disordered the city had become.[59] After one o'clock in the morning of June 3, about eight Spring Streeters, having drunk several glasses of "beer and gin and brandy," saw a carriage on Broadway near Art Street. One of the young toughs (all seventeen to twenty-one years old) threw a stone at the vehicle. Lambert and his companions, who had rented the carriage to attend an earlier uptown wedding, were walking behind it and immediately ran over to the Spring Streeters to have a word with them. Instead of being deferential or contrite, the gang members, described as young "mechanics or butcher's boys as their sleeves were partly rolled up," blew cigar smoke in the gentlemen's faces, called them dandies, and tried to trip them. A scuffle ensued. During the fight one Spring Streeter struck Lambert in the stomach with

57. *John Y. Dixon v. Daniel Stevens,* Dec. 29, 1828, box 7441 (1829), NYCSCPCC; *MCC,* XV, 418, XVIII, 573, 692, XIX, 20, 21, 35, 89. See also Stephen F. Ginsberg, "The History of Fire Protection in New York City, 1800–1842" (Ph.D. diss., New York University, 1968), 239–247.

58. For examples of these attacks, see *National Advocate,* Dec. 7, 1818; *Commercial Advertiser,* Dec. 5, 1818; *Gazette,* Dec. 7, 1818; *Weekly Visitor,* Dec. 12, 1818; *Cornelius B. Hulsart et al. v. Wm. Costello et al.,* Apr. 19, 1829, box 7441 (1829), NYCSCPCC. For Forty Thieves, see *Gazette,* Apr. 2, 1828.

59. On the background of the Spring Streeters, see *Evening Post,* June 4, 1825.

a hard blow. The merchant collapsed in the street and quickly died.[60] Although later convicted of only manslaughter, each rioter was given a heavy seven-year sentence which included three months in solitary confinement. The incident distressed commentators, who believed that young workingmen, like the Spring Streeters, should not be allowed to revel in the streets until all hours of the night, and they argued for better control of such youths. The *National Advocate* declared, "Here are seven [eight] lads apprentices to mechanical trades, carousing, drinking, and fighting at 1 o'clock in the morning; disturbing the public peace; assailing peaceable travellers, and finally causing the death of a worthy citizen. These things were not so in former times."[61]

The *National Advocate* was right. Certainly there were bands of young men and even gangs before. But while reveling on occasion, these youths had usually respected their betters. If they participated in rituals of misrule, they did so along well-worn paths of traditional behavior; and if they fought with competing gangs, they tended to follow set rules and quickly dispersed when confronted by the authorities. The violence and disrespect of the Spring Streeters was new, and it was evident not only in the murder of Henry Lambert. The specter of disorder also appeared in the rise in street and tavern rowdiness among the young and lower classes, in the disruptions of theatrical performances and outdoor spectacles, in the Callithumpian processions, and in the activities of the Highbinders, Old Slip Rangers, the Forty Thieves, and other gangs. Combined with the increased violence in opposing middle-class culture, in strikes, in ethnic and racial conflicts, and in politics, these disturbances marked a growing resistance to all authority. In turn, the magistrates and the middle class they represented became even more convinced of the illegitimacy of all mobs and demanded that the disorder be checked.

60. *Ibid.*, June 4, 25, 1825.
61. *National Advocate,* June 25, 1825.

TEN

Policing the City:
Changing Notions of Riot Control

Where danger is greatest, there should the sentry be placed, and the police should be the Cerberus of society, guarding from danger every man's door, protecting from oppression the innocent and helpless.

Charles Christian, *A Brief Treatise on
the Police of the City of New York,* 1812

Drastic changes within New York City and within the American nation in the half-century following the Revolutionary war altered public attitudes toward the concept of police. Previously, Americans rejected any suggestions of a regular police force because it conjured up images of occupying British redcoats, monarchical tyranny, and the infringement of liberty.[1] Civic leaders did use the term *police,* but when they did so, they referred to it in a very broad way. *Police,* as Noah Webster put it, was the equivalent of the whole "government of a city or place," in essence "the corporation or body of men governing a city." This police was responsible for every facet of municipal control, including the laying out of wharves, commerce, health regulations, and sanitation as well as the maintenance of law and order. But in the early Republic, the term *police* began to be applied exclusively to the men hired to enforce the law. The police became, in the words of police magistrate Charles Christian, "the Cerberus of society, guarding from danger every man's door, protecting from oppression the innocent and helpless."[2]

One reason for this change was the complete abandonment of the old ideal of a single-interest society. A new ideology grew out of the republicanism of the Revolution, which by the 1820s and 1830s embraced free competition between groups and individuals as the best means of achieving the public good. No sooner was the republican crisis of corruption and faction met in the 1760s and 1770s than men began to set themselves apart from one another and the mythical united community became divided into a host of communities organized along political, ethnic, racial, religious, neighborhood, and class lines. As these new groups defined themselves in increasingly particularistic terms, the purpose of government changed. City officials still regulated the city, but the new doctrine of laissez faire downplayed this traditional function. The police, by concentrating on protecting property and maintaining order, no longer acted as the guardians of public welfare, but became umpires guaranteeing fair competition.

Although the middle class welcomed this open competition, at times it led to a frightening vision of the urban world. Many middle-class reformers agreed with Charles Christian that "the obvious inequalities of for-

1. Charles Christian, *A Brief Treatise on the Police of the City of New York* (New York, 1812), 28–29; James F. Richardson, *The New York Police: Colonial Times to 1901* (New York, 1970), 21–22.

2. Webster is quoted in Roger Lane, *Policing the City: Boston, 1822–1885* (Cambridge, Mass., 1967), 1. Christian, *Brief Treatise on Police,* 28–29.

tune" which set men off from each other, as well as the baser passions apparent in "the insatiable appetite for animal gratification . . . in weak and depraved minds," created a "wretchedness," inevitable "in such a heterogeneous mass," which had to be controlled.[3] A police force, then, became one means to control that "heterogeneous mass."

There was yet another reason, connected to the governmental response to urban growth, for the development of police forces in the early nineteenth century. In New York City and other urban areas, there was a gradual delegation of authority in all facets of government. The size of New York made the personal intervention of "the corporation or body of men governing" the city more difficult, and it became necessary to assign specialized agents to tasks which were once a part of the magistrates' duties. The city just became too big for personal government. From this need to delegate authority grew a professional (or at least semiprofessional) police force devoted full time to guarding the public peace.

This development was gradual and piecemeal; reorganization of the various police officers into a single department did not occur until 1845. But even that date, often seized upon as the beginning of the professionalization of New York's police, really marks just another step in a continuing process.[4] Starting in the early 1800s, the idea began to emerge that men should be hired to guard the public peace. In other words, by the 1830s an odd assortment of constables, marshals, and the city watch, numbering several hundred strong, already had become the frontline defense against crime and public disorder.

Charges that these pre-1845 police officers were political appointees more concerned with collecting fees than preventing crime and that they were both corrupt and inefficient are well founded. But the post-1845 regular police force was little better. It, too, was permeated with political hacks who had corrupt and criminal connections.[5] Thus, the actual establishment of a regularly organized police force in 1845 was only a small

3. Christian, *Brief Treatise on Police,* 28–29.
4. Richardson, *New York Police.*
5. So political were the post-1845 police that in 1857 two competing forces were set up, one the creature of the Democratic city government, the other of the Republican state government. In 1857, the intense hatred between these two police forces erupted into riot and made effective control of crime and crowds almost impossible. Despite a few moments of glory for the New York Police Department, politics and corruption continued to play an important role into the twentieth century. James F. Richardson, "Mayor Fernando Wood and the New York Police Force, 1855–1857," *New-York Historical Society Quarterly,* L (1966), 5–40.

improvement over the previous irregular police of constables, marshals, and the watch.[6] Moreover, while the model of the London police, organized in 1829, may have been important in persuading New Yorkers to pass the 1844 law, the idea in the 1810s, 1820s, and 1830s that a police force ought to exist to battle crime and disorder resulted from developments within New York City.

The Magistrates

These local developments can be seen in the changes in riot control from the eighteenth century to the early nineteenth century. In the late eighteenth century the key police officers were the magistrates of the city corporation. First among them was the mayor, who was expected to appear personally at the scene of every major disturbance and to assert actively his authority to disperse the mob. But the mayor was not to face civil disorder alone; other city officials ought to intervene at any sign of trouble. The city recorder, who ranked second in importance among the magistrates, as well as the aldermen and assistant aldermen all shared responsibility with the mayor for the maintenance of public peace.[7]

The broad and overlapping nature of civic offices enhanced the police power of the magistrates. In the late eighteenth century no one drew fine distinctions between the executive, legislative, and judicial duties of the city magistrates. The mayor, besides being the chief executive of the city, was a member of the Common Council and the head judge of the city's civil and criminal court. The aldermen and assistant aldermen worked with the mayor as executors of the law, sat in the Common Council, and served as judges in the court system. The city recorder, although primarily a judicial officer, also was a member of the Common Council and acted as an executive officer.[8] This overlapping of functions had important

6. Richardson, *New York Police,* 23–82.

7. James Hardie, *The Description of the City of New-York; Containing Its Population, Institutions, Commerce, Manufactures, Public Buildings, Courts of Justice, Places of Amusement, &c., to Which Is Prefixed a Brief Account of Its First Settlement by the Dutch, in the Year 1629, and of the Most Remarkable Events, Which Have Occurred in Its History, from That Time to the Present Period* (New York, 1827), 302–303.

8. Sidney I. Pomerantz, *New York, an American City, 1783–1803: A Study of Urban Life,* 2d ed. (Port Washington, N.Y., 1965), 36–40, 136–137, 308–309; Paul O. Weinbaum, *Mobs and Demagogues: The New York Response to Collective*

ramifications. Each magistrate possessed considerable personal power; if a rioter refused to keep the peace, in all likelihood the poor fellow, when brought to trial, would have as his judge the same magistrate who was an eyewitness to his misbehavior.

The magistrates combined this diffuse official power with unofficial influence from wealth and social standing. Although membership in the Common Council was slightly more open to the nonelite after the Revolution than it was during the closing years of the colonial period, most magistrates continued to be members of the city's social and economic leadership.[9] Even magistrates who came from humbler origins had achieved a high social status by the time they reached office. Stephen Allen, for example, born into an artisan family, served briefly as a sailmaker's apprentice but soon after the Revolutionary war established himself first as a hardworking journeyman and then as a master sailmaker. Showing just those virtues extolled by the rising middle class, he branched out and not only made sails but opened a chandler's business and acted as a supplier to other sailmakers. By the time he entered politics in the early nineteenth century, he was an affluent merchant who viewed his term as mayor, from 1821 to 1824, as a capstone to years in public service. Salaries for municipal office were low or nonexistent; yet, as Stephen Allen no doubt knew only too well, numerous fees and vast patronage powers bolstered a magistrate's economic situation. De Witt Clinton, a member of one of New York's leading families, gave up a seat in the United States Senate for the wealth, prestige, and power of being mayor of the city of New York.[10]

Magistrates put their public and personal authority to good effect during eighteenth-century riots. In an effort to avoid an anti-importation riot in 1768, William Smith and the governor "advised the Magistrates to patrol their Wards," where they knew many of the residents, and "with two or three respectable Citizens . . . propagate their Sentiments to render Riots unpopular by preingaging the Voice of the discreet Inhabitants."

Violence in the Early Nineteenth Century (Ann Arbor, Mich., 1979), 112–116; Charles P. Daly, *Historical Sketch of the Judicial Tribunals of New York from 1623 to 1846* (New York, 1855), 64–65; Stephen Allen, "The Memoirs of Stephen Allen (1767–1852): Sometime Mayor of New York City, Chairman of the (Croton) Water Commissioners, etc., etc.," ed. John C. Travis, 80, 88, typescript, NYHS.

9. Bruce M. Wilkenfeld, "The New York City Common Council, 1689–1800," *New York History,* LII (1971), 249–274.

10. Allen, "Memoirs of Stephen Allen," 41–104; Weinbaum, *Mobs and Demagogues,* 112–116; Pomerantz, *New York,* 40.

The success of this form of riot control can be gauged by the response of eighty volunteer firemen, who, after listening to an address from the mayor, "promised to stand by him in preserving the Peace of the City."[11] Some thirty years later, Mayor Richard Varick showed continued adherence to this gentlemanly mode of persuasion when faced by the bawdy-house rioters. Varick revealed, according to one newspaper, exactly the mixture of qualities most admired in an eighteenth-century public official. In persuading the mob to disperse, he exhibited a "spirit and firmness, tempered with humanity, and moderation," which "illustrated his well known character, as the magistrate and the citizen."[12]

City officials expected that their presence alone would defuse a riot. Not only were they recognizable by their staff of office, but their bearing, their dress, and their wide-ranging personal contacts all contributed to their official and unofficial authority. In fact, many eighteenth-century magistrates thought so highly of their power and prestige that they assumed a strongly worded proclamation would quell a disturbance. New York officials used the newspapers to carry strong statements opposing specific riots and their advice that masters and parents keep apprentices, children, and slaves at home.[13] Still, there were times when neither the assertion of deference nor the high-sounding proclamations of governmental officials worked in controlling a riot. When these means failed, some kind of force was needed.

In England this meant turning to the Riot Act of 1715. This statute allowed a magistrate to declare a gathering of three or more people a riot, read the Riot Act to them, and after an hour-long period of grace, use force and make arrests if the disturbance continued. During the colonial period New York, like several other colonies, exhibited a reluctance to pass a permanent riot act modeled on the English statute. Provincial legislatures may have avoided adopting such laws because they feared that they might lead to arbitrary government or because they reduced their flexibility in dealing with royal officials. They may have believed also that there was no need for a permanent statute when the common law, buttressed by court decisions and the English act of 1715, provided them with a definition of

11. William Smith, *Historical Memoirs of William Smith, Historian of the Province of New York, Member of the Governor's Council, and Last Chief Justice of That Province under the Crown, Chief Justice of Quebec,* ed. William H. W. Sabine, 2 vols. (New York, 1956–1958), I, 48.

12. *Mercantile Advertiser,* July 18, 1799.

13. *Journal,* Oct. 19, 1793.

riot as well as the right to muster the militia for moral and military support in confrontations with a mob. Only in a moment of extraordinary circumstances, during the near rebellion of the Green Mountain Boys in 1774, did the New York legislature enact an antiriot law, and then it was geared specifically to conflicts over land claims, resistance to civil authority, and tumultuous behavior in what later became Vermont. Moreover, like most other colonial riot acts, and unlike the English statute, the New York law had an expiration date: passed on March 9, 1774, it was set to expire December 31, 1775.[14]

After the Revolution and throughout the entire first half of the nineteenth century, no statute was passed in New York to define a riot. Instead, New Yorkers relied on the legacy of the common law. Despite this lack of legislative action, hundreds of indictments and convictions appear in the court records, and the common law tradition served as the rationale for the occasional use of armed force to suppress tumultuous disorder.[15]

Yet, before the 1830s, officials were hesitant to order out the military. Americans still distrusted the army because they feared that it would lead to despotism and arbitrary government. The militia could also pose a threat to the magistrates. Troops were unreliable. By law every adult male in the state under the age of forty-five was supposed to be in the militia. This provision meant that, if there was a wholesale mustering of the troops, many of the men in the riot would be called to arms. No magistrate relished the thought of arming any part of the mob; and, if the object of the riot was odious to the entire community, there was always the possibility that the militia might disobey orders and join forces with the mob. To avoid these potential hazards, officials exercised great care in their mustering of particular militia units. In July 1799, for example, Mayor Varick wisely called upon the Washington troop of horse in order to persuade the bawdyhouse mob to go home.[16] Varick, who was a Federalist, knew he

14. Max Beloff, *Public Order and Popular Disturbances, 1660–1714* (London, 1938), 136–137; Pauline Maier, *From Resistance to Revolution: Colonial Radicals and the Development of American Opposition to Britain, 1765–1776* (New York, 1972), 24–26; New York, *The Colonial Laws of New York from the Year 1664 to the Revolution . . .*, V (Albany, N.Y., 1894), 647–655.

15. Oliver Lorenzo Barbour, *A Treatise on the Criminal Law of the State of New York . . .*, 2d ed. (Albany, 1852), 218–227.

16. *Argus,* July 19, 20, 30, 1799; *Gazette,* July 18, 20, 1799; *Daily Advertiser,* July 18, 20, 1799; *MCC,* II, 560, 563, 567; I. N. Phelps Stokes, *The Iconography of Manhattan Island, 1498–1909 . . .* (New York, 1915–1928), V, 1370.

could depend on this company because it was recruited from the city's elite and its members were also Federalists.[17]

The magistrates were supposed to find help, without the military trappings, in the posse comitatus. Translated literally, *posse comitatus* means "power of the county" and refers to the power the magistrate had to summon the entire community to aid the civil authorities in an emergency. Theoretically, everyone had to join the posse comitatus and support the magistrates in the suppression of a disturbance. In practice, however, the posse comitatus was severely flawed. If the riot acted for the community, then it was difficult, if not impossible, to summon the community to oppose the riot. Moreover, many citizens hesitated to risk life, limb, and property to aid the city officials. Instead of relying upon a general posse comitatus, magistrates called upon the aid of private citizens whom they trusted. For example, on July 4, 1805, the mayor "and a few other gentlemen" suppressed a disturbance between some Irish and native-born Americans.[18] This informal posse comitatus probably was composed of friends and relatives who could be depended upon by the magistrate. The informal posse comitatus was not intended as a force to do battle; rather, it too was a means to add moral and social weight, embodied in the leading gentlemen of the community, to the authority of the magistrates.[19] It was meant to daunt, not duel.

These methods of riot control, merging formal and informal authority, worked best in smaller traditional communities where members of the elite knew most of the people in the mob and where the fabled anonymity of the crowd was a thing of the future. Robert R. Livingston and the sea captains could influence crowds in the street during the Stamp Act disturbances because of such personal connections. Likewise, Mayor Varick could dismiss a cartman in the July 1799 bawdyhouse riot because he was able to recognize him. Dependent upon the magistrate or his gentleman friends for patronage, the laborer knew that his behavior might affect his

17. The Washington horse are identified as "Federal soldiers" in the Republican newspaper *Argus*, Oct. 10, 1799. See also Maier, *Resistance*, 16–20; Robert Reinders, "Militia and Public Order in Nineteenth-Century America," *Journal of American Studies*, XI (1977), 81–101; Paul A. Gilje, "The Baltimore Riots of 1812 and the Breakdown of the Anglo-American Mob Tradition," *Journal of Social History*, XIII (1979–1980), 547–564.

18. *Evening Post*, July 6, 1805.

19. Maier, *Resistance*, 16–20; Gilje, "Baltimore Riots," *Jour. Soc. Hist.*, XIII (1979–1980), 547–564.

employment on the day after the riot, and perhaps for years to come. That knowledge in a face-to-face society acted to restrain rioters from becoming more violent.[20]

The Rise of the Police

In the late eighteenth and early nineteenth centuries, this system of riot control broke down. Private citizens stopped assisting the magistrates and abdicated much of their civic responsibility to city officials. As early as 1793 the magistrates complained that they "saw a number of respectable fellow citizens standing idle spectators" to a riot and witnessing the destruction of private property. At that time the magistrates reminded New Yorkers that it was their duty "to give effectual aid to the magistrates . . . in suppressing all riots and breaches of the peace."[21]

The magistrates, however, were in the process of relinquishing their day-to-day personal role in riot control. After 1800 the increasing size of the city made it difficult for the mayor and the other members of the Common Council to appear at every disturbance. Moreover, the phenomenal population growth made it impossible for corporation officials, even local ward aldermen, to recognize familiar faces in the crowd. Charles Christian, a longtime police magistrate who had confronted many a mob, commented in 1811: "When the population of a city becomes so numerous that the citizens are not all known to each other, then may depredators merge in the mass, and spoliate in secret and safety."[22]

The press of municipal business forced the city administration to divide its responsibilities more carefully. Inch by inch the mayor and the aldermen retreated from the increasing demands of the judicial system and withdrew from the close supervision of the conduct of New Yorkers. In 1797 the state passed a law which permitted the mayor or the recorder to

20. Gilje, "Baltimore Riots," *Jour. Soc. Hist.,* XIII (1979–1980), 547–564; E. P. Thompson, "The Moral Economy of the English Crowd in the Eighteenth Century," *Past and Present,* No. 50 (Feb. 1971), 121–126; Thompson, "Patrician Society, Plebeian Culture," *Jour. Soc. Hist.,* VII (1973–1974), 404–405. For a discussion on the mutuality of deference, see J.G.A. Pocock, "The Classical Theory of Deference," *American Historical Review,* LXXXI (1976), 516–523.

21. *Journal,* Oct. 19, 1793.

22. Christian, *Brief Treatise on Police,* 4.

hold civil court without the presence of any of the aldermen, although aldermen could still act as judges if they so desired. In 1803 De Witt Clinton surrendered his position as chief justice of the civil court to the recorder, and in the early 1820s Stephen Allen abandoned the mayor's chair on the city's criminal tribunal, the court of general sessions. Although the Common Council retained both legislative and executive functions, the management of city affairs became the province of distinct committees of the Common Council. In 1798 there were only four standing committees; six years later there were eight. Special officers were hired to administer city services, and in 1830 a new charter created regular executive departments under the jurisdiction of the Common Council.[23]

In the opening decades of the nineteenth century, the mayor, the recorder, and the Common Council became too busy to control the daily problems of urban disorder. Some sort of specialized force was needed. No model existed. The Metropolitan Police of London was still a dream of a few English reformers. Thus, although there were occasional calls for an overhaul of the peace officers, the professionalization of New York's police was a stopgap development, largely dependent on the personalities involved and the gradual increment in their numbers.

A pivotal figure in the emergence of New York's professional police was the longtime high constable, Jacob Hays. Hays developed a tremendous reputation as a crimefighter and peacekeeper. He first became a peace officer in 1798 when Aaron Burr secured a place for him as one of the city's marshals. Four years later, in 1802, Hays assumed the post of high constable when he was only thirty years old, a position he was to hold for nearly fifty years. By the 1840s he was so respected that the city allowed him to retain the title and perquisites of high constable until his death in 1850, even though the post was legally abolished in 1844.[24]

The high constable in the eighteenth century was an official of the courts, serving its writs and executing its orders. He was not supposed to be a crimefighter. Only as an ancillary part of his job was the high con-

23. Pomerantz, *New York,* 36–40, 50–51, 136–137, 308–309; Weinbaum, *Mobs and Demagogues,* 112; Daly, *Historical Sketch of Judicial Tribunals,* 64–65; Allen, "Memoirs of Stephen Allen," 80, 88.

24. Sutherland Denlinger, "Old Hays—There Was a Cop!" *New York World Telegram,* Mar. 1–6, 1936; A. E. Costello, *Our Police Protectors: History of the New York Police from the Earliest Period to the Present Time* (New York, 1885), 92–97; Richardson, *New York Police,* 16–17; Pomerantz, *New York,* 301, 387.

stable to oversee the peace of the city and supervise the watch and other peace officers.[25] Hays broadened the functions of this office by sheer force of personality, making himself not only a kind of police commissioner but also a super-detective and peacekeeper as well. Characteristically, for several years Hays served as both high constable and a captain of the watch. This double duty enabled him to supervise the peace of the city, day and night, and allowed him to collect salaries and fees from both offices. Hays had an eye for the main chance and concentrated most of his efforts on capturing thieves, collecting rewards, and serving summonses and writs, thereby making himself a rich man. He also claimed to know every criminal in the city. To keep track of them he maintained a record of all the inmates in the state prison, their crimes, their age, their description, and the date of their release.[26] He may even have had some corrupt dealings with the underworld. In 1811 he testified at the court of general sessions in favor of Sarah Woods, whose dance hall was notorious for indecorous behavior. Seventeen years later he personally interfered to prevent a disturbance at the Broadway house of ill fame run by a Mrs. Robbins. Significantly, Hays took no action against Robbins or her girls and arrested only her harassers.[27]

Hays, however, did make himself serviceable to the community when riots broke out. Alone, or with other officers, he would plunge into the middle of an affray, often armed with only the high constable's staff, and with a mixture of force and presence strive to break up the disturbance. By the 1820s Hays had perfected these techniques, and everyone in the city knew that High Constable Hays's appearance on the scene increased the likelihood of a trip to jail. In one riot at the Circus in August 1822, Hays

25. George Austin Ketcham, "Municipal Police Reform: A Comparative Study of Law Enforcement in Cincinnati, Chicago, New Orleans, New York, and St. Louis, 1844–1877" (Ph.D. diss., University of Missouri, Columbia, 1967), 18–25.

26. Jacob Hays, "An Account of Prisoners Received into the New York State Prison from the Commencement of the Institution" (1798–1821), bound MS, Library, Museum of the City of New York.

27. Denlinger, "Old Hays," New York World Telegram, Mar. 1–6, 1936; Costello, Our Police Protectors, 92–97; Richardson, New York Police, 16–17; Pomerantz, New York, 301, 387; Jacob Hays, file, newspaper clippings, Library, Museum of the City of New York; People v. Sarah Woods, Aug. 12, 1811, NYC, Minutes of Cases, Court of General Sessions, New York City, 1811, MS, NYHS; People v. John Anderson et al., Jan. 12, 1829, NYCGS.

came to the aid of Marshal George B. Raymond, who was struggling to keep an unruly crowd under control. Each of the police officers took hold of a leading rioter—Hays was noted for his viselike grip—and they started to drag them off. The mob followed, pelting stones at the two intrepid officers, threatening to stab and otherwise intimidating them. Raymond's left eye was cut and barely open; Hays was struck on the head several times with stones; yet both men held onto their captives, prevented their rescue, and managed to quell the disturbance.[28]

Hays's methods reveal an abandonment of the old techniques of deferential riot control. Hays did rely upon the respect and even the awe that much of the city held for him. However, this was not a respect born of either his social or political position. Rather, it derived from physical intimidation and the probability of punishment. Much of Hays's effectiveness, then, stemmed not only from his authority as a police officer representing the law but also from his tough, hard-nosed reputation. By casting himself in this role, Hays established a pattern of police behavior which was followed by police officers after the establishment of the regular police force in 1845. For, unlike London's bobbies, who relied on the powers of the state and eschewed violence, New York police—the neighborhood cop on the beat—depended upon personal contacts within the community, intimidation, and brute force.[29] In short, the reign of High Constable Hays marked the end of the traditional methods of riot control and the emergence of police tactics that dominated the rest of the nineteenth century.

There were other peace officers, not as famous as Hays, who were equally important in the development of New York's police. Throughout the early national period the number of the city's police officers—constables and marshals for the daytime, and the watchmen for the night—continually increased. The mayor appointed the marshals, and voters elected two constables from each ward.[30] Both marshals and constables originally served, like the high constable, as officers of the court system, issuing and delivering writs, summonses, and warrants; only secondarily were they entrusted to keep the peace. But as early as the 1790s the

28. *Gazette,* Aug. 14, 1822; *Evening Post,* Aug. 13, 1822.

29. Wilbur R. Miller, *Cops and Bobbies: Police Authority in New York and London, 1830–1870* (Chicago, 1977).

30. The high constable, however, was appointed by the mayor (Pomerantz, *New York,* 302).

marshals were under injunction from the mayor to disperse any "riotous or tumultuous Assembly," to be "vigilant in detecting and bringing to justice all Murderers, Robbers, Thieves and other Criminals," and to take "before a Magistrate for Examination all idle Strollers, Vagabonds and disorderly persons."[31] By the early nineteenth century many of these constables and marshals had become full-time professionals at their police work. Some, like Henry Abell, worked their way up from being night watchman to marshal and finally to police justice (a judge in the daily criminal court). Abell, George Raymond, Abner Curtis, and others each remained peace officers for well over a decade and had plenty of time to become experts in catching criminals and controlling riots.[32]

Much less professional and much less effective were the watchmen who patrolled the city streets at night. The watch was designed at first not so much to prevent crime or disorder as to check for fires and the safety of the city streets. The watchmen were therefore not empowered to make arrests unless they actually caught someone in the act of crime. But since much crime and disorder occurred at night, circumstances forced them increasingly into police work. Unfortunately, unlike their daytime counterparts who could earn a living from the fees they collected, the watch was extremely poorly paid. For most watchmen their patrol at night was merely a second job to help support their families.[33] At times their lack of diligence proved embarrassing. Pranksters occasionally "capped" a watchman; that is, they stole his leather helmet, the only insignia possessed by these peace officers. Other tricks were played on careless watchmen. For instance, mischievous neighborhood youths tipped over more than one watchbox occupied by a sleeping or intoxicated watchman. The Common Council prescribed disciplinary action to curb erring watchmen. They dismissed any watchman capped twice and suspended many watchmen for being drunk or failing in their duty.[34]

31. Ketcham, "Municipal Police Reform," 18–25; quotation in Pomerantz, *New York*, 302–303.

32. *MCC*, III, 661, IV, 82, 89, 663, 687, VI, 212, 304, 455, 465, 478, 490, 491, VIII, 646, 661, X, 54, 64, 103, XI, 12, 172, 454, 566, 667, XII, 12, 13, 403, 523, 579, 636, 646, 762, XIII, 102, 233, 391, 639.

33. Pomerantz, *New York*, 303–304; Ketcham, "Municipal Police Reform," 26–40; Richardson, *New York Police*, 19–21; Stephen F. Ginsberg, "The Police and Fire Protection in New York City, 1800–1850," *NY Hist.*, LII (1971), 133–150.

34. Costello, *Our Police Protectors*, 72–73; *MCC*, V, 180, 207, 309.

Yet the steady increase in the size of the watch force did add to its effectiveness. In 1788 there were about 50 watchmen, in 1800 there were 72, but by 1825 they totaled 428, divided into three companies, each with two captains and two assistants.[35] Per capita, in 1788 there was 1 watchman for every 663 persons in the city; in 1825 there was 1 watchman for every 388 persons.[36] This increase in the proportion of watchmen reflects the growing apprehensions of disorder.

Although the entire force was not on duty on any given night, the overall size and organization of the watch meant that the city magistrates had a paid auxiliary force available for the suppression of disturbances. Some watchmen had aided the mayor and magistrates in the riots of the late eighteenth century; by the early years of the nineteenth century these "leatherheads," as they were derisively called, were the city's main shock troops battling the mob.[37] During the Augustus Street riot in 1806, the watch became embroiled with rioters: one watchman was killed, and several others were wounded. The magistrates ordered the watch to the scene during the James Street riot of 1812 and on a host of other occasions. For such service the city sometimes rewarded watchmen with extra pay and gave them compensation in case of injury.[38] This, no doubt, added an incentive to be active in riotous situations. Still, the watch was far from being feared by every mob and many times was derelict in its duty. The press in August 1822, for example, criticized the watch's failure to come to the aid of Hays and Raymond at the Circus disturbance.[39] More serious were the failings of the watch on New Year's Eve in 1828, when the Callithumpians were unimpeded in their riotous progress through the city.

35. Pomerantz, *New York*, 303–304; Richardson, *New York Police*, 19–21; James Hardie, *A Census of the New Buildings Erected in This City, in the Year 1824, Arranged in Distinct Classes, according to Their Materials and Numbers of Stories; Also, a Number of Statistical Documents, Interesting to the Christian, the Merchant, the Man of Industry, and the Public in General* (New York, 1825), 41–42.

36. The 1788 figure is based on the population in 1790 and therefore is slightly distorted. The proportional increase of watchmen per citizen is still valid. Comparison with 1800 shows one watchman for every 840 citizens.

37. Costello, *Our Police Protectors*, 72.

38. *MCC*, I, 774, II, 46, 28, 567, IV, 411, V, 250, XVI, 50, 651, XVII, 38, 200.

39. *Gazette*, Jan. 3, 1828; *Evening Post*, Jan. 2, 1828; *American*, Jan. 3, 1828; Weinbaum, *Mobs and Demagogues*, 53.

Shortcomings like these led to the reorganization of the police force in 1844 and 1845.[40]

Every peace officer from high constable to night watchman was responsive to changes in the political currents of the city. Changes in the city administration led to dismissals and new appointments among both the watch and the city marshals, and the constables were even more vulnerable because they faced an election every year.[41] Yet, despite all these difficulties, a degree of consistency was maintained, especially among the marshals and watch captains, which made the two dozen constables, scores of marshals, and hundreds of watchmen one of America's largest and most efficient police forces by 1834.

Overseeing the entire police force, and themselves an important element in the growing professionalization of New York's police, were the special police justices presiding over the Police Office. The Common Council created the Police Office in 1798 to remove from the mayor the burden of examining petty offenders. Although the police justices were also political appointees, either from experience or temperament they quickly gained expertise at their job.[42] The various police officers brought every criminal, disorderly person, or vagrant to the police office. There the police magistrate on duty examined him that day. (Prisoners taken at night had to wait until morning before their cases were heard.) The Police Office dealt with everything from settling a dispute between two neighbors to handling the first stages of a murder case.[43] The police justice heard complaints, examined the witnesses as well as the accused, and decided whether to dismiss the charges, to impose a small fine or penalty, or, if the case was serious, to pass it on to the higher criminal courts. If the police justice decided to do the last, then he had to issue bond or secure the prisoner in jail, have the clerk take written depositions, and ascertain the facts. On top of all this the

40. For the emergence of police forces in Jacksonian America, see Richardson, *New York Police;* Ketcham, "Municipal Police Reform"; Miller, *Cops and Bobbies;* Lane, *Policing the City;* David R. Johnson, *Policing the Urban Underworld: The Impact of Crime on the Development of the American Police, 1800–1887* (Philadelphia, 1979); Celestine Estelle Anderson, "The Invention of the 'Professional' Municipal Police: The Case of Cincinnati, 1788 to 1900" (Ph.D. diss., University of Cincinnati, 1979).

41. Richardson, *New York Police,* 51–289; Miller, *Cops and Bobbies;* Paul O. Weinbaum, "Temperance, Politics, and the New York City Riots of 1857," *NYHSQ,* LXIX (1975), 246–270.

42. *MCC,* II, 413, IV, 361, XIX, 375.

43. For the records of this court, see NYCMMPO, 1799–1829, 39 vols.

police justice was responsible for dismissing the watch in the morning and often personally took charge if a disturbance broke out. In short, the police justice became a crucial cog in the city's law-and-order machinery.[44]

Taken together, the practices of the police justices, High Constable Hays, the other constables, marshals, watch captains, and watchmen marked an important step toward the establishment of a full-fledged police department in New York City. Throughout the early national period this group of police officials gradually assumed greater and greater responsibility over the day-to-day control of crime and disorder. This development does not mean that officials totally abandoned the older methods of riot control. The mayor and the city magistrates still occasionally went to the scene of a disturbance and—with a small army of constables, marshals, and the watch at their backs—attempted to influence the mob. Even when they did, however, there seemed to be more reliance on the threat of physical coercion than on the exertion of deferential paternalistic authority. Moreover, by the 1820s and 1830s, the magistrates more often than not let the various members of the police force handle the disorder which erupted in the city.

Paradoxically, the emergence of a police force to fight crime and quell disorder increased the level of violence in riots. In the eighteenth century, in England as well as in America, the casualties in popular disturbances were ordinarily rioters. The calling out of the army often led to an excess of force. Hence, we see the deaths in the "massacres" at Saint George's Field in London in 1768 and at Boston in 1770. The increased dependence on the watch, marshals, and constables should have acted to prevent casualties—after all, this police represented something less severe than the mustering of the military, yet was stronger than simple exhortation and persuasion. But the new police, especially the watch, had a particular vulnerability. Deference was in decline, and the mayor and magistrates had increasing difficulties exerting their influence over a mob.

Recruited from the same social stratum as that of many of the rioters, the new agents of law enforcement were less likely to gain the respect of the crowd. Since there were no traditions bolstering the position of the police as protectors of property and guardians of order, and since these officers were often left to enforce unpopular laws or restrain the interest of a neighborhood or local community, they were often viewed with hostility. The political nature of the police officers' appointment and the half-hearted

44. Hardie, *Description of the City of New-York,* 302–303; Pomerantz, *New York,* 304–305.

PLATE 19. The Watchman.
Engraving by Alexander Anderson for Cries of New-York, *1822. Courtesy of the*
New-York Historical Society.

commitment of watchmen to the job further undermined their positions.
Hence there were the capping and harassment of individual watchmen and
the concerted plans to "trip up the watch." The only way for this police to
gain respect was, as with High Constable Hays, to use force. But in a society where different groups struggled and competed with one another,
such force only elicited more force from the mob. Violence begot more violence. All too often, both police and rioters sustained injuries. At times
men were killed.

Volcano under the City

They carry guns, pistols, axes, hatchets, crowbars, pitchforks, knives, bludgeons,—the Red Flag. Much of their shouting is done in other tongues, but the cry is in English: "Down with the rich men! Down with property! Down with the police!"

It is an insurrection of evil against law; an uprising of suppressed hellish forces against order.

William Osborn Stoddard,
The Volcano under the City, 1887

William Osborn Stoddard's volcano erupted in July 1863. On the thirteenth of that month resistance to the new draft law led to an outbreak of rioting that quickly engulfed the entire city. Thousands poured into the street, striking out at an incredible array of targets. Quickly, racial antagonism, ethnic hatred, class resentment, and a strident antiauthoritarianism eclipsed the draft issue at the heart of the rioting. For observers like Stoddard, the four days of rioting beginning on the thirteenth threatened to destroy civilization. Mobs attacked the mayor's house, an armory, the *Tribune* building, and the Negro Orphan Asylum and looted and gutted elegant homes and shops on Lexington Avenue. The rioters burned buildings throughout the city and even set whole blocks on fire. On the second day of rioting, raging crowds began to attack blacks, driving them from their homes and jobs, and then, in an act of savagery, strung up captured blacks from trees and lampposts, setting fire to their bodies. Police were unmercifully beaten, killed, and then stripped of any valuables. Soldiers from nearby posts rushed to the scene, only to be overwhelmed by the tumult. Officials called upon the regular army, and troops fresh from the victory at Gettysburg found themselves fighting in the streets of New York. Armed with guns, clubs, stones, and other weapons, the mob showed little fear. Cannons had to be brought into the fray, and soldiers fired point-blank at the mob. Casualties on both sides mounted. The total of deaths is impossible to calculate, but at least one thousand persons lost their lives.[1]

The New York City Draft Riots stand as the most violent and devastating of all American popular disturbances. More people participated, more people died, more property was destroyed, and authority was more challenged than in any other disturbance in our history. The Draft Riots cast a dark shadow on collective action; the reader need go no further than the cover of Stoddard's *Volcano under the City* to know the author's thoughts on rioting. Emblazoned against a red background is the black skeleton of death riding skyward with scythe in hand, sharp spurs digging into his groaning horse. On one side of a black cloud is the date "1863," on the other side an ominous "188?" For Stoddard, and he was not alone in his opinions, the mob was nothing other than a "whooping, yelling, blaspheming, howling, demoniac" mass, "such as no man imagined the City of

1. The best modern account of the Draft Riots is Adrian Cook, *The Armies of the Streets: The New York City Draft Riots of 1863* (Lexington, Ky., 1974). For a popularized account, see James McCague, *The Second Rebellion: The Story of the New York City Draft Riots of 1863* (New York, 1968).

New York to contain." Surprised to find "women among them" and "boys half grown," Stoddard asserted that "none of them seem to be Americans." These foreigners, these half-beasts, in Stoddard's view, constituted the "social volcanic forces" existing in great cities; and "few men have any idea of their extent and power, or how completely they are prepared for an eruption."[2]

The Draft Riots represent, for this study, a view into the future. Although the violence and divisiveness of July 1863 were born of a particular and unique set of conditions, occurring in the midst of a devastating war, they were the climactic expression of the popular disorder that emerged in the first half of the nineteenth century. By 1834 the new pattern of rioting had been set. The "social volcanic forces" were already then starting to boil, and their earth-shattering explosion in 1863 was presaged by the less cataclysmic—yet no less significant—quakes, tremors, and minor eruptions in New York's year of riots—1834.

The eruptions continued after that year, bringing, at times, death and destruction, as attested by the thirty-one fatalities in the Astor Place riot of 1849.[3] Even after 1863 the social volcano was not quieted, and only a few years after the Draft Riots, a major disturbance between Protestant and Catholic Irishmen shocked the city in 1871. Far from dormant, the eruptions persisted, spitting out violence in labor and race riots throughout the nation during the late nineteenth and early twentieth centuries.[4] If bloodletting marred popular disorder after 1834, we must ask, How and why did this type of rioting gain ascendancy?

The purpose of this book has been to explain the changes in rioting, and the changes in the response to rioting, in the earlier period 1763–1834 as a function of broader social, cultural, and ideological transformations. In colonial America, social divisions existed, but the belief in a single corpo-

2. [William Osborn Stoddard], *The Volcano under the City, by a Volunteer Special* . . . (New York, 1887), 9–13. See also Joel Tyler Headley, *The Great Riots of New York, 1712–1873* . . . (Indianapolis, Ind., 1970 [orig. publ. New York, 1873]).

3. Richard Moody, *The Astor Place Riot* (Bloomington, Ind., 1958).

4. For a sampling of this violence, see Richard Hofstadter and Michael Wallace, eds., *American Violence: A Documentary History* (New York, 1970). See also Hugh Davis Graham and Ted Robert Gurr, eds., *Violence in America: Historical and Comparative Perspectives,* 2 vols. (Washington, D.C., 1969).

rate community, even in polyglot New York City, tended to minimize the expressions of those divisions. Moments of popular disorder were seen as a normal and limited expression of public displeasure. Because rioting characteristically represented a community defending perceived rights, it became crucial to the Revolutionary agitation of the 1760s and 1770s. The republican rhetoric of virtue and corruption, with its call for a united community, fitted neatly into the assumptions which had been long a part of the plebeian street culture. In the years after the Revolution, there may have been a new democratic rationale behind government, thereby weakening the role of politics out-of-doors, but the habit and practice of mobbing were not easily erased from general consciousness.

During the 1780s and 1790s, New Yorkers eagerly joined tumultuous crowds in riots against violators of communal morality and in political demonstrations similar to the popular disorder of the 1760s and 1770s. Mobs attacked a medical school and its students in 1788 for allegedly robbing graves. They railed against speculators in 1792, and in 1793 and 1799 they besieged bawdyhouses. Exhibiting a new political awareness, the people in the street participated in a variety of outdoor political activity, ranging from peaceful rallies, like the anti–Jay Treaty meeting in 1795, to street battles with opponents in 1798 and 1799. But the context for this type of activity was changing, and popular disorder of any kind was increasingly discouraged.

The conflict between regular government and mob politics, which was only to be expected after a successful revolution, intensified under the impact of urbanization, immigration, emancipation, and dramatic economic change. The combined weight of these forces shattered any possibility of maintaining the single-interest ideal. As the population of New York City grew, ensuring law and order was increasingly difficult. The introduction of tens of thousands of Irish Catholics convinced many Protestant Americans that their world was about to be swamped by this alien group. With the end of slavery in the North, newly freed blacks and many runaways from the South began to define more clearly for themselves a peculiarly Afro-American identity. Changes in the organization of the workshop cast journeyman and master, and laborer and employer in antagonistic roles. All of these developments combined to distort traditional plebeian crowd behavior into a new, lower-class roughhouse culture evident in tavern and street brawls, theater riots, holiday celebrations, and gang activity.

In opposition to this violence stood a middle-class culture replacing eighteenth-century corporate ideals with a pluralism which allowed peaceful political and economic competition and guaranteed the sanctity of private property. Building upon Revolutionary republicanism, the middle class—composed of merchants, businessmen, lawyers, successful artisans, and remnants of the old elite—seized upon the ideal that private virtue was the best avenue to public virtue and believed that unfettered competition led to the public good. The violent clash between New York's various subcommunities—interest groups—threatened both the open marketplace and the free exchange of ideas. In this so-called democratic environment, riots appeared out of place and were deemed illegitimate. To control an unruly populace, there emerged a new type of police.

But just when the public authorities needed most to control disorder, the same forces which divided the community weakened their ability to deal with the mob. The growth of the city, the increasing heterogeneity of society, and changing economic relations led to the decline of deferential techniques of riot control. Disorder increased, and the new agents of law enforcement proved inadequate to the task. Moreover, mobs unrestrained by informal connections with other groups in society resorted to physical violence with frightening frequency. The various police officers struggling to control the disorder unwittingly contributed to this development by confronting the rioters with coercion and violence of their own. When the force of the mob met the force of the police, there were casualties. A crescendo of violence emerged which was even more distressing to city officials.

In the eighteenth century, ordinarily, the military units called out to suppress a riot inflicted the greatest casualties. This tendency can be seen in New York's largest disturbance before 1800—the Doctors' Riot of 1788. But beginning with the 1799 Saint Patrick's Day riot, the rioters began to inflict casualties against competing groups and against the police. During the early nineteenth century, then, there were countless battles between the police and the mob. All too often, as far as the police were concerned, it was the rioters who seemed to triumph even when the police were lucky enough to make a few arrests. In short, the change in rioting during the early nineteenth century threatened to lead to the mobocracy which so concerned men like Fisher Ames in 1799 and set the stage for the massive violent conflicts of the Jacksonian era and the holocaust of the Draft Riots of 1863.

APPENDIX
Problems in Identifying the Mob

Identifying rioters is difficult. The police arrested only a few persons, if any, at each disturbance. At the June 1814 riot outside Washington Hall, for example, there were 150–200 people. Of those, 20 men were taken in by the police, but only 8 were booked and appear in the court records. There is no sure way to know why the police chose that particular 8 to prosecute. The court depositions indicate direct evidence against these men, and there may not have been any testimony implicating the other, unnamed 12.[1] But there are other possibilities. Political connections and friends in the Police Office might have come into play. The police ordinarily claimed, however, to arrest ringleaders of a riot or those caught in the midst of a disorderly act. The ranks of arrested rioters also included very wealthy individuals as well as a host of poor laborers. This suggests that all social levels were subject to arrest in a riot. It can therefore be assumed that, although only a few rioters were arrested at most disturbances, the sample in the criminal records is generally representative of the people most active in the mob.

Besides the issue of arrest practices, there is also the problem of determining where the identified rioter resided, how he earned his living, and how much property he owned. Again, the inadequacies of American records prevent a quick solution to the problem. (In France and even in England the authorities were very meticulous in collecting information about suspects.) In New York, police officials seldom noted any details about those arrested. Even the written indictments, which were supposed to state the occupation and ward of the defendant, are of little help. Rather than giving accurate information, the indictments tended to list every defendant as being a laborer in the First Ward. Only a few indictments give

1. *People* v. *David Tricedale et al.,* July 11, 1814, NYCGS.

more precise information, usually when directed against a member of the upper classes.

Directories, which were written for commercial purposes, were published nearly every year after the Revolutionary war and listed thousands of New Yorkers' addresses and occupations. But these directories are not very useful in identifying rioters, for not everyone in the city was included in the directories. They were limited to heads of households and did not list all of these; women, blacks, immigrants, and lower-class men were often excluded.[2] More important, even when a directory did list the same name as appeared in the court record, there is no way to be sure that the names referred to the same person. New York contained countless men with common names like John Smith, and even some apparently uncommon names were repeated several times. There were, for example, three or four Isaac Varians.

Tax assessment records and the census present similar problems. Officials were more concerned with the heads of households and the property they owned than with each individual within that household. Such sources do not say who might have lived with the named head of household. Moreover, these records were organized by residence rather than by the alphabet. Without an address it is nearly impossible to use them effectively.

The key to identifying New York rioters is the bail bonds. Because the defendant had to put up money, the magistrates ordinarily included the address and occupation of the accused and the person who swore out surety for him. (Where money was concerned, the officials were always more careful.) Furthermore, the bail bonds provide positive identification even for John Smiths. A bond taken out by a rioter included a promise not to disturb the peace or harass the complainant, and it is therefore possible, using the complainant's name and the date, to connect the bond to a particular case of riot. (This identification would have been easier had the bond stated the crime, but for some reason it seldom did.)

Unfortunately, there is not a bail bond for every rioter arrested. Some rioters were never bailed. For others, the bonds have long since disappeared. There are a few bonds from the 1790s. The record is much better after 1800 up to 1824; but, thereafter, until the 1840s, there are no bail bonds to be found.[3]

These bail bond identifications are supplemented by other sources. Oc-

2. The city directory for the appropriate year was checked for each rioter.
3. NYCSCPC Bonds, boxes 7839–7856 (1791–1824), NYCA.

casionally the court records themselves reveal the occupation or address of the accused in either the rare detailed indictment or within the testimony of the deposition. Newspaper accounts of riots or subsequent trials sometimes mention the names and occupations of rioters. Finally, some names were distinct enough that the directory was used to identify the rioter with relative confidence.

Bibliography

NOTE ON THE SOURCES

Court records and newspapers are the two best sources for studying New York City rioting. Both are faulty because they reflect the views and interests of the city magistrates and the upper levels of society. Yet they do allow a glimpse at lower-class interests through the detailed descriptions of mob activity. The court records are especially good for this. Often the actual depositions sworn to by witnesses and participants exist along with the none-too-informative indictments. Although the depositions were written down by a clerk, they were usually given within a day of the riot and represent the language and the passions of the deponent.

Most of the court records are kept in the New York City Municipal Archives and Record Center. The New York City Court of General Sessions Records (NYCGS) are the most informative. During my research they were a recent acquisition of the Archives and were only just being boxed when I was working with them. Therefore, citations are by date only. There are also some cases from the higher criminal court, the Court of Oyer and Terminer (NYCOT), kept within the General Sessions files. The New York City General Sessions records are of cases actually brought to trial. The New York City Supreme Court Police Court Cases (NYCSCPCC), however, are the records of the cases in which the prosecution was dropped before trial. They too are very useful. Although separately cataloged, both the General Sessions and the Supreme Court Cases records form a single body of unexploited criminal records. Also helpful are the New York City Supreme Court Police Court Bonds (NYCSCPC Bonds), which enabled me positively to identify many rioters, and the New York City Magistrate's Minutes of the Police Office (NYCMMPO), which list the daily activities of the Police Court. Nearly forty volumes of the Magistrate's Minutes were read; and, despite the lack of excessive descriptive material in them, no other source gave me a better eye-level view of New York street life.

Newspapers were scanned and many fruitless hours passed without a single reference to a riot. Until the 1820s newspapers avoided coverage of riots and crime. When an incident was reported before the 1820s, it was frequently in very small print buried behind all of the other news items. There were several important riots that were hardly mentioned at all. However, the lack of other available sources and the rare reference to an otherwise undocumented disturbance made the reading of newspapers indispensable.

UNPUBLISHED SOURCES

Allen, Stephen. Court Minutes, 1821–1822. NYHS.
———. Letters, 1821–1849. NYHS.

———. "The Memoirs of Stephen Allen (1767–1852): Sometime Mayor of New York City, Chairman of the (Croton) Water Commissioners, etc. etc." Edited by John C. Travis. Typescript. NYHS.

Anderson, Alexander. "Diarium," 1793–1795. Microfilm. Columbia University Library, New York City.

Anderson, John. "Diarium Commentarium Joannis Anderson," 1794–1798. NYHS.

Bayer, Goldsbrow. Goldsbrow Bayer Papers, box 1. NYHS.

British Regiment Footguards. Orderly Book, Aug. 14, 1776–Jan. 28, 1777. Microfilm, reel 3, no. 37. NYHS.

Bruce, David. "Autobiography of David Bruce; or, Then and Now." NYHS.

Clinton, De Witt. Papers. Microfilm. Columbia University, New York City.

———. Session Minutes, 1807, 1808, 1812. NYHS.

Constable, William. Letters, 1752–1803. Constable-Pierrepont Papers. NYPL.

Craigie, Andrew. Andrew Craigie Papers, boxes 6, 7. American Antiquarian Society, Worcester, Mass.

Duane, James. "New York City Mayor's Court and General Sessions Trials for November Term, 1787." NYHS.

Furman, Gabriel. "The Customs, Amusements, Style of Living, and Manners of the People of the United States, from the First Settlement to the Present Time ca. 1844. NYHS.

Gage, General Thomas. "New York, Orderly Books, I, Aug. 25, 1766–July 1, 1768, Oct. 29, 1771–July 10, 1774." NYHS.

Hays, Jacob. "An Account of Prisoners Received into the New York State Prison from the Commencement of the Institution" (1798–1821). Library, Museum of the City of New York.

———. Newspaper clippings on file on Jacob Hays. Library, Museum of the City of New York.

———. "Personal Ledger." Library, Museum of the City of New York.

Hone, Philip. "Philip Hone Diary," 1826–1835. Microfilm. NYHS.

Jay, Peter Augustus. "New York City, Court of General Sessions Minutes, 1819–1820." Photostat. NYPL.

Livingston, Robert R. "Letters of R. R. Livingston." Box 3. Livingston Family Papers. NYPL.

———. Papers, 1792–1795. Microfilm. NYHS.

Matteson, David Maydole. "Notes on Riots." Manuscript Division, Library of Congress, Washington, D.C.

"Misc. Riots, 1834." Miscellaneous microfilms, reel 34. NYHS.

New York City. Census and Jury List, 1819, First Ward. NYCA.

———. Census and Jury List, 1819. Microfilm. Historical Documents Collection, Queens College, City University of New York.

———. Court of General Sessions, 1791–1835. NYCA.

———. Court of General Sessions, Minutes of Cases, 1811. NYHS.

———. Filed Papers of the City Clerk, 1784–1829. NYCA.

———. Magistrate's Minutes, Police Office, 1799–1830. NYCA.

———. Mayor's Court Minutes, 1816–1817. NYHS.
———. Minutes of the Court of General Sessions of the Peace, 1812–1813. Historical Documents Collection, Queens College, City University of New York.
———. Minutes of the Court of Oyer and Terminer, 1784–1826. Historical Documents Collection, Queens College, City University of New York.
———. Supreme Court, Police Court, Bonds, 1791–1825. Boxes 7839–7857, 7963. NYCA.
———. Supreme Court, Police Court, Cases, 1808–1834. Boxes 7432–7447. NYCA.
———. Tax Assessments, First–Tenth wards, 1795, 1808–1835. NYCA.
New York City Courts. "A General List of All Persons Indicted and Convicted in the City and County of New York from the End of the American Revolution to the Year 1820." Microfilm. Historical Documents Collection, Queens College, City University of New York.
New York City Manumission Society. "Records of the New York City Manumission Society." Microfilm. NYHS.
Police File. "Police File," 1824. Library, Museum of the City of New York.
"The Panic of 1792." New York City, miscellaneous box 14: 1792. NYHS.
Seventh Regiment File, Minute Book, Second Company, 1834. NYHS.
———, Orderly Book, Fourth Company, 1834. NYHS.
Webb, John. New York City Manuscript Minutes of the Proceedings of the Court of General Sessions of the Peace, April term, 1825. NYPL.

NEWSPAPERS

Newspapers are here cited by their most common full titles, disregarding the minor changes that most of them underwent in the years covered; larger changes are noted. In the notes a newspaper is cited by the shortest form that distinguishes it from other newspapers simultaneously published; all are understood to be of New York City unless identified otherwise.

New York City

Albion. 1825–1830.
American. 1819–1829.
American Citizen. 1801–1810.
American Minerva. 1794–1796. See also *Minerva.*
Argus. 1795–1799.
Chronicle, New-York. 1769.
Columbian. 1810–1817.
Commercial Advertiser. 1800–1834.
Courier. 1815–1817.

Courier, Morning, and New York Enquirer. 1829–1834.
Daily Advertiser, New-York. 1785–1798.
Daily Advertiser, New-York. 1817–1820.
Diary. 1792–1796.
Evening Post, New-York. 1748–1752.
Evening Post, New-York. 1794–1795.
Evening Post, New-York. 1801–1835.

Freedom's Journal. 1827–1829.
Gazette, Gaine's *New-York; and the Weekly Mercury.* 1768–1776.
Gazette, New-York. 1795–1829.
Gazette, New-York: or, the Weekly Post-Boy. 1747–1766. Title changes.
Gazette, Weyman's *New-York.* 1766.
Gazetteer, New-York. 1783–1787. See also *Rivington's New-York Gazetteer.*
Herald. 1794–1797.
Herald, New-York. 1806, 1812.
Independent Gazette. 1783–1784.
Independent Journal. 1783–1788.
Journal, New-York. 1766–1776.
Journal, New-York. 1784–1799.
Man. 1834–1835.
Mercantile Advertiser. 1799–1806.
Mercury, New-York. 1753–1766.
Military Monitor. 1812–1813.
Minerva. 1796–1797. See also *American Minerva.*
Morning Chronicle. 1804–1807.
Morning Courier. 1803.
Morning Post, New-York. 1783–1792.
Morning Post, New York. 1811–1812.
Mott and Hurtin's New-York Weekly Journal. 1795.

National Advocate. 1813–1828.
Packet, New-York. 1784–1791.
Post-Boy. See *Gazette, New-York: or the Weekly Post-Boy;* and *Weekly Post-Boy, New-York.*
Public Advertiser. 1808–1812.
Register of the Times. 1796.
Republican Watch-Tower. 1810.
Rivington's New-York Gazetteer. 1774–1783. Title changes variously.
Shamrock. 1811–1817.
Spectator. 1797–1831.
Statesman. 1822–1830.
Sun. 1834.
Time-Piece. 1797–1798.
Transcript. 1828.
Truth Teller. 1825–1828.
War. 1812–1814.
Weekly Journal, New-York. 1733–1751.
Weekly Post-Boy, New-York. 1745–1747.
Weekly Visitor. 1817–1820.
Workingman's Advocate. 1834–1835.

Outside New York

Albany Register. 1808.
Baltimore Whig. 1812.
Boston Gazette. 1770, 1785–1786.
City Gazette (Charleston, S.C.). 1825.
Columbian Centinel (Boston). 1807, 1810.
Connecticut Gazette (New London). 1776.
Federal Republican (Georgetown, D.C.). 1812.
Maryland Republican (Annapolis). 1812.
Massachusetts Centinel (Boston). 1785, 1788.
Niles' Weekly Register (Baltimore).

1814–1816. See also *Weekly Register.*
Pennsylvania Evening Post (Philadelphia). 1776.
Pennsylvania Gazette (Philadelphia). 1760.
Pennsylvania Packet (Philadelphia). 1783–1784.
Poulson's American Daily Advertiser (Philadelphia). 1812.
St. James Chronicle (London). 1776.
Weekly Register (Baltimore). 1811–1814. See also *Niles' Weekly Register.*

DIRECTORIES

Duncan, William. *The New-York Directory, and Register.* . . . For the years 1791, 1792, 1794, 1795.

Franks, David C. *The New-York Directory.* For the years 1786, 1787.

Longworth, David. *The American Almanack, New-York Register, and City Directory.* . . . For the years 1796–1835.

Low, John. *The New-York Directory, and Register, for the Year 1796.* New York, 1796.

New York Directory, and Register, for the Year 1790, The. New York, 1790.

[Stanford, Thomas Naylor]. *The Citizens Directory and Strangers Guide through the City of New York.* 1814.

OTHER PUBLISHED SOURCES

American Convention of Abolition Societies. Reports of the American Convention of Abolition Societies on Negroes and on Slavery, Their Appeals to Congress, and Their Addresses to the Citizens of the United States. *Journal of Negro History,* VI (1921), 310–374.

The American Register; or, General Repository of History and Science. 7 vols. Philadelphia, 1807–1811.

Ames, Fisher. *Works of Fisher Ames.* Boston, 1809.

[Anderson, Alexander]. *Cries of New-York.* New York, 1822.

Another Citizen. *To the Respectable Public.* [New York], 1774.

Another Citizen. *To the Inhabitants of the City and County of New-York.* [New York], June 5, 1774.

Asbury, Francis. *The Journal and Letters of Francis Asbury.* Edited by Elmer T. Clark *et al.* Nashville, Tenn., 1958.

Aspinwall, Thomas, ed. *Aspinwall Papers.* 2 vols. Massachusetts Historical Society, *Collections,* 4th Ser., IX–X. Boston, 1871.

Barbour, Oliver Lorenzo. *A Treatise on the Criminal Law of the State of New-York; and upon the Jurisdiction, Duty, and Authority of Justices of the Peace, and, Incidentally, of the Power and Duty of Sheriffs, Constables, &c. in Criminal Cases.* 2d ed. Albany, 1852.

Bridges, William. *Map of the City of New-York and Island of Manhattan; with Explanatory Remarks and References.* New York, 1811.

Broad, Amos. *A Discourse, Delivered on the Thirteenth September, 1814, to a Detachment of the United States Army, (Stationed at Brooklyn, Long Island) under the Command of Colonel Berrian.* New York, 1814.

Burnett, Edmund C., ed. *Letters of Members of the Continental Congress.* Vol. VII. Washington, D.C., 1934.

Carter, Clarence Edwin, ed. *The Correspondence of General Thomas Gage with the Secretaries of State.* . . . 2 vols. New Haven, Conn., 1931–1933.

[Cheetham, James]. Lysander. *Annals of the Corporation, relative to the Late Contested Elections, with Strictures upon the Conduct of the Majority, in Seven Numbers.* New York, 1802.

Christian, Charles. *A Brief Treatise on the Police of the City of New York.* New York, 1812.

———. *Notes on the Police of the City of New York by Charles Christian, Late One of the Special Justices of the Peace, Respectfully Addressed to His Excellency the Governor and the Honourable the Members of the Legislature of the State of New York.* New York, 1818.

A Citizen. *To the Inhabitants of the City and Colony of New-York.* [New York], 1774.

A Citizen. *To the People of New-York.* [New York, 1774].

A Citizen. *To the Public: Stop Him! Stop Him! Stop Him!* New York, 1774.

Clap, Caleb. "Diary of Ensign Caleb Clap, of Colonel Baldwin's Regiment, Massachusetts Line, Continental Army, March 29 until October 23, 1776." *Historical Magazine,* 3d Ser., III (1874), 133–138.

Clinton, George. *Public Papers of George Clinton, First Governor of New York, 1775–1795—1801–1804.* Vols. I, II, VIII. Edited by Hugh Hastings. New York, Albany, 1899–1904.

Colden, Cadwallader. *The Colden Letter Books.* 2 vols. New-York Historical Society, *Collections,* IX (1876), X (1877). New York, 1877–1878.

———. *The Letters and Papers of Cadwallader Colden.* Vol. VII. New-York Historical Society, *Collections,* LVI. New York, 1923.

Coleman, William. *Reports of Cases of Practice, Determined in the Supreme Court of Judicature of the State of New-York; from April Term, 1794, to November Term, 1805, Both Inclusive, to Which Is Prefixed, All the Rules and Orders of the Court to the Present Time.* New York, 1808.

Commons, John R., *et al.,* eds. *A Documentary History of American Industrial Society.* Vols. II–IV. Cleveland, Ohio, 1910.

Davis, John. *Travels of Four Years and a Half in the United States of America during 1798, 1799, 1800, 1801, and 1802.* Edited by A. J. Morrison. New York, 1909.

Dix, John A. *Sketch of the Resources of the City of New-York, with a View of Its Municipal Government, Population, &c. &c., from the Foundation of the City to the Latest Statistical Accounts.* New York, 1827.

Documents Relating to the Colonial History of the State of New Jersey. Archives of the State of New Jersey, 1st Ser., XIX. Paterson, N.J., 1897.

Duer, William Alexander. *New-York as It Was during the Latter Part of the Last Century: An Anniversary Address Delivered before the St. Nicholas Society of the City of New-York, December First, 1848.* New York, 1849.

Dunlap, William. *Diary of William Dunlap (1766–1839): The Memoirs of a Dramatist, Theatrical Manager, Painter, Critic, Novelist, and Historian.* 3 vols. New York, 1931.

Dwight, Timothy. *Travels in New England and New York.* Vol. III. New Haven, Conn., 1822.

Eaton, Th[eophilus]. *Review of New-York; or, Rambles through the City: Original Poems, Moral, Religious, Sarcastic, and Descriptive.* New York, 1813.

Edwards, John. *Account of the Trial of John Edwards of the City of New York, Who Was Prosecuted for "Collecting or Promoting an Assembly of Persons, under* *the Pretence of Public Worship in a Public Street, on Sunday, June 16, 1822,"* with a Short Account of His Life, an Address to the Mayor and Corporation, and Advice to the Police Magistrates, &c.* New York, 1822.

Force, Peter. *American Archives.* 4th, 5th Ser. Washington, D.C., 1837–1853.

Foster, Sir Augustus John. *Jeffersonian America: Notes on the United States of America Collected in the Years 1805-6-7 and 11-12.* Edited by Richard Beale Davis. San Marino, Calif., 1954.

Francis, John W. *Old New York; or, Reminiscences of the Past Sixty Years.* Rev. ed. New York, 1866.

The Free Citizens. *To the Public.* New York, 1774.

A Freeman. *To the Public.* New York, 1774.

Gordon, Thomas, trans. *The Works of Tacitus.* 2 vols. London, 1728–1731.

[Greene, Asa]. *A Glance at New York: Embracing The City, Government, Theatres, Hotels, Churches, Mobs, Monopolies, Learned Professions, Newspapers, Rogues, Dandies, Fires and Firemen, Water and Other Liquids, &c. &c.* New York, 1837.

Hall, Benjamin H., ed. "Extracts from the Letter Books of John Thurman, Junior." *Historical Magazine,* 2d Ser., IV (1868), 283–297.

Hamilton, Alexander. *The Papers of Alexander Hamilton.* Vol. I, *1768–1777.* Edited by Harold C. Syrett and Jacob E. Cooke. New York, 1961.

Hardie, James. *An Account of the Malignant Fever, Lately Prevalant in the City of New-York.* New York, 1799.

———. *A Census of the New Buildings Erected in This City, in the Year 1824, Arranged in Distinct Classes, according to Their Materials and Numbers of Stories; Also, a Number of Statistical Documents, Interesting to the Christian, the Merchant, the Man of Inquiry, and the Public in General.* New York, 1825.

———. *The Description of the City of New-York; Containing Its Population, Institutions, Commerce, Manufactures, Public Buildings, Courts of Justice, Places of Amusement, &c., to Which Is Prefixed a Brief Account of Its First Settlement by the Dutch, in the Year 1629, and of the Most Remarkable Events, Which Have Occurred in Its History, from That Time to the Present Period.* New York, 1827.

Haswell, Charles Haynes. *Reminiscences of an Octogenarian of the City of New York (1816 to 1860).* New York, 1896.

Hicks, Whitehead. *To the Inhabitants of This City.* New York, 1770.

Hone, Philip. *The Diary of Philip Hone, 1828–1851.* Edited by Allan Nevins. Vol. I. New York, 1927.

An Honest American. *To the Respectable Public.* New York, 1774.

Hosack, David. *Memoir of De Witt Clinton: With an Appendix, Containing Numerous Documents Illustrative of the Principal Events of His Life.* New York, 1829.

Jay, John. *The Correspondence and Public Papers of John Jay. . . .* Edited by Henry P. Johnston. 4 vols. New York, 1890–1893.

King, Charles. *Progress of the City of New-York, during the Last Fifty Years, with Notices of the Principal Changes and Important Events: A Lecture Delivered before the Mechanics' Society at Mechanics' Hall, Broadway on Twenty-Ninth December, 1851.* New York, 1852.

La Rochefoucauld Liancourt, François Alexandre Frédéric, duc de. *Travels through the United States of America, the Country of the Iroquois, and Upper Canada, in the Years 1795, 1796, and 1797, with an Authentic Account of Lower Canada.* Translated by H. Neumann. 2d ed. 4 vols. London, 1800.

Legion. *To the Publick.* New York, 1774.

Low, Isaac, *et al. To the Respectable Publick.* New York, 1774.

Lyon, Isaac S. *Recollections of an Old Cartman.* Newark, N.J., 1872.

[McDougall, Alexander]. A Son of Liberty. *To the Betrayed Inhabitants of the City and Colony of New York.* New York, 1769.

A Merchant. *The Times, Mankind Is Highly Concerned to Support That, Wherein Their Own Safety Is Concerned, and to Destroy Those Arts by Which Their Ruin Is Consulted.* [New York, 1770].

[Mitchell, Samuel Latham]. *The Picture of New-York; or, the Traveller's Guide, through the Commercial Metropolis of the United States.* New York, 1807.

Morgan, Helen M., ed. *A Season in New York, 1801: Letters of Harriet and Maria Trumbull.* Pittsburgh, Pa., 1969.

Muhlenberg, Henry Melchior. *The Journals of Henry Melchior Muhlenberg.* Vol. I. Translated by Theodore G. Tappert and John W. Doberstein. Philadelphia, 1942.

New York. *The Colonial Laws of New York, from the Year 1664 to the Revolution.* . . . Vol. V. Albany, N.Y., 1894.

————. *General Index to the Legislative Documents of the State of New York, from 1777 to 1888, Inclusive.* 6 vols. Albany, N.Y., 1891.

————. *Messages from the Governors.* . . . Vol. II, *1777–1822.* Edited by Charles Z. Lincoln. Albany, N.Y., 1909.

New York City. Common Council. *Minutes of the Common Council of the City of New York, 1784–1831.* 19 vols. New York, 1917–1930.

————. *Minutes of the Common Council of the City of New York, 1784–1831: Analytical Index.* Edited by David Maydole Matteson. 2 vols. New York, 1930.

The New-York City-Hall Recorder . . . Containing Reports, of the Most Interesting Trials and Decisions Which Have Arisen in the Various Courts of Judicature, for the Trial of Jury Causes in the Hall, during That Year, Particularly in the Court of Sessions, with Notes and Remarks, Critical and Explanatory. Vols. I–VI. New York, 1817–1822.

New-York Judicial Repository. Vol. I, nos. 1–6 (1818–1819).

New-York Magazine, and General Repository of Useful Knowledge. Vol. I, nos. 1–3 (1814).

Nichols, Thomas Low. *Forty Years of American Life.* New York, 1864; rpt., New York, 1937.

Niemcewicz, Julian Ursyn. *Under Their Vine and Fig Tree: Travels through America in 1797–1799, 1805, with Some Further Account of Life in New Jersey.* Translated and edited by Metchie J. E. Budka. New Jersey Historical Society, *Collections,* XIV. Elizabeth, N.J., 1965.

O'Callaghan, E. B., ed. *Documents relative to the Colonial History of the State of*

New York; Procured in Holland, England, and France. Vols. VI–VIII. Albany, N.Y., 1855–1857.

Parker, Amasa J. *Reports of Decisions in Criminal Cases Made at Term, at Chambers and in the Courts of Oyer and Terminer of the State of New York.* Vols. I–VI. Albany, N.Y., 1855–1868.

Plain English. *To the Inhabitants of New York.* [New York, 1774].

A Reporter. *A Graphic Account of the Alarming Riots at St. Mary's Church (Philadelphia) in April of 1822, Together with the Most Important Extracts from the Decisions of the Chief Justices Tilghman, Duncan, and Gibson, relative to the Charter of Said Church, Including Letters from Hon. J. R. Ingersol and Thos. Kittera, Esq.* [Philadelphia], 1844.

St. Méry, Moreau de. *Moreau de St. Méry's American Journey (1793–1798).* Translated and edited by Kenneth Roberts and Anna M. Roberts. Garden City, N.Y., 1947.

Scull, G. D., ed. *The Montresor Journals.* New-York Historical Society, *Collections,* XIV. New York, 1881.

[Seabury, Samuel]. *The Congress Canvassed; or, An Examination into the Conduct of the Delegates, at Their Grand Convention, Held in Philadelphia, Sept. 2, 1774: Addressed to the Merchants of New-York.* [New York], 1774.

[————]. *Free Thoughts on the Proceedings of the Continental Congress, Held at Philadelphia, Sept. 5, 1774. . . .* [New York], 1774. Evans No. 13602.

Shamrock Society of New York. *Emigration to America: Hints to Emgirants from Europe, Who Intend to Make a Permanent Residence in the United States, on Subjects Economical and Political Affecting Their Welfare; Drawn Up Especially for Their Use, in July Last.* London, 1817.

Shewkirk, Rev. Mr. "Diary of Rev. Mr. Shewkirk, Pastor of the Moravian Church, New York." *Memoirs of the Long Island Historical Society.* Vol. III, *The Campaign of 1776 around New York and Brooklyn.* Edited by Henry P. Johnston. Pt. II, 101–127. Brooklyn, N.Y., 1878.

Smith, William. *Historical Memoirs of William Smith, Historian of the Province of New York, Member of the Governor's Council, and Last Chief Justice of That Province under the Crown, Chief Justice of Quebec.* Edited by William H. W. Sabine. 2 vols. New York, 1956–1958.

Society for the Reformation of Juvenile Delinquents. Annual Reports of the Managers of the Society for the Reformation of Juvenile Delinquents in the City of New York. Vols. I–V. New York, 1825–1830.

[Southwick, Henry C.]. *The Trial of Amos Broad and His Wife, on Three Several Indictments for Assaulting and Beating Betty, a Slave, and Her Little Female Child Sarah, Aged Three Years, Had at the Court of the Special Sessions of the Peace, Held in and for the City and County of New-York, at the City-Hall, of the Said City, on Tuesday, the Twenty-eighth Day of February, 1809.* New York, 1809.

Stanford, John. *A Catechism for the Improvement of Youth in the State Prison of New York.* New York, 1814.

Steiner, Bernard C., ed. *The Life and Correspondence of James McHenry, Secretary of War under Washington and Adams.* Cleveland, Ohio, 1907.

[Stoddard, William Osborn]. *The Volcano under the City, by a Volunteer Special.* . . . New York, 1887.

Tappan, Lewis. *The Life of Arthur Tappan.* New York, 1870; rpt., New York, 1970.

Thurman, Ralph. *To the Inhabitants of the City and County of New-York.* [New York], 1775.

To the Public. Apr. 19, 1774. New York. Evans no. 13671.

To the Public. Apr. 19, 1774. New York. Evans no. 13672.

To the Public. May 17, 1774. New York.

To the Public. May 18, 1774. New York.

To the Public. Sept. 28, 1774. New York.

To the Public. Affidavit of Thomas Mesnard, Dec. 30, 1774. New York.

To the Sons of Liberty in This City. Feb. 3, 1770. New York.

[Trenchard, John, and Thomas Gordon]. *Cato's Letters; or, Essays on Liberty, Civil and Religious, and Other Important Subjects.* 3d ed. 4 vols. London, 1733.

The Trial of Gulian C. Verplank, Hugh Maxwell, and Others, for a Riot in Trinity Church at the Commencement of Columbia College, in August 1811. New York, 1821.

An Unbiased Irishman. *Orangism Exposed, with a Refutation of the Charges, &c. &c., Brought against the Irish Nation, by Lawyer David Graham, of New-York, in His Defense of the Orangemen, Tried in This City, on the Thirteenth and Fourteenth Days of September, 1824, for Assault and Battery on a Poor Irishman, on the Twelfth Day of July, 1824.* . . . New York, 1824.

Volney, C. F. *A View of the Soil and Climate of the United States of America.* . . . Translated by C. B. Brown. Philadelphia, 1804.

Wansey, Henry. *Henry Wansey and His American Journal, 1794.* Edited by David John Jeremy. Philadelphia, 1970.

Warden. D. B. *A Statistical, Political, and Historical Account of the United States of America, from the Period of Their First Colonization to the Present Day.* 3 vols. Edinburgh, 1819.

Wheeler, Jacob D. *Reports of Criminal Law Cases, Decided at the City-Hall of the City of New York, with Notes and References.* 3 vols. New York, 1854.

———. *Trial of John Moore, John Mullen, John Lowry, and Henry Bush, on an Indictment for an Assault and Battery on James Murney, on the Twelfth of July, 1824, before the General Sessions of New York on Monday and Tuesday, the Thirteenth and Twenty-fourth Days of Sept. 1824.* New York, 1824.

White, Philip L., ed. *The Beekman Mercantile Papers.* Vol. I. New York, 1956.

Willett, William M., ed. *A Narrative of the Military Actions of Colonel Marinus Willett, Taken Chiefly from His Own Manuscript.* . . . New York, 1831.

Wyche, William. *Report of the Trial of Henry Bedlow, for Committing a Rape on Lanah Sawyer, and Arguments of the Counsel on Each Side, at the Court of Oyer and Terminer, and Gaol Delivery for the City and County of New-York, Oct. 8, 1793.* New York, 1793.

Index

Abell, Henry, 278
Abolitionists, 162–163, 167, 251. *See also* Slavery, anti-
Abyssinian Baptist Church, 154
Actors, British, and theater riots, 247–251
Adolescence, 22–23. *See also* Youths
African churches, 153–156, 169
African Church on Sixth Avenue, 156
African Ebenezer Church, 154
African Free School, 157–158
African Grove, 156–157, 169
African Methodist Episcopal Zion Church, 154
African Methodist Union Church, 156
African Mutual Relief Society, 169
African schoolhouse, 167
Afro-Americans. *See* Blacks
Albany Committee, 75
Alien Act, 129
Allen, Stephen, 270, 275
Allicote, Joseph, 50
Amalgamation, fear of, 162–163
American Revolution, symbols of, 39–41, 43, 45–59, 65–68, 101, 106
Ames, Fisher, 3, 5, 6, 35, 288
Anderson, Alexander, 87, 89
Anderson, Joshua, 248–249
Anglophobia, 247–251
Anonymity, crimes of, 173–175
Anthony Street, 127, 128, 154, 161, 166, 239, 240, 255
Anthony Street Abyssinian Baptist Church, 167
Antiauthoritarianism, 47
Anti-Catholicism, 28, 130–131. *See also* Irish: prejudice against; Paddies; Pope Day
Antifederalists, 97–99
Apprentices: in mobs, 5, 141, 226,

253, 258, 271; as Highbinders, 130–131; as cheap labor, 191; anti-evangelicalism of, 215–218; and Stephen Allen, 270. *See also* Mechanics; Youth groups; Youths
Arsenal, 141; in riot of April 1834, 134, 141
Artisans. *See* Mechanics
Asia, HMS, 62, 63
Association, the, 59, 60, 63
Astor Place, 286
Augustus Street, 130–133, 136, 142

Bail bonds, 290
Bakers, 194, 195, 196, 218, 243
Balloon ascension, 252
Bancker Street, 239
Bank of the United States, 83
Baptists, 207, 214; mob harassment of, 208
Barbers, 106
Barclay Street, 130–131, 150–151, 159
Barricades, 168
Battery, the, 62, 63, 104, 106, 241, 257, 259
Bawdyhouses, 24, 47, 85–91, 130, 181, 237–239, 272–273, 276. *See also* Prostitution
Bedford Street Church, 208
Bedlow, Henry, 87–89
Beekman Slip, 66
Bethel Church, 208
Blackbirders, 150–152
Black Cat, 173–175, 198
Black cockade of Federalists, 108
Blackened faces, 16, 43
"Black-Eyed Susan," 247
Blacks: attacks on, 15, 153–170, 258, 259, 260; in conspiracies of 1712 and 1741, 15; holidays of, 19; in

303